COLONIAL SETTLERS

AND

ENGLISH ADVENTURERS

Abstracts of Legal Proceedings in
Seventeenth-Century English and Dutch Courts
Relating to Immigrant Families

A Source Material Guide

By

NOEL CURRER-BRIGGS

GENEALOGICAL PUBLISHING CO., INC.
Baltimore   1971

Published in England by
PHILLIMORE & COMPANY LTD.
Chichester, Sussex
Under the Title
English Adventurers and Colonial Settlers

American Publisher
GENEALOGICAL PUBLISHING CO., INC.
Baltimore, Maryland
1971

Library of Congress Catalog Card Number 70-177281
International Standard Book Number 0-8063-0488-X

Made and printed in Great Britain
Bound in the United States of America

CONTENTS

v

CONTENTS (contd.)

FOREWORD

This volume of abstracts from the legal records of various English
Courts and two Dutch Notarial Courts supplements my earlier miscellany
published under the title "English Adventurers and Virginian Settlers":
"Virginia Settlers and English Adventurers". Much of the material collected here was assembled in the course of a search to establish the English
origins of a Virginian settler named Thomas Kirby, who migrated to America
in the 1630s. Details of this search and the sources examined have been
described in the Foreword to my previous book. What remains here consists
of material relating to those branches of the Kirby family not closely related
to the Virginian branch, but among which are to be found several who emigrated to New England at about the same time. The cases in Parts I and
II, therefore, have been chosen with the same considerations in mind as
those which prompted the selection of documents in "Virginian Settlers".

Among the earliest emigrants to Massachusetts were a young farmer and
his brother, Thomas and Richard Chadwell. Thomas was among those who
came with John Winthrop in 1630, and he settled in Summer Street, intending to farm there. However, in 1637 he forsook the land and established
himself at Butt Point as a shipwright and neighbour of one Richard
Hollingworth. It is uncertain whether Richard Chadwell was a member of
the Winthrop expedition, for his name first appears in New England records
in 1637 among those of the founders of Sandwich. It is possible that he
came in the "Blessing" in 1636, one of those ships which engaged in the
trade between Britain, the West Indies and New England. In the minutes
of the Providence Island Company's meeting of June 1636 there is a request
to grant Lt. Chadwell and Mr. Hungerford eight servants if they will stay
in Providence Island, together with instructions to the Governor to admit
them to any vacant places suitable to their "qualities, they being of good
birth and rank". However, neither seems to have been enthusiastic to
settle in the West Indies for Hungerford eventually settled in Connecticut
and Chadwell in Massachusetts.

The Chadwells were Cotswold sheep-farmers. Traces of them can be
found in villages along the Gloucestershire/Oxfordshire borders as early
as the 14th century. At the end of the 15th century a John Chadwell was
a tenant of the Talbots at Great Rissington, while another John, or perhaps
the same, held land at Burford and Lt. Barrington. A letter dated 20 July,
1501, from John Greville of Milcote, Warwickshire, to his cousin, William
Greville of Arle, near Cheltenham, afterwards a well-known judge, concerns the sale of some land in Charlton Kings and informs his kinsman that
John Chadwell has been appointed his attorney in the matter. At about this
time, or a little later, one branch of the family established itself in Wiltshire near Savernake Forest. A William Chadwell appears in the Court
Rolls of Burbage in 1558 and 1561; the 1576 Subsidy Rolls show that he
was assessed at the large sum 'of £20, while at Gt. Bedwyn his relative
John Chadwell was assessed at a mere £3. At the Lent Assizes in the
same year Thomas Chadwell, as shoemaker of Gt. Bedwyn was bound over
to keep the peace and fined £5 for causing a riot.

The documents in this collection are mainly to do with that branch of
the Chadwell family living in Oxfordshire and Gloucestershire, and in
particular with those Royalist members of it, who suffered from their

* To avoid confusion male members of the Chadwell and Currer families
  mentioned in this Foreword have been given reference numbers,
  details of which are given in Appendix I and II.

adherence to the King. Further material connected with this large family
will be published in subsequent volumes of this series. In so far as
American readers will be interested in this family for the links it provides
with other 17th century emigrants, it is as well to give a brief description
of the main areas in which it is to be found in England.

1. Chadwell of Gt. Rissington and Burford

William Chadwell of Rissington died in 1529. From him the senior
branch of the family descended. He left three sons, Richard (202), John
(203) and Robert (204)* and two daughters. Richard inherited his father's
lands in Rissington after his mother's death and John moved to Broadwell,
north of Stow-on-the-Wold, where he founded a family, which during the
next century increased in wealth and influence. Of Robert little is known.
He is probably to be identified with Robert Chadwell of Shipton-under-
Wychwood, who died in Burford in 1617, and may have been the ancestor
of the Chadwells of Stanton Harcourt. In 1559 Richard bought the Manor
of Nether Hampen in the parish of Shipton Oliffe. Though little more is
known about him, he clearly prospered for on his death he left his son,
Richard (307) not only his estate in Rissington and Nether Hampen, but
also the lease of the Rectory of Chipping Norton to his younger son,
Michael (308). In 1620 this lease became the subject of a lawsuit between
Michael's son, Edward (420) and William Leigh of Addlestrop, details of
which can be found in this volume (Item No. 105). When he died in Burford
in 1591 he was the owner not only of the Manor of Nether Hampen, but also
of 200 acres in Gt. Rissington, nine cottages and a barn in Stow-in-the-
Wold and 120 acres in Maugersbury and Swell. In 1589, on the marriage
of his eldest son, Simon (409) to Elizabeth, daughter of Edmund Bray of
Taynton, Oxfordshire, and later of Gt. Barrington, Gloucestershire,
Richard (307) had settled the Manor and lands at Gt. Rissington on them,
and went to live in Burford, where he took an active part in the public
life of that thriving little town. Burford records contain numerous references to members of the Chadwell family, but none figures more often
than Richard. He became a Bailiff of Burford in 1573, and held that
office the following year when Queen Elizabeth I visited the town. He
served a second term in 1585 and was made an Alderman in 1586. He was
closely associated with his father-in-law, Simon Wisdome (whose daughter
Anne he married), in the foundation of Burford Grammer School, and was
able to send his own eldest son, Simon (409) to Oxford University. Besides
his lands in Oxfordshire and Gloucestershire, Anne Wisdome brought him
estates in Molesworth and Sawtry in Huntingdonshire, and when Simon
Wisdome died in 1587 he left his son-in-law all his property in Burford
and Signet despite the fact that he had a son and grandson of his own.

Richard Chadwell (307) left four sons and one daughter. Simon (409)
the eldest lived at his house, Cookseys, in Gt. Rissington until 1611,
when he removed to Molesworth in Huntingdon, but soon after his mother's
death, he returned to Oxfordshire and settled in Taynton, where he was
still living in 1625. It is not known exactly when he died. He had at
least ten children among them Edmund (572), Simon (573), born in 1594,

John (574) and Michael (575), born in 1598. Edmund became a soldier.
His cousin, Sir Giles Bray wrote to Secretary Conway in June 1625
asking him to bestow some preferment on Edmund Chadwell in " the employment now on hand for Cadiz. He would have tendered his services to you
before this, only I employed him in conducting our Oxfordshire recruits to
Plymouth. He did the Queen of Bohemia some service in the Palatinate
under my uncle, Sir Francis Vere, with loss of blood."

John (410) and Richard (412), the second and third sons of Richard
Chadwell (307) of Burford, were lawyers. Like their brother Simon
(409) they lived for a time outside Oxfordshire in Huntingdonshire and
Northampton. They were both in Northampton in 1613 and lived there
until about 1620 when John went to Ireland and Richard returned to
Oxfordshire. Richard (412) married Katherine, the daughter of Edward
Hungerford of Windrush, and died at Foscot in the parish of Idbury in
1635 without issue. He left his estate to his widow and her brother,
another Edward Hungerford. The relationship between this branch of
the Hungerford family and those of Connecticut has not been firmly established. This branch was also related to the Ayleworth family, one of
whose members, Francis Aylworth was in Massachusetts in 1630.

2. Chadwell of Broadwell, Gloucestershire.

John Chadwell (203) of Broadwell died in 1572 leaving a widow and a
son William (306). He had owned land in Broadwell as well as Gt. and Lt.
Rissington and Burford. William added to this and when he died in 1613
he owned property not only in Broadwell but also in Donnington and
Maugersbury, which he divided between his two sons, William (413) and
Thomas (415). William (413) was prosperous enough to buy the Manor of
Broadwell in 1619 for £3,240 in partnership with Anthony Hodges, to
whom he was related by marriage (Richard Hodges, Anthony's brother,
being William Chadwell's brother-in-law). The Hodges were an old-
established family, owning a great deal of land near Stow-on-the-Wold,
which ultimately descended to the Leighs of Addlestrop, by whom it is
still owned. Anthony Hodges and William Chadwell bought the Manor with
the intention of dividing it between them, for in 1622 they came to an
agreement whereby Hodges retained the Manor House and Chadwell kept
rather more than half the land.

At the beginning of the 17th century the Manor of Hidcote Bartrim
belonged to Anthony and William Freeman, the brothers-in-law of the
elder William Chadwell (306), and ancestors of the Freeman-Mitford
family, now Lords Redesdale. The Freemans of Oxfordshire are known
to have Virginian connections too. He held his part of the Manor from
1625 to 1631 when he sold it to the Rutters. The younger William Chadwell
(413) married Anne, the daughter of Thomas Widdowes of Moreton-in-
Marsh, in 1605. They had three sons and three daughters. William (516),
born in 1613 matriculated at Exeter College, Oxford in 1631 and was
called to the Bar in 1641. He represented the Borough of St. Michael
in Cornwall in both Parliaments of 1640 until disabled in January 1644
for joining the King at Oxford. He was one of the Royalist Members who
sat in the Oxford Assembly, and compounded for his delinquency in 1646
(See Item. 118).   He ultimately returned to legal practice and succeeded William Thursby in 1660 in the Office of Custos Brevium in the
Court of Common Pleas.

3. Chadwell of Chipping Norton, Oxfordshire.

The son and grandson of Michael Chadwell (308) of Chipping Norton had a much stormier history than their cousins of Broadwell and Rissington. Michael (308) was a wealthy man, yet his son, Edward (420) found himself imprisoned in the Fleet for debt, and his grandson, Michael (522) after being accused of murder and acquitted, died heavily in debt, as a result of his espousal of the Royalist Cause. Edward Chadwell married twice. His first wife was Elizabeth Markham, daughter of John Markham of Astwood, Northamptonshire, by whom he had two daughters, Anne and Joyce, and his second was Juliana Beaufew (or Beafoy), the daughter of Thomas Beafoy of Edmondscot, Warwickshire, by whom he had one son, Michael (522). By his first marriage he was related to Sir John Conway, later Viscount Conway, Secretary of State to James I and Charles I. The majority of the lawsuits in this collection conern Edward Chadwell and his son Michael (Items 102, 106, 109-111) and arose from Edward's improvidence and his son's attachment to the Royalists. At the end of the Civil War Michael found himself in Durham from where he compounded for his estates in 1649 (Items 119,120). According to the schedule he then submitted he owned lands and houses in Chipping Norton and Over Norton worth £167 before the war, and debts amounting to nearly £2,000. His fine was fixed at a sixth at £505 15s. 4d. but following a petition to the Committee for Compounding asking for this to be reduced in view of various "extents and engagements" upon his estate, he came to London, was arrested on suspicion of murder and gaoled at Oxford. At his trial he was acquitted, but because of this incident he had not been able to pay his Composition Fine, so the Committee increased it to £632 3s. 9d., which landed him even further in debt. He died in 1656 in Durham.

4. Chadwell of Ebbesbourne Wake, Wiltshire.

As mentioned earlier, one branch of the Chadwell family settled in the neighbourhood of Savernake Forest during the 16th century. The 1623 Visitation of Dorset takes note of the family, and gives details of the arms bourne by Edmund Chadwell (352) of Ebbesbourne Wake just over the county boundary in Wiltshire. They are the same as those appearing on the monuments of the Chadwells of Broadwell - "Argent, a fess dancette azure." There is, however, some doubt as to the family's entitlement to these arms, since no record of any grant can be found in the College of Arms. Nevertheless the history of Woodstock Manor recording the Visitation of Oxfordshire by Somerset Herald (John Phillipott) in 1634 contains an account of the defacement of the arms used by one Francis Gregory because he was not able to prove his lawful right to them, and shows that Somerset Herald was assisted by John Chadwell of Woodstock, who signed the memorandum. It is strange, therefore, that the Chadwell's own arms should be suspect. The Visitation of Dorset pedigree starts with William Chadwell (150) of Burbage, who was living in 1576. His son Edmund (251) married Anne More, the daughter of John More of Mottesfont, Hampshire, and they had a son, Edmund (352) and daughter, Eleanor, who married one William Gould. The younger Edmund (352) married Elizabeth Hooper, daughter of Thomas Hooper of Baveridge, Dorset by whom he had eight sons and three daughters. The eldest son, yet a third Edmund Chadwell (453) married into the prosperous Wiltshire family of Mompesson, which had numerous connections with New England. Of the remaining sons, Francis (454), Oliver (455), William (456), Nicholas

(458), Joseph (459) and Thomas (146) all went to London, where they entered various trades and professions. Oliver became a goldsmith and probably a Quaker, for he left the Society of Friends £20 in his will. William became a button-seller and Thomas a clothworker. It is possible that Francis also became a goldsmith, since his son John (564) and grandson, Thomas (668) were goldsmiths and jewellers. John (457), the sixth son of Edmund (352) entered the church. He took his M.A. at Wadham College, Oxford in 1663 and in due course became vicar of Farnham Hampshire, and later of Mappowder, Dorset, where he died unmarried. He was for some years the recipient of an annuity of £9 from his patron, Sir Winston Churchill, ancestor of the Dukes of Marlborough and his famous namesake.

5. Chadwell of Stanton Harcourt, Oxfordshire.

There are numerous scattered references to the name Chadwell in Oxfordshire records of the 17th century, but many of them cannot be accurately linked to the main lines of descent. The family of Richard Chadwell (412) or (444) of Upton Burford lived on at Upton until the death of Lawrence (546) in 1684. This was a less prosperous branch judging from the Hearth Tax returns of 1665. David Chadwell (545) probably a brother of Lawrence moved first to Westwell, where he signed the Protestation Oath in 1641, and subsequently to Lechlade, where his name appears in the 1671 Hearth Tax returns. The Chadwells of Stanton Harcourt were mostly labourers and their names occur from time to time in the Churchwardens Accounts and as recipients of Poor Law charity. A Samuel Chadwell (591) was an officer in the "London" in 1654 and saw action against the Dutch. A Thomas Chadwell, born in about 1602, who married in 1632 Bridget Gaunt, the daughter of Francis Gaunt of Greenwich, ultimately befame in 1644 a Maker of Writs De Diem Clausit Extremum in the Court of Wards and Liveries, and he succeeded one John Mostyn, who had deserted his post to join the Royalist army, it may safely be assumed that Thomas Chadwell did not share his Oxfordshire relatives' political views, and that he is not to be confused with either of his contemporaries, Thomas Chadwell of Donnington (415) or Thomas Chadwell of Lt. Barrington (529), who were both Royalists. He may, however, be the same Thomas Chadwell who was ordered in 1666 to be "attached for speaking scandalous words of the Bishop of Chichester" and sent to the Gatehouse Prison for his offence.

6. Chadwell of Lt. Barrington and Stroud, Gloucestershire.

This branch of the Chadwell family can be traced back to John (189) who owned two houses in Burford High Street in 1516, and who witnessed the will of William Buscy, vicar of Lt. Barrington in December 1497. This house belonged to Thomas Chadwell (224) of Lt. Barrington in 1552 and was still owned by his great-grandson, Thomas (529) in 1652. The search for the connecting links has been much hampered by the loss of the earliest registers of Little Barrington and the inaccessibility of other local records to do with the parish. Thomas (224), who died in 1554, was probably the son of John (189), and he left a daughter, Alice, and son, Richard (325), who inherited his property. There follows a gap until 1601, when we have the will of another John (426), who died at about the age of 36 and was the eldest of three brothers. This will, which will be published in a subsequent volume of this series, is of importance in providing one of the few clues to the identity of the brothers Thomas and

Richard who emigrated to America in the 1630s. The will leaves a legacy to an unborn child, whose birth and sex have not been firmly established, although there are faint reasons for believing that he may have been Samuel Chadwell of the "London" mentioned above. John Chadwell (426) goes on to leave all his lands and tenements to his son Thomas (529) and to Thomas's male heirs, and in default of such heirs, then to the unborn child if it shall be a boy. If neither has heirs, then the entail goes to John's brother, Simon Chadwell (427), and for default to his brother Moses (428). The Inquisition taken after John's death in September 1604 shows that Thomas (529) was six years and nine days old at the date of his father's death, which establishes his birthday as 1 August 1595. By relating the evidence of this will to Smyth's "Survey of Men and Armour in Gloucester-shire" of 1608 it is possible to show that there were two Simon Chadwells then living, both of them about forty years old, one living at Gt. Barring-ton and the other at Stroud. As it is known that Simon Chadwell (409), the son of Richard Chadwell of Burford (307) was born in about 1566, it is not unreasonable to assume that the other Simon Chadwell was one who was born in 1568 and who removed from Little Barrington to Stroud and from whom it is possible to trace several generations of descendants in that town. It is not known where Moses Chadwell (428) was in 1608, for Smyth omitted Lt. Barrington from his survey. He was certainly there in 1605, for he witnessed the will of his neighbour Reynold Cocke of Lt. Barrington in that year. That the Massachusetts family descends from him is the more likely because the emigrant Thomas baptised his eldest son Moses in Massachusetts in 1637 and the names Thomas, Richard, Benjamin and Samuel occur both in the American and Stroud/Lt. Barrington branches of the Chadwell family. Thomas (529) had a numerous family; his eldest son, Thomas (630), born in 1631, went to live at Kempley in north-west Gloucestershire, where he became a clothier, John (631) married but had no surviving children and died in 1695 at Black Bourton, Oxfordshire; Samuel, (632) his third son, died without issue in 1677 at Lt. Barrington and his youngest son, William, (633) who was born about 1645 became curate of Wick Rissington in 1668 and vicar of Lt. Barrington in 1669 and later moved to Shilton, Oxfordshire, where he was still living in 1695. This branch of the family lived at Upper Lypiatt, a hamlet on the outskirts of Stroud. They were related to the Arundels, another prosperous cloth-ing family with American connections.

The third main group of documents in this volume relates to the Currer family of Craven in Yorkshire. Their claim to be included in a book of Anglo-American source material is different from those of the Kirbys and Chadwells, for apart from Sarah Currer, the daughter of John Currer of London, (414), who owned an estate in what is now North Carolina, and whose will is published in "Virginian Settlers" (Vol. II), they did not found a family in America, though some of their remoter descendants emigrated to the Middle West in the 19th century. The collection of documents in this volume are mainly concerned with Henry Currer (601) and his close relatives. Henry Currer was born in 1621 and in his early twenties join-ed the Earl of Newcastle's army in support of the King. During the period immediately before and throughout the Civil War he was the agent of the Earl and Countess of Pembroke's Craven estates, and Governor of Skipton Castle. Skipton belonged to the redoubtable Lady Anne Clifford, Countess of Pembroke, Dorset and Montgomery, who steadfastly refused throughout the Civil War and Commonwealth to come to terms with Parliament.

Skipton was first attacked by the Roundheads in 1642, when Sir John Mallory of Studley was governor. It held out for three years when it surrendered, but shortly after, it was possibly retaken and occupied by the Royalists and changed hands finally in May 1648. The order of Parliament for the slighting of the castle were given in October 1648 and the work began in December. The west end of the walls were pulled down around the breach made by the Parliamentarian artillery. The whole of the castle old building was unroofed, the lead and wood sold and the upper parts of the walls pulled down to about half their height. Details of these operations appear in item 129 of this volume. The Countess of Pembroke came to Skipton in July 1649, stayed ten days and moved on to Barden Tower. The following February she came again to Skipton and remained nearly a year, causing boundaries to be ridden and generally making repairs. During this time she occupied those parts of the castle which had not been slighted.

The Currer documents in Part IV are interesting mainly for the light they throw on a prominent Yorkshire family in the 17th century. References are made to members of other families, such as the Saltonstalls and Copleys, which had New England and Virginian connections, and for this reason the collection can be of use to the American as well as the English genealogist.

Part V of this volume consists of brief abstracts from Chancery proceedings between the years 1550 and 1625 (PRO Class numbers C.1.; C.2 Eliz; and C.2 Jas I). They concern families living in the counties of Norfolk, Suffolk, Essex and Yorkshire, but also include a few cases relating to Kent, Hertfordshire, London and Cambridgeshire. All the families have to do with Virginia or New England, but, of course, only a tiny fraction of the cases themselves. Unlike the first three sections of the book, these abstracts, some 620 in number, have been reduced to the barest essentials and form little more than an extended guide or index for the genealogical enquirer. In order to cover the year 1550, which was chosen arbitrarily and in order to ensure that the immediate premigration generation was adequately covered, it was necessary to search PRO Ref. C.1., which gives neither an alphabetical index nor specific dates. Several of the cases, therefore, may have taken place in any of the years between 1547 and 1551. References under class C.1. are as follows:-

C.1/1223 - C.1/1285 cover the period 1547 to 1551; items 155-169

C.1/1286 - C.1/1324 cover the period 1551 to 1553; items 170-188

C.1/1325 - C.1/1397 cover the period 1553 to 1555; items 189-208

C.1/1398 - C.1/1488 cover the period 1555 to 1558; items 209-232

The handwritten index to PRO Refs. C.2. Elizabeth and C.2. Jas I gives only the names of the plaintiff(s) and defendant(s). The printed index gives more details, but only contains a selection of the cases. It was necessary to include cases involving the relevant names even though they might not have originated in any of the counties mentioned above. Neither index gives dates to the cases consistently, hence most dates have had to be omitted, except on the rare occasions where they are given. It has been found convenient to present the findings in cases where a fair amount of detail is given under the following headings:-

A. PRO Reference
B. Plaintiff(s) and Defendant(s)
C. Subject
D. Location
E. Date (where given)

However, since many of the cases deal only with personal matters (abbreviated to P.M.) or debts, these have been grouped together under their relevant class numbers, and give only the names of plaintiffs and defendants and the subject, since neither date nor location is usually given.

Parts VI and VII are made up of some sixty extracts from the notarial records of Rotterdam and Amsterdam between 1644 and 1669. They have been translated from the Dutch and relate to the activities of certain English and Dutch merchants trading with Virginia and New England. Their selection was made in connection with the search for Thomas Kirby, and so their interest is somewhat limited. They do, however, offer the English and American searcher an idea of the enormously valuable material that is to be found in Dutch records, and which may often help to fill in gaps left by the destruction of English records. The Dutch spelling of English names presents problems for the translator. Wherever there are doubts these are left as in the original, but where positive identifications can be made the commonest English spelling has been used; e.g. Brooke for Broocq, or Broeck; Kirby for Kerckbij or Kirkbij; Postlethwaite for Postelwit and Booker for Boucker.

PART 1

C2 Chas I K. 17/33 and K. 15/45
20 May 1631

Bill of Complaint of Thomas KIRBY
of Birchington, Thanet,
    versus
Robert WHITE and Susan his wife
and Mercy HUFFAM.

Thomas KIRBY of Birchington in the Isle of Thanet, Kent, yeoman, is the
administrator of the goods and chattels of John KIRBY, his late son.
Susan HUFFAM, daughter of Mercy HUFFAM, late of Birchington, widow,
by the means of Thomas PARAMOR, the elder, of Monkton, Kent, Esq., was
to marry the said John KIRBY, they both being under the age of 21. Thomas
KIRBY not much liking the marriage, assured nothing at all to his son or to
Susan for her jointure in case she should outlive his son. Susan and John
were married about Whitsuntide 12 months ago. Thomas KIRBY agreed that
he should dwell in one of his houses in Birchington, and also occupy 20 acres
of land belonging to it, paying £15 a year rent. He also gave his son John
three cows, and allowed them to be pastured in his pasture ground and suffered his son to occupy 100 acres more, for which John was to pay £56 a year.
He also gave John four wagon horses. John took possession of the house and
lands at Michaelmas after his marriage and sowed ten acres with wheat.
John and his family were all maintained in this house with meat and drink at
Thomas's expense until the death of John, which was a little time after
Christmas immediately following. John was to have had as a marriage
portion with Susan £150, viz. £100 from Mercy HUFFAM and £50 from an
uncle. During John's lifetime Mercy paid him £100 in money and goods,
but reckoned to make it up with one gold ring which was used as a wedding
ring, reckoned at 30 shillings, and a riding suit for Susan, which Mercy
reckoned at £3, was to make up the £100, as well as goods and household
stuff which Mercy reckoned at £15, which was hardly worth that. However
John and Susan accepted it as such. Mercy after confessed that all the £100
was paid to John, and that if Susan had died before John he could challenge
nothing as due from her. After John's death, Susan was in the house where
he died, and had possession of all his goods and ready money amounting to
about £59. At the instigation of Mercy and Thomas PARAMOR she would
not be at any charge or allow anything, not so much as a sheet, to bury him,
but put all the charge and trouble on Thomas KIRBY, his father. Shortly
after the funeral, although Susan was under 21 years and not fit to manage
her husband's estate, nevertheless, by the advice of Mercy and Thomas
PARAMOR she took letters of administration of John's goods at the time of
his death, and finding herself unable to manage the business, she agreed,
with the consent of Mercy and Thomas PARAMOR, to renounce the administration, and to consent to Thomas KIRBY taking it over, on condition that
Thomas KIRBY should allow her to have £100 in money and goods which had
come with her from Mercy, and the £50 which was still due from her uncle,
which was not then paid, and on condition that he should give her another
£100 and so have all the goods. Thomas PARAMOR agreed to stand surety
and a bond was drawn up, but he refused to sign it. Eventually an agreement was reached whereby the plaintiff would pay £150 to Susan in repayment
of her jointure, and she yielded up the administration of John's estate to his
father. This agreement was dated 18 February 1629/30 and was granted by
Sir Nathaniel BRENT, Commissary of the Lord Archbishop of Canterbury
within whose diocese John died. Thomas KIRBY put in an inventory of his

1

son's goods and credits and made an account of them and paid Susan and
Thomas PARAMOR, who was ordained to be her guardian, £301 6s. 0d.
£120 he paid out of his own purse and Thomas PARAMOR became bound
to make good to Susan the sum of £301 6s. 0d. Thomas KIRBY was to
hold all the goods and chattels that were his son's at the time of his death
for ever. Susan remarried one Robert WHITE of Southwark, soap boiler,
and all four conspired to get new letters of administration in the name of
Robert WHITE in order to obtain the £301 6s. 0d. and in order to frustrate
what had been done since Susan was still under 21 years old. Thomas
KIRBY asks the Court to compel them to give an account of their proceedings.

9 June 1631
Answer of Mercy HUFFAM.

She says that John KIRBY, the plaintiff's son, married Susan, her daughter,
and that they went to live in part of the plaintiff's house at Birchington and
occupied 20 acres of land belonging to it and 140 acres more, part of St
Nicholas Court land, most of which was then sown with corn. John was to
have this, together with corn growing on the 20 acres which was to be
harvested at the plaintiff's expense. John KIRBY was to occupy the house
and land rent free for the first year after his marriage and also the plaintiff
was to furnish John with stock for the farm (or for a better one) and John
was to pay no rent for the house and twenty acres so long as he held it rent
for the 140 acres. The marriage was agreed to on this basis and took place
accordingly. The plaintiff fulfilled most of his agreement as regards housing
and giving them the land. She denies that the plaintiff paid for the maintenance of John and Susan after they went to live at the house in Birchington,
because she bore part of the cost herself. Immediately after John's death,
which was in the January following his marriage, the plaintiff took possession of the house and lands and also converted to his own use wheat sowed
upon 15 acres by John and also a great part of the ready money that had been
his son's. It is true that Susan's portion was £150, of which Mercy was to
pay £100 and the other £50 to be paid by an uncle. She says she did pay
John KIRBY £85, and that the remaining £15 was owing to him at the time of
his death. Included in the £85 was the gold ring mentioned in the bill and
£3 spent on a riding suit for Susan. She denies delivering goods or household
stuff which she reckoned at £15, or any other goods, towards the payment of that
£15 residue of the £100, or that John and Susan accepted it as such. It is true
that after John's death, Susan on the advice of Thomas PARAMOR Esq., did take
letters of administration of her late husband's goods. Having taken them (she
then being under the age of 15 years) and fearing she should not compass the same
without some loss and trouble in regard the plaintiff had possessed himself of a
great part of her husband's estate, the defendant was content to compound with
the plaintiff to renounce the administration to him. He would suffer her to have
full portion of £150, and he would give her £100 more or something to that effect.
She believes Thomas PARAMOR offered to become bound to the plaintiff for the
performance of the agreement, but she denies that the agreement was ever concluded or broken. In fact it was not concluded. However there was an agreement made between Mr. George STANCOMBE, clerk, on behalf of the plaintiff
and her, on behalf of Susan, by which Susan was to have £150 over and above
the portion she had had when she married. Thomas PARAMOR consented to
this so that they might make general releases to each other and avoid further
lawsuits. By the agreement Susan renounced her letters of administration and
the plaintiff had the letters granted to him. She says that the agreement was
afterwards broken by the plaintiff. It is true that John KIRBY had credits to

2

the value of £10 and upwards at the time of his death in divers dioceses in the province of Canterbury, and letters of administration were granted out of the Prerogative Court of Canterbury on behalf of Susan, she being then within the age of 17 years, and thereby the letters granted to the plaintiff became void in law. Susan afterwards married Robert WHITE, who had since taken out letters of administration, which he did without this defendant's knowledge. She denies all combination and confederacy or that they have embezzled any plate or that the plaintiff to their knowledge paid £301 6s. 0d. as is alleged in the bill and all other charges in the bill levelled against them.

Answer of Thomas PARAMOR (Document damaged - No date)

This defendant's answer is practically the same as that of Mercy HUFFAM.

26 May 1631
Answer of Robert WHITE and Susan.

This answer is likewise similar to that of Mercy HUFFAM.

*****

C2 Chas I K. 3/12
8 November 1625

Bill of Complaint of Adam KIRBY
of Alkham, Kent,
    versus
John KIRBY and William WOOLLETT.

In August 1623 Adam KIRBY was indebted to one William WOOLLETT of Alkham, yeoman, for the sum of 39/7. Three years ago Adam became bound to WOOLLETT in the penal sum of £4 10s. 8d. for payment at Michaelmas next following. At the time of payment Adam KIRBY did not pay the 39/7 because there were other reckonings and demands between them, which were, together with bill, referred to the arbitration of Stephen WARD and Michael HUFFGATE. Adam KIRBY afterwards paid William WOOLLETT the sum of 30 shillings, part of the said 39/7, and in satis-faction of the other 9/7 William WOOLLETT hired from Adam KIRBY two horses and one of his servants to work for him. This labour, together with the carriage of one load of corn for William WOOLLETT, was more in value than 9/7. William WOOLLETT sued KIRBY and won.
In March 1623 Adam KIRBY and William WOOLLETT sowed together "to halves" 23 acres of barley and oats on land belonging to William WOOLLETT in Alkham, viz. 11 acres of barley and 12 acres of oats which Adam har-vested wholly at his own cost, and stored in William WOOLLETT'S barn at Alkham. He should have had half the barley and half the oats as well as half the straw. But William WOLLETT would not let him have more than 3 quarters of barley and 10 quarters of oats. The total yield was 22 quarters of barley and 40 quarters of oats. It was worth at least £26 and the cost of sowing it £15. He accuses William WOOLLETT of taking all

the rest, plus the straw and aftermath, and KIRBY was compelled to seek
fodder for his cattle elsewhere and some died for want of it.
John KIRBIE of Alkham, yeoman, about 7 years ago claimed title to 30 acres
of Adam's land in Alkham.   An agreement was reached between them, which
is since lost or unlawfully held by John KIRBIE.   John has made an entry
upon Adam's land and has sued him for the 30 acres with intent to recover
the land.   Since it is against all equity that William WOLLETT should take
the most part of the barley, oats and straw, whereas one half only is his due,
and whereas John KIRBIE sues Adam for the title of the land he craves the
Court to issue a writ against them.

   Answer missing.

*****

3.   C2 Chas I K.3/22*
        19 October 1633

        Second Answer of John KIRBY one of
        the defendants to the Bill of Complaint of Adam KIRBY.

In obedience to an order of this Court made 16 November last, and of a
report by virtue thereof made 12 May last by Sir Edward CLARK, Kt.,
for further Answer to the said Bill of Complaint, John KIRBY says that
he knows nothing of the fine or of the indenture to lead to the use thereof.
He knows nothing of the release mentioned in the bill supposed to be made
by John KIRBY, the father, or whether the said John KIRBY made any
subsequent release.   He knows nothing concerning the rent charge mentioned
in the bill, supposed to be granted by the plaintiff to Michael KIRBY, or
whether there is any such rent charge granted.   He denies that the plaintiff
at any time kept his father and mother and his brother Michael and his sisters.   He says that the yearly value of the land in question was £14 per
annum, and was never worth more.   As for the promise mentioned in the
bill, he says, as in his former answer, that he never made any such promise.   He says that he has the award mentioned in the bill made by Robert
BROOM, and also the award made by Francis ROGERS, which he has in
his custody and that they are too long to be recited in his answer but he is
prepared to produce them in Court.   He says, that the rent charge of £10
per annum granted to William GILLETT and assigned over to John LOTT was
issuing out of 18 acres of land in Alkham, Kent called Nack Wood and Cross-
croft.   He says it is true that he agreed to pay this rent charge of £10 to
John LOTT.   He denies that at any time he made any other agreement concerning the rent charge granted to GILLETT.   All of which he is prepared
to prove.

        *Bill missing, but probably connected with Item 2.   See also Items
        4, 5 and 6 below.

                        *****

4

Bill missing.   Answer of William
PROWD to the Bill of Complaint of John
KERBY.

William PROWD says that there was a lawsuit as is alleged in the bill,
and that Adam Kerby the other defendant asked him to one of the clerks
to the commission to set down the depositions of such witnesses as the
parties should bring before the Commissioners to be examined.   This
defendant, being well acquainted with all the commissioners, whose
names are Thomas EALES Esq., William NETHERSOLE, gent, Peter
PYARDE, an attorney-at-law, Stephen HOBDAY, yeoman, agreed and
went with KIRBY to the house of one William POLLARDE in Canterbury
where the commissioners were sitting and examined witnesses on behalf
Adam KIRBY, who was then the plaintiff as well as on behalf of John
KIRBY and John DILNETT.   Peter PYARDE, one of the commissioners,
with the consent of the others and of Adam and John KIRBY, caused one
John (?BINGHAM), servant and clerk of Peter PYARDE, to engross the
depositions of the witnesses to be examined.   At the end of the first day
on which the commission sat and examined witnesses, either Peter PYARDE
or John (?BINGHAM), his clerk, conveyed all the depositions and interrogatories to Peter PYARDE'S house in Canterbury.   Such depositions
as were not engrossed were thereupon engrossed John (?BINGHAM) at
Peter PYARDE'S house and left in his custody to be sent by him to this
Court by one Henry (?RACKHAM), gent, then of Canterbury.   This defendant denies that Adam KIRBY and he conspired to upset the plaintiff's
case in any way, or that he wilfully or corruptly altered the depositions
in any way contrary to the declared statements of the witnesses.   He also
denies that he made any alterations in the interrogatories.   He also denies
the discovery mentioned in the bill and all other unlawful practice alleged
against him.   He further says he believes that Adam KIRBY exhibited a
new bill of complaint into this Court against John KIRBY, the now plain-
till and others, to which John KIRBY put in an Answer in the Court.   In
order to make the present plaintiff give a better answer to the new bill,
Adam KIRBY obtained an order of reference from this court dated 16
November 7 Chas I (1631) to Sir Edward CLARK, Kt, one of the masters
of this Court, to consider Adam KIRBY'S new bill and the defendant's
plea and answer, which had been alleged to be insufficient.   After perusal,
Sir Edward CLARK pronounced the plea and answer to be insufficient, and
a subpoena was awarded against John KIRBY.   After John KIRBY had made
a better answer to Adam KIRBY'S second bill, Adam KIRBY replied to it
by serving John KIRBY with a subpoena.   After this Adam KIRBY came to
this defendant and asked him to be one of his commissioners with John
STANLY, Alderman of Canterbury, Thomas ELWIN an Attorney in H.M.
Court of King's Bench and one Francis ----- of Canterbury.   This defendant agreed and took the names of the commissioners up to London, and
delivered them to Thomas SUMMERS, one of the Clerks of this Court.
He told him that Adam KIRBY wanted a commission the next vacation to
examine the witnesses in his lawsuit then pending before this Court, and
that John KIRBY and Mr. Francis LOVELACE Esq., his counsel, refused
to join in the commission with him.   He also said that Mr. SUMMERS
would within a month after the end of Trinity Term, send the commission
to Adam KIRBY to Canterbury.   This was sent about four days before
Michaelmas last so that Adam KIRBY could not, by virtue of that commission, examine any witnesses.   The examination eventually took place in
John STANLY'S house in Canterbury on 31 March last (1634).   After

April last this defendant and Francis HAWLETT went to the parish of
Alkham, Kent, 12 miles from Canterbury, to the house of one Adam
CHANDON, a lame man nearly 80 years old, and Elizabeth his wife
about 60 years old, whom not being able to travel to Canterbury, this
defendant and Francis HAWLETT examined. ..... (Three lines inter-
polated and illegible.) ..... The defendant denies all other charges
mentioned in the bill.

*****

5.   C2 Chas I K.12/67
        Sworn 12 June 1634.

        Bill missing.   Answer of Adam
        KIRBY to the Bill of Complaint of John KIRBY.

The defendant says that he believes that John KIRBY, deceased, late
father of the plaintiff and of this defendant, was seised in fee tail of the
messuage and lands mentioned in the bill, and not in fee simple; and of
one half of another messuage or tenement and land in fee simple in the
parish of Ringwolde (Ringwould) Kent, being all lands of the nature and
tenure of gavelkind partable amongst the heirs according to the custom
of gavelkind used in the county of Kent. (The next sentence is erased
in the original.) And also that John the father was seised in fee of
half of other lands lying in Ringwolde in the said county. The defendant
says that his father, by a deed dated 30 October 1601 did convey to him
and his heirs half his messuage, tenements, lands and hereditaments with
their appurtenances in the parish of Ringwolde and elsewhere in the
county. Further John KIRBY, the father, did about August 1608, by
his will, give all his houses, lands etc. in the parish of Alkham to this
defendant and his heirs male forever. After making this conveyance and
will, John KIRBY, the father, finding himself and Alice his wife, the
defendant's mother, to be old, sickly and poor, partly by reason of their
great charge in bringing up many of their children, did about that time
yield up to the defendant the full possession of all the aforesaid lands.
Thereupon the defendant entered into them and dwelt in the principal messuage. He was reputed sole owner for about 20 years even until the death
of the defendant's father who died about 10 years ago. During all this
time the defendant kept his father and mother and one or two of his sisters
who were then young maidens. John KIRBY the father, in order to streng-
then the defendant's estate and title in the said premises, about February
14 Jas I (1617) released to the defendant and his heirs all rights to his
lands in Alkham. Thereupon the defendant, by his father's appointment
and for the maintenance of Michael KIRBY, his youngest brother, and
for his portion which John KIRBY his father intended to give him (Michael
KIRBY), granted Michael KIRBY an annuity of £10 a year to be issuing
out of all the lands in Alkham for 4 years. John KIRBY, the now plaintiff
was then also present at the house of one Stephen PILCHER of Coldred,
Kent, yeoman, where the deed of Release of the annuity was executed.
Intending to settle the estate in Alkham and Ringwolde upon this defendant
and his heirs for ever, according to his former deeds and his will, John
KIRBY, the father made a deed dated June 15 Jas I (1617) agreeing with
one William EDWARDS that he John KIRBY sr, should levy a fine before
the Court of Common Pleas of all the aforesaid lands etc. in Alkham.
This fine was levied and acknowledged accordingly. It was declared in

the indenture that the fine was to the use of the defendant and his heirs, and the defendant further says that about 16 years ago (1618), as far as he remembers, the plaintiff, having wasted his means and become indebted to many men, came to him and his father and asked them to help him pay £10 to one LUSHINGTON, one of his creditors. Whereupon this defendant, taking compassion on his brother, let him have cattle worth £10 to pay LUSHINGTON. About that time the plaintiff asked his father and this defendant to grant him a newly built house and a barn and 18 acres of land (part of the aforesaid lands formerly conveyed to this defendant). This defendant and his father consented to the plaintiff's request. A conveyance was drawn up, and the defendant and his father by their joint deed dated 19 Jas I (1621) conveyed to the plaintiff and his heirs the new messuage, barn and 18 acres in Alkham. At the same time they released their right and title to him and his heirs forever, he being then in possession and on the strength of that the defendant procured £10 towards the payment of the plaintiff's debts. The plaintiff has ever since by force of that deed peace-ably enjoyed the premises. About that time and according to the agreement the defendant's father, to prevent all trouble which might arise after his death between the defendant and the plaintiff, directed Adam KIRBY and John KIRBY to make releases to one another concerning their several parts of the lands. Accordingly the plaintiff and defendant went together from Alkham to Dover to one Thomas WATKINS, gent, who made two deeds of release, one from the defendant to the plaintiff of the new house, barn and 18 acres in Alkham, and the other from the plaintiff to the defendant Adam KIRBY of the other house, barn and about 13 acres of arable land, 7 acres of pasture, 6 acres of woodland, wherein this defendant was then and for many years before had been living by force of the former conveyance and fine. Both releases were sealed and delivered in the presence of Thomas WATKINS each to the other and they were at the special request of the plaintiff left in Thomas WATKINS' custody to be delivered by him to one Charles TRIPP Esq., then a Counsellor at Law for John KIRBY, who was appointed by them both to make further deeds and covenants between them concerning the quiet enjoyment of the lands. But Charles TRIPP died before anything more could be done. The defendant greatly suspects that the plaintiff has got releases into his custody. Long before that time, it was further agreed between John KIRBY senior and John KIRBY junior that whereas John sr had by his deed dated March 7 Jas I (1609) granted a rent charge of £10 per annum issuing from the lands in Alkham to one William GILLETT on the condition for the redemption of the said rent charge by the payment of £100 to the said GILLETT at a date mentioned in the indenture which one John LOTT about 11 Jas I (1613) bought from GILLETT, that the plaintiff should during the lifetime of his father pay to John LOTT the rent of £10 a year according to the covenant. John KIRBY jr paid John LOTT for about 2 or 3 years, but because John KIRBY jr ceased paying the rent to John LOTT, and also because Adam KIRBY gave out that the lands out of which the rent was due had formerly been conveyed to him by his father before granting the rent charge to GILLETT; and because they were thus not liable for the rent, John LOTT sued Adam KIRBY and his father and the plaintiff for the rent. Thereupon Adam and John KIRBY being unwilling to contend the suit referred the matter to arbitration. John LOTT and Adam and John KIRBY agreed together to appoint Francis RAYWORTH the elder, gent, and Thomas WATKINS as arbitrators to settle their differences with Robert BROOM, clerk, as umpire, in case the arbitrators should not make an award between the parties within the specified time limit. Accordingly Adam KIRBY came bound to John LOTT for £100 to perform the award of the arbitrators, and he similarly became bound to his brother for £100 and likewise John LOTT and John KIRBY jr each became bound to him (Adam KIRBY) in a similar way. Robert BROOM made his award as follows: John KIRBY jr should pay John LOTT 40/-

towards the redemption of the annuity, Adam KIRBY should pay John LOTT
in full discharge of the rent due at Lady Day next following, £120, £10 in
November 1620 and £110 more on 25 March next following.
Robert BROOM'S award was published but not delivered to Adam KIRBY
until the first payment of £10 and the second payment of £110 were due,
and then it was delivered to Adam KIRBY in Alkham in the presence of
witnesses, namely Benjamin KLOOKE and John MARSH of Alkham and
others.   Adam KIRBY was holding the award behind him when KLOOKE
snatched it from him and gave it to John MARSH, who with the plaintiff
have ever since kept it from the defendant.   In November 19 Jas I (1621)
Adam KIRBY was arrested and imprisoned in Dover at the suit of John
LOTT upon an action of debt on the said bond of £100.   He was detained
in prison for the space of 3 or 4 months until such time as he was forced
to satisfy John LOTT and to pass over to the plaintiff, John KIRBY jr and
Michael KIRBY, his brother a messuage, barn and stable and 5 or 6 acres
of land in the town of Folkestone of the yearly value of £6 per annum which
he, Adam KIRBY, had bought in 1623.   John KIRBY sr being sick caused
Adam and John jr to come before him, and straightly charged them to agree
together and live together as loving brethren should do.   He charged Adam
to suffer John jr quietly to enjoy the new house, barn and 18 acres and in
like manner he charged John jr to let Adam enjoy the other messuage and
barn etc. wherein he Adam had lived for at least 20 years.   About 3 or 4
days after the death of John KIRBY sr John jr said he hoped to live ..
(4 lines ruled out) .. Not long after John jr and Michael KIRBY sold the
house, barn, stable and 5 or 6 acres of land in Folkestone for £100 or
£120 and therewith John jr paid John LOTT £100 and Adam likewise paid
him £10, part of the £120 awarded to him as aforesaid.   Adam likewise
gave John jr certain calves and sheep, which were then well worth £10,
towards a further payment of the said £120.   During all this time Adam
occupied house, barn, stables, 13 acres of arable, 7 acres of pasture and
6 acres of wood in Alkham according to the former agreement and release.
Since the death of John sr John jr and John MARSH got possession of the
release and either cancelled it or made away with it.   After about 16
April 1626 or 1627 John jr caused Adam to be again arrested in Dover
and imprisoned for a debt of £100 which John jr supposed he owed him,
which Adam had entered into for the performance of Robert BROOM'S
award.   Adam lost the case and was detained two months in prison.   The
plaintiff made a forcible entry into his house etc. at Alkham and evicted
him from all his lands and has kept possession of them ever since and
taken the whole profits thereof for his own use.   After 20 May the plaintiff and John MARSH came to Adam in prison and there Adam charged the
plaintiff with having done him a great wrong first by getting him and his
father to assure to him (the plaintiff) the new house and barn and to give
him £10 and then to force him to prison.   John jr and John MARSH persuaded Adam to refer all differences to arbitration of Francis ROGERS DD.
In order to be released from prison he agreed to do this.   He became
bound to John jr for £100 for the performance of the award of Francis
ROGERS.   Shortly afterwards John jr and John MARSH went to Francis
ROGERS while Adam still remained in prison, and induced him to make an
award.   Adam hearing from John jr that Francis ROGERS had made his
award was then suffered to be·set at liberty but only to go from the prison
to Alkham where the plaintiff and John MARSH were in company with Francis
ROGERS and others.   There the plaintiff, John MARSH and Francis
ROGERS procured the sum of £50 and tendered the same to Adam which was
not by the award to be paid to him until 3 months after, which Adam was
forced to receive on pain of return to prison.
They threatened Adam and compelled him to draw up a release to the plaintiff which they pretended was awarded by Francis ROGERS of the afore-

said lands etc.   Later Adam being at liberty found that the award was not
good in law and that he had been wronged and deceived by it, and that it
was but a confederacy between John KIRBY jr and John MARSH to imprison
him with the object of defrauding him of all his lands and money and of
freeing the rent charge.   (document torn) ...
He denies collusion with William PROWD and denies that William PROWD
altered the depositions in any way.   He also denies that PROWD kept any
commission or deposition of any kind, or that he knew anything as is alleged
in the bill touching this defendant's witnesses.   He also denies the discovery mentioned in the bill and any other fraudulent practices alleged
against him.   He also denies that John KIRBY, the father, or Alice, his
wife, were seised in their demesne as a freehold during their lives, with
remainder to the plaintiff the heirs males and to the right heirs of John
KIRBY sr.   He denies that the plaintiff became bound in obligations such
as are alleged in the Bill, and also that the plaintiff has paid the portions
mentioned in the Bill.   He also denies that after the death of John sr and
Alice, his wife, the messuage and premises came to the plaintiff and denies
that the plaintiff ought to have had and enjoyed the same.   He also says
that John KIRBY sr understood all the deeds and that nothing was concealed
from him ..... (A large part of this document is blurred and illegible and
consists of denials of all the charges alleged in the bill.)

C2 Chas I K.26/70

The Replication of Adam KIRBY
Plaintiff to the several Answers
of John KIRBY and John DILNETT.

Adds nothing.

The joint Rejoinders of John
KIRBY and John DILNETT to
Adam KIRBY'S Bill of Complaint.

They maintain everything contained in their answers to be true.   They
maintain that John KIRBY the father was defrauded, as is alleged in their
answer, and that the matter touching the deed of feoffment was true.   They
maintain that their father made the deed of feoffment to BENNETT and
MARSH; that the plaintiff did join their father in a deed of feoffment and
John jr further says that the plaintiff by his deed of 20 May Chas I for £50
paid to him by this defendant made a release to him and his heirs of the
house and lands mentioned in the answer.

*****

C21 K.3/10

Interrogatories to be administered
to witnesses to be produced on
behalf of Adam KIRBY Plaintiff
against John KIRBY, Francis ROGERS,
John MARSH and others.

1. Do you know the plaintiff and defendant how long have you known them ?

2. Did you know John KIRBY deceased, father of the plaintiff and of John KIRBY the defendant; was he seised in fee simple of half a messuage and certain lands in Ringwold, Kent, and other lands in Alkham Kent; of what nature and tenure are the lands and what are they worth when let by the year ?

3. Did John KIRBY, the father, in his lifetime, convey to Adam KIRBY the plaintiff one half of the messuage and tenement in Ringwold and half of his lands elsewhere in Kent; have you heard John KIRBY, the father, confess that he made such a deed ?

4. Has Adam KIRBY, during his father's lifetime, sold his title to the messuage in Ringwold; to whom has he sold it, and has the party to whom he sold the said half messuage peacably enjoyed it ever since ?

5. Did John KIRBY, the father, make a will, and is this writing now showed to you his will; who wrote it and where, were you a witness to it; was John KIRBY in perfect mind and sense when he made it; where was he, how many miles from his dwelling, whence caused this his will to be made; are the other witnesses alive or dead now; did you see the testator make his mark and set his seal to it ?

6. Did John KIRBY, the father, yield up possession to the plaintiff Adam of one barn, one messuage and lands in Alkham, the lands in question; did Adam occupy them to the death of his father; was Adam reputed sole owner of them; did he maintain and sustain his father, mother and brother Michael and two of his sisters; how long since John KIRBY, the father died ?

7. Did you know that John, the father, and Adam conveyed to John KIRBY, the defendant a messuage and 18 acres in Alkham; were you a witness to the deed; was there any timber then given to build him a house; was the land, timber etc. given in performance of an agreement formerly made between the three of them ?

8. Has the defendant John ever since enjoyed peaceable possession of the messuage and 18 acres; how many years is it since he first had the estate in it; has he sold any of it, how many acres has he sold and to whom and for how much, and has he sold any other land ?

9. Was John KIRBY the defendant, by agreement with his father and brother to pay Adam £10 a year for the 18 acres etc. for 10 years or else pay his brother Michael and his sisters the legacies given by John their father in his will ?

10

10. Have you heard that John KIRBY, the father, before he died charged his sons Adam and John to live peaceably together as brothers should, and that Adam should let John enjoy the barn and 16 acres in Alkham, and that John should let Adam live in the house at Alkham ?

11. Have you heard John the defendant say he would be glad to take the barn and 18 acres in satisfaction for his portion of land which he should have from his father; what legacy was he to pay to his brother Michael and his sisters and did the father give the defendant John the land in question to pay out of it the said legacies ?

12. Did John, the father, thereupon demand and require John, the son, to deliver to him a deed to be cancelled, formerly made by him, the father, to Peter BENNETT and John MARSH in trust to the use of the father and his wife for their lives and after to the use of the defendant John KIRBY, and what answer did the latter make to his father ?

13. Was it agreed between Adam and the defendant John that they should make releases to each other of all the cont-roversies and demands between them; did the defendant John make such a release and what was the substance of it ?

14. Why was the release made between the plaintiff and John KIRBY the defendant ?

15. Who gave them instructions for making of the releases, and what were they; why are they not to be seen and where are they; were the releases left with Mr. Charles TRYPP, deceased ?

16. Were the releases made for the assuring of certain lands of which the plaintiff was then in possession by previous conveyance of John KIRBY, the father ?

17. What other thing can you say to prove that John, the father, conveyed the lands in question to the plaintiff ?

18. Did you see the releases sealed by John, the father, to the plaintiff, and by the plaintiff to the defendant, and were you a witness thereto ?

19. Who else were then present besides yourself at the seal-ing of the release, declare their names and all matters touching the same and touching the controversies between the then parties.

20. Were the controversies between the plaintiff and John KIRBY and John LOTT of Chillenden all referred to arbitrament of Francis RAWORTH, late of Dover, gent; deceased and Thomas WATKINS, gent, and ·to the umperage of Robert

BROOME, Clerk, the then Minister of Ringwold, and did they make an award and what was the substance of it ?

21. Did you know that Adam KIRBY paid in money or cattle the sum of £10 to Ingram LUSHINGTON or Symon LUSHINGTON and was it the proper debt of John KIRBY or not; why did Adam KIRBY pay it, and what can you say to prove that Adam has sustained a wrong by John KIRBY touching the lands in question or paying of money to John LOTT in discharge of one annuity of £10 per annum granted by John KIRBY, the father, to William GILLETT to be issuing out of the lands at Alkham and in paying the arrears on the annuity according to the award of Robert BROOME ?

22. Was the annuity discharged by the sale of Adam KIRBY'S land in Folkestone, and should Adam by any agreement made by him with his brother have to him and his heirs and lands in question, or not, declare what you know.

23. Did Joseph MARSH, the son of John MARSH, one of the defendants serve on the jury at Maidstone which tried the case there between John DILNETT and Adam KIRBY, and did John MARSH procure Christopher SPICER to travel to the Assizes to serve on the jury; was it not 30 miles from SPICER'S dwelling to Maidstone; what reward have Joseph MARSH and Christopher SPICER received for so travelling, and of whom did they receive it ?

24. How much money have John or Joseph MARSH lent to John KIRBY the defendant since they first commenced suit against each other ... (The rest of this question is interlined and impossible to read.)

25. Did John KIRBY, the defendant ask Adam to ask their father to settle the messuage and 18 acres of land on him, the defendant, and was John to pay Adam £10 a year in consideration thereof, or pay Michael KIRBY, their brother, and their sisters their portions.

26. Did John KIRBY, the defendant, after his father's death ask John MARSH what he should do with the lands that his brother Adam then occupied, and what advice did MARSH give; how long had Adam KIRBY dwelt in the house and lands in question ?

27. When John KIRBY, the defendant, had caused Adam to be arrested and imprisoned in Dover, did he obtain possession of the house, barn and lands then in Adam's possession and occupation ?

28. Where was Adam when John the defendant obtained possession of the houses and lands, and who was in possession when he took them; what company had John when he took possession and what were their names ?

12

29. When Adam was in prison in Dover, did John KIRBY
    and John MARSHE come to him, and what communication
    did they have with him; did they persuade Adam to lay
    the case before Francis ROGERS, then Minister of the
    parish of Denton for his arbituration ?

30. Did Adam, during his imprisonment give a bond of £100
    to stand by the award of Francis ROGERS, and did John
    KIRBY likewise give a bond to stand by it ... (The rest
    of this question is heavily interlined and nearly illegible.)

31. Did John KIRBY cause Adam to be arrested in Dover on
    a bond of £100 to stand by the award of Robert BROOME ?

32. Was Adam bailed out of prison to go to Alkham to hear
    the award of Doctor ROGERS, or was he suffered to go
    there without putting in bail, and was he then returned
    to prison in case he did not agree to the award ?

33. Is it the general opinion of the people of Alkham that John
    MARSHE is the instigator behind John KIRBY in his
    actions against Adam, and do you believe that John KIRBY
    has greatly wronged his brother ?

34. Was it on John MARSH'S advice that John had Adam
    arrested so that he could seize his lands?

35. In what way has Adam KIRBY been defrauded and de-
    ceived by John KIRBY, Francis ROGERS and John
    MARSHE; is ROGERS' award just and if not why not ?

36. Was John KIRBY endebted to Adam when he had the latter
    arrested on the bond of £100 ?

37. Did John MARSHE and Peter BENNETT persuade John
    KIRBY, the father, to make a deed of his lands in Alkham
    to them to certain uses specified in the deed, and did
    John, the father, say that it was not made according to
    his mind and therefore he would have it cancelled ?

38. Did you hear John KIRBY, the defendant, say that although
    his father had given a greater part of his lands to Adam than
    he had given him, yet he hoped to live as well with his
    smaller portion as Adam would with his larger share, or
    words to that effect; what else have you heard him say on
    this subject ?

39. Did Adam assign over to John certain cattle and sheep and
    was John KIRBY to pay in consideration thereof £29 to John
    LOTT as part of the arrears of the annuity of £10 per annum
    granted by their father to William GYLLETT, and assigned
    by GYLLETT to LOTT ?

40. Did John MARSHE about 7 or 8 years ago ask you to ride
    to Maidstone Assizes to serve on a jury there to try a suit
    between John DILNETT, and Adam KIRBY in an action of

trespass and ejectment; what reward did MARSHE offer you, and who else did he persuade to do the same beside yourself ?

41. Did ROGERS, before he made his award, know that Adam had been arrested and imprisoned at Dover ?

42. Was Francis ROGERS minister at Alkham when he undertook the award, or was he then dwelling at Denton and minister of that parish; who was minister of Alkham when the award was made ?

43. Were there any other controversies between Adam and John when they entered bonds of £100 to each other to abide by ROGERS' award other than an action of debt commenced by John against Adam then before the Mayor and Jurats of Dover held at the Guildhall there on a bond of £100 to stand by an award of Francis RAWORTH and Thomas WATKINS or the umperage of Robert BROOME ?

44. Did ROGERS make his award before Adam was set at liberty and was it read to him while he was in prison; who read it to him ?

45. Did ROGERS, as a Justice of the Peace, sign any warrant for the apprehension of Adam KIRBY, and for what cause; were you constable at the time ?

46. When Adam KIRBY first examined witnesses at Canterbury by virtue of HM Commission ... (interlined and illegible) ... was ROGERS examined by the commissioners on behalf of John KIRBY, the defendant; how was his deposition taken; did Francis ROGERS then and there fall out with Adam KIRBY and beat him ?

47. Was Benjamin CLARK, deceased then examined on behalf of KIRBY ?

48. Did you ever hear John KIRBY say that if he could get his brother Adam arrested and put in prison he would then get him to come to an agreement with him ?

49. When you were at Maidstone Assizes to hear the case of DILNETT v. Adam KIRBY, did you hear John KIRBY offer to give Adam the messuage and barn and half the lands in Alkham then in Adam's occupation; for what reason did John make this offer ?

50. Illegible.

51. Nearly illegible, but deals with the will of John KIRBY, the father.

52. As 51 also about the will.

53. Did you write this deed of release now showed to you
and did you see John KIRBY, the father, write his mark and
set his seal thereto and deliver it as his act and deed to
Adam KIRBY ... (Nearly illegible, but concerns the
witnesses to the deed.)

54. What other thing can you say to prove that the plaintiff
ought to have the messuage and lands in question and
satisfaction for his lands in Folkestone which John KIRBY
the defendant, sold, if he did not redeem the annuity and
arrears thereof to John LOTT, and for the sheep and cattle
which the plaintiff had delivered towards the payment
thereof ?

*****

C21 K.3/10

DEPOSITIONS taken at Canterbury
31 March, 16, 17 and 19 April 10
Chas I on behalf of Adam KIRBY
Plaintiff against John KIRBY
Francis ROGERS and John MARSHE,
defendants by virtue of HM
Commission forth of His Highness'
Court of Chancery to John STANLEY,
Esq., Thomas ELWIN, William PROWD
and Francis HAWLETT, gents or to
three or two of them directed
for the examination of witnesses
between the said parties.

Michael KIRBY of Alkham, Kent, husbandman, aged 50.

1. The parties to the case are his brothers John and Adam.
He has known John MARSHE 40 years and Francis ROGERS
about 20.

2. He knows John KIRBY, the father, who was his father.
John KIRBY, the father, was long reputed the owner of
lands in Ringwold mentioned in the interrogatory, but
he does not know of what tenure he held them.   He gave
half these lands to Adam.   He was also seised in fee
simple of two messuages and over 40 acres of land in
Alkham of the tenure of gavelkind, and that these lands
are well worth £30 per annum.

3. He has heard his father say he gave Adam half his lands
in Ringwold and elsewhere in Kent.

15

4. He knows that Adam sold his share of land in Ringwold during his father's lifetime and that the party who bought it has enjoyed it quietly ever since.

6. He well knows that the father yielded up possession to the plaintiff the messuage and lands mentioned in this interrogatory, and that Adam was reputed sole owner. He agrees that Adam maintained the family and that John, the father, died about ten years since.

7. He agrees that the lands were so conveyed to John, the son and that he was a witness to the deed.

8. It is 14 or 15 years since the conveyance was made to John, the son, and of late years he has sold away to Joseph MARSHE the messuage, barn and 12 or 13 acres of land for £80. John KIRBY did not at any time hold by lease any of his father's lands other than the said messuage, barn and 18 acres.

9. Long before the messuage, barn and 18 acres were conveyed to John it was agreed that John should pay Adam £10 a year for 8 years and that he should enter bond to pay this deponent and his sisters certain legacies; he should release all his right and title to Adam in the old messuage, barn and about 30 acres while Adam should release his right and title in the other messuage, barn and 18 acres.

10. He agrees that this happened and that John for his part has enjoyed peaceably the messuage and 18 acres in Alkham ever since. About 9 years ago John dispossessed Adam of the old messuage and 30 acres and Adam was demnified thereby at the least £200.

11. He agrees and says that John entered several bonds to pay him and his sisters £20 given them by their father's will.

12. When the father and Adam conveyed the messuage and 18 acres to John KIRBY the defendant, the father asked John to give up the deeds mentioned in this interrogatory to be cancelled. But the son said that he had not got them in his keeping, but that he would never use them to harm Adam.

13. He has nothing to add to his answer to the 9th interrogatory.

14. The reason for making the releases was so that John and Adam should each enjoy their respective lands in peace.

16. Nothing to add beyond what he said in the 6th and 9th interrogatories.

17. Nothing to add beyond what he said in the 6th, 7th and 9th interrogatories.

21. He remembers this incident because John was not able to pay the £10 himself. Adam was hindered of £200 at least

by reason of John's dispossessing him. He also sold his house and land at Folkestone to pay John LOTT the annuity and arrears of £120.

22.   John LOTT was paid £120 as deposed in the last answer.

25.   He agrees.

26.   There was such a speech in Alkham after the father's death and John KIRBY did ask MARSHE'S advice about the land.   Adam had lived there for more than 20 years.

27.   When John caused Adam to be arrested, this deponent kept possession of the messuage and 30 acres for Adam, but his brother John came and dispossessed him.

28.   When John KIRBY came to dispossess them he brought one John PARKER and others whose names he does not know.

29.   John KIRBY sent this deponent to Adam in prison and asked him to agree to sign a bond of £100 to abide by the arbitration of ROGERS if he, John, would do the same.

30.   Adam agreed and became bound as stated, and so did John.

32.   Adam was discharged from prison after signing the bond and went to Alkham, but he did not put in any bail to answer the action so far as this deponent remembers.

33.   It is true as set down in the interrogatory.

34.   When John KIRBY and John MARSHE were together at Dover, this deponent remembers them sending him to ask Adam to join them at Dover to sign an agreement.   When Adam came they had him arrested and imprisoned, and by that means persuaded him to become bound in £100 as aforesaid.   The lands are worth more than £20 a year and Adam is demnified £200 by John as a consequence of his proceedings.

35.   By reason of his imprisonment at Dover.   The award was not fair because our father gave the messuage and lands in question to Adam and his heirs and the messuage and lands and 18 acres to John for his heirs, which is and was formerly agreed between them.

36.   Yes.

37.   John MARSHE persuaded John KIRBY, the deponent's father to make the assignment, but whether Peter BENNETT did he knows not.   He has heard his father say the deed was not made according to his liking and he would have it cancelled.

39.   Yes, but whether John KIRBY paid John LOTT the £29 he does not know.

41.   He did know of Adam's imprisonment, because John KIRBY, the defendant sent this deponent to Denton to tell ROGERS

about it.

42. Francis ROGERS was Minister of Denton when he made the award and dwelt there. One Master HARBER was minister of Alkham at that time.

44. Yes.

46. While we and the commissioners were writing depositions at Canterbury of a sudden we heard a great noise and falling out in another chamber in the said house wherein the commissioners did then sit, and thereupon they sent the clerk to learn what the matter was. Then came Francis ROGERS and Adam KIRBY before the commissioners, and Adam complained that ROGERS had hit him with his fist in the face, which ROGERS did then confess to be true.

50. It is true that John MARSHE and John KIRBY did (after this deponent had been examined before the commissioners in Canterbury) find fault with him because he had declared that John LOTT had been paid £120 in discharge of the annuity by the sale of Adam's house and lands in Folkestone.

52. John KIRBY, the father, lay sick 14 days before he died. This deponent's sister, Christian HANDON, widow, did attend him. Neither Francis ROGERS nor John MARSHE visited him during the time of his last sickness. He never heard of his father's making a will either during his last sickness or within 20 years of his death.

53. He was present at the house of one Steven PILCHER of Coldred in Kent, yeoman where his father John KIRBY caused Mr. Thomas WATKINS of Dover to write a release which is now showed to him. He saw his father sign and seal it.

54. In all conscience and equity Adam KIRBY ought to have to him and his heirs the messuage, barn and 30 acres and also the £10 paid to Ingram LUSHINGTON or Simon LUSHINGTON and much more money for the cattle and sheep which John KIRBY the defendant had of him and also the year's rent of the lands in question besides his costs and charges at law.

Richard SIMMONS of Swainfield, Kent, yeoman aged 57.   16 April 1634 at Canterbury.

1. He has known the plaintiff and defendant for about 16 years.

6. Adam KIRBY, being in this deponent's debt during the lifetime of John KIRBY, the father, in the sum of £16, and for the true payment thereof, Adam, then being in possession of the lands etc. in question, did by his deed about 15 years

18

ago grant an annuity or rent charge of 32/- a year to be paid out of the lands, and John and Michael KIRBY became bound in an obligation of £30 to him as security for its payment.

46. He remembers Francis ROGERS striking Adam KIRBY with his fist during the examination at Canterbury.

John LOTT of Chillenden, Kent, yeoman, aged 80. 17 and 18 April 1634.

1. He knows John KIRBY, Adam KIRBY, John MARSHE and Francis ROGERS, and has known them for about 20 years.

2. He knew the father, but not what estate he had of the lands in Ringwold, but he knows that father enfeoffed his son Adam in half the said lands and that Robert BROOME, clerk and minister of Ringwold did by virtue of a letter of Attorney give state and seisin of the lands to the plaintiff. The lands were formerly worth £20 per year.

3. He knows this to be true.

6. About 30 year ago John KIRBY, the father, gave up possession of the messuage and lands in question to the plaintiff, and the plaintiff did maintain his family there until his father died.

7. Yes   John KIRBY the son was to pay an annuity to this deponent of £10 a year which the father had formerly made to GYLETT, but which GYLETT had assigned over to him. However the son only paid 2 years, and there were arrears of £22, of which Adam paid £20 and John, the defendant paid £2.

8. Yes.   John, the son, has had the land for about 16 years. He has sold the messuage and 13 of the 18 acres to Joseph MARSHE.

9. He does not know.

10. This answer repeats the story as above concerning the dispossession and imprisonment of Adam.

11. The defendant said that he would be glad to accept the lands as his portion at the house of and in the presence of this deponent in Chillenden.

20. RAWORTH and WATKINS could not agree on an equitable award (interlined and nearly illegible.)

21. John KIRBY, the defendant, by selling Adam's house and lands at Folkestone, raised money to pay this deponent £120.

24. £10

25. John, the father, said in this deponent's hearing he
would give his son John timber to build a house and
barn at Chalksale and he knows this was done and
the house and barn built.

26. Adam had enjoyed the premises about 30 years at the
time his father died.

33. It is.

34. He can add nothing to his former answers except that
Adam paid this deponent two instalments of £10, which
John should have paid, and is thereby wronged by John.

35. He does not think ROGER'S award is fair.

38. He agrees that John did make the statement attributed
to him in the interrogatory.

39. Yes.

41. Yes.

42. ROGERS was living at Denton.

43. No, there were no other suits besides the one mentioned.

46. He saw Francis ROGERS strike Adam KIRBY.

50. When this deponent was examined at Canterbury, John
MARSHE and John KIRBY were very angry with him for
saying that they had sold Adam's land in Folkestone to
pay him this deponent.

John PARKER of Alkham, Blacksmith aged 30.

1. He has known the plaintiff and John KIRBY and John
MARSHE all his life and Francis ROGERS 14 years.

27. He, together with John KIRBY, the defendant, and Thomas
PARKER, this deponent's brother, while Adam was imprisoned at Dover, obtained possession of the messuage
and lands mentioned in this interrogatory from Michael
KIRBY, who then kept possession of it.

DEPOSITIONS taken at Alkham on
14 and 15 April 1634 on behalf
of Adam KIRBY.

20

Elizabeth HAMMON, wife of Adam HAMMON, of Alkham,
yeoman, aged 60.

1. She has known John, Adam KIRBY and John MARSHE for
   40 years and Francis ROGERS for 12.

2. John KIRBY was her father, and she knows he was the
   owner of the lands in Alkham.

11. Within three days of the death of John KIRBY, her father,
    and before he was buried, she heard her brother John
    KIRBY, the defendant, say that he would hold himself
    contented with the messuage and 18 acres which their
    father had formerly given him, wherein he then dwelt,
    and he hoped to live as well as his brother Adam who
    had more land.

Michael SPAREPOYNT of Caple, Kent, husbandman, aged 50.

1. He has known John and Adam KIRBY 40 years, and John
   MARSHE 40 years, and Francis ROGERS 20 years.

2. He knew John, the father, for he is married to one of his
   daughters.

6. He knows Adam lived in the house for 12 years till his
   father died and did maintain his father and mother.   The
   father died about 9 years ago.

7. He remembers the agreement mentioned, and also that the
   father gave John the defendant, timber for his house and
   barn.

8. Yes for about 20 years until he sold some part of it to
   Joseph MARSHE.

9. Yes.

10. Four days before he died the father commanded his sons
    John and Adam to live peaceably together, but John caused
    Adam to be arrested and imprisoned and while in prison
    dispossessed him of the lands in question.

21. It was John, the defendant's proper debt and Adam paid it.

22. It was paid out of the sale of the Folkestone lands.

25. He can add nothing to his former answers.

27. John, the defendant, did obtain possession in this way.

38. He did hear the defendant remark to this effect.

50. John KIRBY and MARSHE were very angry with him for
    deposing as he did in Canterbury.

52. John, the father, was ill two or three weeks before he
    died and was looked after by his daughter Christian
    HANDON and the then wife of Michael KIRBY.   He has
    heard of no will made by John, the father.

                        *****

8.   C2 Chas I K.11/42
        8 November 1641

        Bill of Complaint of Adam KIRBY
        of Canterbury, yeoman.
         versus
        Mary FURSER.

In October 1638 Adam KIRBY, at the request of one Mary FURSER of
Canterbury, widow, did carry out of the yard of the said Mary a great
quantity of dung, being about 20 loads, to her ground which lies within
the liberty of the city about two miles distant.   Mary FURSER promised
to pay Adam KIRBY a sum such as it was reasonably worth.
He also in July 1639 and July 1640 did work for her in her pasture ground
in the parish of Northgate, making several haystacks, in which work he
occupied a whole week, for which she promised to pay him.
In February 1639/40 he kept one gelding for her for 6 weeks for which
she promised to pay.   In November 1639 Mary FURSER, having occasion
to use some straw to make a hovel in her yard, asked to buy two loads of
straw from him whereupon he delivered them to her.   Also in November
1639 he delivered her one load of wood, in the years 1638 and 1639 at
several times he lent her several sums of money, in all amounting to £8.
During the winter quarter 1639/40 he sold and carried to and for one
William WATMORE, gent, 250 loads of dung to the full value of £10, for
which the said William WATMORE promised payment.   Notwithstanding
Adam KIRBY performed all the work for Mary FURSER for which she
ought to give him reasonable satisfaction, yet she refuses either to
account with him or to give him recompense.   William WATMORE is
since deceased and Mary WATMORE his wife refuses to discover to him
whether she is executrix or administratrix and she also refuses to give
him satisfaction for the dung and carriage.   He therefore seeks remedy
at law.

        C2 Chas I K.11/42
        Sworn 23 January 1641/2

        Answer of Mary FURSER, widow,
        to the Bill of Complaint of Adam KIRBY.

                        22

She denies that the plaintiff ever carried out of her yard a great quantity
of dung to her ground.   She also denies that he ever did any work for
her or make any stacks of hay then or at any other time mentioned in the
bill.   She denies that he kept a gelding for her for 6 weeks or otherwise, or that he delivered her 2 loads of straw or a load of wood or that
he ever lent her any money.   She denies making any promises such as
are alleged in the bill, all of which she is prepared to prove before the
Court.

*****

C21 C.8/8 and C2 Chas I C35/2.
16 June 1642

Bill of Complaint of Edmund CASTLE,
plaintiff, versus John KIRBY defendant.

Elizabeth KIRBY, wife of the defendant John KIRBY, was granted a
portion on marriage.   If she died without issue it was agreed she should
leave £40 for the use of the plaintiff's children, whose mother was her
only sister, Joanne.   In November 1640 the defendant, John KIRBY,
became bound for £80 to pay the plaintiff £40 nine months after Elizabeth's
death.   He refuses.

Answer missing.   Replication of
Edmund CASTLE.
Hilary Term 1642

He re-iterates the truth of the Bill.   Elizabeth, the defendant's late
wife, before she married him intended to give or lend a good part of her
estate to the plaintiff's children if she died without issue.   On her death,
without issue, therefore, the sum of £40 became due as alleged.
The following witnesses testify to the truth of the plaintiff's case:-

William THURLBY, of Dover, Kent, gent aged 25.
John MARSH of Dymchurch, yeoman aged 30.
Elizabeth, the wife of George DALLIDOWNE, feltmaker, of Dover
    aged 44.
Richard HARNBROOK of --------- Kent, yeoman aged 40.
Richard LUSHINGTON of --------- Kent, yeoman, aged 23.
Francis RAWCHE of Dover, Kent, gent aged 49.

*****

23

10.   C 9/316/89
       6 July 1700

       Bill of Complaint of Roger KIRBY
       of Cranbrook, Kent, Esq., and
       Katherine his wife, versus,
       Richard WEBB and Matthew LANT
       and John BREWER.

In 1694 the plaintiffs had occasion to borrow £700 and applied to John
BREWER of West Farleigh, Kent, Esq., to lend it to them.   They
mortgaged by way of security one fourth part of their manors of
Sissinghurst, Copton, Stone and other manors and several messuages
and lands belonging to them in the parishes of Cranbrook, Frittenden,
Hedcorne, Biddenden and elsewhere in Kent and Sussex and all the manor
of East and West Barmeing in Kent and several other messuages to John
BREWER with the proviso that if they should pay the £700 with interest
at a certain date mentioned in the indenture this grant to be void and John
BREWER was to reconvey the premises back.   But they, having no
counterpart, cannot set forth the same exactly.   They are informed that
John BREWER assigned the premises to Matthew LANT of the -----
Temple in London Esq., whose money the said £700 was, and that one of
them at Michaelmas 1696 or 1697 entered the premises, and has ever
since taken the profits of the manors of East and West Barmeing of about
the yearly value of £200.   The plaintiffs have asked BREWER and LANT
to come to an account with them, but they by combination with Richard
WEBB of Barmeing, gent, the tenant in possession, refused to accept the
same, pretending that the mortgage is either to BREWER, or assigned to
Matthew LANT, and that they have leased the premises to WEBB for 5
years, which have not yet expired, and that they will not accept the mortgage money until it has.   In fact BREWER and LANT have let the property
to WEBB at a low rent, and refuse to let the plaintiff know the term.
There is also an agreement between the three of them whereby BREWER
and LANT reserve to themselves all the hops and hop gardens, and that they
should have a lease back of some part of the hop gardens to themselves,
from which they have made £200 last year over and above the rent paid by
WEBB, which they will not bring to account with the plaintiffs.   Richard
WEBB has cut down several willows and other timber, and in particular
much young growth of not more than 5 or 6 years' standing, and he commits
other waste and destruction upon the property.   They ask the Court to
compel BREWER and LANT to accept the principal sum and terminate the
mortgage and to compel Richard WEBB to deliver possession of the premises
and to stop felling timber.
The answers of BREWER, WEBB and LANT constitute a denial of the charges.

                              *****

11.   C2 Jas I B.3/7
       31 May 1617

       Bill of Complaint of Roger
       BATHERNE of Penhowe, Mon-
       mouthshire, Esq., versus,
       Walter KIRBY and Anthony
       ROBINSON.

                              24

Roger BATHERNE at the persuasion of one Walter KIRBY of the city of
Gloucester married one Margaret KIRBY, widow, late wife of one Thomas
KIRBY who has 3 children living by her former husband. Thomas KIRBY
was the brother of Walter KIRBY, and at the time of his death possessed
the manor of Abbots Barton in the city of Gloucester and 249 acres in the
city of Gloucester and 26 acres of pasture belonging to the manor of Abbots
Barton lying in the fields called the Hill and Overhide, and one pasture
called Oxlease containing 34 acres and also 33 acres of meadow called
Frise meadow, 12 acres of meadow called Walham, 20 acres of meadow in
Sudmead, one pasture called Byrchea 12 acres, and a windmill in a field
there, together with all commons, tithes etc. He held, by virtue of an
indenture of lease dated 20 September 2 Jas I (1604) made by the mayor
and burgesses of Gloucester. Thomas KIRBY died intestate 4 years ago
greatly indebted. This was unknown to Margaret his wife but known to
Walter KIRBY his brother. The plaintiff Roger BATHERNE knew nothing
of this. The only relief Margaret had for herself and her three children
was the lease Walter KIRBY had of the land which he concealed from
Roger BATHERNE. Having effected a marriage between him and his
sister-in-law about a year ago, Walter KIRBY to his sister-in-law's
great undoing and to the avoiding of the lease which John KIRBY, his father
had, which is yet unexpired, maliciously seeks to exclude BATHERNE
and his wife and the children from the manor of Abbots Barton and all the
other premises. Notwithstanding since the marriage between Roger
BATHERNE and Margaret KIRBY to Walter KIRBY has made a lease of the
Abbots Barton property to Anthony ROBINSON for 3 years dated 9 August
14 Jas I, and ROBINSON brought an action against John BUTLER, John
GWILLIAM, Josias WOOLLEY and Giles WILKINSON as tenants of the
land to which they pleaded not guilty and so the matter came to trial at
Common Law. Roger BATHERNE does not know by what title Walter
KIRBY could pretend to avoid the lease made by the mayor of Gloucester.
At the trial he said that Margaret had taken letters of administration of
her late husband's goods, and since he had married Margaret he was
possessed of the premises. But in answer to this Walter pretended that
he had a remnant of a lease in being for 4 years made about 60 years ago
to John KIRBY, his father, and devised to Walter and so the lease made by
the mayor was void. Albeit Roger BATHERNE'S counsel showed a mortgage of John KIRBY'S lease made to one Peter RUMNEY which was forfeited whereby he had no power to make his will thereof and showed several
assignments whereby the lease had come to Thomas KIRBY and proving that
Walter KIRBY permitted an agreement to be had between Elizabeth, the
wife and executrix of Peter RUMNEY and Bridget KIRBY, the wife of the
said John KIRBY, after the deaths of their respective husbands to be made
and the estate to be invested in Elizabeth RUMNEY, and proving that
Thomas KIRBY and the tenants quietly held the Barton with his knowledge
and privity from 20 September 1604 (being 8 years after Thomas had taken
the lease). He also showed that Walter KIRBY knew that Margaret, after
her husband's death, was possessed of the Barton for 4 years during her
widowhood; all which being given in evidence Walter KIRBY by indirect
means with the help of Anthony ROBINSON, who, at the time of the trial
was one of the sheriffs of Gloucester, caused a jury to be returned which
brought in a verdict against BATHERNE. (The remainder of this document is too blurred to read coherently.)

4 June 1617
(partially damaged.)

Reply of Walter KIRBY and
Anthony ROBINSON.

The manor of Abbots Barton belonged to the mayor and burgesses of
Gloucester and in November in the third or fourth year of Philip and
Mary they granted it to John KIRBY, now deceased, the defendant's
father, from Michaelmas 15 (?6-?) for the term of 60 years.   John
KIRBY was so possessed when in February 1577 he made his will in
which 'he demised the premises to Bridget KIRBY, then the wife and
mother of the defendant for her life, the profits to go towards the up
bringing of their children and the payment of certain legacies.   He
also devised by his will that if Bridget should (die before the end of
the term) that then Thomas KIRBY, son of John and Bridget and brother
of this defendant, should enjoy the premises during the remainder of
the term, or for as long as he should live.   He also willed that if the
said Thomas (? should die without issue before the end) of the term, then
this defendant should enjoy the said premises for the rest of the term
unexpired.   He made Bridget sole executrix.   John KIRBY shortly after
wards died and Bridget proved his will and entered into possession and
brought up the children and paid the legacies according to her
husband's will. Bridget died 36 years ago and after her decease
Thomas KIRBY took possession by virtue of the request made to him and
so possessed he died 4 years ago.   The defendant goes on to say that he
was not more than 16 at the time of his father's death, and having lived
for the most part of his time in places far removed from the said premises
did not learn of the bequest made to him until about a year ago, at which
time he took a copy of the will out of the prerogative court.   He there
upon took counsel's advice, and being advised that he ought to have the
premises during the residue of the term, about a year ago he entered the
premises.   As the possession of the premises was wrongfully detained
from him by the plaintiff and his tenants, he Walter, last August for the
lawful recovery of his possessions, made a (grant) of the premises to
Anthony ROBINSON which is the lease mentioned in the Bill, or so he takes
it to be.   Anthony ROBINSON for his part says that being a cousin to the
wife of Walter KIRBY, at the request of Walter and his wife he accepted
the lease.   They both say that in October last Anthony ROBINSON was
elected sheriff of Gloucester but was not sheriff at the time of the making
of the lease.   Anthony ROBINSON by force of the lease, or grant made
by Walter to him, entered the premises and was possessed thereof until
John GWILLIAM, John BUTTLE, Josias WOOLLEY and Giles WILKINSON,
tenants under the plaintiff's pretended estate, entered and dispossed him.
Last Michaelmas term he brought an action against them in the court of
King's Bench and a venire facias was awarded to Toby BULLOCK the other
sheriff of Gloucester for a trial.   Toby BULLOCK was ordered to name
jurors for the trial.   In due course the jurors appeared in the court of
King's Bench and were duly sworn and the case was long and deliberately
debated in the presence of the plaintiff himself.   The jury gave a verdict
for Walter KIRBY and Anthony ROBINSON against John GWILLIAM etc.
and judgement was given accordingly.   They hope that this court will up
hold this verdict since it appears to him that the plaintiffs are seeking to
frustrate the will and true intent of the testator his father.   They both of
them deny all the other charges in the bill and in particular Walter KIRBY
denies that he obtained the plaintiff's consent to the marriage with Margaret
KIRBY his sister-in-law without revealing his brother's debts of which he
has no knowledge.   He denies all the other charges in the bill.

Bill of Complaint of Joseph
HARDING versus Walter KIRBY.

About three years ago Walter KERBIE possessed the lease of a messuage
and certain lands in Lawrence Weston in the county of Gloucester and of
the manor of Abbots Barton in the city of Gloucester and of so much of the
lands belonging to it as amounted to a third part of the said manor, by
force of a lease made by the mayor and burgesses of Gloucester to John
KERBIE his father for 60 years which will expire at Michaelmas. The
rest of the messuage or farm was then detained from him by Margaret
BATHERNE, widow, John REYNOLDS and John COUCHER, Edmund
CLEMENTS, gent Richard KNIGHT, John WYMAN, John GWILLIAM,
Francis BIRCH, John SHAYLE, William BARTON, George WORRALL,
gent, John COUCHER, Lawrence WILSHERE and others. Three years
ago Walter KERBIE let a close, part of the said premises, to Robert BISHOPP,
gent, for a term yet enduring at a rent of £14 per annum, and another
close to Josias WOOLLEY for a term yet enduring at a rent of £16. About
January last twelve months ago KERBIE assigned over all his right and
terms in the premises at Lawrence Weston and the two closes just mentioned to Francis GRIFFIN, gent, towards the satisfaction of a judgement
of £600 which GRIFFIN had against him, and GRIFFIN received the rents
until Michaelmas last. KERBIE in Michaelmas term 16 Jas I exhibited
a bill of complaint in the High Court of Chancery against Margaret
BATHERNE, John REYNOLDS etc. etc. etc. for the recovery of the
residue of the farm and for the recovery of the mean profits during the
time they were detained. In Trinity term 17 Jas I he had a decree made
by the Court for the possession of the land against all the defendants, but
by the neglect of his counsel the mean profits of the land were omitted
from the decree. In June 17 Jas I all the aforesaid defendants were served
with a writ of execution and several notes of its substance were delivered
to them and possession of the greater part was yielded up to KERBIE
accordingly. In the same month one Thomas HYETT, gent, Joseph
HARDING'S near kinsman, was arrested and imprisoned in Gloucester by
the then sheriff of the city of Gloucester on an execution awarded by the
Court of King's Bench on a judgement of £201 10s. 0d. at the suit of
Elizabeth FIELD on a bond of £200 wherein he stood bound to her as surety
for KERBIE and for the proper debt of the said KERBIE. Thomas HYETT
remained in prison for three weeks and KERBIE asked HARDING to do his
best to find £201 10s. 0d. for Thomas HYETT'S release. He promised
that he, KERBIE, would pay it whenever he should be asked to do so.
Thereupon HARDING borrowed £100 and got several of his friends to
become bound with him for its payment. At KERBIE'S request he paid
the sheriff and Thomas HYETT paid the rest and was released at the
beginning of July. Walter KERBIE was then arrested for £32 at the suit
of one HILL and was imprisoned in the Northgate where he remained for
5 or 6 weeks until Joseph HARDING paid the £32 to the sheriff and ten
more besides for KERBIE'S expenses to procure his release. KERBIE
then owed HARDING £150 and HARDING also stood bound as surety for
him for several bonds amounting to over £80 principal debt which he has
since paid. All these sums paid by HARDING and HYETT for KERBIE
amount to more than £400 for the satisfaction of which KERBIE in August
17 Jas I assigned over his term of years in the farm of Abbots Barton to
Joseph HARDING and also agreed that HARDING should receive the arrears

of the mean profit from the persons aforesaid.   By force of this deed
HARDING entered and held the bond farm for a short space until the
beginning of September following, about which time the sheriff apprised
the lease although it was not then extent and took possession of the farm.
After this an agreement was reached between GRIFFIN, KERBIE and
HARDING that for the freeing of KERBIE and the farm from the judgement
HARDING should pay GRIFFIN £48 more in November last and enter a
bond for £82 to GRIFFIN on 24 June then next coming, which HARDING did.
It was also agreed that GRIFFIN should convey to HARDING'S use all the
interest which KERBIE had passed to him.   This he did, and conveyed his
right in the lands in Lawrence Weston and in the Barton farm to John
TROTMAN, gent, to Joseph HARDING'S use.   The plaintiffs have combined
with John REYNOLDS, Edmund CLEMENTS, John COUCHER, Richard
KNIGHT, contrary to this decree and in contempt of court have entered
upon the possession of several pastures, part of Barton farm, and detained
them from HARDING.   And the hayward has also entered part of the lands
of Barton farm and keeps possession of them from HARDING, and KERBIE
has got the assignment and deeds made to HARDING and all other deeds
concerning the premises and detains them from HARDING not only as
touches the Lawrence Weston land but the Barton land as well
Margaret BATHERNE, John REYNOLDS etc. have detained the mean
profits from HARDING although they have been frequently asked to pay
them and he therefore requests them to make answer to this Bill and give
account of their actions.

6 October 18 Jas I (1620)

Answer of Edmund CLEMENTS, one of the
defendants, to the Bill of Complaint of Joseph HARDING.

CLEMENTS says that Walter KERBIE was possessed of the premises in
Lawrence Weston and at Abbots Barton mentioned in the bill and also
acknowledges KERBIE'S decree from the Court of Chancery for the
possession of the Barton farm lands but not for the mean profits then in
arrear.   He further says that amongst others he was served with the
decree and that Walter KERBIE, partly for the consideration mentioned
in the bill and partly in trust for the intended good of his children, assigned over his interest in the Barton farm lands to HARDING.   Long
before the decree was granted he, CLEMENTS held a close of 12 acres
from Roger BATHERNE Esq. but that shortly after KERBIE got possession of the farmhouse and the lands belonging to it by a verdict at
Common Law.   But before KERBIE assigned it over to HARDING, KERBIE
entered the pasture lands, which were then in the occupation of this defendant, and let them to Toby CLEMENTS, this defendants son, for the
rest of the term KERBIE had in the farm at a rent of 20 marks per annum.
Toby CLEMENTS paid KERBIE a whole year's rent beforehand and
accordingly enjoyed the same for the greatest part of the term as tenant
of KERBIE.   If there by any rent unpaid he thinks that Toby CLEMENTS
will be ready to pay it to those who have the right to it.   He denies all
plots and combinations and contempt of Court.   As concerns the arrears
of rent he says that HARDING in his bill confesses they were not mentioned in the decree, and if there by any behind this defendant is informed
that they are payable to Walter KERBIE who is a miserable poor man and
lies in the common gaol of Gloucester, where he has long remained, and

28

not to HARDING. But Edmund CLEMENTS hopes that the Court will not
order him to pay for the close either to KERBIE, or any of his assigns,
because he paid a great fine for his interest and his rent in due manner
to BATHERNE.

6 October 1620

John REYNOLDS' Answer.

John REYNOLDS says that Thomas KERBIE, late of the city of Gloucester,
gent, was in his lifetime husband of Margaret BATHERNE, widow, one of
the defendants mentioned in the bill. He was possessed of the site of the
manor and farm of Abbots Barton and other lands belonging to it by virtue
of a demise for term of years made to him by the mayor and burgesses of
Gloucester which yet remains in force and is yet unexpired. Thomas
KERBIE died thereof possessed and Margaret BATHERNE, his then wife,
took letters of administration of all the goods and chattels of her husband.
By virtue of this she became possessed amongst other things of the Abbots
Barton farm. By her deed of 20 March 12 Jas I (1614) in consideration
of the sum of £166 she let John REYNOLDS several pieces of arable land
amounting to 20 acres for 21 years by virtue whereof he is possessed of
the same for the rest of the 21 years and has taken the rent and profits
from the land. He says that in Trinity term 17 Jas I Walter KERBIE had
a decree from the Court of Chancery, but for various reasons an order
was made by this Court on behalf of this defendant and the other defendants
against Walter KERBIE. By this order this defendant conceives himself
to have full authority to possess the premises demised to him by Margaret
KERBIE, and he denies all the charges brought in the bill against him.
He knows nothing of any of the other matters mentioned and asks that the
case be dismissed against him.

*****

C 22/662/1

Elizabeth KERBY plaintiff versus
Robert CARPENTER defendant. Gloucester.

Interrogatories on behalf of plaintiff.

1. Do you know the parties; did you know Robert KERBY
    father of the plaintiff; when and at what age did he die ?

2. Do you know the value and nature of Robert KERBY'S
    goods at his death ?

3. How did Robert KERBY settle his personal estate, names
    of his children; what legacies did he leave them ?

4. Did Robert KERBY desire that Henry HOLFORD and
    the defendant should be his exors ?

5. Did Henry HOLFORD and the defendant prove his will ?

6. Anything else material.

Depositions of witnesses on behalf of
the plaintiff taken at the house of
John TAYLOR, by the Sign of the
George, Gloucester, before Anthony
EDWARDS, . . . WATS and Robert
TAYLOR gent.

16 Jan. 1649/50.

Thomas PEARCE, Gloucester, gardener,
aged 50.

1. Knows parties; knew Robert KERBY father of the plaintiff.
    The plaintiff was about 7 years old on his death.

2. The defendant lived with Robert KERBY as a servant for
    about 9 months; when he left Robert KERBY was worth
    £300 and upwards; Robert KERBY lived for about 9
    months after he left; the greatest part of his estate
    consisted in moneys and the rest in goods, corn and
    household stuff.

3. Robert KERBY has often spoken in the deponent's presence
    that he would commit the tuition and breeding of Rose KERBY
    and the plaintiff to Henry HOLFORD, gent, deceased, and
    the defendant, and that he would give each of his daughters
    £100 apiece, and further said that £8 interest from each
    £100 was sufficient to maintain a girl.

4. He has heard Robert KERBY ask the defendant to under-
    take the tuition of one of his daughters and the other he
    was desirous to commit to Mr. HOLFORD, to which request
    the defendant yielded. After the death of Robert KERBY
    the defendant took Rose into his custody and Mr. HOLFORD
    took the plaintiff.

Elinor PEARCE, wife of Thomas PEARCE,
aged 48.

1. Has heard that Robert KERBY died about 14 years since
    and that the plaintiff was aged 7 at his death.

4. Rose KIRBIE was the elder sister.

30

Richard HARRIS, Whaddon, yeoman,
aged 39.

1.   As before.

2.   The estate of Robert KERBY was reported to be worth
     £400; Robert KERBY would give no more than £200 for
     the benefit of his two daughters, saying that £100 was
     enough for a girl's portion.

3.   He knows that one John HAYWARD, clerk, whose sister
     Robert KERBY married, after the death of Robert KERBY
     took letters of administration of his will.   After admin-
     istration was obtained Henry HOLFORD and the defendant
     produced a nuncupative will, whereby they destroyed the
     administration and took the deceased's goods into their
     hands.

5.   The plaintiff is aged 21 and upwards;   does not know that
     she has received any part of the £100 from the defendant
     or HOLFORD.

Margaret ......, widow,
aged 4..

3.   Was present with John HUNT, her late father and one
     Margaret WALKELEY, widow, when she heard Robert
     KERBY say that he did and would appoint HOLFORD and
     the defendant as exors. and bequeathed £100 apiece to
     his two daughters.

Jeffery BEALE, Gloucester, gent,
aged 47.

2.   While the plaintiff lived as a servant with this deponent,
     he went to Richard HAYWARD the plaintiff's uncle to
     demand a portion.   Deponent and Richard HAYWARD had
     conference with the defendant, to which the defendant
     replied that he had already disbursed what he had of
     Robert KERBY'S goods to Rose the plaintiff's sister and
     that Henry HOLFORD had the money.   Since this suit
     started this deponent and William WINTLE of Gloucester,
     with whom the plaintiff was then living, went again to the
     defendant, who protested that he had only £30 left of Robert
     KERBY'S money, which he was willing to pay to the plain-
     tiff by annual instalments of £10;   later the defendant
     privately promised to pay £40.

Margaret WALKER, Gloucester, widow,
aged 54.

3. The morning before Robert KERBY died he sent for one
    Mr. BROADGATE, then of the city of Gloucester, to put
    in writing what he had willed and declared, which he did
    and Robert KERBY signed it.

Katherine KNIGHT, Gloucester, widow,
aged 50.

3. Robert KERBY said he would give £100 to each of his
    daughters and that the rest should be spent at his funeral.

Ann HAYWARD, wife of Richard HAYWARD,
of Barnwood, yeoman, aged 44.

2. She has heard that Robert KERBY gave £150 apiece to each
    daughter. The defendant and HOLFORD dealt very hardly
    with the two children in so much that some of the children's
    friends near in blood did commiserate their hard usage and
    poor keeping, wanting clothes, diet, needful changes of
    apparel and other things fit for them to prevant them from
    vermin, whereby they were sorely pestered, and upon this
    deponent's husband's charge, viz. the eldest daughter until
    the said defendant fetched her from this deponent. And this
    deponent's said husband and his mother kept the plaintiff at
    their charge until she was able to go to service, where in
    she ever since and now does employ herself, having no other
    help or means to maintain herself.

Sarah WEBB, wife of Richard WEBB
of Gloucester, Smith, aged 56.

2. Money and personal estate of Robert KERBY was worth
    £280 or thereabouts and he had besides £40 in goods.

3. John HAYWARD is brother of this deponent.

5. About three years after HOLFORD took the plaintiff to his
    custody he maintained her in a mean condition, in so much
    that this deponent being her aunt reflected her love upon
    her (and for that Mr. HOLFORD was minded to depart from
    Gloucester to London) took the plaintiff into her custody and
    kept her at her grandmother's charge until she was about 14
    years old, since which time she has lived in service. She
    is now about 23. Before this suit began the defendant offered
    to give £60 to the plaintiff in six-monthly installments of £10.

John HAYWARD, Nympsfield, clerk,
aged 50.

2. After Robert KERBY'S death this deponent had his goods
under letters of administration granted by ordinary of this
diocese of Gloucester to the value of £240 in bonds and other
things and also a house.

William WINTLE, Gloucester, haberdasher,
aged 27.

5,6. On his visit to the defendant, the defendant offered to pay
£30 or £32, and that she should also have the lease which
was mortgaged, part of her father's estate.

Interrogatories on behalf of
Robert CARPENTER defendant.

1. Do you know the parties and Robert KERBY ?

2. Were you present when Robert KERBY made his will; did
he give £100 apiece to his two daughters; did he say £100
was enough for two wenches ?

3. Did Robert KERBY appoint Mr. HOLFORD and the defendant
as exors and direct that they should each bring up one of the
daughters ?

4. How long did Mr. HOLFORD keep the plaintiff; did he keep
her until she was taken from him by widow HAYWARD, her
grandmother ?

5. Did the defendant breed up Rose KERBY in a fitting manner
according to her quality; for how long; was she since
married to one Giles NURSE yeoman; did the defendant
pay £100 to Giles NURSE for her portion; did Giles NURSE
seal a release to the defendant for the same ?

6. Anything else material.

Depositions of witnesses on behalf
of defendant, taken at the George Inn,
Gloucester.

16 Jan 1649/50

Margaret HARGEST, Gloucester, widow,
aged 40.

1. Knows parties.

2. Was present when Robert KERBIE made his nuncupative
   will, bequeathing £100 to each of his daughters.   Robert
   KERBY then confessed that his estate was worth £300,
   saying that £100 was enough for wenches, and that the
   rest should see him well buried, and that he would have
   nothing to do with the HAYWARDS, being his wife's kindred
   further than 12 pence apiece would go.

Margaret WALKER, Gloucester, widow,
aged 54.

2. Robert KERBY said he would give no greater portions
   unto wenches if he had never so much.

Edward TYTHER, Gloucester, gent,
aged 38.

5. The defendant kept Rose very sufficiently and in decent
   apparel until Giles NURSE married her, when the defendant,
   paid the portion to Giles NURSE, for which he took a receipt,
   to which this deponent was a witness.

*****

34

Bill of Complaint of Anthony WHITE,
Vicar of Wargrave, Berks, John SANDERS,
of Hambledon, Bucks, gent, Francis WEBBE
of Wargrave, yeoman, Overseers of the Will
of Suzan KIRBY, widow, late wife of Adam
KIRBY, the elder, of Wargrave, deceased,
whose executrix she was, versus William
KIRBY and Adam KIRBY.

Adam KIRBY, the elder, in his lifetime possessed a large and valuable
estate which far exceeded his debts and legacies. He also owned a
large freehold estate of land in Wargrave, Berkshire. By his will he
bequeathed his house in Wargrave, in which he lived, to his wife Suzan,
during the minority of their son, Adam, for the upbringing of the rest
of their children. He gave his four daughters, Suzan, Elizabeth, Agnes
and Frances £50 each. Amongst other legacies he gave his son George
£100 at 21 or on marriage which his wife was to keep during her widowhood towards George's education and upbringing. She lent the £100
bequeathed to George to William KIRBY, another of Adam KIRBY'S sons
and as well as another £100 and took a bond for £400 for its repayment
using the interest from the loan for George's maintainance and to bind
him apprentice. George was apprenticed draper in 1623 for 8 years,
but left his apprenticeship and became apprentice to Richard FYNCHER,
Skinner, in 1624. He was made free of the Skinners Company in 1631.
Suzan made her will on 4 November 1624 in which she made the following
bequests:- That whereas her late husband gave his son George £100
when he should reach the age of 21 or marriage, which was in the hands
of her son William KIRBY, who stood bound for the payment thereof, her
will was that her overseers (the plaintiffs in this case) should employ
it for the best use of George. She also devised to him her own gift of
£10 to be paid to her overseers for his benefit. She also gave her
grandchild Adam KIRBY son of her son Adam, £30 to be paid at 21, and
if he should die, this legacy to go to his brother Anthony KIRBY. She
further devised to the 6 children of one Francis THACKHAM 10s. apiece.
All legacies to be paid within six months of her death by her executor,
Adam KIRBY her son. She died leaving enough to satisfy her debts and
legacies, and Adam proved the will and proceeded to execution, and
possessed himself of the estates of his late father and mother. Suzan
has now been dead more than six months, indeed nearer 12 months, and
the legacies were due to be paid within six months of her death. The
plaintiffs have asked Adam for the money, viz. the £100 devised to
George by his father, £10 devised to him by his mother, the £30 devised
to Adam the grandchild, and the various other smaller legacies to the
children of Francis THACKHAM, they all being under 21 years of age
and unmarried.

Although Adam KIRBY, the son, did in the lifetime of his mother waste
a great part of the estate left to him by his father, so that his mother
did not think fit to trust him with the several sums of money abovesaid
she entrusted the plaintiffs, her friends, to dispose of them instead.
Yet Adam, in agreement with his brother William, in whose hands the
money is, now refuses to let the overseers, the plaintiffs, have the
money to be disposed according to the terms of Suzan's will. Further

he is threatening to sue out the bond from William to use the money for himself, and to prevent the overseers. fulfilling their trust on behalf of the minors, George, Adam and the THACKHAM children. They ask for a writ to be issued to Adam and William to compel them to perform the proper execution of the will.

C2 Chas I. W.71/51
28 November 1625

Answer of William KIRBY to the
Bill of Complaint of Anthony WHITE and others.

He acknowledges the fact of his late father's estate as set out in the Bill. He says his mother committed £190 to his hands and took a bond for the payment thereof in her own name for £400, and since her death Adam KIRBY his brother as executor has received £60 of it with £14 interest and threatens him for the rest, and says he will sue him unless he pays it. He utterly denies agreeing with his brother to withhold it from the overseers, and is very desirous to pay it to whom the Court shall award so that he may give up his bond of £400; and he has not been overhasty to part with it by reason of the bequest of £100 and its employment for the benefit of his brother, George. But as a wellwisher to both his brothers Adam and George, he wishes the plaintiffs and executor were well agreed, and that this cause might come to an end without further trouble.

C2 Chas I W. 71/51
1 December 1625

Answer of Adam KIRBY to the
Bill of Complaint of Anthony WHITE and others.

He recites the terms of his father's will, but says that Suzan was left the house and lands in Wargrave for the benefit and bringing up of all the children, and not just of Adam as the bill suggests. Suzan, after her husband's death, possessed herself of his estates and educated his children except Adam the defendant, who went to service soon after his father's death and maintained himself without any assistance from Suzan his mother. He says his mother did not pay or put into safety all the legacies made by his father, nor did she settle George's £100 in William's hands as is alleged. It came into William's hands as follows: Suzan KIRBY (?asked) William to lay out the £100 in barley the year before she died and to convert it into malt for her use and benefit, she thinking to have the profit of it for herself. He suggests that William persuaded her to do this and then kept the profit from the sale himself. As regards the £400 bond, he says that Suzan took it not only for the £100 she made over to William, but also for £100 which he owed her, and for some of his other debts, he sold his lands to his brother William, and because William was not able to pay him so much ready money as the lands were sold for, he asked Suzan to take the money he owed her from William. She therefore took the bond of £400 for the money which was owing her by him (Adam) as well as for the money which William had received for

the malt. He says that Suzan was so far from thinking the money safe
in William's hands (he owed several other large sums of money to several
other people) as that she told him (Adam) that she would either get in her
money when the time was expired, or get William to give better security
for it. He does not believe that Suzan used the interest for George's
education, but thinks she bestowed £20 with the placing forth apprentice of George, whom she first placed with a Girdler giving with him
£10, but a short time after the Girdler broke, and so she placed him a
second time, this time with a Skinner in London to whom she gave £10.

He admits to Suzan's will of 4 November 1624 and the items recited from
it in the bill, but says she also left several other legacies which were
not recited, viz: £5 to Anthony WHITE, the plaintiff, a jug to her son
William, divers other goods to George, £5 to her daughter Margaret
THACKHAM, divers things to her daughter Elizabeth WHITE, wife of
the plaintiff Anthony WHITE, £15 to each of her daughters Agnes,
Frances and Suzan KIRBY, 20/- to her brother MARBROUGH. He says
these ought to have been paid within one month after her death. She
only appointed the plaintiffs overseers, but him she appointed executor,
which showed she did not mistrust him, as is alleged in the bill. He
says that at her death his mother had goods in the house of the plaintiff
Anthony WHITE which he has not given over and that she had several
bonds (Document damaged and sense difficult to determine). He denies
collusion with his brother William, but says that he will sue his brother
if he does not pay him the money which he has of their mother's.

*****

C8/76/130
19 May 1637

Bill of Complaint of Castle BRANGWIN,
infant, by his guardian Ann BRANGWIN,
his mother, plaintiff versus Nathaniel
KIRBY, defendant.

Peter KIRBY and William KIRBY his son were seised of one messuage
and lands in Charlton-on-Otmoor, Oxon. On 16 June 1625 in consideration of £129 they conveyed the property to Richard ALLEY alias
LEVERETT. Half an acre, part of the property, lies in a furlong
called Mill Furlong between the lands of Thomas MIN on both sides.
Final concord was shortly afterwards levied. On 3 March 1625/6
Richard ALLEY enfeoffed Francis BRANGWIN father of the plaintiff.
Francis BRANGWIN died two years since and the property ought to
descend to the plaintiff. Nathaniel KIRBY, son and heir of William has
entered the lands, claiming the greatest part of them, including the
half acre. He has got into his possession the title deeds.

37

.. June 1637

Answer of Nathaniel KIRBY.

Does not believe that Peter and William KIRBY were seised; does not know of the conveyance to ALLEY. Believes that Peter KIRBY was seised in tail to him and his heirs of two yardlands, of which the half acre is part and that he died seised, when they descended to William the defendant's elder brother as son and heir. William died without issue, whereby they ought to descend to the defendant. Any conveyance made must have been in trust for Peter and William in the nature of a mortgage. At the time of William KIRBY'S death, the defendant was aged 15.

*****

16.   C2 Chas I K.12/60
         11 November 1641.

         Bill of Complaint of Adam KIRBY
         of Wokingham, Berks, Scrivener,
         versus Richard CARTER and Joan
         his wife.

The plaintiff and one Thomas SMITH of Buscott in the county of Berks, yeoman, about September 4 Chas I 1628 borrowed from Isabel DEAN of Henley-on-Thames, Oxon. widow, the sum of £10, upon receipt of which by the appointment of Isabel DEAN, they entered into an obligation of £20 to one Joan DEAN, spinster, daughter of the said Isabel. They delivered this bond to Isabel for her security at such time as was then agreed upon. But before the repayment of the money one Richard CARTER, then of Henley, tallow chandler, was a suitor in the way of marriage to Joan and so far succeeded with her that she made him a promise of marriage which was altogether distasteful to Isabel her mother, since Richard CARTER was then a widower and a man of mean estate and Joan a very young maid. Isabel was able to give in marriage with Joan a portion twice as much in value as Richard CARTER'S whole estate was then worth. Whereupon Isabel would not allow the bond to remain in her daughter's name, but sent to Adam KIRBY to renew the bond and make it in her own name; she found that her daughter would not be ruled by her, but would marry CARTER against her will. Thereupon Adam KIRBY and Thomas SMITH about 11 or 12 years ago entered into a new bond of £20 to Isabel for the repayment of the £10 borrowed. Adam KIRBY sent the bond by his wife to Isabel. When she received it she caused one Elizabeth SPIER, widow, another of her daughters, who then lived in the house with her mother, to search amongst her papers for the other bond entered into with Joan DEAN. Elizabeth SPIER, finding it, gave it to Adam KIRBY'S wife to be cancelled. But when Adam KIRBY received the bond from his wife never thought of cancelling it, but put it into a box amongst other papers and kept it for 3 or 4 years in his own custody. At the end of this time he removed from Wargrave, where he then lived into Gloucestershire some 50 miles distant, and in the removal of his goods the box wherein the bond then was, was lost together with other papers. Since that time the bond has come into the hands of Richard CARTER, who also has long since married Joan DEAN. Although Adam KIRBY made a new bond with Isabel DEAN in her own name and notwithstanding that Richard CARTER has been often informed by Isabel, and that Joan DEAN, now the wife of Richard CARTER, well knows that the bond was made to her in trust only, yet, nevertheless, Richard CARTER and Joan his wife have lately put it in suit, meaning thereby to force Adam KIRBY to pay the money again to them.

15 November 1641

Answer of Richard CARTER and Joan
to the Bill of Complaint of Adam KIRBY.

Joan CARTER says that Adam KIRBY and Thomas SMITH on 27 September 4 Chas I (1628) did borrow £10 from her mother, which Isabel had intended as part of her portion. For security of repayment Isabel then directed that the obligation of £20 mentioned in the bill should be made to this defendant, Joan, and in her own name. As Isabel had given the money to Joan to this end, the plaintiffs became jointly and severally bounden to her with interest. She further says that the obligation was sealed and delivered by the plaintiffs to her for her own use and not for the use of her mother, and that it has been ever since kept for her use and benefit and not otherwise. About ten or eleven years since the defendants married with Isabel's approval. They deny that the plaintiff and Thomas SMITH did enter a new bond of £20 to Isabel as the bill suggests. They also deny that the plaintiff sent any new bond by his wife to Isabel DEAN or that Elizabeth SPIER did ever deliver the bond now in question to the plaintiff's wife to be cancelled. They further say that what new bond the plaintiffs gave Isabel in her own name or what money they have paid her upon any bond they do not know. They deny that they were informed by Isabel or that Joan knew that the bond in question was made to her, Joan, in trust and that the money lent was Isabel DEAN'S own money. Richard CARTER denies that Isabel DEAN at any time asked him to deliver up the bond to be cancelled, but he admits that in June 1639 he caused the plaintiff to be arrested upon the bond and presently afterwards being set at liberty offered to make a composition pretending he was unable to pay the whole debt, whereupon the suit was stayed in the hope of obtaining a composition, but the plaintiffs failing to pay the debt, or any part of it, Richard CARTER caused the bond in question to be put in suit for recovery of debt. The plaintiffs have severally pleaded performance of the bond and these defendants intend to prosecute the suit further.

*****

17. C2 Chas 1 W.20/30
29 October 1647

Bill of Complaint of William WELLS
of Gaddesden, Hertford, yeoman, and
Jeremy WELLS of London, fishmonger,
son and heir apparent, versus
Richard KIRBY and Ellen his wife
(document slightly damaged.)

William WELLS had one daughter named Ellen who had for her marriage
portion £80 . . . . . Richard KIRBY of London, joiner, person of little
or no worth, having a desire to marry the said Ellen, had about 1½ years
since in the presence of William CARPENTER, the elder, of London,
brewer, and William CARPENTER, the younger, brewer, then friends
and creditors of the said KIRBY, some speech with William WELLS who
in conclusion consented.   He told them that Ellen had about £20 of her
own money when Richard KIRBY should take a house and have occasion
to use it.   Jeremy WELLS also promised to see this made good.   Jeremy
WELLS may have given an undertaking that on William WELLS' death, if
KIRBY would relinquish all future expectations from him, he would give
KIRBY £50.   It was not intended that KIRBY should receive any such sum
in marriage with Ellen other than the sum of £80, nor was William WELLS,
who had many other children to provide for, fit to part with more.   Shortly
afterwards Richard KIRBY and Ellen the daughter married, and the present
estate of Ellen, (which then happened to be in the hands of one John
SOUTHEND on mortgage and which William WELLS promised to KIRBY)
fell short by £15 of the sum of £80.   Before Richard KIRBY had taken
any house to live in, William WELLS paid to him the £15, whereupon
KIRBY, offering to give William WELLS an acquittance for no more than
he had received . . . . . KIRBY did at that time give William WELLS a
general release dated 2 . . . . . 1646.   (Damaged passage.)   The two
CARPENTERS, Richard KIRBY and Ellen combined together to charge
William WELLS with an action for £80 more as part of the marriage agreement, and thereupon, it so happening that Jeremy WELLS having brought
an action of assault and battery against KIRBY the matter was heard at
Guildhall and judgement given against KIRBY.   Damages were likely to
be given for Jeremy WELLS, but the judge in regard of the nearness of
relation between them, and to prevent all occasion of further quarrels
amongst them, ordered an arbitration between them.   Afterwards John
DIGBY of London, milliner, and . . . . . WATSON, gunsmith, being two
of the jury (both of them nominated as arbitrator by the said KIRBY)
persuaded William WELLS to refer all other matters outstanding between
Richard KIRBY and Jeremy WELLS to them.   By a bond dated 9 June 1647
Jeremy WELLS and Richard KIRBY became mutally bound to each other
to stand by the arbitrament of DIGBY and WATSON, the arbitration to be
given before 1 July next following.   In due course DIGBY and WATSON
heard the cases and after some dispute asked KIRBY what it was he would
insist upon from William WELLS.   Richard KIRBY replied that he wanted
only £4 10s. claiming that John SOUTHEND had left so much unpaid either
of principal or interest due to Ellen; and upon being further asked if that
was all he claimed, he answered that it was.   The arbitrators both
seeming satisfied as to the amount concerning William WELLS persuaded
the latter to pay KIRBY £4 10s. in order to end the matter, which he
accordingly did.   William and Jeremy WELLS then thought that all

40

difference as concerned William were at an end, and in fact KIRBY was so satisfied with the settlement that he shortly afterwards told some of his friends that he had received the £4 10s. and that he had had as much from William WELLS as he could in conscience expect. Concerning the battery committed by Richard KIRBY on Jeremy WELLS, the arbitrators declared that Jeremy should have his costs and damages. Notwithstanding they afterwards drew up an award, whereby William or Jeremy should pay Richard KIRBY £10 on October 1 1647 and £10 more on July 1 1648 and that the plaintiff should further pay £60 within 3 months after the death of his father, William WELLS, without any satisfaction to Jeremy for his costs of suit, contrary to their own declarations as aforesaid.

6 November 1647

Demurrer and Answer of Richard
KIRBY and Ellen, his wife.

Richard KIRBY demurs from answering because he says the whole bill is built up upon the pretence that he asked more in marriage with Ellen than was agreed.

*****

C2 Chas I K.19/55
9 July 1649

Bill of Complaint of Richard KIRBY of St.
Botolphs without Aldgate, London,
citizen and joiner, versus William
WELLS and Mary his wife.

About 3 years ago Richard KIRBY, who was living in the Minories, in the parish of St. Botolphs-without-Aldgate, married Ellen, the daughter of William WELLS. He was a joiner and stockmaker of guns, pistols, muskets; patronelles and such like, and was employed not only by the State, but by nobleman and gentlemen of quality, who entrusted their arms to him for repair. While he was away on business his wife Ellen was left in charge. But William WELLS and Mary, his wife, Ellen's father and mother, Jeremy WELLS and Mary, his wife, Ellen's brother and sister-in-law, ... WARREN and ... WRIGHT, and several other people as yet unknown, have combined to defraud the plaintiff of his estate and goods and have persuaded Ellen to elope, taking with her all his goods, wares, bonds, bills, writings and estate and have served a warrant on him for a breach of the peace. He was tried and committed to the Compter of the Poultry in London, and during his imprisonment they went to his home and took away all his household goods, including bedding, brass, pewter and iron ware, some in use, others unfinished, made for sale, and all his working tools and a great store of his customers' goods which had been

41

entrusted to him to make or finish consisting of muskets, guns, fowling pieces, birding pieces, pistols, carbines, patronelles, callivers, locks, stocks and barrels for guns ready, finished and unfinished, amounting in value to £200.

When he came out of the Poultry he went home and found his loss. He asked William WELLS where his things were, but WELLS refused to tell him. He asks the Court to compel them to give an account of their action.

C2 Chas I K.19/55
16 July 1649

Answer of William WELLS and Mary
his wife, and Jeremy WELLS and
Mary his wife to the Bill of Complaint of
Richard KIRBY.

They say that the bill of complaint has been brought frivolously in order to involve the defendants in causeless expense. They acknowledge the plaintiff's marriage with Ellen, daughter of William and Mary WELLS and that the plaintiff was a joiner by trade, but by whom he was employed they do not know. They say that if he was entrusted by people with their goods, it is not material to the case. They know nothing about his credit or repute before he was married, but they do say that before he married Ellen he was a very poor man. Since his marriage he has been a very contentious and troublesome person, and has spent and wasted most of the portion he had in marriage with Ellen by lawsuits, which tend almost if not altogether, to her utter undoing. They know nothing about his wares which he said he had left in the custody of his wife when he went abroad for his affairs, or of what their value was, if he left any, or what became of them except that Mary WELLS, the wife of William WELLS has been at his house above 12 months last past. None of the others have been to his house at any time, and Mary has only been there at such times as she was desired to go by the plaintiff, or his wife, but not since he was committed to prison. They deny all manner of combination and confederacy as is most scandalously alleged. They also deny persuading Ellen to elope, or to bring with her any bonds, bills, writings etc. They deny procuring a warrant for his arrest, but they say they believe it is true that about the time mentioned in the bill he was committed for some misdemeanour to the prison of the Poultry Compter upon the complaint of several of his own near neighbours, but this was done before these defendants had notice of it, except Mary, the wife of William WELLS, who casually passing by the plaintiff's house on the day he was committed to prison, saw a great tumult at his door in the street. They deny breaking into his house and taking away his household stuff, and are confident that the plaintiff has invented this story. They deny that he has asked them at any time to restore it to him. They do not believe that he has in fact lost any goods whatsoever whilst he was in prison, unless his landlord has distrained anything in his house for his rent, which the plaintiff owed him. They have been informed that his landlord had lately threatened to distrain his goods if he could find enough in the plaintiff's house to give him satisfaction for what was due to him for rent. They deny all the other charges in the bill.

*****

42

C5/383/113.   See also C5/170/19 (Item 25, below)
14 January 1655/6

Bill of Complaint of Ralph SHERWOOD
of Slade End, Brightwell, Berks, and
Alice his wife, versus Joan and
Richard KIRBY.

The plaintiff, Ralph SHEROOD of Slade End, Brightwell, Berks and Alice,
his wife, late wife of John KIRBY deceased, who was executor of James
KIRBY late of Brightwell, yeoman, deceased shows that James KIRBY
made a will dated 12 November 1644, appointing his son John KIRBY,
executor.   Among other legacies to his children, he devised to his
daughter Mary SADLER, £100 to be paid within 6 years of his death
with a proviso that Jacob SADLER, her then husband, should at the
same time add £200 of his own and make her a jointure of £300, or else
Mary should have in lieu of the £100 an annuity of £6 per annum to be
paid quarterly during her life, and the £100 to be distributed among her
children at their ages of 21 years.   On 12 November 1644 John KIRBY
became bound in a bond for £1,000 to Joane KIRBY of Brightwell, widow,
and Richard KIRBY of Wallingford, draper to see the legacies paid to
his brothers and sisters.   James KIRBY died soon after making his will,*
and John proceeded to probate, took possession of his father's personal
estate and was ready to pay the £100 to Mary SADLER should Jacob agree
to pay the £200 mentioned in the proviso.   John KIRBY married the plaintiff, Alice, and waited for Jacob SADLER to pay the £200, but he did not.
In due course John KIRBY made his will, appointed Alice, the plaintiff,
his executrix and died.   She took possession of his estate and was ready
to pay Mary SADLER the £100, but Jacob never paid the £200.   Alice
then married the plaintiff Ralph SHERWOOD.   Jacob SADLER is dead
without paying the jointure and there is now no means of obtaining payment.
The plaintiffs have continued to pay the annuity of £6.   Mary SADLER,
now a widow living at Soningwell, Berks is not content with the annuity,
although she knows that under her father's will the £100 is due to her
children-; viz. Jacob, Thomas and Jane SADLER, who claim it.   This
puts the plaintiffs in a great straight, not knowing what they should do,
since Mary and her children cannot agree among themselves.   The
children have combined with Joan KIRBY and Richard KIRBY to persuade
the plaintiffs to give them not only the £100, but also to continue paying
their mother the annuity of £6, whereas they know that the plaintiffs are
willing to pay the £100 to whomever Mary SADLER and her children agree
shall receive it, or to whomever the Court shall direct, so that they
shall be free of it.

7 April 1656

Answer of the children by Richard
KEATE, gent, their guardian.

They have seen the Answer of their mother, Mary SADLER and believe
all contained in it to be true, and believe the £100 belongs to their mother,
and they disclaim all interest therein.

24 Jan 1655/6

Joint Answer of Joan and Richard
KIRBY and Mary SADLER, and her
children to the Bill of Complaint of Ralph
SHERWOOD.

They acknowledge the terms of James KIRBY'S will and add that in the
last clause of his will he declared that Mary SADLER, his daughter,
should have £50 added to the £100 to make up her portion to £150 at the
time her husband made up her jointure to £300, which was given to him
by Jacob SADLER, his father.   Mary believes this last clause repeals
the proviso, as being contrary in case the testator had intended the
proviso to stand.   But Richard KIRBY says he wrote and framed the
bill on James KIRBY'S instructions, and that the proviso was inserted
to stir Jacob SADLER, whom Mary had married against her father's
wishes, to make some provision for her.   The testator never intended
that the proviso should be stood upon by his executor, but that the £100
should be paid notwithstanding.   The testator also declared that Mary
had nothing from him yet and though she had played the fool, meaning in
her marriage, and would not have provision made for her by Jacob her
husband, yet she should have the £100.   James KIRBY died possessed
of a great personal fortune to the value of £1,000 or thereabouts.
Richard KIRBY believes John KIRBY would have paid the legacy of £100
had he lived without taking any notice of the proviso.   The plaintiffs are
liable as successors of John and James KIRBY to pay the legacy.   Jacob
SADLER died two years since without making a jointure, but did receive
a legacy of £300 from his father, Jacob SADLER, deceased, as appears
by an acquittance signed by Jacob SADLER, the younger, to Thomas
SADLER, the executor of Jacob, the elder.   Joan and Richard KIRBY
have taken steps to try to obtain from Thomas SADLER the £300 which
Jacob inherited from his father for Mary SADLER so that the £100
jointure legacy may be lawfully paid to her.

*****

20.   C5/511/61
           23 October 1671

           Answer and Plea of Peter KIRBY to
           the Bill of Complaint of Richard
           KIRBY and William DICKINSON and
           Jane his wife.

           Bill Missing.

Firstly Peter KIRBY says that Peter KIRBY deceased, father of the
plaintiffs Richard and Jane, was in his lifetime seised in fee simple in
the messuages, lands and premises mentioned in the bill and also that
he made his will dated as in the bill of complaint and demised thereby
the said premises to his son Nathaniel KIRBY, deceased, the father of
this defendant Peter, and to his heirs male, on condition that he should

* See Vol. I part I Section 7.   Will No. 183.

at his entry into the property give sufficient security to pay the other children of the said Peter KIRBY the following legacies:- to John KIRBY £10, to the plaintiff Richard KIRBY £10, and to Robert KIRBY £10, to the plaintiff Jane £20, to Amy KIRBY £20 to his sons at the age of 26 and to his daughters at the age of 21. If any of the children should die the survivors should be their heirs. He also made further bequests in such manner and form as is set out in the bill of complaint. The defendant also believes that Peter KIRBY died shortly afterwards seised of the premises, and that Jane, his widow, and executrix proved the will, and also that the said Jane and Richard ALLEY alias LEVIRETT and William KIRBY named in the bill, entered the premises and took the profits for ten years towards the payment of the testator's debts and the education of the plaintiffs Richard and Jane and the other children. The ten years expired in 1635, and immediately after Nathaniel KIRBY entered on the premises and enjoyed it during his life, but the defendant Peter KIRBY does not believe that the premises were, or are of the yearly value of £33 as is alleged, or that they are above the yearly value of £30. He agrees that Richard attained the age of 26 at the time mentioned in the bill, and the plaintiff Jane likewise attained the age of 21 about the time mentioned in the bill, in the lifetime of their brother Nathaniel. The defendant believes that John, Robert and Amy died after the death of Peter KIRBY the testator, but whether any of them attained their resp- ective ages of 26 and 21 he does not know, but he believes that if they died before their respective ages their legacies of £10 apiece bequeathed to John and Robert and the legacy of £20 to Amy became due and accrued to the plaintiffs Richard and Jane and Joan KIRBY, and that in such case, a third of it amounting to 20 marks belonged to Richard and another third to Jane. He goes on to say that he can prove that John KIRBY, if he had lived would have been 26 in 1639 and Robert KIRBY would have been 26 in 1648, Amy KIRBY would have been 21 in 1641. He says that he does not doubt that Nathaniel, his father, paid the plaintiff William DICKINSON and Jane his wife the legacies due to Jane by the will of Peter KIRBY the testator, by his conveying a certain cottage in Charlton-upon-Otmoor (Oxfordshire) to William DICKINSON and Jane, his wife, and that they have been ever since in possession of it. Of what estate they have in it he does not know. He believes that immediately after Richard and Jane attained their ages of 26 and 21 respectively, the late unhappy war and distraction in this kingdom came on, and continued, but he denies that it was due to the war that the plaintiffs could not take their remedy at law against Nathaniel for the recovery of any legacies due to them or that after the war was over, they forbore to prosecute Nathaniel upon his promise to pay the same. He has heard of no such thing, or that Nathaniel pretended to have had serious losses as a result of the war, and complained that it had impoverished him. He believes that Nathaniel died seised of the premises, but he denies that he died about 12 years, since he believes that he died (?27) years ago. He further says that he does not know whether Nathaniel died before he had paid the legacies to the plaintiffs, but believes that he did fully satisfy the plaintiff, William DICKINSON and Jane, his wife, for their legacies by the grant of the cottage. Nathaniel, or this defendant's guardians since the decease of Nathaniel, have long since paid the plaintiff Richard not only the legacy of £10 given to him, but also all such dividends of the other legacies which might belong to him by the deaths of John, Robert and Amy. He cannot but admire that the plaintiff should be so unjust and vexatious as to demand the same again of this defendant and to sue him in this Court.

At the time of the death of this defendant's father, he was but an infant of very tender years, and after his father's death his eldest son and heir did enter the premises and held them as issue in tail by virtue of the will of the said Peter KIRBY. By virtue of this he has, since the decease of his father, received the rents and profits, but he denies that William DICKINSON and Jane his wife married after the death of this defendant's father, since he can prove they were married in the lifetime of his father. He denies that they ever requested him to pay their leg- acies and that he knows the sum of money due as of right to them or that the sum of £63 6s. 8d. belongs of right to the plaintiff Richard KIRBY. In fact he refuses to pay any such sums to the plaintiffs, and he has been informed that Richard and Jane attained their respective ages and that John, Robert and Amy died before achieving their ages, anything to the contrary notwithstanding. He denies that he claims the premises by any settlement prior to the will of his grandfather Peter, or that Amy, Robert and John attained their respective ages as is suggested in the bill. He confesses that he claims the legacies have been paid and that he claims to derive his title to the premises from the said will as heir at law to his grandfather. He denies that he or his father have any private or other estate in the premises.

*****

21.   C 22/662/34   (See C5/511/61)

Interrogatories to be administered
on behalf of the defendant, Peter
KERBY, yeoman.

1.   Same as for the plaintiff

2.   When did Nathaniel KERBY, the defendant's father die; were you at his funeral, were you clerk of the parish; why was the burial not registered in the Church Book; how many years is it since the death of Nathaniel ?

3.   Did you know that Nathaniel, or the defendant, or some person for the defendant has paid Richard KERBY the plaintiff the legacy which was given him by the will of Peter KERBY his father; how much was he paid, when and by whom; what have you heard Richard confess about this ?

4.   Did you not know that Nathaniel made a grant of the cottage and some land in Charlton to William DICKINSON and Jane, his wife, the plaintiffs; what term was the grant, what was the yearly value of the premises; how long have they been in possession; have they not acknowledged themselves content with the legacy they received under the will of Peter KERBY the grandfather ?

5.   If there be any other matter relative to the cause state it.

Robert MYNNE of Oxford, yeoman,
aged 54.

1.   He has known all the parties ever since he can remember.

3.   He knows that Robert PHIPPS, who married Elizabeth
      ..... (?MYNNE), who was the defendant's guardian paid
      Richard KERBY £24 4s. 8d. in several payments, viz:
      £10 on June 24 1651, £6 14s. 8d. in May 1653, £7 10s. 0d.
      in September 1651, for a legacy which was given to him John
      and Amy KERBY by the will of Peter, the grandfather, which
      belonged to him by the deaths of John, Robert and Amy.
      Richard signed an acknowledgement when he had received the
      last payment and promised to give an acquittance for it when
      one Mr. William DICKINSON, who was Richard's brother-
      in-law, and with whom he did business, came home.   Richard
      insisted that DICKINSON only should write the acquittance.
      He remembers this because he was tenant to Elizabeth, the
      wife of Robert PHIPPS out of whose lands the money was
      raised.

4.   He has heard that Nathaniel gave William DICKINSON and
      Jane a cottage and lands worth 30/- per annum in lieu of
      the legacy.   He thinks they have had possession of it for
      about 35 years.

Robert PHIPPS of Yarnton, yeoman,
aged 45.

1.   He has known the plaintiff and defendant about 23 years.

3.   He says he married Elizabeth MYNN the defendant's
      guardian who paid Richerd KERBY £24 4s. 8d. for the
      legacy in the manner stated by the last deponent.   About
      half a year before he made the first payment his wife was
      sued by the plaintiff for payment of the legacies and was
      advised by her attorney, Mr. Peter LANGSTON, to pay
      them, and she accordingly did so.

4.   Three years ago the defendant asked the plaintiff how he
      held the cottage etc., and he answered in right of his
      wife's portion and legacies, but in fact he only holds in
      right of her portion.

Oliver PANGBOURNE of Charlton,
Innkeeper, aged 54.

1. He has known all the parties as long as he can remember.

2. He says Nathaniel died about 27 years ago or more. He was at the funeral, and one James WITHAM was then clerk of the parish, but he was sick at the time and one William WITHAM who is now clerk executed the office of clerk and dug the grave. Nathaniel was buried in the Churchyard of Charlton, and by reason of the Wars and Troubles there was no resident parson there and so the Register of Burials was then omitted.

Mary WADDAMS, wife of Thomas
WADDAMS of Charlton, aged 69.

4. She has heard Jane DICKINSON declare that she holds the cottage as her portion.

Matthew ALDRIDGE of Charlton,
husbandman aged 35.

1. He has known the parties for several years.

4. As the last deponent's answer.

Mary ALDRIDGE, wife of Matthew
ALDRIDGE, aged 35.

4. As above.

William BRYAN of Charlton, yeoman
aged 45.

4. As above.

William DORLE, als. WITHAM of
Charlton, collarmaker, aged 55.

2. He repeats the deposition of Oliver PANGBOURNE.

*****

C 22/662/34. (See C5/511/61)

Interrogatories to be administered
to witnesses on behalf of Richard
KERBY and William DICKINSON and
Jane, his wife plaintiffs, versus
Peter KERBY defendant.

1. Do you know the parties to this case; did you know
   Peter KERBY the defendant's grandfather and Nathaniel
   KERBY, John KERBY, Robert KERBY, the sons of Peter
   the elder, all now deceased ? Do you know the 2 messuages, in Charlton-upon-Otmoor whereof Peter, the
   grandfather died possessed and devised by him for the
   payment of his debts, now or late in the occupation of
   Matthew ALDRIDGE of Burnham and William BRYAN;
   what was their yearly value ?

2. This writing dated June 1625 containing eight sheets of
   paper beginning "In the Name of God Amen. I, Peter
   KERBY etc. etc." and ending "Richard ALLEY, his
   mark, William KERBY, his mark" Is it a true copy of
   the Will of Peter the testator, and how do you know ?*

3. Do you know the dates when the Plaintiffs Richard
   KERBY and Jane DICKENSON, and when John KERBY,
   Robert KERBY and Amy KERBY were born and when
   they died.   Are these notes shown to you true copies
   of the Register Books of the Church of Charlton test-
   ifying the baptisms of Richard, Jane, John, Robert and
   Amy KERBY and the burials of Amy KERBY ?

4. When did Jane, the relict of Peter KERBY, the testator
   die ?

5. Do you know or believe that John KERBY died before
   attaining the age of 26, where did he die, how did he
   come to his end and your reasons ?

6. Do you know or believe Robert KERBY is dead, where
   and how did he die, what induces you to believe he is
   dead; when did he depart from Charlton or other place
   of residence, whither went he and when was he last heard
   of; did he die before attaining the age of 26 ?

7. Are you acquainted with the handwriting and usual marks
   of Nathaniel KERBY and of William DYNHAM, gent and
   Henry DAY; did any of them subscribe their names to the
   indenture now showed to you, being a lease of a cottage
   and 4 acres in Charlton made by Nathaniel to the plaintiffs William DICKINSON and Jane for the term of their
   lives attested by the said William DYNHAM and Henry
   DAY; are they in their handwriting; are DYNHAM and

* See English Adventurers and Virginia Settlers Vol 1, Will 194.

DAY long since dead; do you believe Nathaniel really made the indenture ?

8. Do you believe Jane KERBY, sister of Richard KERBY was paid her legacy of £20, and her dividends of her brother's and sister's legacies; what was paid to her or her husband William DICKINSON.

9. Illegible.

Depositions taken at Merton, Oxfordshire
on Monday 15 April 24 Chas II (1672)
before Marmaduke KEEN, Henry CLOPTON,
William HOPKINS and Richard PRATT,
gents on behalf of the plaintiffs.

Francis BLOWER of Bicester, Oxon., gent,
aged 40.

2. Yes. Last Saturday he examined it with the original in the Registry of the Diocese of the Bishop of Oxford at Oxford and believes it to be a true copy of the will of Peter KIRBY.

Robert MINN, formerly examined on
behalf of the defendant and now on
behalf of the plaintiff.

9. He refers to what he has already deposed on the part of the defendant, and as to the rest he says that the money was paid in satisfaction of the legacies and not for any collateral respects to the plaintiff Richard KERBY that he knows of.

Anthony FRANKLIN of Bicester, gent,
aged 34.

3. The writings now showed to him are true copies of the Church Books of Charlton, for he examined them this day April 15.

Oliver PANGBOURNE, formerly examined on
the part of the defendant now on behalf
of the plaintiff.

1. He knows the parties to the case and also knew John, Robert, Amy and Nathaniel KERBY and the lands

mentioned, which are worth £30 a year.

4.   Jane, the relict of Peter KERBY died about 3 or 4 years
     since.

5.   He believes so, but does not know when he died.

6.   Robert KERBY left Charlton about the beginning of the
     late wars.

7.   He believes the mark of Nathaniel KERBY, now shown him,
     is genuinely his mark.

8.   He has heard it commonly reported that William DICKINSON
     or Jane his wife received the legacy of £20 and the dividends
     of her brothers' and sisters' legacies.

Mary WADDAMS, wife of Thomas
WADDAMS of Charlton-upon-Otmoor
formerly sworn on behalf of the
defendant now on behalf of the
plaintiff.

4.   She thinks Jane, the relict of Peter KERBY died about
     2 years ago.

5.   John KERBY was in this country about 37 years since,
     but she never saw him since.   She has heard that he was
     killed with a coach in London not long after his being in
     the country and this she believes by reason that such news
     was sent down to his friends.

6.   Robert KERBY died about 28 years ago as she has been told
     and believes.

8.   She has heard that Mr. William DICKINSON sued the relict
     of Nathaniel KERBY for a legacy and dividends and that he
     succeeded in his suit and was paid.

John DUNKIN of Merton, Oxon., gent,
aged 56.

7.   He knew the handwriting of Mr. William DYNHAM and
     believes the writing now shown him to be his.   He thinks
     Mr. DYNHAM has been dead about 30 years.

Thomas INGRAM of Charlton, blacksmith,
aged 60.

5.	He has heard that John KERBY died about 30 years ago by a fall from a coach, but how old he was when he died he does not know.

6.	Robert KERBY went into the army about the beginning of the late wars, and he has never heard of him since.

William INGRAM of Charlton, labourer,
aged 45.

6.	He has heard that Robert is dead and has not heard of him since the fight at Branford in the late Civil wars.

*****

23.	C.8/262/31 (See also C.22/642/50)
18 June, 1680

Bill of Complaint of John HORNE
of Berkhampstead St. Mary, Herts.,
gent and his wife Mary plaintiffs,
versus, John NASH and Richard KIRBY.

John NASH of Berkhampstead St. Peter, dyer, was seised in 1668 of a copyhold messuage and land in Berkhampstead St. Peter and a copyhold meadow called Herringhangers in Berkhampstead St. Peter.   He borrowed of Frances WETHERID, widow, and her son Francis, £100.   For security NASH surrendered the lands to them on 30 September 1669.   The mortgage was assigned to Jeremy WELLS.   NASH continued in possession.   In December 1674 WELLS made his will and died.   In October the plaintiff John HORNE married Mary WELLS.   One Richard KIRBY of Abergavenny, Mon. pretends that he is cousin and next heir to Jeremy WELLS (since Jeremy WELLS died without issue) and threatens to enter the lands. Since Jeremy WELLS' death NASH has refused to pay interest to the plaintiffs.

3 December 1680

Answer of John NASH one of the
defendants.

The surrender to WELLS was not in the nature of a mortgage.   NASH continued in possession until Jeremy WELLS' death in December 1674 under a three year lease of 2 September 1671.   Jeremy WELLS was uncle of Richard KIRBY.   John NASH has kept possession since Jeremy WELLS' death as tenant to KIRBY.

8 July 1680

Answer of defendant, Richard
KYRBYE.

NASH was an indigent man and low in the world. The surrender to
Jeremy WELLS was absolute. His real estate ought to descend to Richard
KYRBYE as the only son, and heir of Elinor KIRBY deceased and heir to
Avies DEANE this defendant's aunt deceased, who were sisters and co-
heirs of Jeremy WELLS.

*****

C.22/642/50
October 1681

Interrogatories on behalf of
plaintiffs in suit of John HORNE
gent and wife Mary (relict and
executrix of Jeremy WELLS gent)
plaintiffs, versus Richard KIRBY
and John NASH defendants.

1.   Do you know the parties ?

2.   Did NASH borrow £100 from Judith WETHERID, widow,
      or Francis WETHERID gent, as security; did he surrender
      certain copyhold land by way of mortgage, held of the manor
      of Berkhampstead St. Peter and Berkhampstead St. Mary
      alias Northchurch, Herts., were the lands afterwards
      forfeited for non-payment ?

3.   Did Jeremy WELLS pay the £100 to Judith WETHERID and
      did he then accept a surrender of the lands as security ?

4.   Did NASH continue in possession of the lands after their
      surrender to WELLS ? Did he pay WELLS the interest ?
      Did WELLS look on the lands merely as security for the
      mortgage and not as part of his real estate ? Did NASH
      declare it to be a mortgage ?

5.   Are these true copies of the court roll ?

6.   Are the plaintiffs lawfully married ?

7.   Do you know of a bond in £2,000 entered into by Jeremy
      WELLS to Thomas WELLS and William WELLS ?

8.   Did the estate settled on the plaintiff Mary by Jeremy
      WELLS fall very much short of the value specified in
      this bond ?

9. Has NASH since WELLS' death continued in possession of the lands; is he now in possession; had he ever paid interest to the plaintiffs ?

10. What is the yearly value of the lands ?

11. Anything else relevant.

15 October 1681

Depositions on behalf of plaintiffs,
taken at Berkhampstead St. Peter.

Joseph SAYER, rector of Berkhampstead
St. Mary, aged 50.

1. Does not know defendants.

6. Plaintiffs were married on 3 October 1678 at Berkhampstead St. Mary.

John WHEIPLEY, Berkhampstead St.
Peter, tailor, aged 48.

1. Knows all parties except KIRBY for 3 or 4 years, has known KIRBY for about one year.

10. Lands are worth £8 per annum and could be sold for £160

Mrs. Judith WETHERID, Berkhampstead
St. Mary, widow, aged 60.

1. Does not know KIRBY.

Francis CLERKE, Berkhampstead St. Peter,
gent, aged 70.

1. Has known KIRBY about 2 years.

William WELLS, Ivinghoe, Bucks.,
gent, aged 50.

1. Knows all parties

Edmund NUBOULT, Berkhampstead St. Peter,
clerk, aged 38.

1. Has seen KIRBY.

*****

C.5/170/19
1 December 1690

Bill of Complaint of James KIRBY
of Slade End, Brightwell, Berks,
versus   Hugh COALES.

The plaintiffs, James KIRBY of Slade End, Brightwell, Berks., gent,
and Richard BLACKALL of Wallingford, gent, lent money to Hugh
COALES of Wallingford, haberdasher to pay his debts.   He claimed to
be the owner of 3 messuages in Fish Street, Wallingford in the occupation
of Nicholas LANGFORD, ... MAXEY and Joseph CORDER.   He affirmed
that the property was free of all incumbrances and that he had full authority to convey them to the plaintiffs, and as such proposed to sell them
to the plaintiffs three years ago.   After paying him for them, they discovered that the property was charged but Hugh COALES promised to save
them harmless.   They find now that the property was already mortgaged.

        Answer missing.

                    *****

C.7/194/24
16 June 1693

Bill of Complaint of Richard KERBY,
late of Abergavenny, Monmouthshire,
Joiner, versus   Michael BOHUN, gent.

Eleven years ago the plaintiff was sent on business by John ARNOLD Esq.,
his then master to Monmouth where he was brought before the Magistrates
and required to give bail to appear at the next Quarter Sessions to be
held at Monmouth to answer certain charges levelled against him.   For
want of bail he was sent to prison until one Michael BOHUN of Monmouth
(defendant to this bill) and one Walter ROGERS at John ARNOLD'S request
bailed him out.   When he was brought to trial nothing was charged against
him and he was discharged without any cost to his bailees except £3 paid
to the gaoler for his keep.   When the plaintiff came back to London on
his lawful occasions, BOHUN sued him for the £3 and he has been in
Newgate Prison ever since.

        Answer of Michael BOHUN, gent.

Richard KIRBY was outlawed on 6 June 30 Chas II (1690) at the suite of
James PRICE in a Plea of Debt, and is still outlawed.

                    *****

                    55

27.   C.5/122/11
         undated

         Breviate of Bill of Complaint of Martha
         BARNARD of Ramsden, Oxon., widow versus
         Richard KERBY senior, Richard KERBY,
         junior of Alvescott, Oxon., and John
         HAYES defendants.

Whereas Richard KERBY senior theretofore of Ramsden yeoman, now of
Alvescott, Oxon., was seised in fee simple in ground called Lambert
Layes coppice in Ramsden, with common of pasture, and a parcel of fern
ground on Ramsden Heath, Richard KERBY agreed to sell the same to
Richard HAYTER, senior, of Burford, conveyed by feoffment of 30 April
1651 for £18 10s. 0d.   To the end that the said Richard KERBY senior,
Richard KERBY junior, and Martha KERBY and John HAYES may be made
to answer, and that Richard KERBY senior may declare if he excuted the
feoffment, and that they may set forth whether they do not threaten that
the plaintiff should not enjoy the said gound.

         At Alvescott.
         25 April 1696

         Answer of Richard KERBY senior, and
         Richard KERBY junior and Martha
         KERBY and John HAYES defendants.

They do not know of any contract with Richard HAYTER for the sale of the
cottage and grounds called Lambert Layes coppice etc.   Richard KERBY
senior says that it is true that he and Martha, his late wife, being seised
in tail of one messuage and two yardlands in Ramsden (whereof the cottage
etc. was part), he conveyed it by lease and release of 21/22 January
1657/8 to James WHITE of Cogges, yeoman, except half an acre lying near
the heath with a cottage thereon erected, which are the premises claimed
by the plaintiff, for £805, with a covenant to levy a fine and to suffer a
recovery.   The fine and recovery were levied and suffered to the intent
that the entail might be cut off.   Richard KERBY senior further confesses
that he sold the wood growing in Lambert Layes coppice, except that in
the hedgerows, to Richard HAYTER for £18 10s. 0d., but he did not
grant the ground of the cottage or coppice or any plot or commons to him.
Shortly afterwards, in 1655, the wood and trees were cut down and the
defendant Richard KERBY built the cottage at his own cost and permitted
the mother of the defendant John HAYES, she being destitute of an habitation and being aunt to this defendant, to dwell therein for life.   The
defendant never conveyed it to her or to any other person named in the bill
under whom the plaintiff claims to derive a title.   Richard KERBY senior,
and Richard KERBY junior his eldest son and heir in tail demised the
cottage on 20 March 1678/9 to Martha KERBY one of the daughters of
Richard KERBY senior for 1,000 years at a peppercorn rent.   This demise
is attested by Walter KERBY and Alexander MAY.

                          *****

                           56

C.22/986/51
1698

James KIRBY, plaintiff, versus
Mary ELDRIDGE an infant by Mary
ELDRIDGE, widow, her mother and
guardian.

Interrogatories for the plaintiff.

1. Do you know parties; did you know Richard the said
   infant's father ?

2. Did you know Jane ELDRIDGE, widow, the defendant's
   grandmother ?

3. Are the writings shown you true copies of court rolls
   of the manor of Brightwell ?

4. Do you know the manor of Brightwell, Berks; can a
   copyhold tenant surrender his estate into the hands of
   two customary tenants out of court, or into the hands of
   the steward of the manor or clerk out of court; will such
   surrender be good to pass the estate in case the same be
   afterwards presented by the homage in open court; at
   what time has the person to whom the surrender is made
   to bring in the surrender and have the same presented ?

5. May a copyholder mortgage a copyhold estate ?

6. Is the clerk of the Bishop of Winchester usually the steward;
   will a surrender to him be good ?

7. Did the plaintiff lend Richard ELDRIDGE any money; how
   much and when ?

8. Was the plaintiff pressing Richard ELDRIDGE to pay the
   money ?

9. Did Richard ELDRIDGE ever request the plaintiff to forbear calling in the money due ?

10. Anything else material.

Depositions taken on behalf of the
plaintiff, taken at the house of
Thomas MAXEY innholder (the White
Hart inn) Wallingford, Berks., before
Jonathan SAYER, Gilbert TROW, Richard
PUSEY.

4 May 1698

James KERBY junior, Wallingford,
gent, aged 17.

57

3., 10.   The five writings are true copies of court rolls.
           Records were in books and not in rolls.

John FULLER, senior, Milton,
Berks., yeoman, aged 70 and
upwards.

4., 5.   Has known manor of Brightwell since 1689.   In
           1689 this deponent lent £300 to Richard ELDRIDGE
           gent and took a mortgage by surrender as security.

7.   Two or three years after the above loan, the plaintiff
           and one Richard BLA... by Richard ELDRIDGE'S
           direction paid his deponent £300 to discharge it.

Daniel THOMAS, Reading, Berks.,
capmaker, aged 38.

8.   In March 1693 deponent arrested Richard ELDRIDGE
           at the plaintiff's suit for £1,300 and took him to the
           White Hart Inn, Wallingford, where the plaintiff
           came and pressed Richard ELDRIDGE to repay
           £750 due on a mortgage;   Richard ELDRIDGE
           admitted the debt and mortgage and undertook to
           surrender the property absolutely at the next court.

Thomas HADDUCKE, Reading, Berks.,
periwig maker, aged 32.

8.   Arrested Richard ELDRIDGE in March 1693 as above.

John KIRBY Brightwell, yeoman,
aged 23.

1.   Knows the parties.

2.   Did not know Jane ELDRIDGE; has heard that she
           died in late February or early March last as he was
           invited to the funeral.

9.   On orders of the plaintiff he went 3 or 4 times to demand
           money of Richard ELDRIDGE.

58

William LEAVER junior, Brightwell,
Berks., yeoman, aged 41.

2.   Knew Jane ELDRIDGE.

4.   Has known manor of Brightwell for 20 years; such
     mortgages by surrender are the custom of the manor;
     he is a customary tenant.

5.   Copyholders may mortgage copyhold estate.

8.   Was with the plaintiff and Richard ELDRIDGE when
     Richard ELDRIDGE was under arrest.

John FORD, Sotwell, Berks., yeoman,
aged 40 and upwards.

7.   Since the death of his uncle James FORD, he found it
     entered in James FORD'S books that James FORD about
     1684 had lent Richard ELDRIDGE £200 on a mortgage of
     copyhold estate.   As executor he called in the mortgage.

Interrogatories on behalf of
defendant.

1.   Do you know the parties, Richard ELDRIDGE, Richard
     ELDRIDGE'S father John and Jane, widow of John ?

2.   Did John ELDRIDGE die seised of a copyhold estate in
     Brightwell; did Jane hold the same in widowhood; was
     this estate left incumbered with mortgages when John
     ELDRIDGE died; was part sold to pay them off ?

3.   What is the copyhold estate now worth to be sold ?

4.   Has Richard ELDRIDGE mortgaged the estate since the
     death of John ELDRIDGE to plaintiff ?

Depositions on behalf of the defendant.

William LEAVER junior, Brightwell,
Berks., yeoman, aged 41.

1.   Has known the parties for 10 years; knew Richard
     ELDRIDGE who is reported to be dead beyond the seas,
     having been absent about two years; knew John ELDRIDGE
     who died in February last.

2. John ELDRIDGE died seised and Jane held the same in widowhood; John died seised of another estate in Brightwell which was not held by Jane, part of which was copyhold and part freehold; John ELDRIDGE left the estate much incumbered; to pay the mortgages, Richard sold the following lands:- parcel of land in Mackney in Brightwell to John LEAVER for between seven and eight hundred pounds, part of which was paid to Thomas RYMER a mortgages; about a yard-land in Sladend field in Brightwell to John ELDRIDGE for sum unknown.

3. Estate is worth £1,200

4. Was present when Richard ELDRIDGE mortgaged the estate to the plaintiff, but cannot remember the particulars.

*****

C.22/664/44. The Bill and Answer to which the following depositions refer are missing, but see item 30 for Richard KYRBY of Landbeche.

C.22/664/44
January 1561/2

Interrogatories on behalf of Richard
KYRBY plaintiff, versus Randall HALL.

1. Do you know parties ?

2. Do you know if the defendant has any knowledge of
   the law or of making evidences ?

3. Do you know that the defendant came to the plaintiff's
   house on the eve of the Ascension about 4 o'clock,
   desiring him to seal an indenture of the Manor of
   Landbeche ?

4. Did the defendant bring with him a lease ready written ?

5. Did the defendant say to the plaintiff "If you seal not
   this indenture presently you forfeit a bond of £200",
   and did the plaintiff seal the same ?

6. Did the plaintiff read the indenture before sealing;
   is or was he able to read it ?

7. Is the plaintiff very aged and impotent ?

18 January 1561/2

Depositions of witnesses on behalf
of Richard KERBY plaintiff.

Richard BALLDRYKE, Landbeche,
aged 40.

3. Knows of visit to the plaintiff's house. He was present.

5. The defendant made the statement alleged. The bond to
   be forfeited under the award. KIRBY then sealed the
   indenture, whether for fear or not the deponent does not
   know.

6. The plaintiff did not read, and was unable to read the
   indenture by reason of an impediment both in his sight
   and speech, but the indenture was read to him by Henry
   GODBOD.

7. The plaintiff is of four score years of age or thereabouts
   and has great impediment in his speech and is impotent so
   that he is not able to make himself ready without help of
   others.

Thomas WARD, Landbeche, aged 60.

Henry GODBOD, Landbeche, aged 33.

William SAMPSON, Landbeche, aged 60.

The answers of the above add nothing.

15 January 1561

Depositions on behalf of plaintiff
Richard KIRBY before Mr. Andrew
PERNE and Richard BRAKYN Esq.

Mr. Francis HYNDE, Maddingley, Cambs.,
Esq., aged 30.

1. There were contentions between the plaintiff and the
    defendant; one was for the assurance of one third of
    the lands of the plaintiff to the wife of the defendant;
    another was for £35 for marriage money due to the
    defendant and for arrears of rent to value of £10 due
    to defendant.

2. The plaintiff and defendant agreed to submit to the
    award of deponent and others.

3. By the award the plaintiff was bound to make a lease
    of the manor of Beche for two years to the defendant
    to begin after the end of an existing lease to the def-
    endant.

4. Paper lease was drawn up by the defendant.

5. He knows nothing.

6. After the award the plaintiff showed this deponent a
    lease in reversion of the manor of Landbeche to Edward
    STEWARD and George HASELL for 40 years.

7. Upon a fault found in the lease by the plaintiff, the
    defendant agreed to its emendation; does not know
    whether the plaintiff refused the offer.

8. After the award was made, arbitrators went to the
    plaintiff's house, when the plaintiff said he could not
    perform the award, since he had made a lease to
    STEWARD and HASSELL.

Thomas WARD, Landbeche, aged 60.

Adds nothing.

Henry ....., Landbeche, aged 34.

Adds nothing except that the plaintiff signed the emended lease
to HALL, he being one of the witnesses.

William SAMPSON, Landbeche, aged 60.

Illegible.

Bill and Answer missing.

*****

C.2. Eliz. H.8/9
29 October 1596

Bill of Complaint of Christopher
HODSON of Shenley, Herts, gent.
versus John HOLFORD.

About the beginning of the Queen's reign one Richard KIRBYE of Landbeche
in the County of Cambridge gent (See item 29) was seised of the Manor of
Landbeche, called Brayes.   By a deed made between him on the one part
and Edward STYWARD and George HASYLL on the other part, he let the
manor to them for a term of years, by force of which they entered into
possession.   George HASYLL was possessed of one ninth part of the
manor called Brayes, as well as a tenement in Landbeche called Yeald
Hall by force of a lease from one John MARTIN of Woodhurst, Huntingdon,
gent.   In the 22nd year of Eliz. George HASYLL assigned his leases as
above to one John NEWSHAM of Chesterton, gent who entered into possession.   John NEWSHAM then assigned his rights to Robert SHUTE, then
second Baron of the Exchequer Court and Thomasyn, his wife.   Robert
SHUTE then died and the leases came to Thomasyn, his widow by survivorship.   She then assigned them to John HUTTON Esq. and Edmund BENDISH,
gent, who in consideration of the sum of £660 sold the leases to the plaintiff.
However all the original leases from Richard KIRBYE and John MARTIN
have got into the hands of John HOLFORD of Long Stanton, Cambridgeshire,
gent, who refuses to give them up.

Answer missing.

*****

31.   C3/407/30
        19 February 1638/9

        Bill of Complaint missing.

        Answer of Henry PEIKE one of the
        defendants to the Bill of Complaint
        of Matthew KIRBIE plaintiff.

It is true that the defendant about 18 or 19 years since had the reversion
of a copyhold messuage and lands at Over, Cambs., after the death of
Robert PEIKE his father, who is at this time living, which are of the
annual value of £11, and that the plaintiff of his own accord at about the
same time solicited the defendant to buy his reversion, offering his £50.
The defendant sold the property to the plaintiff and received £5, with
bond for payment of £45 within one year.   Only £25 has been paid.   On
30 May 1624 the defendant in London received a new bond, brought by
Mr. COTSFORD, in which the plaintiff with one William EATON bound
themselves in £40 to pay £20, dated 15 May 1624.   The money was not
paid, the defendant did not give a bill of discharge.   Denies combination
with the other defendant Richard MILLER.   Richard MILLER had a
mortgage on the plaintiff's estate; he was lord of the manor of Over.
Admits that in Trinity term 1631 he put the bond in suit against the plaintiff, and again in Hilary term last.   He denies that he had the latter case
tried in the plaintiff's absence, the plaintiff being employed as a surveyor
of lands, since the plaintiff was in town at the beginning of the suit.

                              *****

32   C2 Chas I M.34/33
        9 June 1641

        Bill of Complaint of Christopher
        MILES of Broughton, Hunts., yeoman,
        versus Matthew KIRBY, gent.

Three years ago Christopher MILES lent William MILES of Broughton,
Hunts., yeoman deceased, £100, for which he promised repayment at a
time shortly then to follow.   He also promised to give a bond of £200
for the repayment, which was by William MILES'S direction then made
but not sealed by him.   Nevertheless the plaintiff did become bound for
him to one Sybil BRIGGS for the payment to her of £30 which he,
Christopher, owed her, and William MILES promised to make payment
to her on the plaintiff's behalf.   But William MILES did not pay the £100
to Christopher during his lifetime and he died 1½ years ago intestate,
being at the time of his death not indebted to any person other than the
plaintiff.   William MILES died possessed of a personal estate far sur-
mounting all his debts, and left Anne MILES, his wife.   Anne MILES
after the death of William took out letters of administration possessed
herself of her late husband's estate.   Christopher MILES asked Anne
to make payment for she well knew it to be a just debt.   But in order to

avoid payment she gave out that she had not assets to satisfy it, and to
that end, by combination with Matthew KIRBY of Over in the county of
..... (Cambridge), gent, her own brother, and John BOYDEN of St. Ives,
Huntingdon, yeoman, and Alice his wife, daughter of the said Anne, she
pretended that her late husband was indebted to divers other persons to
whom in truth he was not indebted, and that she has paid them several
sums of money.   She and the other confederates have secretly sold and
converted to their own use all the personal estate of William MILES.
The plaintiff requests the Court to compel Anne MILES and the other
confederates to disclose the estate of the late William MILES, and to
account for the sums they have expended.

        Answer of Matthew KIRBY, gent,
        and Seakin BOYDEN and Alice his
        wife to the Bill of Complaint of Christopher
        MILES.

They say they have no knowledge of any loan by Christopher MILES to
William MILES, and they do not believe that William MILES received
£100 from the plaintiff at any time.   They deny that William MILES gave
a bond of £200 to the plaintiff, or that he gave directions for any such
bond to be made.   Alice BOYDEN says that while she lived with William
MILES, which was for at least ten years, (she being his daughter-in-law
by virtue of William MILES' marriage with her mother) Christopher
MILES often came to his house, and not long before William MILES' death
borrowed money from him.   They do not know that Christopher MILES
became bound for William MILES to Sybil BRIGGS for the payment of £30
andthey believe this to be untrue.   Further, they deny that he paid Sybil
BRIGGS anything out of his own money.   But it is true that about 2 years
before William MILES died intestate he was not indebted to anyone for any
sums greater than the value of his personal estate.   Seakin BOYDEN and
Alice say that they have cause to think that William MILES, before
BOYDEN became a suitor to Alice, his daughter, in marriage, the better
to persuade him did faithfully promise him that if he (Seakin BOYDEN)
would marry Alice he (MILES) would give him £150 with her as dowry.
Although Seakin BOYDEN married Alice, William MILES never paid this
in spite of being asked to do so.   Indeed he was so far from paying it,
that when Anne MILES, wife of the said William MILES, for the better
advancement of her daughter's marriage, sold certain lands which were
part of her own jointure amounting to £73, William MILES took all this
money and then again faithfully promising to pay it to Alice towards her
advancement in marriage but notwithstanding Anne MILES agreeing to
the sale as aforesaid, William MILES was forced to dispose of the £73
to pay part of his debts to prevent the clamour of his pressing creditors.
Anne MILES took letters of administration of all her husband's personal
estate and possessed herself of so much as she could quietly obtain.   But
they deny that they combined or confederated with Anne MILES to avoid
payment of any of William MILES' just debts, or that they tried to circumvent the plaintiff of any just debt due to him.   Anne MILES, on the contrary
has paid several people large sums of money to satisfy William MILES'
debts, in fact more money than the personal estate of her husband already
amounted to.   They also deny that they converted or disposed of any part
of William MILES' estate to any use of any other person whatsoever, but
Seakin BOYDEN confesses that Anne MILES sold him 2 horses, 2 cows,

and 160 sheep and indemnified him from such sums of money as he at her
request stood engaged for with her. BOYDEN shortly after made a bona
fide sale of the sheep etc. for the sum_ of £57 6s. 0d. BOYDEN further
says that by reason of the goods conveyed to him he disbursed out of his
own money £79 13s. 8d. towards the payment of William MILES' debts,
and in fact has disbursed much more money than he has received so far.
He hopes that Anne MILES will not suffer him to become so much demnified
in his estate as he yet is, and therefore he believes that those goods of
William MILES hereafter expressed and yet remaining in his custody by
Anne MILES, to wit 1 great bible, 2 little books, 1 joined bedstead with
tester and balance, a featherbed, pair of pillows, a mattress (numerous
articles of furniture and household stuff - document torn). They say they
know not of any further goods of William MILES but what is already
inventoried by Anne MILES, and already exhibited to the Ecclesiastical
Court, except one bond of £200 entered into by one John THREDDER of
Wistowe, Hunts., to William MILES and that only for performance of
certain covenants to be made and performed by THREDDER. They believe
that much of William MILES' goods were sold at a lower rate than they
were valued at owing to the troublous times that immediately ensued.
They further deny all combination and fraud but they confess that the last
time they saw Anne MILES was at Abbots Ripton, Hunts, about a fortnight
since.

*****

33.   C.7/201/103 and C.6/111/71
November 1650 and April 1653

William KIRBY of Abchurch Lane,
Citizen and Merchant Taylor of
London and Elizabeth, his wife,
daughter and heir of John MADDY
of Buckden, Hunts., yeoman,
deceased by Elizabeth, his wife,
(John MADDY was son and heir to
Dorothy MADDY of Buckden, widow),
versus Thomas JACKSON, gent.

- November 1650

The plaintiff Elizabeth's grandmother, Dorothy MADDY of Buckden was
seised in reversion in fee after the death of Ann BYWATER, long since
deceased of a freehold messuage and 25 acres called Le Hyne in Buckden.
In 1613 she surrendered the reversion to John MADDY and Elizabeth, his
wife, and the survivor of them. They were admitted tenants after the
death of Anne BYWATER. John MADDY went as a soldier in Count
MANSFIELD'S voyage and was killed. He left the plaintiff Elizabeth his
only child and heir, then aged 6. Shortly afterwards the mother died,
and soon after that William CLEMENT of Houghton, Hunts. claimed the
property was mortgaged to him by John MADDY and took possession of
it in 1615. At his death he left it in his will to his son John CLEMENT,
who sold it to one ..... HALSTEED, who sold it to John WILLIAMS of
Houghton, yeoman, who sold it to Thomas JACKSON of London, gent,

66

who has enjoyed it for the past 12 years and is still in possession. The plaintiffs have asked him to give them possession since his title is not good and he has refused.

Plea and Demurrer of Thomas
JACKSON, gent.

As the mortgage is alleged to have been made 35 years ago he pleads it must long since have been settled, and states his title must be good by virtue of the sales which have taken place meanwhile.

*****

C.21/K.2/9
1652

William KERBY and Elizabeth his wife,
plaintiffs, versus Thomas JACKSON,
defendant.

Interrogatories on behalf of the
defendant.

1. Do you know the messuage in Buckden, Hunts., now in question; was it about 16 years since in the possession of (WILLIAMS) Esq.; did he hold the same and 16 acres of land; of whom did he buy it; did the seller know that it was originally mortgaged; had the property been sold four times without any claim being made ?

2. Did the defendant JACKSON buy the property about 16 year ago and did he pay WILLIAMS £140 for it about June 1635; did the defendant know of the mortgage ?

3. Has the defendant enjoyed quiet possession until of late ?

4. In what condition were the premises on the death of ..... ; what did William CLEMENT senior lay out in repairs shortly after he came in; did it cost him £40 ?

5. In what condition were the premises when JACKSON came in; did he spend £140 in repairs ?

6. Did John MADDIE deceased, father of Elizabeth KIRBIE, the plaintiff, sell all his estate in Buckden ?

6 April 1652

Depositions on behalf of defendant
Thomas JACKSON taken at Buckden before
Cadwallader POWELL, Robert DICKMAN
and Henry REUVAN gents.

John HALSTED, Woodhurst, Hunts.,
clerk, aged 60.

1. It is 16 years since the messuage was in possession of
    John WILLIAMS Esq.; he purchased it of John HALSTED
    clerk, i.e. this deponent; who does not know of prior
    mortgage.

John LAWRENCE, Fen Stanton, Hunts.,
yeoman, aged 68.

4. On death of ..... the inn called the Vyne was very much
    in decay; he laid out £150 in repairs.

5. Premises were very old and ruinous when ..... entered.

6. John MADDEY confessed that he had sold all his estate
    in Buckden, including the Vine.

..... LANGTHORNE, Buckden, Hunts.,
....

Adds nothing.

John GRIGGS, Buckden, Hunts.,
labourer, aged 65.

4. Thomas BYWATER and his wife Anne having but a life
    estate in the Vine, cut down all the trees in the orchard,
    pulled down a barn and hovel and allowed the messuage
    to fall to ruin; William CLEMENT spent £40 on repairs.

Richard CASE, Buckden, Hunts,
labourer, aged 75.

Richard USHER, junior, Buckden,
carpenter aged 46.

Rowland LOVELAND, Buckden,
carpenter, aged 58.

The answers of the above add nothing.

..... RAYMONT, senior, Buckden,
yeoman, aged 65.

4. John MADDIE was grandchild of Anne BYWATER.

..... TAWYER, Buckden,
blacksmith, aged 50.

1. Messuage descended from William CLEMENT senior
    to his son John; John surrendered it to his brother
    William; William surrendered it to John HALSTEAD,
    clerk; John HALSTEAD surrendered it to Mr.
    WILLIAMS; Mr. WILLIAMS to JACKSON; no claim
    of a mortgage was made during this time.

John JACKSON, Buckden, gent.,
aged 51.

2. Thomas JACKSON, paid £140 to Mr. WILLIAMS for
    the property in June 1635.

3. At the Manor Court of 5 October 1635 Thomas JACKSON
    was admitted tenant.

..... April 1652

Depositions taken at Buckden on
behalf of plaintiffs.

Interrogatories are too badly damaged
to be transcribed.

John BRADSHAW, Buckden, yeoman,
aged 7..

1. Knows parties.

2. Knows messuage called the Vine; the defendant John
    MEDBERY holds it of Thomas JACKSON.

Robert RAYMONT, Buckden, yeoman,
aged 65.

Adds nothing.

..... MOTLEY, Brampton, Hunts.,
gent., aged 21.

Recites copy of court roll 9 April 1613 ...

Henry BURDER, Buckden, yeoman,
aged 70 and upwards.

1.   Has known the plaintiff Elizabeth KERBY for two years,
     JACKSON for 20 years, MEDBURY for 8 years; knew
     MADDEY junior and his wife Elizabeth (knew him for
     30 years but not his wife), does know Elizabeth the
     plaintiff, the daughter of John MADDEY; knew John
     MADDEY senior and wife Dorothy for 20 years; knew
     Anne alias Agnes BYWATER, grandmother of John
     MADDEY junior for 20 years.

..... MADDEY, Great Paxton, Hunts.,
husbandman, aged ...

1.   Knows that John MADDEY and Elizabeth were parents
     of Elizabeth the plaintiff.

Elizabeth IRELAND, wife of
Henry IRELAND of Buckden,
labourer, aged 50.

1.   Deponent is daughter of John and Dorothy MADDEY.

Richard RAYMONT, Buckden,
labourer, aged 50.

Adds nothing.

John JACKSON, Buckden, gent.,
aged 51.

No trace of the mortgage has been found in the Court Rolls.   John MADDEY
senior the husband of Dorothy was buried at Buckden 8 April 1611; Anne
BYWATER was buried at Buckden 28 January 1616.   Plaintiff Elizabeth was
baptised at Ramsey, Hunts., 28 November 1613.   John MADDEY junior and
Elizabeth ROGERS were married (at Buckden) 20 December 1612.

*****

C.5/421/171 and C.6/22/113
7 May 1663

Bill of Complaint of Henry PEARSON
of Southampton in Long Island in
America, versus John KIRBY of
Olney, Bucks.

In May 1639 (before Henry PEARSON went out of England) he lent Job
BRYMLEY of Olney, Buckinghamshire, yeoman, £120, at the rate of 5%.
For security Job BRYMLEY mortgaged 3 acres of land to the plaintiff in
Olney with the proviso that Job BRYMLEY should pay PEARSON the interest
of the £120 by half-yearly instalments for 5 years and the principal sum of
£120 at the end of the 5 years, otherwise the land would be forfeited.
However Job BRYMLEY neglected to pay PEARSON the interest and principal at the end of 5 years and died in debt to the plaintiff.   He left the three
acres at his death to his daughter Jane, who afterwards married Daniel
HOWES of Olney, yeoman.   Henry PEARSON having occasion to go to the
parts beyond the seas did by his letter of attorney, appoint Edward FULLER
of Olney, gent, William GEYNES of the same town, and Thomas CONSTABLE
of the same town, mercers, all now deceased, his attorneys, amongst other
things to receive the interest money during the 5 years, and the principal
at the end of it.   He left with them the deed of mortgage the better to enable
them to maintain his title to the lands.   By virtue of this they entered,
received the profits, and shortly after died.   Daniel HOWES, in right of
his wife Jane, entered the land and sold it to John KIRBY of Olney, haberdasher of hats, charged with the payment of the £120.   Notwithstanding
John KIRBY bought the three acres charged with the payment as aforesaid,
and notwithstanding he was abated the sum in his purchase price, yet he
refuses to pay the principal sum of £120 as he ought to do.   John KIRBY
being a soldier in the Parliament army against the King by some indirect
means has gotten into his hands the mortgage deed so that the plaintiff is
unable under the Common Law to make his title to the lands and so cannot
recover possession of them.

20 May 1663

Plea of John KIRBY to the Bill of
Henry PEARSON.

He refuses to acknowledge any of the matters contained in the bill, and for
plea he says that the plaintiff claims title by force of a deed of mortgage
which has come into the hands of this defendant.   Now since the plaintiff

has not made oath that he has not the deed in his custody, or lost it, or knows not what is become of it, (which he ought to have done) and for many other defects in the bill, John KIRBY pleads not to be compelled to make answer.

*****

36.   C.6/22/133
        7 November 1664

        (Bill Missing, but see item 35)

        The Answer of John KIRBY.

He knows nothing of £21 mentioned in the bill of complaint or any other money lent by the plaintiff to John BRIMLYE, or that BRIMLYE made any mortgage to the plaintiff of 3 acres of land mentioned in the bill. He knows of no trust which the plaintiff may have reposed in Edward FULLER, William GEYNES and Thomas CONSTABLE. He does not know of any Power of Attorney the plaintiff may have given them. He denies ever having seen any mortgage deed or counterpart. He admits that about 8 or 9 years ago, he bought the 3 acres of land in Olney in question from Daniel HOWES and Jane his wife, and paid £15 for it. He enjoyed peaceful occupation of it for 4 years before the deaths of William GEYNES and Edward FULLER, who, although they lived in the same town, never claimed the land by virtue of any pretended mortgage.

*****

37.   C9/407/481
        - July 1668

        Bill of Complaint of John KIRBY of
        Olney, Bucks, Haberdasher of hats,
        versus Dudley POPE.

The plaintiff is the eldest son and heir of Matthew KIRBY late of Over, Cambs, gent, deceased. In June 1639 Matthew KIRBY was lawfully seised by copy of the court roll of the manor of Over by the surrender of one Henry PIKE, one of the customary tenants of the manor; of the reversion after the death of one Robert PIKE, father of Henry PIKE, of a messuage, 9 acres of arable, 6 roods of marsh ground and 6 roods of meadow in Owze fen in the parish of Over and 2 roods of meadow in Southton fen, 10 acres of pasture of the yearly value of £25, under a condition to pay £62 to Rachel PIKE, a sister of the said Henry; £12 within six months after the death of Robert PIKE, to Anne PIKE sister of Henry; £10 within six months after the payment to Rachel, to Ruth PIKE another sister £8 within six months after the payment to Anne; to Rose PIKE another sister £15 within 6 months after the payment to Ruth; to Thomas PIKE brother of Henry £15 within 6 months after the payment to

Rose; to Francis PIKE another brother £10 within 6 months after payment
to Thomas; to John PIKE another brother £15 within 1 year after the
payment to Francis; and also 20 shillings each to Rachel and Anne PIKE,
daughters of John PIKE, at 18 years, should they all be living at the times
in question. Matthew KIRBY having paid £200 purchase money to Henry
PIKE and having compounded with Robert PIKE the father who had interest
in the premises for the term of his life, for an annuity of £12, and the
sheriff of Cambridge having taken the body of Matthew KIRBY upon execution
for £60, was constrained to borrow £60 from Joseph PARKER, late of Over,
gent, to procure his liberty, and for security agreed on 12 June 1639 to
surrender the reversion of the messuage and premises into the hands of
Sackville WADE then and still lord of the manor to the use of Joseph PARKER.
An agreement between Joseph PARKER and Matthew KIRBY was left in the
custody of Matthew KIRBY. Joseph PARKER afterwards being minded to
dispose otherwise of the money he had lent to Matthew KIRBY, one Dudley
POPE Esq. a counsellor-at-law pretending much love and kindness to
Matthew KIRBY in regard the latter had married one Mary POPE his only
sister, the plaintiff's mother, did agree to pay PARKER the £60 for which
the premises were mortgaged. POPE would hold and enjoy the 8 acres of
arable and close of 10 acres and two roods of meadow in Southton (value
£14 a year) until such money as he should deposit with PARKER for Matthew
KIRBY, and the sums of money to the PIKES might be fully paid. It was
also agreed that Matthew KIRBY should hold the messuage and homestead,
one acre of arable 6 roods of marsh and 6 roods of meadow in Owze Fen
for the payment of £12 a year to Robert PIKE, and afterwards to himself
and his heirs according to the custom of the manor, and also the two closes
8 acres of land and 2 roods of meadow after the money due from Dudley
POPE to Joseph PARKER and the PIKES should be paid. On 6 April 1641
Matthew KIRBY persuaded Joseph PARKER to surrender the reversion of
the messuage etc. into the hands of Sackville WADE to the use of Dudley
POPE. The latter was thereupon admitted tenant and has ever since held
it under the same conditions as Joseph PARKER. Matthew KIRBY died in
July 1662 until which time he had enjoyed the messuage, 1 acre of land,
6 roods of marsh and 6 roods of meadow and Dudley POPE has ever since
enjoyed the rest according to the agreement made between them. Robert
PIKE, who was to have £12 a year during his life, died in July 1642. Rose,
Thomas, Francis and John PIKE and several other PIKES who were to
receive sums of money, died before Robert PIKE and never received any
part of the money. Therefore Dudley POPE did not lay out more than £100
which has been repaid to him out of the profits of the premises in his own
use. He ought in equity to surrender all the premises to the use of the
plaintiff and to account to him for the overplus of the rents etc. received
by him. Dudley POPE was near Matthew KIRBY at the time of his death.
He intends to disinherit the plaintiff of the property, (albeit he well knows
it ought of right to come to him as eldest son and heir of Matthew KIRBY)
and although he has been fully paid for what money he has disbursed.
Soon after Matthew KIRBY'S death he got custody of the deed of agreement
made between Joseph PARKER, himself and Matthew KIRBY, and now
pretends that Matthew absolutely surrendered the premises to the use of
PARKER and that PARKER surrendered them to the use of him, Dudley
POPE, without condition. He also claims that the plaintiff is his heir at
law, his only sister's son, and says that if he the plaintiff will forebear
to prosecute him he will consider him in his will. Since Matthew KIRBY'S
death he has taken possession of the premises which were in the latter's
possession and refuses to account to the plaintiff for them and to surrender
them to his use.

Answer missing.

*****

38. C.5/502/23
13 December 1674

Bill of Complaint of Jane HOW,
versus Mary KIRBY, widow of
John KIRBY of Olney, Bucks.

About ..... years ago Job BRINGLEY, father of Jane HOW, widow, of
Olney, died possessed of two messuages and lands amounting to about
2 acres in Olney, of a yearly rental of £4, leaving them to the plaintiff
and her sister Elizabeth.   After their father's death Jane married Daniel
HOW, since deceased, and Elizabeth married Henry HUGHES, by whom
she had a son, Henry HUGHES.   After her marriage, Jane had occasion
to need £16, and prevailed upon her husband to join with her in a mortgage
of her half of the premises to one Robert THROCKMORTON who agreed to
lend her the £16.   For security she joined with her husband in levying a
fine to THROCKMORTON.   Not long after Elizabeth died, and after that
her son Henry HUGHES, and the plaintiff inherited her half of the property
as heir at law.   Robert THROCKMORTON later made a conveyance of the
mortgage to John KIRBY and he entered into the premises on the strength
of this conveyance and possessed himself of both halves.   About .....
years ago John KIRBY died, leaving Mary his wife, his executrix, who
possessed herself of both halves of the property and refuses to come to an
account with the plaintiff, or to redeem the mortgage, for she has got into
her hands all the deeds of the property, thus preventing Jane HOW from
proving her title.

Answer missing.

*****

39. C.9/393/10
- October 1694

Breviate of Bill of Complaint of
John KIRBY of Haddenham, Isle of
Ely yeoman, plaintiff, versus
Barron BRITTON, gent and William
SPARROW, gent, defendants.

One Barron BRITTON, late of Sandy, Bedfordshire, deceased conveyed
to William SPARROW, gent, his brother-in-law, certain lands in Sandy·
and elsewhere in Huntingdonshire and Bedfordshire in trust for a jointure
for his wife Martha BRITTON, and shortly after died.   About 14 years
since the plaintiff married Martha, and for some short time after Barron
BRITTON paid the plaintiff according to the settlement, but has several

74

then rented at 100 marks per annum situated in St. John Street in the parish of St Sepulchre's without Smithfield Bars, London, called the Windmill, was to be sold, and not having the means to take it, he asked William STRETTON to lend him the purchase money. William bought the lease of the Windmill for John YORKE and lent him £150. This inn comprised all or most of John YORKE'S estate which at the time of his death was valued at £12,000. Afterwards to requite some of the kindness and friendship that William STRETTON had shown him, John YORKE and Ellen invited themselves to dinner to William STRETTON'S house and told him that because they had no children of their own, he would like to take one of William STRETTON'S children to be educated and brought up by them. He promised William STRETTON to give a portion for her preferment in marriage as if the child were their own. William STRETTON freely gave his consent and bid John YORKE make free choice of one of his own sister's children, who was then deceased, he William being then married to another wife whose name was Anne BRABANT, daughter to Susan BRABANT, by whom he had also several children then living. John YORKE requested that he might choose one of STRETTON'S own children by his then wife, which STRETTON consented to. John and Ellen YORKE took home with them Priscilla STRETTON, William's daughter, and used her with all fatherly respect and regard for many years. About 14 years ago the plaintiff Richard KIRBY, then dwelling in St. John Street where he had lived for many years before, having affection for Priscilla, understood that John YORKE intended not only to give a good portion with her but, also that he would bestow a great part of his lands upon her (he and Ellen still having no children of their own). Mr. William KING of Lincolns Inn, an attorney in the Court of Common Pleas, Richard KIRBY'S master, was then lately dead and had turned over his practice to Richard KIRBY, who was then an attorney of the court, so he became a suitor to Priscilla in the way of marriage. After some negotiation Priscilla agreed to marry him, and John YORKE consented to give her a portion of £500, their diet during the lives of John and Ellen, and after its decease the greatest part of his lands worth £400 per annum to the issue of Richard and Priscilla if any. Richard and Priscilla married shortly after. Shortly afterwards John YORKE fell sick and about November 1613 he made his will in which he appointed Ellen (being then a woman of about the age of 87) sole executrix, leaving her in lands, goods and chattels £12,000 at the least. He made no provision either for the plaintiff's portion of £500 or lands to be conveyed to him, the plaintiff having issue by Priscilla now living. Not long before his death John YORKE charged Ellen to make good his promise and to care for Priscilla and her children since he had omitted them in his will. Ellen took upon her the sole administration of his goods etc. and proved the will in the Prerogative Court of Canterbury. Since that time the plaintiff has asked her many times to make good the testator's promise, which she said she would. To that end she disbursed several sums of money for the plaintiff, he being at that time in debt, by reason he had forborne his portion for many years and neglected his practice to follow the affairs of Ellen. He entered into a bond with Ellen for £200 for the payment of £100 and another £60 for the payment of £30, payable at a date long since past. Ellen assured him that they would never be put in suit against him but would only remain as a tie to bind him to such serviceable affairs for her as he without any such obligations he would willingly have done. About March last past he had a conversation with Ellen concerning the bonds and his portion of £500 and asked her to cancel them that he might receive the residue of his portion. Ellen answered that she intended to deliver them up forthwith. After John YORKE'S death Ellen had many suitors of good reckoning who did much importune her to consent to marry, amongst them one Edmund

WRIGHT, gent, a young man of weak estate. In order to effect his purpose
and to work himself into her favour he, knowing that the plaintiff and Priscilla
were then very inward with Ellen, solicited them to give way for his access
to her and entreated them to do their best for him and to further his suit.
The plaintiff, reposing great confidence in WRIGHT and thinking him an
honest man often moved Ellen on his behalf and caused his wife to do the
same. But Ellen grew in great dislike with him and wish him to avoid her
house, telling him that she then intended not to marry. Whereupon WRIGHT,
growing quite out of hope and in a manner desperate, then resolved to go
into the country to live there, being then utterly hopeless of her favour.
The plaintiff wrote to WRIGHT in the country who forthwith came to London,
and was admitted to his former favour. There he spoke to the plaintiff concerning his intended marriage, and the plaintiff pointed out to him how dangerous this might be to him (the plaintiff) if it were effected unless some provision
were taken for Priscilla and their children. WRIGHT affirmed that if the
plaintiff and his wife would continue their endeavours for him, he would give
the plaintiff £500, should he ever marry Ellen. WRIGHT married Ellen in
May last and now denies his promise, and has Ellen to deny her promise to
deliver the bond for cancellation and to make up the portion to £600.
WRIGHT and Ellen are now threatening to put the bonds in suit.

20 October 1623

Answer of Edmund WRIGHT and
Ellen, his wife to the Bill of Complaint
of Richard KIRBY.

Ellen WRIGHT denies that William STRETTON ever lent John YORKE any
money and helped him when they married but says that she married him for
love. She further says she doubts is STRETTON ever lent John YORKE
any money, but that if he did it was repaid, though she does remember
lending William STRETTON'S last wife £10 to bury STRETTON. About 25
years ago after the death of William STRETTON'S second wife, he entreated
John YORKE and herself to keep one of them for him, and out of good will
towards him, he being their neighbour, and not to requite any kindness
formerly done by him, they took Priscilla, then a little girl. They brought
her up as if she had been their own child, but she denies that John YORKE
promised to give any portion for her, or that he promised the plaintiff that
if he married Priscilla he would make her worth £500. She also denies
that John YORKE promised to settle the greatest part of his lands on Priscilla
or her children in his will. She has heard that the plaintiff had married a
former wife, with whom he had had a very mean portion. After they had
married John YORKE voluntarily bestowed £50 on Priscilla and permitted
them to lodge gratis at his house should they wish. After John YORKE'S
death she continued to do the same for a long time, and therefore the un-
thankful disposition of the plaintiff is herein plainly shown. Instead of
gratitude for his goodwill and charity of John YORKE and herself towards
Priscilla, the plaintiff now troubles her, being weak and aged above 80
years of age. Last April he drew his knife upon the defendant Edmund
WRIGHT and swore he would cut his throat. Regarding John YORKE'S
will, she refuses to state the value of his estate since it has nothing to do
with the plaintiff. He was certainly not indebted to the plaintiff or his wife
by deed or promise. John YORKE left in his will some mourning garments
to the plaintiff and his wife and a legacy of £50 to John KIRBY, the plaintiff's
son which the plaintiff cunningly got into his own hands. She denies promising to make good any promises of John YORKE. She says that the plaintiff,

as it seemed to her, was indebted to one John ATTREE, since deceased, and failing in payment, the plaintiff was arrested and imprisoned for the debt and at the mediation of Edmund WRIGHT she agreed to lend him £100 to get him out of prison and took a bond of £200 dated April 1615 of which he repaid £20. He was also indebted to Sir James PITT, and the defendant lent him £30 on bond dated 20 February last for the repayment in May last, but he has not repaid her any of this. She had been unwilling to have Priscilla's name linked with that of the plaintiff in the bonds. About 8 years ago he was indebted to several people for sums amounting to £400 which he was unable to pay, and for which he broke with his creditors and absented himself in the country, from where he pleaded with Ellen by his letters to free him from his trouble, so she entreated Edmund WRIGHT to take some pains therein on the plaintiff's behalf. On the initiative of WRIGHT the creditors were persuaded to accept lesser sums, so that his whole debts were compounded for £200, which Ellen paid. She denies that any of the sums given to him were in payment for services he rendered to her in his capacity as an Attorney in the Court of Common Pleas. She denies making any promise not to put the bonds in suit against him. She says it is true that the plaintiff and Priscilla and one William YORKE and Mary his wife did in March and April last solicit her with both fair speeches and threats to have their bonds and bills given to them, but she refused because they were for money which she lent the plaintiff. She denies any promise to increase the £500 portion to £600, and says there is nothing due to him from her out of her estate or her former husband's.

Edmund WRIGHT denies that the plaintiff used his good offices to further his marriage with Ellen.

*****

41.   C.2 Jas I K.7/29 and Chas I K.26/93
           27 November 1623

           The Bill of Complaint of William KIRBYE
           of Grays Inn Lane, victualler, and
           Richard KIRBYE of Hammersmith, glasier,
           versus John ROBINSON and John TENDRINGE.

About 10 years ago, John ROBYNSON of Hammersmith, innholder engaged the plaintiff William KIRBYE to serve as tapster, in which capacity he continued to serve for three years. During this time he was forced to trust travellers, who resorted to his house at Hammersmith for their meat, drink and lodging, which, at the time of his departure, amounted to £20 or thereabouts. About Easter 19 Jas I (1621) upon the compromise of Robert BELL, an arbitrator chosen on behalf of William KIRBYE and of John TENDRINGE, an arbitrator chosen by John ROBINSON for the determining of all controversies depending between them he (William KIRBYE) assigned the debts to John ROBBINSON. In spite of this in Easter Term 19 Jas I ROBINSON began an action in the Court of Kings Bench against William KIRBYE for 200 marks and obtained a judgement by default through the negligence of William KIRBYE'S Attorney. The following June ROBBINSON threatened to take out an execution against William KIRBYE if he did not submit all differences outstanding between them to the arbitrament of John TENDRINGE. They then did submit their differences to John TENDRINGE, who on June 28 said that William KIRBYE should become bound in six bonds

78

should remain in the hands of one Mr. HATTON, Scrivener until the releases were made. William KIRBYE'S sureties were William BALDOCK and Richard KIRBYE. They have paid £13 and ask the Court to enforce ROBBINSON and TENDRINGE to give them the general release according to the arbitration award.

6 December 1623

The Joint and several Answers of
John ROBINSON and John TENDRINGE
to the Bill of Complaint of William
KIRBYE and Richard KIRBYE.

John ROBINSON says he did employ William KIRBYE as a tapster in his inn. He reposed a special trust in him and for sums of money received by the said William KIRBYE, until such time as he discovered that William KIRBYE had misemployed and wasted a great deal of it. When he found out, he pressed KIRBYE to account for it, and he agreed that he was endebted to him (ROBINSON) to the sum of £55, by which unfaithful dealing ROBINSON himself endebted to one RAWLE a vintner in Fleet Street for wine which KIRBYE had received the money for and misemployed. KIRBYE was arrested and he and John TENDRINGE became bound to RAWLE for the payment of £30, and so secured his release. Whereupon he caused William KIRBYE to be arrested for the debt, but he found sufficient bail. He obtained judgement against KIRBYE with costs amounting to £66, but KIRBYE went to arbitration and John ROBINSON agreed to reduce the debt to £22 10s. 0d.

*****

C.2 Chas I C117/63
29 April 1645

Bill of Complaint of Katherine
COOPER of Westminster, widow, relict
and executrix of John COOPER of Westminster
deceased, cordwainer, versus Roger KIRBY.

Allen BIGMORE of London, currier, deceased, was seised of an estate of inheritance in a messuage and tenement in the parish of St. Margaret's, Westminster in a place there called the Sanctuary, situated on the right hand of the way leading from thence to St. Margaret's churchyard consisting of several rooms, chambers, cellars and shops which were in the occupation of Alice PARK, widow. By his indenture of June 1612 Allen BIGMORE let the said messuage and other premises to Alice PARK for 12 years viz. to 1624 for a yearly rent of £3. In January 1612/3 he granted the reversion to Thomas SALISBURY for 12 years to commence in 1621. In July 1613 he let the messuage to Thomas SALISBURY for 31 years to begin at Michaelmas 1633 for the yearly rent of 12 pence payable to him, Allen BIGMORE, his heirs and assigns. Thomas SALISBURY, being possessed of the said lease in September 1632 sold it for £30 to John COOPER. About 16 years ago, Allen BIGMORE died, and after his death Margaret BIGMORE, widow, claiming to be his relict and late wife, brought a writ of dower against Thomas SALISBURY or Alice PARK, as occupants of the messuage and recovered several rooms and parts of it, to wit, the shop, the room behind the shop, the upper chamber next over the street. John COOPER after this assignment of dower and not knowing anything of it married Thomasine, Allen BIGMORE'S daughter, and shortly afterwards was acquainted by Margaret BIGMORE of the assignment of dower, by reason of which in October 1632 Margaret BIGMORE and John COOPER came to an agreement by which John should have the 3 rooms for 31 years, if Margaret should so long live and he agreed that she should have in exchange the chamber over the shop, the chamber behind that and the chamber over the last mentioned chamber for the term of 31 years. Margaret BIGMORE afterwards married Roger KIRBY who in the right of his wife possessed himself of the 3 chambers and in February 1641 they let John COOPER the 3 last mentioned rooms for 7 years to begin Lady Day next ensuing at a rent of £4. Thomasine, daughter of Allen BIGMORE being dead, John COOPER about 8 years since married the plaintiff, and in September 1643 having made his will, he died possessed of all the aforesaid premises, bequeathing them to the plaintiff. The 31 years lease is all or most of the means she has for her livelihood and for the education of 2 small children which she had by her said husband. The indenture of lease for 31 years, the deed poll, the agreement, the indenture of the 7 year lease have fallen into the hands of Roger KIRBY and Margaret his wife, or of one Mark SHARP and Thomasine his wife, Richard KNAPP, one of the children of the said Thomasine, or Francis CLARK, or one of them, and with theirconsent Thomasine the wife of Mark SHARP, pretending to be the next heir at law to Allen BIGMORE and that the premises are descended to Thomasine as sister and next heir of Allen BIGMORE, they and Roger KIRBY, Margaret his wife, Richard KNAPP and Francis CLARK sealed a lease upon the premises to Richard KNAPP who thereupon brought an action of trespass against the plaintiff. Not having the deeds by which she might maintain her rights in the property, Richard KNAPP obtained a verdict against her. Before or since this time Roger and Margaret KIRBY made a secret conveyance of the dower to Mark SHARP, Thomasine his wife and Richard KNAPP, or one of them, and permitted them to avoid the agreement concerning the dower, and to destroy the lease of 7 years, whereas the presises ought to belong to the plaintiff. Allen BIGMORE conveyed the premises to some person or persons in fee simple, fee tail, or some other estate of inheritance, and after his death it did not descend to Thomasine, the wife of John COOPER as daughter and next heir. He had no intention that it should come to his daughter or to Thomasine, his pretended sister now wife of Mark SHARP. Roger and Margaret KIRBY in order to get possession of the dower have executed some lease of ejectment upon the premises and have caused the plaintiff to be arrested and intend to proceed against her.

Answer of Roger KIRBY damaged.

*****

43.   C.2 Chas I K.22/35
12 February 1648/9

Bill of Complaint of Dunstan KIRBY
of Hammersmith, Middlesex, yeoman,
son of Henry KIRBY of Hammersmith,
versus Ellen STOCKWOOD.

The plaintiff, Dunstan KIRBY, is the godson of Dunstan STOCKWOOD
late citizen and draper of London, deceased. On 8 October 1641 Dunstan
STOCKWOOD, who owned good personal estate consisting of plate, ready
money, leases, messuages and lands, etc., as well as wares in his shop
and other securities, and of a great quantity of low wines and hot waters
and stills to make hot waters of, amounting in all to the value of at least
£3,000, made his will. Amongst other legacies he bequeathed to Dunstan
KIRBY, the son of Henry KIRBY, the sum of £20 to be paid at 21 years and
made Ellen STOCKWOOD his then wife sole executrix, who proved the will.
In January 1647/8 the plaintiff attained his age of 21 years and the legacy
of £20 ought to have been paid to him. He went to Ellen STOCKWOOD and
asked her to make payment but she refused. She pretends that she has not
yet got possession of the personal estate of her late husband with which to
pay the legacy. She says that soon after her husband's death she had an
inventory made of his personal estate and a valuation, but it was imperfect.
The goods were valued at less than their real worth, so that the true value
of every particular cannot be known, and such leases as she has brought
into the inventory did not contain details of their length of time to run or
of the rents due upon them. Ellen STOCKWOOD refuses to make a true
inventory and to reveal her late husband's personal estate as she ought
to do. The plaintiff shows that Dunstan STOCKWOOD was at the time of
his decease possessed of a very great quantity of hot waters which he
considered to be of great value, and Ellen has not set down in the inventory the quality of the hot waters on purpose to conceal their value. Ellen
STOCKWOOD pretends she has paid money for Dunstan STOCKWOOD'S
debts, but will not set out the details. She also pretends she has laid out
a great deal of money in rebuilding or repairing his houses, of which she
has the benefit, but does not say how much. And now she pretends she has
fully administered her husband's estate and has no assets to pay his legacies.
He prays the Court to compel her to give a true account of her administration
of the will.

   Answer missing.

   C2 Chas I K.27/102 (22/35)

   Replication of Dunstan KIRBY.

He says that Ellen STOCKWOOD'S answer is insufficient and untrue and
replies that he does not believe Dunstan STOCKWOOD'S debts were
doubtful and desperate at the time of his death, but might have been
recorded is she had taken pains to do so. He says she has possessed
herself of a greater part of her husband's estate than is mentioned in her
answer, and has undervalued it and concealed much of it. He denies that
she has disbursed money for building as she pretends, and is she has,
she ought not to be allowed to take this from legacies demised by her
husband, for such building was for her own advantage, and she was in
no way bound to undertake it.

                              *****

                               81

44.   C.10/59/93
             18 May 1659

             Bill of Complaint of Henry KERBY,
             Citizen, and Weaver of London,
             versus John TWISTLETON.

The plaintiff on 20 March 1653/5, owner of a messuage called the Katherine
Wheel in the parish of St. Giles in the Fields worth £20 per annum, told a
friend, William EDWARDS of Blackwall, yeoman, that he would demise the
property to one John TWISTLETON, citizen and cordwainer of London.
In 1658 after much negotiation the plaintiff and John TWISTLETON agreed
to terms for the latter to buy the remainder of the lease of the Katherine
Wheel. TWISTLETON wished to pay with certain bonds in his possession.
The bond holders were :- Edward ABBOTT of London, merchant; George
ABBOTT of London, Esq., William SCOTT of Conghurst, Kent, Dorothy
CRANFIELD, widow, late wife and administratix of William SCOTT.

             C.10/86/46 and C.10/108/84
             December 1665

             Further Bill of Complaint of
             Henry KERBY, versus John
             TWISTLETON.

TWISTLETON mortgaged the premises to Richard YOUNGE and James
NOELL although he had not properly obtained possession from the plaintiff.
Henry KIRBY was imprisoned in the Fleet for failure to pay debts incurred
by him and Isabella, his wife. Also mentioned in this case; Peter TROVELL
and Hannah, his wife. Henry KIRBY also described as distiller in 1667 and
John TWISTLETON as victualler of St. Martins in the Fields. In 1662 John
TWISTLETON is described as of St. George's, Southwark, James NOELL
as of Noble Street, citizen, and goldsmith.

                              *****

45.   C5 615/76 (See 47 below, C.10/493/135)
             11 November 1664

             Bill of Complaint of Richard KIRBY
             of London gent, versus William
             GANDY.

In 1659 William GANDY of Chancery Lane, citizen and Merchant Taylor,
became bound with Richard KIRBY as his surety for Richard KIRBY, the
plaintiff's debt in 2 bonds each of the penalty of £100 for the payment of
£50 with interest. The plaintiff not being able to pay the money at the
stated time, William GANDY came to him and asked him to give him a
warrant of attorney to enter judgement against him for his collateral
security in case he died. The plaintiff, Richard KIRBY, not having any
money at that time to discharge William GANDY, because he was engaged
in a great building project which required the expenditure of a considerable
sum of money, William GANDY came to the plaintiff's lodgings on 1 December

1661 and asked him to discharge him from the obligations or otherwise to give him further collateral security. In order to satisfy William GANDY he told him that he had an interest in a lease of 7 tenements in High Holborn, of which $2\frac{1}{2}$ years was yet to run from Christmas 1661. These tenements were in the occupation of the following; viz:- GAVILL at a rent of £28 per annum, John WHITE at £22 per annum, Francis LUTTRELL Esq. £21 per annum, Robert FLAXMAN gent, £10 per annum, Walter CLUNIE, gent, £45 per annum, Bartholomew SIMMONS £18 per annum, Stephen WARE the younger £20; in all a yearly value of £164 whereof £20 per annum was to be paid to the ground landlord. These premises were mortgaged by the plaintiff to George WELLS of Marylebone, brickmaker, for £100 and interest, for which George WELLS stood engaged as bail for him at the suit of Thomas MEDLICOT of the Inner Temple. If William GANDY would pay off the money due to Thomas MEDLICOT so that George WELLS might be discharged at bail and be accountable to the plaintiff for such moneys as he should receive from the premises over and above what he should pay to MEDLICOT, then he would arrange for George WELLS to assign the mortgage to William GANDY as a security to him. William GANDY agreed and paid Thomas MEDLICOT £100. The assignment from WELLS to GANDY was sealed in December 1661. It was nevertheless agreed that the assignment was drawn absolutely without any condition, yet the mortgaged premises should only remain as security for the £100 he paid to Thomas MEDLICOT and a collateral security for the several obligations wherein he stood bound to the plaintiff which William GANDY then took upon himself to discharge. (A long passage giving minute details of rents received from the various tenants whose names appear above which from the basis of the complaint inasmuch as William GANDY, refuses to give an account of what moneys he has received.)

*****

C7/22/19
May 1667

Richard KIRBY of London, gentleman,
versus John BARRY of Inner Temple,
Barrister.

John BARRY married Katherine KIRBY, the plaintiff's sister on 20 October 1651. A marriage settlement of £700 was to have been paid to her, but the defendant has not paid it. The plaintiff's records were destroyed in the Fire of London 1666. The plaintiff and his sister are son and daughter of Elizabeth KIRBY (alive and a widow in 1651, but dead in 1667). Other persons mentioned in the case; John BILLINGSLEY of London, gent, co-trustee with the plaintiff of the marriage settlement. Mr. ALCOCK, milliner. Elizabeth BAMFORD, widow.

*****

83

47.   C.10/493/136 (See 45 above, C.5/615/76)
        November 1674

        Richard KIRBY of London, gent,
        versus Thomas BLOUNT.

In 1660 the plaintiff took a large piece of ground to build on of the Hon.
Christopher HATTON, now Lord HATTON, in Great Street, Hatton Garden,
Middlesex, and also of Symon BENNETT Esq. and others by lease for 42
years. Rent £23 10s. 0d. per annum. In 1661 the plaintiff built two houses
on the lands at his own expense, but had not enough money to finish them.
He entered into negotiations with Thomas BLOUNT of the Inner Temple,
London, gent, to whom he had formerly sold a larger house in Lincolns Inn
Fields concerning the mortgage of the lease. BLOUNT agreed to finish the
houses if the plaintiff would make over the lease to trustees for him. In
1662 the plaintiff caused George WELLES, brickmaker, to whom he had
mortgaged the lease, and Thomas OSBORNE, to whom he had made over the
redemption, to assign their interest to Thomas BLOUNT. BLOUNT has
failed to finish the buildings; the lead and other materials have been stolen,
but after much persuasion the plaintiff bought extra timber and finished the
woodwork, and got BLOUNT to complete the work in 1664. However, BLOUNT
persuaded him to go abroad, in order, as the plaintiff alleges, to secure the
buildings for himself. The plaintiff refused to go abroad. BLOUNT then
divided the bigger house into two, and in 1664 let one part to one ....
CHAMBERLAINE and the other to Roger SCATTERGOOD, linen draper,
and the other smaller house to John JORDAN, bricklayer.

                         *****

48.   C.5/170/87
        30 June 1685

        Bill of Complaint of Joseph KIRBY one
        of the Proctors of the Arches Court
        of Canterbury in London, versus William
        SUTTON.

In October 1679 the plaintiff and Susanna, his present wife, having placed
their affections on each other applied to William SUTTON of St. Mary
Somerset, London, haberdasher, Susanna's father for his consent to their
marriage. William SUTTON agreed to the proposal, and the marriage treaty
was drawn up to arrange the marriage portion. It was agreed that William
SUTTON should give £250 with his daughter, a peice of plate worth £8 or
£10 in lieu of a wedding dinner. £200 should be paid on the date of the marriage
and the remaining £50 within 12 months, with interest. William SUTTON should
give the plaintiff his bond for the £50. The marriage took place in October 1679
and William SUTTON accordingly gave the plaintiff a peice of plate (though not
of the value agreed on) and paid the £200 as agreed. A receipt expressly
stating that this was the first payment of the total sum of £250 was given by
and accepted by William SUTTON. Soon after William SUTTON sealed a
bond for the remaining £50 and this was likewise acknowledged, but it was
not sealed at the time and the plaintiff did not distrust SUTTON. However
it was not sealed and William SUTTON gave an undertaking not to become

                         84

engaged by any bond to any of his children to the detriment of the plaintiff in relation to this debt of £50. In June 1679 William SUTTON paid Susanna, the plaintiff's wife his daughter, £10 as part of the £50 and promised to pay the remaining £40 at the time agreed in the contract. But when this time arrived it had still not been paid. About Christmas 1679 the plaintiff's wife, on the instigation of her father, asked the plaintiff not to take it ill that the £40 was not paid, and to tell him that he would receive it in the Spring. In 1682 Susanna was at her father's house and remembering the payment was still due she shut the door of the room where they were and her father asked her whether he had given her husband any note for the £50. She declared doubtfully that if she were assured there were no such note, and that if she died of the child she was then with, he would never pay it to the plaintiff, but to his eldest daughter Elizabeth. He continued to put off the payment which was not delayed since June 1679. On 21 August 1683 the plaintiff wrote a letter to him demanding that the £40 be paid by the following October to this effect, viz. "Sir, my wife presses me to write to you about the £3 16s. 0d. due on the account of Betty's board to 6 August with which I was never concerned, having given it to her for her better maintenance in clothes, she hath several times spoke about it and hath been told that nothing can be done without your order and sought this the best and privatest opportunity. I am also to tell you of the £40 which you know was to be paid 4 years since. I think it ought to be clear so that no after disputes may happen between those that survive on either side therefore let the 5th year growing to an end pray let it be paid without any manner of delay by the time being 17 October next about 2 months. I pray your answer and am yours in all duty, J. KIRBY. August 21, 1683." The letter was delivered to William SUTTON who in answer wrote as follows: "These for Mr. Joseph KIRBY. Loving son, my love to you and these is to let you understand it has been my continual care to take care to pay you. My house in Soho is on sale and in case it be let or sold I shall then presently give you full satisfaction and to your own content (and what I) write is very true. And although the spirit of building is on me, yet nevertheless you shall have full content and I find my daughter does help to inflame my accounts therefore pray let that be at an end now presently, because I am at a very great and extraordinary charge besides striving to get something of an estate, and on 13 September next I shall pay you £15 and if you press me for it again I shall then, rather than disappoint you, borrow it then for you. Your real father William SUTTON, when time will serve you will find it so. August 26, 1683." Notwithstanding this promise and although the house in Soho was sold, William SUTTON has still not paid the £40 and now absolutely refuses to pay it. William SUTTON and his wife Susanna have constantly acknowledged the debt and promised to pay it, but they have not offered to let the plaintiff and his wife take up any goods and commodities or household furniture or suchlike towards satisfaction instead. Although the plaintiff's house being fully furnished, and such goods as were proffered were of no use to them, and he therefore would not and has not accepted such in lieu of the payment of £40. The plaintiff acknowledges that as to the interest on the £40 William SUTTON did agree to pay and did pay it from October 1679 to April following and so consistently from year to year till April 1684, sometimes paying it himself and sometimes by the hand of Susanna his wife in several small sums of money except some part thereof which the plaintiff's wife had in a piece of silk to the value of about 30 shillings which she was forced to take up of one Mr. GODOWN, a silk weaver, at the request of her parents. In April last the plaintiff sent a friend to William SUTTON to demand the money or to have a note or some security for it, but SUTTON now refuses to acknowledge the debt or to admit the above quoted letters, or that he has ever paid interest on the principal. He and his wife now refuse to pay, pretending that the marriage treaty contained no such agreement.

12 May 1685

Bill of Complaint of Joseph
KIRBY, versus William SUTTON.

This bill begins by reciting the marriage contract of 1678 but differs from
the other bill by stating that William SUTTON agreed to pay shortly before
the marriage to a considerable part of the sum agreed, and £150 more soon
after the marriage should be effected. William SUTTON in part performance
paid the first sum, and William SUTTON, being a person of great dealings
desired the plaintiff to leave the remaining £150 till such time as the plaintiff should have occasion for it, telling him that it would do him a kindness
and the plaintiff no prejudice. He agreed to pay the plaintiff the usual interest
on it. The plaintiff agreed. William SUTTON kept the money a long time and
paid the interest for it, but of late he and his wife have paid £100 of the principal so that there still remains £50 to be paid plus interest. The plaintiff
wants to have his money but William SUTTON taking advantage that the plaintiff has no security for it, and knowing that neither the plaintiff or his wife
kept any account of what money either of them had received, has taken displeasure against the plaintiff, and he and his wife have conspired together
to deprive him of his £50. They refuse to disclose how and to whom and when
they have paid the interest and principal thus disabling the plaintiff from
bringing an action for the moneys outstanding. Two years ago William SUTTON
and his wife asked the plaintiff if he would allow one Elizabeth SUTTON,
spinster, one of their daughters, to board with the plaintiff and said they
would give an allowance to him for her keep, to which the plaintiff consented.
Elizabeth SUTTON has lived with the plaintiff for 2 years which he considers
is reasonably worth £20 per annum, during which time William SUTTON or
his wife have paid the plaintiff's wife several small sums of money, but how
much the plaintiff cannot remember, having kept no account. He believes
there is still due to him at least £20. William SUTTON refuses to come to
an account and to disclose how much is has paid, or to say how much is due
for Elizabeth's board, or to make any satisfaction for it. He asks that William
SUTTON be required to present accounts so that a settlement can be arrived at.

29 May 1685

Answer of William SUTTON and
Susanna his wife and their
Demurrer to the Bill of Complaint
of Joseph KIRBY.

William SUTTON says he plainly told the plaintiff that he designed £250 for
his daughter's fortune but could and would only pay £200 immediately and
that he intended to pay her £50 more. He could not punctually promise it,
for having 2 other daughters and a son to provide for and the greatest part
of what he had being out in trade, he did not know by reason of the uncert-
ainty of trade and of the circumstances of others to whom he had given credit
what condition he might be in. But he told the plaintiff that after he had
married his two other daughters and given them £200 apiece he would then,
if he were in a condition to do so, not only pay him £50 more, but as much
as he should bestow on any of the other daughters that so he might prefer
them in an equal manner. He goes on to say that either before or soon after
the marriage in about October 1678 he paid the plaintiff £200 and the plaintiff
seemed to be satisfied with it. He has several times since given the plaintiff
not only several other small sums of money, but also he has given him and his
wife several gifts such as a piece of plate worth £6, a parcel of land for a
cistern, silks, deals, coals, linen and suchlike to the value of £40 or up-

86

wards, and that he will according to his promise make up the plaintiff's wife's fortune equal if not superior to either of her sisters who as yet remain single. He says that since the marriage he has had considerable losses and stands engaged to pay several debts. He is grown into years and not so capable of business as formerly, whereby he has been obliged to take other measures in relation to himself and family than what he did formerly. He craves the benefit not only of the Act for the Prevention of Frauds and Perjuries but also of the Statute for Limitation of Personal Actions. He denies asking to have £150 interest, or that he ever paid such interest to the plaintiff, or that he or his wife paid the plaintiff or his wife £100 as part of the £150. But whatever sums he may have paid after the payment of the £200 was out of mere goodwill or in requital for the kindness the plaintiff had shown to his other children, and in particular to Elizabeth, whose sojourn with the plaintiff was more for the affection between her and the plaintiff's wife. He admits having given the plaintiff small sums of money from time to time but cannot say how much, since he never expected to be called to account for them, though he thinks he may have given the plaintiff or his wife £10, and Susanna, the other defendant thinks she may have given them several small sums of money of 40 or 50 shillings. As to the rest of the bill, they demur to answer.

*****

C.9/344/24
11 February 1709/10

Bill of Complaint of Susanna KIRBY
of London, widow, versus Richard
and Elizabeth IVES and Thomas and
Elizabeth TYMME.

William SUTTON, late of London, deceased, was seised in fee of a good estate of inheritance in 3 messuages or tenements in Castle Alley in Thames Street in the parish of St. Mary Somerset, London, worth £40 per annum and several other messuages in the City of London and elsewhere. In August 1698 William SUTTON died intestate not having made any conveyance, or settlement, or other disposition of his estate. He left George SUTTON, his only son and heir, the plaintiff, and Elizabeth, now the wife of Thomas TYMME, and no other issue. On the death of William SUTTON, the premises descended to George SUTTON, the plaintiff's brother, who about two or three years after the death of his father, being then in the East Indies, died intestate leaving at his death Sarah, his widow, since married to one .... ABRAHAM, and one daughter of about 3 years old, who likewise died soon after her father. After the death of George and his daughter the premises descended as of right to the plaintiff and Elizabeth her sister as heirs at law of her brother, or his daughter, subject only, as is claimed, to the dower of Sarah, the widow. The plaintiff hoped to have been let into possession of that part justly belonging to her. But Thomas TYMME and Elizabeth, his wife, and .... ABRAHAM and Sarah, his wife, have combined with one Richard IVES of the parish of St. Mary Somerset, and Elizabeth, his wife, and several other persons unknown to defraud the plaintiff of what justly belongs to her. Thomas TYMME and Elizabeth have got possession of two of the three houses in Castle Alley worth £25 and have been in possession ever since the death of William SUTTON (George being then in the East Indies and not knowing of his father's death). Richard and Elizabeth IVES have been in possession of another messuage in Castle Alley worth £15 and up- wards. Thomas and Elizabeth TYMME now pretend that the messuages which they occupy were settled upon them by William SUTTON, whereas they know this to be false. For if Thomas and Elizabeth were in possession for any time during William SUTTON'S life, it was only on the latter's suffrance, and they were only tenants paying him a yearly rent. Richard and Elizabeth IVES for their part pretend that their house was bought from William SUTTON by Elizabeth IVES' first husband, except that a rent of £6 per annum was paid in lieu of the full purchase price and they had the option to purchase it. The plaintiff says that this is not the case. They also pretend that they have all along paid their rent to Thomas and Elizabeth TYMME who pretended they were also entitled to the premises as well as to the other 2 houses. The TYMMES have lately turned their 2 houses into one and threatened to pull it down, or otherwise dispose of it, and refuse to produce the deeds for the plaintiff although she has frequently asked for them.

1 March 1709/10

Answers of Richard and Elizabeth
IVES to the Bill of Complaint of
Susanna KIRBY.

They admit the intestacy of William and George SUTTON and that the plain- tiff and Elizabeth TYMME are co-heirs to George SUTTON'S daughter. They believe that about 40 years ago William SUTTON demised a messuage in St. Mary Somerset in the ward of Queenhithe to one Edward MOORE and his wife for a long term of years at a rent of £6 per annum. This they believe came to be vested in Christopher BEAUMOND, Elizabeth IVES' former hus- band, who died intestate several years ago. After his death letters of admin- istration were granted to Elizabeth his widow, who afterwards married Richard IVES. They have thus accordingly enjoyed the premises for several years. William SUTTON was not only the lesser of the messuage but also built it, and they do not believe that George SUTTON and his daughter were ever seised of it as heir at law to William SUTTON, or that William SUTTON'S widow was entitled to any dower in any of the messuages. They have been informed that when William SUTTON made the lease he was not owner of the freehold but only possessed a long lease. For this reason the plaintiff can- not claim any right to them as heir at law. The reversion and inheritance have been claimed by the executors of Henry Frederick THYNNE Esq. by whom a bill has lately been exhibited against this defendant Richard for that purpose. They believe that the messuage was broken open and robbed during the lifetime of Christopher BEAUMOND, and several writings and other things stolen or destroyed, so they have lost the benefit of such further information as otherwise they might have had. They believe that William SUTTON was owner of some other property in London, but what they do not know. They refuse to give an account of the rents they have received until such time as the plaintiff shall prove her title to the property. They deny ever having paid rent at £6 a year to George SUTTON, or his daughter, or that they claim any other title save by virtue of the lease made to Edward MOORE.

88

1 March 1709/10

Answer of Thomas and Elizabeth
TYMME to the Bill of Complaint
of Susanna KIRBY

They say that they married in the lefetime of William SUTTON who agreed
for Elizabeth's marriage portion to convey to them by an indenture dated
20 January 1 William and Mary two messuages in St. Mary Somerset
abutting to the west of Castle Alley, to the east on George Yard, to the
north on a dye house then in the occupation of William ANDREWS. In
this indenture William SUTTON stated that he was seised in fee simple
from encumbrances. The defendants by claim to these tenements on the
basis of this conveyance and deny ever having paid rent for them to William
SUTTON and say that the plaintiff has no right or title to any of them.
They deny that Richard IVES and his wife are their tenants of the other
messuage mentioned in the bill.

*****

C.8/360/114
8 January 1699/1700

Bill of Complaint of Thomas
HOUGHTON of St. Dunstans in
the West, London, gent, versus
Edward KIRBY.

In 1692/3 the plaintiff employed one Edward KIRBY tailor to make up two
suits of clothes. Eventually KIRBY presented a bill for £10 16s 7d.
without allowing for money already paid by the plaintiff. KIRBY is suing
him in the Petty Bag Office. (Followed by lengthy particulars of legal
process.)

*****

C2. Jas I K.4/56
31 January 1606/7

Bill of Complaint of William KIRKBY
of the city of Winchester, gent, and
Elizabeth his wife, Executrix of the
last will and testament of William BURTON,
late of Winchester, gent, deceased, versus
Elize HUGHES.

Ellis (Elize) HUGHES, Clerk was seised in the right of his Church of the
Vicarage of Sparshott, Hampshire. On 24 October 12 Eliz (1569) he made
a lease of a corn a barn and the tythes of the Vicarage to William KENDGE
of Sopley, gent for 60 years pay £20 a year, 8 bushels of wheat and 8

89

bushels of malt. Failure to pay the rent gave the vicar authority to re-possess the premises. KENDGE conveyed the premises to one Richard BURTON, late father of William BURTON, deceased, for £100. Richard BURTON made his will on the .... day of .... in the .... year of our Sovereign Lady Queen Elizabeth making his son William executor. He died shortly afterwards in Winchester. During the 28 year of Elizabeth (1585) Ellis HUGHES and William BURTON agreed that BURTON should relinquish the barn, corn and tythes to HUGHES who was to pay BURTON £20 for 7 years. In 1603 William BURTON fell ill, and continued sick for 3 years, during which time HUGHES ceased paying his rent. BURTON died and HUGHES continued to refuse to pay his rent to the plaintiffs his heirs and executors.

20 April 1607

Answer of Ellize HUGHES to the
Bill of Complaint of William KIRBYE.

He says it is correct that he was lawfully possessed of the premises in right of his Church and Vicarage of Sparshott. He admits to making the lease of the chamber to William KINDGE and says that it was a room over the parlour there, and agrees that the terms were as set out in the bill. He takes it to be true that KYNDGE let the premises to the late Richard BURTON under the terms set out in the bill. However after Richard BURTON'S death, about the 38th year of Elizabeth (1595) William BURTON broke the condition of the bond wherein Richard BURTON became bound to HUGHES and for this reason wilfully forfeited it. Whereupon William BURTON, understanding that HUGHES intended to commence a suite on the bond against him unless he were prepared to yield up his (HUGHES') estate to him, entreated him earnestly to deal in a friendly manner with him, saying that he, William BURTON, had no children, and that if HUGHES would deal friendly with him over the premises he would at his death leave him a great part of his goods, since he and his father had enjoyed the premises for a long time at less than its real value. Where-upon HUGHES agreed to pay William BURTON £100 (i.e. £20 a year for 5 years) - the amount disbursed by Richard BURTON for the premises. Whereupon William BURTON took the £100 and resigned the premises to HUGHES. BURTON asked, and HUGHES agreed, that interest should be paid on the £100, and he appeared to be satisfied with the arrangement. HUGHES says he paid four instalments of £20 and during the fifth year, being short of money he only paid £10 and obtained BURTON'S consent to forbear the rest for the next year, which he duely did. He also paid him £30 in respect of the interest. He denies ever agreeing to pay William BURTON or his executors or assigns £20 a year for ten year.

*****

52.   C.22/664/64
          January 1608/9

          Thomas KIRBY Esq., plaintiff,
          versus John BRYAN, defendant.

Interrogatories to witnesses on
behalf of plaintiff.

1. Do you know the parties ?

2. Illegible.

3. What sum of money did Valentine KNIGHT in his
    lifetime ...... Thomas KIRBY Esq. deceased or
    how stood he indebted to him ?

4. Was the said Valentine KNIGHT in his lifetime
    lawfully seised of the manor of Tusbury, (Timsbury,
    Hants ?)

5. Did Valentine KNIGHT by his will direct that the
    manor should be sold by John BRYAN, the defendant,
    his brother-in-law for the payment of his debts ?

6. What was the annual value of the manor, and for how
    much could it be sold ?

7. Has John BRYAN sold the manor; to whom and for
    how much; how much has been paid; what security
    has he for the payment of the rest ?

8. What debts has John BRYAN discharged since the sale ?

9. Has John BRYAN enough money in hand to discharge
    the debts due to the plaintiff ?

10. Has John BRYAN put all or some of the money to other
    use ?

11. Anything else relevant.

14 January 1608/9

Depositions of witnesses on behalf
of the plaintiff taken at Winchester
before ...... Esq. and John WHITE,
gent.

Charles DEN(HAM) ...... Hants., gent.,
aged 58.

1. Knows parties

2. Knew Thomas KIRBY Esq., deceased and Valentine
    KNIGHT deceased.

3. Valentine KNIGHT ...... in his lifetime with Thomas
    KIRBY Esq. deceased (in two bond of) ...... pay
    ...... of £100.

4.   Valentine KNIGHT was seised of the manor of
     Tymsbury and died seised.

5.   By his will Valentine KNIGHT appointed the manor
     to be sold ......

6.   Illegible.

7.   John BRYAN has sold the manor to William WALLER
     Esq.; (? thinks it was sold for) £600; (? thinks John
     BRYAN received) £200.

8-11 Illegible

(Willi)am KYRBY of Winchester,
aged 30.

2.   Has seen two obligations for payment of £50 (rest
     illegible)

(John) BOD...., Winchester, ...

Was a servant to Thomas KYRBY decease. Valentine KNIGHT owed Thomas
KYRBY £100.

                              *****

53.   C.2 Jas I. K. 8/8
             May or June 1616

             Bill of Complaint of William
             KIRKEBY of Winchester, Hants.,
             gentleman, and Elizabeth, his
             wife, Executrix of the will of
             William BURTON, gentleman,
             versus Peter BLAKE, Esq.

William BURTON owned two tenements in Kingsgate Street, Winchester
valued at £100 and upwards. One Peter BLAKE Esq. asked BURTON to
let them to him at a yearly rent. On 27 March 25 Eliz (1583) Peter BLAKE
took a 21 year lease from the Michaelmas next following at a rent of £7 a
year. A schedule was attached of all the household stuff which BLAKE was
to give up at the end of 21 years. Peter BLAKE held the property for some
(?) four years and then let it to one PISTON for a much greater rent than he
was paying BURTON. About ten years ago William BURTON made his will,
and having no issue, appointed Elizabeth, his then wife, since married to
William KIRKEBY, his executrix, and shortly after died. Elizabeth proved
the will and took over the administration of his estate. William BURTON gave
many legacies to charity. Before his death he told Elizabeth what rents were
due to him and handed her a paper book written in his own hand, showing what
rents were then due to him. In this book it was plainly stated that Peter
BLAKE owed William BURTON at the time of his death £24 10s. 0d. or 3½

years rent at £7 due in 1589, 1590 and 1591. William BURTON intended during his lifetime to sue Peter BLAKE for this rent, however Peter BLAKE pacified him and he took no legal action before he died. After his death Elizabeth, at the instance of William KIRKEBY, her second husband, wishing to fulfil the legacies and settle her late husband's estate, asked BLAKE for the rent of £24 10s. 0d., but he refused to pay it; whereupon they sued him upon the original Articles of Agreement in the Court of Kings Bench, but Peter BLAKE pleaded that the indenture of lease had no counter-part, either because it was lost during William BURTON'S sickness (he having been sick 3 years before he died), or because (as the plaintiffs say) Peter BLAKE had it and would not produce it. The result was that the case could not proceed. Now Peter BLAKE knowing that William KIRKEBY and Elizabeth have no remedy at Common Law, continues to refuse payment, so they ask this Court to compel him.

6 June 1616

Answer of Peter BLAKE Esq., to
the Bill of Complaint of William
KIRKEBY.

(Part of this document is obliterated and nearly unreadable). The original agreement of 27 March 26 Eliz is acknowledged, but the household stuff is alleged to have been very scanty and decayed. BURTON is said to have re-entered the property after PISTON'S death and to have removed much of the household stuff. Since it is now 26 years since the time when it is alleged the rent was not paid, he cannot remember with accuracy what happened, except that he and BURTON met in Winchester at the house of BURTON'S father-in-law, one Mr. WHITE, and BURTON abated the rent by £8 and bills were exchanged for the arrears of rent. (The rest of this document is too decayed for sense to be extracted from it.)

13 February 1616/7

Second Answer of Peter BLAKE
to the Bill of Complaint of William
KIRKEBY.

He says that William BURTON never made a lease by indenture dated 27 March 26 Eliz of the two tenements in terms suggested in the bill and that he never held the property on such terms. Nevertheless for the greater enlightenment of the Court and in pursuance of its order, he acknowledges that BURTON by certain articles dated 27 March 26 Eliz did let the two tenements to him for 21 years at a yearly rent, and that in April immediately following, before any payment of rent was due, they made a new agreement at a new rent, and he took a new lease from BURTON for 31 years. To this was attached a schedule of household stuff to be delivered up at the end of the lease viz; doors, wainscot, glass, casements, windows, benches, floors boarded, portals, studies and closets and such like being annexed as part of the freehold, saving a few shelves of little value which he paid for since they were moveables. But since all this took place 31 years ago, he cannot really remember the details. Having obtained the lease, Peter BLAKE, who lived most of his time in London at the Temple, and as the tenements were let at a greater rent by BURTON then he could seldom let them again (sic) and thereby often standing tenantless to his great loss, came to Winchester to BURTON at his father-in-law's house either in 1590 or 1591 to see to these matters. BURTON demanded arrears amounting to £13 2s. 0d. supposed to be then unpaid for the two years 1590 and 1591 and also part of 1589. They settled for £7 10s. 0d. or £6 10s. 0d. (damaged text) ... Peter BLAKE gave back some of the household stuff, viz; a cupboard, a pair of andirons and other things he cannot now remember as part payment for the rest and BURTON accepted PISTON as tenant and took rent from him. Soon after PISTON died, and BURTON continued to let the tenements for 16 or 17 years and in the end William KIRKEBY and Elizabeth sold their interest in the property for a good sum of money ... (The rest of the text is too fragmentary to make sense.)

*****

54.

C2 Chas I K 24/3 (see also K 22/51, K 27/125)
10 October 1628

The Bill of Complaint of Dorothy KIRKBYE,
late wife of Gerrard KIRKBYE, Esq., deceased
of Stanbridge, Hants., Administratrix of the
goods and chattels of the late Gerrard KIRKBYE
deceased, versus Sir William PAWLETT and
Sir John PAWLETT.

During her widowhood, Susan KIRKBYE of Stanbridge, intending to marry Launcelot WARNEFORD, wished to make provision for her young children by her former husband. By a tripartite indenture dated 15 June 20 Jas I (1662) between Launcelot WARNEFORD (1st party), Susan KIRKBYE (2nd party) and Sir William PAWLETT of Edington, Wiltshire and Sir John PAWLETT of Hidestreet near Winchester (3rd party) she sold Sir William and Sir John a number of goods and chattels mentioned in a schedule attached to the indenture to raise portions for her younger children, Richard KIRKBYE, Elizabeth KIRKBYE and Dorothy KIRKBYE, the surplus, if any, to be used for Gerrard KIRKBYE. £150 was raised and secured by Gerrard KIRKBYE. The agreement specified that WARNEFORD, Susan KIRKBYE and the PAWLETTS should assign all the goods to Gerrard KIRKBYE and a deed was made to this effect on 12 May 1 Chas I (1625) whereby Gerrard undertook to pay £150 to the younger children within 6 months of Susan's death. Sir William and Sir John have not yet sealed and delivered the deed, and will not authorize the plaintiff to receive the goods or sue for them. The goods remain in the hands of Launcelot WARNEFORD and Phillip GIFFORD, Susan being lately dead. They and John ROLFE have removed them from the house at Stanbridge to a place unknown. The plaintiff is ready to perform her duty to Richard, Elizabeth and Dorothy KIRKBYE, and to pay them their portion, yet she is prevented by the defendants, who likewise refuse to give her the inventories.

C.2 Chas I K 22/51
17 January 1628/9

The joint and several Answers of
Launcelot WARNEFORD, Phillip
GIFFORD and John ROLFE to the
Bill of Complaint of Dorothy KIRKBYE,
widow.

Launcelot WARNEFORD admits that Susan KIRKBYE, whom he afterwards married, was seised for life as her jointure in the Manor of Stanbridge Ranvills and certain lands in Roke in the parish of Romsey, out of which Gerrard KIRKBYE, her eldest son, had a rent charge of £40 p.a. for life. She also possessed certain goods, details of which he cannot remember, and having another son and two daughters who had no provision made for them, a tripartite indenture was made between himself, Susan and Sir William and Sir John PAWLETT for the purpose set out in the bill. After his marriage to Susan he gave Gerrard £20 p.a. above the £40 he already received out of the estate as well as maintaining Susan's younger children. The goods set aside for the younger children's portions still remained to be disposed of by the trustees, Sir William and Sir John PAWLETT. He kept one part of the indenture uncancelled in his custody for about 2 years until negotiations were begun concerning the marriage of Gerrard to the plaintiff. Part of the terms of the settlement was that some of Susan's jointure lands be set apart so that Gerrard's annuity of £60 be increased to £120 p.a., and also that the inheritance of 10 or 12 tenements, worth about £80, be settled on Gerrard and Dorothy and their heirs. WARNEFORD would not agree to these terms unless the tripartite indenture were cancelled, and the goods granted to Sir William and Sir John PAWLETT in trust for the younger children be regranted to him and Susan for their own use and the younger children's portions be found out of the plaintiff's marriage portion by Gerrard. To this Gerrard consented. Accordingly assurances were drawn up settling £120 p.a. on Gerrard and the plaintiff and providing for the younger children's portions to be paid for by Gerrard. Then the tripartite indenture was cancelled. He says that he has used these goods, some of which wore out in the course of usage and others he has replaced by new. During Gerrard's lifetime his ownership of them was never challenged. The plaintiff continues to enjoy the £120 p.a., and all Susan's jointure lands, together with Gerrard's estate, have descended to his son and heir, Thomas KIRKBYE. On Susan's death, being compelled to leave Stanbridge House to the plaintiff, and for the placing of some of his goods and books be brought from Oxford, he took a chamber in the house of the defendant John ROLFE for part of his goods, and another chamber for the other part in Phillip GIFFORD'S house. Some of his goods he has locked up in the barn at Stanbridge, but he has left a great deal in Stanbridge House for the plaintiff's use. As to the deed made 21 May 1 Chas I, he says that Gerrard, out of the moneys he received with the plaintiff as her marriage portion, was to pay £300 as parriage portions for his sisters Elizabeth and Dorothy. WARNEFORD borrowed this £300 at interest from Gerrard until it should be needed for his sisters' portions. For security (until such time as he could give security by bond) he gave Gerrard the deed of 21 May, which was to be made void when WARNEFORD became bound to Gerrard. With his eldest brother Thomas WARNEFORD he did become bound to Gerrard in the sum of £600. He has paid interest on the £300 to Gerrard's sisters who are well contented therewith.

Phillip GIFFORD says he knows nothing about the matters mentioned in the bill except that on the death of Susan, Launcelot hired a room or two in his house to keep his goods in.

John ROLFE says the same and that Launcelot locked up the room he had hired and took away the key so that he has no idea of what is in it.

C 2 Chas I K 24/3
19 January 1628/9

95

The Joint and several Answers of
Sir William PAWLETT, Sir John
PAWLETT, two of the defendants,
to the Bill of Complaint of Dorothy
KIRKBYE, widow.

They say that Susan KIRKBYE, intending to marry and to make provision for
her younger children, did make a trust as mentioned in the bill, and that there
was a schedule of goods attached, which they have not of late seen. Sir
William says he was not privy to the agreement made by Gerrard KIRKBYE
and never saw the deed of assignment. Sir John says he takes it there was
such a deed of assignment made by Launcelot and Susan, and that they were
parties to it, and that the consideration of the making of the deed was £150
intended for the three younger children. He believes the recital of the terms
in the bill is correct. Sir John says the deed was left with him to be sealed
by him and Sir William, but that before he sealed it he remembered that
Gerrard KIRKBYE, whom it principally concerned, asked to have it from
him, to which he agreed provided it was returned to him quickly. But Gerrard
died still having it in his custody and without returning it. They both say they
never had any possession of the goods and that the plaintiff never requested
them to enable her to sue for them. They deny taking the deeds away from the
house at Stanbridge.

C2 Chas I K 27/125

Dorothy KIRKBYE'S replication

She reaffirms all points in her bill, and adds that upon her marriage to
Gerrard KIRKBYE or upon the drawing up of the marriage settlement she
says there was never agreement made by Gerrard or any of his friends or
herself that the tripartite indenture should be made frustrate, or that the
goods granted to Sir William and Sir John in trust for Gerrard and the
younger children should be regranted to WARNEFORD and Susan his wife
for their own use, as WARNEFORD pretends in his answer. Whereas
WARNEFORD claims that Gerrard was to pay the younger children's portions
out of Dorothy's marriage portion as he and his wife, Susan, had no part of
it, and also had given up part of Susan's jointure towards the maintenance
of Gerrard and Dorothy, she replies that it is true that, out of affection for
Gerrard, her eldest son, and in view of his marriage and for the bettering
of the younger children's portions; and in consideration of an annuity of
£40 p.a. to be paid to WARNEFORD for 7 years (Deed of 20 April 1 Chas.
I) Susan did convey part of her jointure lands towards the maintenance of
Gerrard and Dorothy and towards a jointure for her. Gerrard, for his part,
disbursed out Dorothy's jointure lands towards the provision of portions for
the younger children £500, never intending to yield up his interest in the
goods and chattels mentioned in the tripartite indenture and schedules.
Concerning the indenture of 12 May 1 Chas. I between Sir William PAWLETT,
Sir John PAWLETT, Launcelot and Susan on one part and Gerrard on the
other, she says that this was made bona fide for the benefit of Gerrard and
the younger children and not for security of £300 lent by Gerrard to
WARNEFORD till WARNEFORD should be able to give other security by
bond as he claims in his answer. This is still in force and entitles her to
the goods as administratrix of Gerrard's will. She does not believe that
WARNEFORD voluntarily joined in the conveyance of his wife's jointure to
to Gerrard out of affection, but for consideration of the annuity it brought
him.

*****

96

C.2 Chas. I K 3/41
30 January 1628/9

Bill of Complaint of Dorothy KIRBY,
widow, of Gerrard KIRKBY late of
Stanbridge Erles, Hants, Esq.,
deceased, on her own behalf as well
as on behalf of Thomas KIRKBY, her
son, an infant, and son and heir of
Gerrard KIRKBY, versus Launcelot
WARNEFORD, Philip GIFFORD and
John ROLFE.

Gerrard KIRKBY in his lifetime was seised of an estate of inheritance in
the Manor of Stanbridge Earles, Roke and Stanbridge Ranbells and of other
lands in Romsey, Michelmersh, Tymbesbury and Hursley in the county of
Southampton. It comprised :-

 one barn and one close of arable land (20 acres),

 one close of arable and pasture called the Fatting
 Leas (23 acres),

 one meadow called the long meadow next the water
 (15 acres),

 another meadow called the Long Meadow next the
 coppice (19 acres),

 another called Gadmeade (13 acres) late in the tenure
 of William GOSLINGE,

 a messuage and tenement and 2 watermills, one called
 Wheat Mill and the other a Malt mill,

 one meadow called the Coniger (12 acres) now or late
 in the tenure of John HAMON,

 three fields (40 acres) now or late in the tenure of
 George ROLFE,

 another arable field called Rokewood (8 acres),

 a parcel of the croft close next adjoining the cottage
 now or late in the tenure of Robert BEDFORD containing 6 acres and now or late in the tenure of Launcelot
 WARNEFORD,

 and several messuages, lands and tenements now or
 late in the several tenures of John WOOLLES, Thomas
 BONABY, George ROLFE, Andrew HICKMAN, John
 ROLFE, Richard COLLINS, John MOULD, Elizabeth
 KIRKBY, William SPAINE, William COLES, John
 PALMER, William JOHN, Robert BEDFORD or their
 several assigns.

All the above are part of the Manor of Stanbridge Earles and Roke and were
conveyed to the use of the late Gerrard KIRKBY and Dorothy (plaintiff) for
her jointure and to their male heirs. All the residue of the manor was to be
to the use of Susan WARNEFORD, mother of Gerrard, for life, and after
her decease to the use of Gerrard and his male heirs. So seised Gerrard

died in April last (1628), Thomas being his son and heir. After Gerrard's
death, Dorothy entered upon the property and is lawfully seised in her
demesne as of freehold, the inheritance thereof expectant to Thomas.
Susan WARNEFORD died in August last. After her death the premises
conveyed to her for her life accrued to Thomas in possession, who is lawfully seised in fee tail accordingly as son and heir of Gerrard, from whom
the reversion in fee is also descended. But Launcelot WARNEFORD Esq.,
Bachelor of the Civil Law, late husband of the said Susan, Phillip GIFFORD
of Lockerly, Hants., gent, and John ROLFE of Roke and Roger HIDE have
wrongfully taken into possession the deeds, court rolls and evidences concerning the manor which rightly belonged to Dorothy and Thomas her son,
and have taken away the trunks, boxes and desks wherein the evidences were
kept. They have wrongfully made entry into the premises, and have let the
land to persons unknown, to Dorothy's great prejudice and the disinherison
of Thomas her son. She has asked them to deliver up the deeds, but they
refuse.

C.2 Chas. I K 3/41
18 April 1629

The joint and several Answers of
Launcelot WARNEFORD, Philip
GIFFORD and John ROLFE to the
Bill of Complaint of Dorothy KIRKBY,
widow.

Launcelot WARNEFORD says that when the marriage between Gerrard
KIRKBIE and Dorothy was first mooted on 25 March 1625, an agreement
was made between William PARGETER, Dorothy's father, and him and
Susan WARNEFORD his then wife (who then had a jointure in the Manor of
Stanbridge and in most of the other lands mentioned in the bill) and Gerrard
KIRKBYE, by which the assurance of Dorothy's jointure and securing the
inheritance of the manor were agreed. It was further agreed that if Gerrard
KIRKBYE should die without male issue, the inheritance of the manor should
come to Richard KIRKBYE, his brother, upon payment of certain portions to
the daughters of Gerrard; and further that Richard KIRKBYE should be paid
£20 per annum out of the premises until he reached the age of 21, and afterwards £30 during his lifetime. It was further agreed that of all the particular
parcels of land mentioned in the bill to be Dorothy's jointure (except the
several tenements in the occupation of several persons and except Rokewoods
and Croft Close) he, Launcelot WARNEFORD, should have a certain estate
for ten years from the date of the articles, but Rokewood and Croft Close for
ten years only is Susan WARNEFORD so long lived. He should be paid, if
Susan his wife lived less than 7 years after the date of the articles, £40 p.a.
which was intended to be charged out of the manor. Is Susan died within
7 years, then the £40 was to be paid to him half yearly for the residue of
the 7 years, the first payment to begin half a year after Susan's death.
According to the articles it was agreed that conveyance should be drawn up
by indenture whereof he should have one part for the benefit of himself and
Richard KIRKBYE his son-in-law (stepson), who was wholly dependent on
him. But shortly after, before the defendant had any draught on paper of
the conveyance or was able to see the contents thereof, William PARGITER
procured one part of the conveyance of the manor ready engrossed in parchment (indented without any counterpart or paperbook). It was to be then
sealed by the defendant and his wife, and returned again to William

PARGITER in London (insomuch as he had not time to consider whether all
intentions of the articles were provided for) or else the intended marriage
was to break off upon return of the messenger with the indenture unsealed.
WARNEFORD, not suspecting but that everything was done according to
the meaning of the articles, and hoping to have the counterpart, he and his
wife then sealed the one part of the conveyance and returned it by the messenger, and shortly after the marriage took effect. Gerrard and Dorothy,
by force of the conveyance, took possession of the premises and held them
during Gerrard's life, and she still holds them except for three grounds
called Rokefields, of which, as yet, this defendant was never out of possession. He also confesses that he and his wife also held the residue of the manor
during her life. She died last August. He ought to hold the same lands
limited to Dorothy's jointure (except the tenements etc.) for the residue of
the term of ten years. WARNEFORD asked William PARGITER for the
counterpart of the conveyance to be sealed by him and Gerrard KIRKBYE
as was promised and as he was entitled; but neither in Gerrard's lifetime
nor since has he got it so that he is induced to think that the articles were
incompletely drawn forasmuch as Dorothy in her bill makes no mention of
any limitation touching Richard KIRKBY. Consequently he and Richard
KIRKBYE are remedyless at Common Law. He further says that after the
marriage of Gerrard and Dorothy, William PARGITER came to Stanbridge
with one KNIGHT, a solicitor, to see the evidences and court rolls of the
manor. At that time they took some away with them; some other Gerrard
had at another time. He thinks that Dorothy has these, or that they are in
other hands, but he also has some which he thinks he may lawfully keep for
Richard KIRKBY'S benefit and for his own, and he intends to keep them.
All the premises are kept from him, except Rokefield and the annuity is as
yet unpaid, which ought to have been paid within 6 months after the death of
Susan. He denies keeping any boxes or trunks etc. Phillip GIFFORD and
John ROLFE say that neither of them has ever had any court rolls, deeds or
evidences of the Manor of Stanbridge nor anything to do with them. They all
three deny entering the manor or doing anything to the plaintiff's hurt, save
that WARNEFORD confesses that he has since his wife's death entered the
lands called Rokefields (part of the lands that according to the articles ought
to be to him for the residue of the said ten years).

C.2 Chas. I K 15/16 (see also K 3/41)
18 May 1629

Answer of Roger HYDE to the Bill of
Complaint of Dorothy KIRKBY, widow.

The defendant was for some 20 years, during the lifetime of Thomas KIRKBY,
Esq. deceased, late father of Gerrard KIRKBY, steward of the Manor of
Stanbridge Earles and continued steward during Thomas KIRKBY'S lifetime.
As far as he remembers he kept one court after his death for Susan his wife.
He entered into a book all proceedings of these courts for his own private
rememberance, and such presentments and other things as were done before
the court. He did this rather in respect that sometimes court books by
negligence being lost, great trouble and vexation has resulted. Out of these
private court books he says that he always, upon demand of the Lord of the
Manor, engrossed such grants and acts in parchment, for which the Lord of
the Manor paid him. He says he has always been ready to do this for the
plaintiff if the plaintiff asked him for any court rolls, and he further says
that if she wishes still to have any court rolls engrossed and will pay him
for engrossing them, he will be ready to do them for her. As for any other

court books, rolls or deeds etc. concerning the manor and lands, he says
he has never had them in his custody for at least ten years, at which time
there was a question in the Court of Wards about the wardship of Gerrard
KIRKBY. As soon as this question was determined about 8 or 9 years ago,
he gave them all back again to Susan KIRKBY, and he says that since then
he had had none of these documents in his custody, or knows who has any
of them. He denies meddling with any trunks, boxes or desks as complained
of in the bill and denies all the charges in the bill concerning the transfer of
land.

*****

56.
        C. 2 Chas. 1 K 8/51 and K 22/43
        26 November 1629

        Bill of Complaint of Elizabeth KIRKBY
        and Dorothy KIRKBY daughters of
        Thomas KIRKBY Esq. and Susan his
        wife, both deceased and sisters of
        Gerrard KIRKBY Esq. also deceased,
        versus Thomas and Launcelot WARNEFORD.

Thomas KIRKBY died about 10 years since (1619). The plaintiffs and Gerrard
KIRKBY being all young and the plaintiffs being left unprovided for by their
father, Susan their mother, having a personal estate worth at least £1,000
left to her by her husband Thomas the plaintiff's father, and the managing
of the lands of inheritance of Gerrard during his minority being of the value
of £400 per annum, she married Launcelot WARNEFORD, gent, about 7
years ago (1622). Afterwards by virtue of this marriage he took all the
profits of the lands until about 5 years since (1624) when Gerrard KIRKBY
came of age (b. ca. 1603). Launcelot, Susan and Gerrard, knowing that the
plaintiffs ought to be provided for out of their father's estate, agreed between them that the plaintiffs should have £150 apiece for their preferment
in marriage. Gerrard thereupon gave Launcelot WARNEFORD £300 for the
benefit of the plaintiffs and took an obligation of £600 in his (Gerrard
KIRKBY'S) own name for the assurance thereof in respect of the fact that
the plaintiffs were then both under 21, and from Launcelot WARNEFORD
and Thomas WARNEFORD Esq. his brother on condition that Thomas and
Launcelot WARNEFORD should pay £300 to the plaintiffs within six months
after their marriage, with the consent of their mother and brother, with the
use and interest in the meantime. Up till about one year ago (1628) Launcelot
WARNEFORD paid the plaintiffs at the rate of 8 per cent, that is to say to
each of them £12 apiece yearly as long as Susan his wife and Gerrard KIRKBY
lived, and for some time after. But since both Susan and Gerrard died about
2 years ago and taking advantage of the condition of the obligation which was
so uncertainly written that no suite may be taken on the bond of £600, and
because no precise time of payment was expressed in it, Launcelot WARNE-
FORD now refuses to make any further allowance to the plaintiffs and refuses
to give any other security for it albeit that both have now attained the age of
21. Consequently no consent is required from their mother and brother who
are anyway dead. He well knows that the £300 was never intended to be kept

100

by him without interest being paid on it, especially as the plaintiffs have no other means to live by. The plaintiffs therefore, being now of age, hope that the Court will hold it reasonable that they themselves should now manage their own estate. They have requested Launcelot WARNEFORD to give them security in their own names for the payment of £150 apiece, and also to pay them the back interest for the time he has failed to make the payment of it, particularly as Launcelot, refusing to do it, and Dorothy KIRKBY, widow, administratrix of Gerrard KIRKBY'S will, to whom obligation belonged, also refuses to pay them the £300 or make them an allowance. They are also in jeopardy of losing the principle of £300 if either of them do not marry speedily, or if Thomas WARNEFORD should die, his lands being entailed, and Launcelot WARNEFORD being decayed in his estate since he became bound as aforesaid.

C.2 Chas. I K 22/43
8 January 1629/30

Answer of Thomas and Launcelot
WARNEFORD to the Bill of Complaint
of Elizabeth and Dorothy KIRKBY.

Launcelot WARNEFORD acknowledge the identity of the plaintiffs, but says that Thomas KIRKBY'S estate was not as big as the plaintiffs state in their bill. In fact it only amounted, according to him, to about £200, and the lands were worth £240 a year. He says that Susan, his wife, when she married him, took the goods which belonged to Thomas KIRKBY, her former husband, which were not disposed of by her after his death, and had the profits of the lands for about 5 years until Gerrard came of age. Launcelot further says that there was an agreement between him, Susan and Gerrard that the plaintiffs should have £150 each for their portions and as a result of this agreement Gerrard did give Launcelot £300 as the bill says. He denies receiving any profits from the above mentioned lands howbeit both he and Thomas WARNEFORD, the other defendant, both confessed that Launcelot received £300 for the plaintiff's preferment in marriage, and that they both became bound to Gerrard KIRKBY in his own name for the assurance thereof with the condition for payment as is set forth in the bill. He further says that he and his brother paid the interest on £300 at 8 per cent quarterly every year to the plaintiffs since they became bound until Michaelmas last. He intended to go on paying them but the plaintiffs then sued him. He denies ever intending to take any advantage of the bond, though he himself did write it as near as possible as he could according to the agreement between him and his late wife and Gerrard. He denies ever refusing to make any further allowance. All the same he has refused and still does refuse to give any other security than he and his brother have already given, for he hopes to prove that the security he has already given is sufficient. He further says that it was not intended that the £300 be kept by him without consideration, and he is ready to pay the residue which now amounts to ? £8 and will be ready from henceforth to pay the interest. He also says he hopes that the court will not compel him to give further security to the plaintiffs. Thomas WARNEFORD says that his lands are entailed, but he holds others in fee simple to the value of ? £150.

C.2 Chas. I K 8/51
5 April 6 Chas (1629/30)

The Answer of Dorothy KIRKBY, widow
of Gerrard KIRKBY.

Dorothy KIRKBY acknowledges the agreement between Thomas and Launcelot
WARNEFORD and her late husband Gerrard KIRKBY concerning the £300.
She also confirms that her husband died 2 years since and that she undertook
the administration of her late husband's estate and thereby became entitled
to the bond in question taken in trust for the benefit of the plaintiff.

*****

57.   C.9/112/6
29 April 1689

Bill of Complaint of John KERBY Citizen
and Tallowchandler of London, son and
heir of Launcelot KERBY, late of
Winchester, deceased, versus Ann KERBY,
Elizabeth COLEMAN, Thomas WESTCOMBE,
Robert BEALE, Thomas GEORGE, John
VIBERT and others.

Launcelot KERBY died on 29 December 1685. At the time of his death he
was seised of a small real estate consisting of 3 messuages, 2 malthouses,
2 orchards, 3 gardens and one rood of ground in the parish of St. Maurice,
Winchester which descended on the plaintiff as son and heir, then an infant.
He was also seised of a great personal estate and died indebted to several
persons upon bond viz:

To	Elizabeth COLEMAN, spinster	£ 20
	Thomas WESTCOMBE	£ 80
	Robert BEALE	£100
	Thomas GEORGE	£ 40
	John VIBERT	£ 6 3s. 0d.

Amounting in all to £246 3s. 0d.

Launcelot died intestate and Letters of Administration were granted to Anne
KERBY his relict, the plaintiff's mother-in-law (stepmother?) who possessed
herself of the personal estate and sufficient to pay all his debts with a great
sum plus which she ought to pay. Being an infant, Anne entered upon the
real estate and has ever since received the rents and profits. She has the
deeds and writings concerning it. The plaintiff has now attained 21, and
Anne ought to deliver up the deeds to him. But Anne KERBY, desiring to
defraud the plaintiff of the premises. She and the creditors now put the
same in suite against him as heir of his late father in the names of the

obligees aforesaid. She claims that the personal estate is not large enough
to satisfy the same.

C.9/112/6
6 June 1689

Answer of Anne KERBY, widow,
to the Bill of Complaint of John
KERBY.

Launcelot KERBY died seised of part of a house and garden on the Lower
Brooks in Tanner St. Winchester late in the occupation of Richard THORNE,
the other part being held of a chattel lease from the Warden and Scholar
Clerks of the College near Winchester in which there was a malthouse, and
of another messuage, orchard and garden in Jurie Street, commonly called
Goale Street, and one other messuage in the parish of St. Maurice in
Winchester, wherein he lived, with part of a malt house and a little piece of
ground. Launcelot KERBY had seven children, to wit:- the plaintiff, John
KERBY and one more by a former wife, and five more by the defendant, the
elder of whom was not ten years old and youngest not nine months at the time
of his death. He had made a draft of his will whereby he devised to the plaintiff his house and garden on the Lower Brooks and some other small legacies,
and with the rest of the real estate made provision for this defendant and the
rest of his children, willing likewise that this defendant should keep the profits
of the house and garden devised to the plaintiff till he reached 21 years of age.
He left some blanks in his will for the legacies to some of his children. A
little before his death being taken with a fit of collick or gripe in the bowels
and having taken some physick for it in the morning of the day he died, and
finding it not pass through him and growing thereupon apprehensive that it
might be mortal to him, (and the plaintiff and defendant and other being then
with him) he said he had made a draft of a will in his own handwriting and
spoke to this defendant to look in his desk for it. She could not find it there
so he said it must be in a box in the room where he used to lay his writings
and calling to the plaintiff bade him fetch it to him presently that he might
perfect it. Whereupon the plaintiff pretended to go for it, but this defendant
and one Mr. JONES, the minister of the parish following, found him tumbling
the papers together, which this defendant conceives he did purposely to prevent
its being found. When they came to him he told them there was nothing like a
will there, though after the death of Launcelot KERBY it was found there mixed
amongst his other papers amongst the middle of the writings in the box. This
defendant and Mr. JONES returned to Launcelot's room and told him that John
could not find the will. He prayed that somebody there would write a will for
him and he should be very short. Thereupon Mr. JONES, the minister, offered
to write it, and one Dr. OVER, his physician offered likewise to write it. Dr.
Over told the defendant to leave the room and led her to the chamber door and
shut it after her. Then, as she was afterwards informed by those that were
there, Dr. OVER, at Launcelot's direction wrote his will for him in these
words :-

"This last will and testament of Launcelot KERBY of Winchester as
followeth; imprimis I give and devise unto my five sons John, Thomas,
William, Henry and Launcelot and to my two daughters Joanna and
Anne all my lands and tenements both real and personal wheresoever
they lie to them and their heirs for ever as they shall attain to the
age of three and twenty to be equally divided between them; and
their mother to have the rents, issues and properties thereof until

the age aforesaid. I make and ordain my loving wife Anne KERBY to be executrix of this my will in witness thereof I have hereunto set my hand and seal on 26 December 1685. Signed sealed and declared in the presence of us."

And after the defendant had been out of the room some time, she went thither again and asked Dr. OVER whether he had done the will, and he said he had. It was done but it lacked witnesses and thereupon two or three witnesses were called in but Dr. OVER then sent one of them to call Mr. JONES the minister to be a witness. In the meantime as this defendant is informed, Launcelot KERBY finding himself declining and in extremity of pain but very sensible and earnest to have all things finished about his will, called that his will might be signed and asked who were there to witness it. They brought it to him, declared in the presence of those that were there that it was his last will (the plaintiff being one of those present), and being in extremity of pain called to them to sign it and not to stay but to seal it with any thing, and being taken with a fit of vomitting as soon as that was over desired them to witness it, whereupon Dr. OVER and four more that were there present did afterwards set their hands as witnesses. But it seems the testator did not sign it and it being laid down upon the bed one Richard HEAMAN took it up and said it was not signed. Whereupon Launcelot KERBY cried out, "Oh bring it round to me," that he might have done it, and put on his spectacles and got himself up and took the pen in his hands to do it, but his physick working upwards choked him before he could do it. After his death this defendant saw Richard HEAMAN with the will in his hands and asked him what he did with it, and he told her he took it up because the plaintiff would have torn it up. However the plaintiff afterwards seemed satisfied with it and declared that he had heard his father cry out to Richard HEAMAN to stand farther off that he might have breath to finish his will and sent this defendant word that when he came of age there should be nothing wanting in him but that his father's will should be performed, and desired her in the meantime to take up the rents. The defendant denies she took up Letters of Administration to her husband but says she proved the will in the Ecclesiastical Court by the oaths of five witnesses whose names were subscribed thereto. By virtue of this she possessed herself of as much of his personal estate as she could, a true inventory of which she has annexed to this her answer.

She denies that the estate was sufficient to pay his debts which Launcelot owed the other defendants to the bill. She denies concealing part of the personal estate. She has exhibited a true inventory of the estate, and knows of no part omitted from the inventory. Launcelot, by reason of the great building of the house wherein he dwelt, had run himself much in debt, and quickly after his death she was pressed by his creditors for payment, and some even sued her. She sold the chattel lease to pay her husband's creditors for he had lived in good repute and she wished to honour his memory and name. A relation of hers, seeing the sad condition she was left in, having six of her seven children in the house with her gave her money to go on with. The debts due to the testator have not been fraudulently compounded for and still justly due. She confesses that she has lived with her children in Launcelot's house since his death and has made malt there in an endeavour to support herself and her family. She admits she has received the rents from the Tanner Street property, but that it was much out of repair and she has been forced to lay out large sums in repairs. She says that the plaintiff requested her to be his guardian before a judge until he came of age, and promised to see his brother and sisters cared for and his father's will performed. She claims no title to the real estate except her title in dower. After his father's death the plaintiff made known his desire to be apprenticed tallow chandler, and the defendant enquired of her relations to find him a place. She paid £18 for him to be apprenticed to Mr. CRANWELL, Tallow Chandler in Shoe Lane in London. She also laid out money for Thomas KERBY, her husband's second son by a former wife, whom he had bound apprentice in London during his lifetime.

Schedule 1.

An Inventory of the goods and chattels of Launcelot KERBY, deceased, late of Winchester, gent, taken 5 Jan. 1 Jas. II 1685/6.

(Details omitted.)

A particular of such debts due to the testator Launcelot KERBY which Anne KERBY has not received, but esteems to be desperate and which were therefore omitted from the inventory.

Debts on Bonds and Bills.

From Henry BADGER	£ 1		
Penal bill from William LANSON for	£15	24 July	1669
Bond from William WADE for	£11	29 August	1663
Penal bill from John GREW for	£ 1 15s. 0d.	24 March	1667
Penal bill from James SMITH for	£ 8 10s. 0d.	29 Sept.	1665
Penal bill from Henry WADE for	£22	2 Oct.	1665
Penal bill for £5 from William WADE		22 August	1663

August 27 1664 then Henry WADE owed £16 5s. 0d. and gave bond for it and he oweth £10 more on another bond.

Penal bill from William SIMS 16 July 1674 for payment of £26 on 23 July 1674.

Book debts desperate   April 8 1678

	£	s.	d.
LARNER of Sutton	10	2	3
Richard BEMISTER	11	14	0
Mr. CARTER	6	19	4
Wid NOYSE	2	4	0
Richard SMITH the goldsmith		18	6
James DANS	1	7	6
Henry BROWN	3	18	5
Mr. ELSTON		7	6
Edward TIPPER	2	3	0
Efram PRIOR		15	9½
Mrs. LARUNS	1	9	7
Abraham MORRIS		8	0

Note: The other defendants give in their answers details of the debts and money transactions which existed between them and Launcelot KERBY.

Schedule 2

A Schedule of the debts due from Launcelot KERBY which have been paid and discharged by the defendant since his death.

	£	s.	d.
Mr. WALDRON	10	0	0
Mr. SNAT	3	16	0
ALLEN at still		3	0
Goody BRODWAY		1	0
Mr. BEALE for wine	1	3	0
Mr. CROPP		3	6
Joan TROADS, my servant for wages		11	3
Mr. BATES		12	10
John COLLINS for timber & work	8	10	0
Mrs. WAVELL for a frize coat for John KIRBY		15	10
James FFORDER for fetching bricks		8	0
Thomas STATFORD		15	0
Giles LARDER	2	4	11
GOLDSMITH for carrying bricks		5	0
Mr. LAMPORD	3	12	6½
Mr. FROST of London	43	10	0
Mr. GRACE		6	3
Mr. FREEMAN	1	3	0
Mr. FISHER		1	0
Goody OSMAN		4	2
William HORRELL		12	1
Goody ADAMS for beer for the workmen		11	2
William WEBB	1	15	11
Poor Rate due before my husband died		17	0
The Minister		6	0
Mr. WESTROME for interest	4	16	0
Mr. WESTROME 1 year's interest	1	4	0
KINON	3	13	0
Mrs. BUTLER		2	4
Mr. PURDY	2	15	0
Mrs. COWELL	18	0	0
Mrs. GOSLING	4	10	0
HAYTER the carpenter		9	2
William OADES		15	10
Interest to BEALE	7	10	0
Nicholas TAILER	6	9	9
Mr. MERRYWEATHER for bricks		1	6
Mr. GOOD for business done before my husband died	4	2	6
The clerk for my husband's knell and one year's duty for quarterage		4	10
Mr. GOFTE	2	10	2
CHOB	1	5	2
Mr. KELLIAR	1	14	3
Lineard ELEY	1	5	0
For drawing the Inventory twice over and Bills out of the books		15	0
John KERBY's schooling		10	0
To George for interest	3	6	0
Mr. CRANLEY for proving the will	1	1	0
To Mr. CRANLEY for exhibiting the inventory		4	4

Funeral expenses

	£	s.	d.
Coffin for my husband	1	13	0
For the cloth		1	0
5 gallons of claret		17	6
6 lbs of sugar		3	0
For my mourning	1	11	8
His shroud		12	2
For digging his grave		2	0
For rosemary			6
For spice			6
For the certificate			2
12 dozen of bread		12	0
For a mourning quoife, hood and ruffles		9	2

An account of the money laid out by the defendant in providing cloths and other things for Thomas KERBY, second son of Launcelot KERBY, deceased, for which he stood obliged by covenant when he placed him apprentice.

	£	s.	d.
April 18th 1686 for cloth to make him a suit	2	4	10
Linen to line his breeches and pockets		2	3
Pair of breeches		9	8
Making his clothes		5	6
Shirts		11	3
Making of shirts and thread		1	2

Schedule 3

A schedule of all the deeds and evidences which the defendant Anne KERBY has or knows of concerning the real estate of her late husband, Launcelot.

One deed of sale dated 20 January 1667 from John GAMLIN and Frances his wife to Launcelot KERBY of a house in Goal St.

One deed of sale dated 7 April 4 Jas. I from Henry DAY and Margery, his wife to Arthur MAINE of a tenement, cottage and garden in Tanner Street.

An old deed of sale from Margaret RANDELL and John BAKER to Nicholas BARNESDALE of a house in Winchester.

A deed of sale dated 28 June 13 Chas. I from Mary MAINE and Steven MAINE to Peter HAWKESWORTH of the corner tenement, cottage and garden in Tanner St.

A deed poll from Mary MAINE and Stephen MAINE to Peter HAWKESWORTH of the aforesaid house in Tanner St.

The release of William SPENSER and Robert SPENSER to Arthur MAINE.

A deed of sale dated 1 September 13 Chas. I from Simon BARKESDALE to William HANCOCK of 4 houses in Winchester and fines thereupon.

A deed poll of the same from William WRIGHT to Nicholas BARNESDALE.

A deed of sale dated 17 May 1659 from William HANCOCK to Launcelot KERBY of a house and garden in the parish of St. Maurice and fine thereupon.

4 old books for the performance of covenants.

A letter of attorney from Wm. HANCOCK to receive possession.

An old lease of the house in St. Maurice parish from Simon BARKESDALE to Thom. VIN expired.

A bond from Joan AUSTIN dated 18 December 1656 for performance of covenants to Launcelot KERBY on the sale of the lease on the Brookes, viz; in Tanner Street.

A deed poll dated 1 December 1637 from Henry MOORE, Simon BARDESDALE and Katherine MOORE to William HANCOCK.

A deed dated 20 March 1657 to lead to the use of a fine from Joan AUSTEN to Launcelot KERBY of the house in the lower Brooks in Tanner Street.

The fine thereupon.

Schedule 4

A schedule of all the rents that the defendant has received of the real estate of her late husband together with that part of the chattel leases let with them under an entire rent which became due since his death and of which remains due.

Received from John WEBB in part of rent for the house and garden and orchard in Goale Street, let at £7 p.a.	£13 5s. 0d.
Received of Richard THORNE and John GILBERT for 2½ years rent for the house and malthouse and garden on the Lower Brooks being most free land and part chattel lease an entire rent.	£22 10s. 0d.

Rents remaining due.

From John WEBB at midsummer next 1689 there will be due	£11 5s. 0d.
From John GILBERT at midsummer next there will be due	£ 9

Schedule 5

A particular of the charges and expenses the defendant has been put to in repairs to the houses and taxes and charges issuing out of the same since the death of her late husband.

		s.	d.
Feb 19, 1685,	for a lock and nails	1	2
	for a window and timber and a panel of a wall	3	0
	for a door and timber, nails and a latch for the washhouse door	5	0

			£	s.	d.
	for mending the lock and putting it on				6
	for another lock and putting him on			1	0
May 3, 1686,	Goodman FOX for lime			11	8
4	John NOICE for two load of sand			10	0
6	for tilepins			4	6
	Goodman FOX for bricks		1	7	6

and many similar items, up to and including April 1689.

*****

C.9/461/80
20 February 1700/1

Bill of Complaint of Launcelot KERBY
of Winchester, gent, and Barbara his
wife, versus Anne KERBY and Thomas
CRAWLEY.

Last June Anne KERBY of Winchester, widow, mother of the plaintiff, earnestly
desired him to settle in Winchester, he then desiring to live in London, and
proposed to him a marriage with the plaintiff Barbara, which she said would be
very much to his advantage. She said that her influence with Thomas CRAWLEY,
the father of the plaintiff Barbara would ensure that she brought with her a very
good estate. She promised to settle on Launcelot in consideration of the marriage a garden, Malt House and messuage of hers worth £20 a year situated in
Winchester, mostly freehold, though part leasehold, and half a meadow at
Chobham in Surrey worth £10 a year. He accordingly acceded to his mother's
desires and abandoned his plan to settle in London where he had completed his
apprenticeship and agreed to settle in Winchester. After some negotiations the
following agreement was reached. Anne KERBY was to settle the aforementioned
property on Trustees for her use for life and after her death to the use of
Launcelot for his life and after his death on Barbara as her jointure, and there-
after to the issue of them both. Thomas CRAWLEY agreed to give a marriage
portion of £500 with Barbara. Launcelot procured deeds of settlement to be
drawn and requested Anne KERBY and Thomas CRAWLEY to sign them, a date
having been fixed for the marriage. But Anne KERBY then decided that she
could get Launcelot a better marriage if he waited and since the agreement had
not been signed by all the parties, she then refused to sign, in spite of the fact
that mutual promises of marriage had been exchanged between Launcelot and
Barbara. Launcelot was very surprised and did not feel himself free to be
discharged from his promise to marry Barbara to whom he had now become
very attached. He asked Thomas CRAWLEY if he would still be prepared to
settle the £500 on Barbara in jointure if they were to marry, he promising to
try to persuade his mother to keep her part of the bargain, but he refused.
He then returned to his mother saying that he had been threatened with a suit
of breach of promise of marriage if he did not proceed with it and after mature
consideration, she agreed to another plan whereby Launcelot should release to
her £300 which was due to him out of the personal estate of his father Launcelot
KERBY, deceased, who had died intestate, of which Anne had taken Letters of
Administration and for legacies given to him by several others of his which she

had received during his minority and likewise for money lent by him to his mother; and also if he, who is eldest son and heir to his mother, would release his title to the residue of her estate and give bond for £250 for the proper burying of her at his own cost after she died, then she would consent to execute the deed mentioned above. Under the circumstances he was forced to accept her proposals. He asked one ..... Attwood of Chichester to stand surety for him and become bound with him to his mother. He then told Thomas CRAWLEY he had prevailed upon his mother to make the settlement, and asked that the marriage treaty be drawn up and to let things proceed. To this he consented. However Thomas CRAWLEY asked Launcelot to make a further agreement that he would be a certain date in the articles of agreement get his mother to settle the messuage etc. and that thereupon Thomas CRAWLEY would pay him £500 as the marriage portion of Barbara. They were married on June 30th last past (1700) with the advice and consent of Anne KERBY, who sent her two daughters to the wedding and a letter confirming her promise. The plaintiff therefore expected that Anne KERBY and Thomas CRAWLEY would have performed their parts of the agreement and make the settlements. But they have both refused and combine together to defraud the plaint iffs of their rights. Anne refuses to make the settlement and Thomas refuses to give the £500 which is due only after Anne has performed her part of the agreement.

*****

59.   REQ 2/231/18
         Undated

         Bill of Complaint of Edward KERBY, Henry
         KERBYE, Thomas KERBYE, John KERBY,
         Ann KERBY and Mary KERBY, children of
         John KERBYE jun late of West Cotton in the
         parish of Hardingstone, Northants., yeoman
         deceased, and Francis MANLEY and Katherine
         his wife, and John FILKINS and Isabel his wife,
         two other daughters of the said John KERBYE
         deceased, plaintiffs, versus Laurence MANLEY.

John KERBYE the elder late of Grafton Regis, Northants, yeoman, grandfather of plaintiffs, being lawfully seised of divers goods, sums of money and chattels delivered £150 to John KERBYE, his son, to be employed for the benefit of plaintiffs. John KERBYE senior also owned a great number of sheep and an estate for the term of years of certain lands called Sewardsley and Thickshawe in Northants. About 4 May 1573 he made his will, appointing his wife, Isabel, his executrix, by which he bequeathed to the plaintiffs 25 score of sheep and his interest in the said grounds wherein they then went, to be employed by John KERBY junior to the use of the plaintiffs in these words, " Item I geve to the children of John KERBYE my sonne all my
         sheepe now goinge within Sewardsley and Thickshawe which
         be about the nomber of xxvtie score sheepe together with my
         whole estate and interest in the same groundes aforenamed to
         be occupied and employed by the said John KERBYE to the use
         of his said Children."
After the death of John KERBYE senior, his wife procured probate of the will at the Prerogative Court of Canterbury, and delivered the sheep and grounds to John KIRBY junior. John KIRBY junior very shortly after died

110

intestate, and his wife Pernell, mother of the plaintiffs, sued out letters of administration ... Pernell married again one Laurence MANLEY of West Cotton gent, to whom came possession of the £150, the sheep and the grounds, and he became bound, together with one Francis MANLEY of the same, gent., to Mr. Richard TALLENTINE, official to the archdeacon of Northampton, in £1,000 for the faithful administration of the estate by Pernell and to educate and bring up the plaintiffs being then very young. When the man children were 21 and the woman children were 18 or if any should marry under age, Pernell should pay to each of them £52 10s. 0d. After which Pernell died. Laurence MANLEY has withheld portions from Edward, Henry and Thomas (who have accomplished the age of 21) and from Katherine, wife of Francis MANLEY and Isabel wife of John FILKINS. The better to effect his purpose, Laurence MANLEY has got the said bond into his hands and has sold all the sheep, some at 9s. apiece and some for more, and the grounds being worth £50 a year, the interest of which amounts to a great sum, Laurence MANLEY has often been gently required to pay the sum of £150 and deliver the sheep and grounds and the interest due, and the said bond, but has refused. Plaintiffs ask that he be subpoenaed to answer.

REQ 2/232/29
10 February 1592/3

Thomas KIRBIE and John KIRBIE and
Oliver FELL junior and Agnes his wife,
plaintiffs, versus Laurence MANLEY

Undated. Interrogatories on behalf of the plaintiffs.

1. Do you know the parties ?

2. Do you know John KIRBIE grandfather of the plaintiffs,
    of what wealth or ability was he at the time of his death ?

3. Did John KIRBIE senior make a will; did he make his
    wife Isabel his executrix ?

4. Did John KIRBIE senior devise to the children of his
    son John KIRBY 25 score sheep and grounds called
    Sewardsley and Thickshawe ?

5. Did John KIRBY junior receive £150 of his father for
    the use of the plaintiffs and their brethren ?

6. Did Isabel KIRBY deliver the 25 score sheep to Laurence
    MANLEY ?

7. Was this done a little before they were shorn, so that
    the wool might be used for the benefit of her son's
    children; how much wool ?

8. Did Laurence MANLEY make an acquittance to Isabel
    KIRBY, acknowledging the receipt of the sheep ?

9. Did Laurence MANLEY marry Pernell, widow of John
    KIRBY junior; what promise did he make at the time
    of his marriage as to the management of the stock left
    to the children and as to increasing it to £800 so that

each child might have £100 at least ?

10. Did the defendant obtain enough of the goods of
    John KIRBY to make up the legacies ?

11. Did the defendant enter a bond to pay £52 10s. 0d.
    to each of the children, over and above legacy given
    by their grandfather ?

12. Did the defendant obtain goods of John KIRBY junior
    to the value of £2,000 ?

13. Was John KIRBY junior in debt at the time of his death ?

14. Did the defendant freely give Thomas KIRBIE one of
    the plaintiffs a lease of a farm in West Cotton ?

24 January 1593/4

Depositions on behalf of plaintiffs, taken
at Westminster.

John WHALLEY, Grafton, Northants.,
yeoman, aged 49.

1. Knows parties.

2. Knew John KIRBIE senior 'he is verelie persuaded
   that he was worth two thowsand poundes in goodes
   and chattels at the tyme of his dethe'; he was
   assessed in subsidies at 100 marks in goods.

3. John KIRBIE senior made a will, Isabel was executrix.

4. John KIRBIE senior devised sheep and grounds as in the
   interrogatory; there were about 24 score sheep and
   ten; John KIRBY junior at this time had eight children
   and his wife was with child of the ninth.

5. John KIRBY junior received £150 of John KIRBIE senior
   before the latter's death for the use of his children;
   he has heard Thomas MEAD and Robert KIRBY a son
   of John KIRBY junior so say and affirm.

6. He knows that Isabel KIRBY delivered to Laurence
   MANLEY the sheep since he was present at the delivery;
   Laurence MANLEY gave Isabel an acquittance in receipt.

7. Sheep were delivered before they were shorn, so that
   the wool might be employed for the use of the children.
   They produced about 47 or 48 todd of wool.

8. Laurence MANLEY made an acquittance to Isabel in
   receipt for the sheep with the legacies. He was present
   at the sealing of the deed. It was dated 16 October 1573.

9. Knows that Laurence MANLEY married Pernell, late
   wife of John KIRBY junior.

10.   Robert KIRBY uncle of the children of John KIRBY
        junior told him that he had been at Peterborough
        and proved a will for John KIRBY's children and
        had made them £5 apiece more of their father's
        goods.

11.   The defendant and one Francis MANLEY entered
        a bond of £1,000 to Richard TALLENTYNE; among
        the conditions one is that the defendant should pay
        the children £52 10s. 0d. apiece.

12.   Nothing.

13, 14 John KIRBY junior was not in debt at his death.

John ROBERTES, Hardingstone, Northants,
gent., aged 77.

1.   Knows parties.

2.   Knew John KIRBIE senior, 'he was accounted a very
        ritche man and worthe ii thowsand poundes.'

3-8   Nothing.

9.   Laurence MANLEY married the late wife of John
        KIRBY junior.

10-13   Nothing.

14.   Deponent being possessed of a lease of a farm in
        West Cotton, being of Her Majesties inheritance,
        he, the said MANLEY, having procured a lease
        of the reversion thereof, deponent caused the
        defendant to come before the Lord Treasurer,
        trusting to procure the lease for the deponent's
        own use. Referred to Sir Walter MILDMAY.
        Deponent allowed to remain for 6 years longer.
        The defendant said 'I have geven it away with one
        of my wyffes sonnes whome she hathe Intreted me
        that I shold be good unto.'

Further interrogatories on behalf of plaintiffs;
(numeration begins at no. 7)
Undated.

7.   Did you know John KIRBY senior, of what wealth
        was he ?

8.   Did he make a will, was Isabel executrix ?

9.   Did he devise the sheep and grounds to the children
        of John KIRBY junior; how many sheep and how
        many children ?

10. As No. 5 in original interrogatory

11. As No. 6

12. As No. 7

13. As No. 8

14. As No. 9

15. As No. 10

16. As No. 11

17. As No. 12

18. As No. 13

19. As No. 14, about seven years since

**

... Sept ....

Further depositions on behalf of plaintiffs.

Thomas (MEAD, Bloxham); Oxon.,
butcher, aged 4(2)

1. Knows Thomas and John KIRBY and the defendant

2. Knew Isabel wife of John KIRBIE senior; she was
his executrix.

4. John KIRBIE senior held grounds and sheep; John
KIRBY junior had nothing to do with them while John
John KIRBIE senior lived.

5. John KIRBIE senior devised sheep and grounds to the
children of John KIRBY junior.

7. Knew John KIRBIE senior, was worth 2,000 marks at
his death.

8. John KIRBIE senior made a will and made Isabel
executrix.

9. John KIRBY junior had eight children.

10. Knew John KIRBY junior received £150 from John
KIRBIE senior to the use of the plaintiffs.

12. Sheep were delivered a little before they were shorn
by Isabel to John KIRBY junior; they produced about
50 todd of wool.

15. Goods received by the defendant were sufficient to make
up sum of £800.

17.   Goods of John KIRBY junior which came to the defendant were worth at least 2,000 marks.

18.   John KIRBY'S only debt was about £20 owed for purchase of a house in Northampton.

William WICKYNS, Towcester, Northants., gent., aged 4(?).

11.   Laurence MANLEY sold 24 score of the sheep to this deponent; 12 score of the best at 10s. apiece and the rest at 8s. apiece.

12.   Sheep produced 50 todd and upwards.

13.   Mentions John WHALLY son of the said Isabel.

Otherwise adds nothing.

Robert KYRBY of Eston Eston (sic) Northants., yeoman, aged 47.

7.   John KIRBIE senior was his father; was worth £3,500 at his death.

10.   John KIRBIE senior gave John KIRBY junior £140 for his children; John KIRBY junior acknowledged receipt on his deathbed.

Otherwise adds nothing.

**

Interrogatories on behalf of defendant Laurence MANLEY.

1.   Do you know the parties ?

2.   Were John KIRBY, late of Grafton Regis, Northants and his son John, late of West Cotton in the parish of Hardingstone, Northants possessors of grounds called Sewardsley and Thickshawe in 1573 ?

3.   Were John KIRBIE senior and junior tenants by lease and how many years were to come in 1573 ?

4.   Did John KIRBY junior take the profits of the grounds from 1573 until his death ?

5.   Did his widow, Purnell, take the profits of the grounds after his death ?

6.   Did John KIRBY junior or Purnell sell or mortgage any of the sheep in 1573 ?

7.   Did Purnell in her widowhood buy a messuage in Northampton from Robert BARNES, and did she join with Henry KIRBY, her son, in the purchase, reserving to herself a life estate, with remainder to Henry ? Did she pay £60 for the messuage ?

8. Was Henry seised of the messuage ?

9. Did Laurence MANLEY give Thomas KIRBY a lease
of a farm in West Cotton in lieu of his legacy; but
afterwards at Thomas's request sell the lease for
£118, which Thomas received in lieu of his legacy ?

10. What other sums of money has the defendant paid to
the other children of John KIRBY junior in lieu of
their legacies ?

**

Depositions on behalf of the defendant (no heading)
Undated.

William COCKYN, Northampton,
glover, aged 44.

9. The defendant gave Thomas KIRBY a lease in West
Cotton in lieu of his legacy and later sold it for £100
and odd at the request of Thomas, and Thomas received
£20, part of this.

10. The defendant gave in this deponent's house £10 to
Henry KIRBY in lieu of legacies. He heard Francis
(MANLEY) who married Katherine, another of the
children of John KIRBY junior, say that he had
received among other things in the time of the defendant's sickness, he then lying at his farm in West
Cotton upon an account between them, the sum of £100
in lieu of legacy to the said Katherine.

Thomas MEAD, Bloxham, Oxon,
butcher, aged 42.

3. John KIRBIE senior held the grounds by lease from Sir
John FERMOR for 7½ years, which was 1½ years unexpired when he died.

6. Pernell did not sell or drive away any of the sheep before
her remarriage.

7. Does not know that Pernell bought a house but thinks that
John KIRBY junior did so.

William WICKYNS, Towcester, Northants.,
gent, aged 43.

Adds Nothing.

George PARE, Spratton, Northants.,
carpenter, aged 50.

9. Knows of gift of West Cotton lease, which was for 21
years and its subsequent sale.

10. John KIRBY, another son, received £45 of the
    defendant, in part of his legacy; the defendant
    has given Edward KIRBY £50 for his legacy;
    has given Henry KIRBY £63 for his legacy;
    Henry also had from his mother one house in
    Northampton; Francis MANLEY had received
    £100 as legacy of his wife Katherine; one FYLKYNS
    who married another daughter of John KIRBY junior
    has received £50

*****

C.3/363/15
29 May 1622

Bill of Complaint of John KIRBY of
Loddington, Northants., labourer,
versus George BASS, Robert LADD,
John CAVE, William THOMPSON and
Henry ALLWOOD.

For the last 30 years the plaintiff has been an inhabitant of Loddington and
lived there all the time by his handiwork as a day labourer. By this means
and by careful endeavour he had got together in ready money and other goods
substance to the value of 20 nobles, and being likewise possessed of other
money, goods and chattels of like value being the property of his 3 children
James, John and Eleanor, given to them by one Ellen BRIGSTOCK, spinster
deceased, their aunt on their mother's side, and by one Stephen (Erle?).
They left this in his hands in trust to be employed in stock or otherwise at
his discretion for their benefit for which he stands chargeable to the children
both in law and conscience. In February 17 Jan. I (1620), being in danger of
becoming destitute of a house for himself, his wife and children by reason of
the transformation of the estates of those under whom he had heretofore lived,
and fearing the strictness and penalties of the laws of this realm that might
happen to him and his family if they should become destitute and without a
dwelling, he entered into communication with one George BASS, late of
Loddington, husbandman, to buy from him a building then used for a kiln house,
and about half a rood of ground belonging to it, being part of an ancient farm
in Loddington wherein George BASS then dwelt. Before any assurance was
made thereof, George BASS and the plaintiff were both content that the bargain should be void and thereupon they entered into speech of another bargain
touching a piece of ground lately used as an orchard 17 yards in length and 10
in breadth containing in all 6 perches of ground. The plaintiff told George
BASS that his intention was to buy the 2 parcels of land, or one of them, to
build a house thereon and to have all easements etc. for that purpose, as
namely to have allowance of stone, straw and timber for building the house,
and to have liberty to place and adjoin the house to an ancient barn of the
messuage and to lap the great timber roof tree and side pieces thereof upon
the gole or hillwale of the said barn. To this George BASS agreed, and
further that he should be permitted to set up his house and to use it as a
dwelling without let or hindrance. Upon a good assurance to be made the
plaintiff, believing in the promises of George BASS, but himself being an
ignorant, unlearned man, the bargain was concluded. Shortly after the plain-

117

tiff paid George BASS £8 6s. 8d. and gave bond for the payment of 5 more pounds at a later date, which was the agreed purchase price. George BASS resorted to John RAND Esq. Counsel at Law, indifferently chosen by both parties, and gave him instructions according to the former agreement, and an indenture of sale was drawn for the piece of ground without any covenants or warranty touching the buildings and enjoying of the intended house. The plaintiff disliked this indenture and wished Mr. RAND to add a covenant or other assurance for that purpose, or otherwise he would not proceed in the bargain, for that it was the only end that he bought the land for. Mr. RAND answered that the same might not conveniently be put into the indenture of bargain and sale, but in some other colateral deed or assurance to be made afterwards, and he advised the plaintiff to accept George BASS'S word in the meantime. Afterwards certain feoffees to whom George BASS had formerly conveyed the lands, viz. Robert LADD, John CAVE, William THOMPSON and Henry ALLWOOD, should join and make him further assurance, and as Mr. RAND said he would devise in what manner George BASS should give warranty that the plaintiff should build a house on the land, as also what further assurance the feoffees should make. George BASS duly sealed and delivered the indentures on this occasion. Later the plaintiff told some of his friends about the bargain. They told him that other persons were interested in the estate of the said lands intended to be bought and sold, and that the assurance BASS had made was insufficient in law, and moreover that trouble might arise if he were to erect a house on the land as a thing contrary to the laws and statutes of this realm if he did not get a good assurance for his own security. They therefore advised him speedily to demand a better assurance concerning the estate and interest of the lands, as well as sufficient warranty that he might peaceably erect a house thereon without lawful encumbrance. But George BASS refused, and meanwhile the £5 became due on the bond which George BASS demanded, but which the plaintiff refused to pay forasmuch as the feoffees in whom the land was then vested had not yet sealed any conveyance to him. However since matters have gone so far he decided to start building his house but it was soon discovered that the ground was part of an ancient messuage given to the inhabitants of Loddington for their support, and that it was prohibited by law to build upon it unless 4 acres of land at least were to be used and occupied with it, and therefore the inhabitants of Loddington said they would complain to the Justices of the Peace for a warrant to stop it, and that if he continued they would cause the same to be reported to the Court of Exchequer to forbid him erecting the house. The plaintiff fearing further damage and trouble was driven to compound with the common informer who was threatening these charges, and to give him a sum of money to desist. He then went to George BASS and told him what had happened and asked him to take back the land and return his money to him, but George BASS refused. He was so stricken with the anxiety of the case that he fell into a great sickness, during which George BASS came to him wishing him to be comforted and not to take any grief for that cause, promising that he should in no way be hindered thereby, and suggested putting the matter to arbitration. The arbitrators having examined the case would not proceed to make a final end on it without the consent of both parties, and George BASS, despite his fair words, obstinately refused to come to an agreement or to take back the ground. He craves the Court to call George BASS, Robert LADD, John CAVE, William THOMPSON and Henry ALLWOOD to account for their actions.

(Answer missing)

*****

C2 Chas. I C 19/27
20 November 1640

Bill of Complaint of Thomas CHAPMAN
of St. John's Chapel, Leicester, versus
Richard KIRBY.

Thomas CHAPMAN, late of Foxton Leicestershire, gent deceased, the
plaintiff's father, was seised of the manor of Foxton, Leics., heretofore
Darbyes manor and after Eatons manor. The manor of Foxton extends to
Gumbley, Leics, near Foxton, within which manor the plaintiff's father had
a court leet and view of franck pledge of all the tenements of the said manor.
Richard KIRBY, late of Gumbley, yeoman deceased, was in his lifetime seised
of a messuage or tenement and two yardlands of arable land, meadow and pasture in Gumbley, heretofore the land of one ... ILSTON. It descended to
Richard KIRBY or to his father, or mother, or some other of his ancestors
from ILSTON. KIRBY dwelt in the house and occupied the two yardlands as
they had formerly been occupied and· used by his ancestors the said ILSTONS.
These premises were time out of mind before held of the manor of Foxton by
fealty suit of court and some other services, and Richard KIRBY while he
lived in the said house and occupied the premises, did usually appear and do
suit both in the court baron and court leet of the plaintiff's father at Foxton
for the said lands and premises, and did such other services there as were
imposed upon him. If by chance he was at any time absent from the court he
was either essoined or .... and so likewise did the ILSTONS, the
ancestors of Richard KIRBY, in their time do suit to the said court baron and
court leet of Darby and Eaton for the house and land they were in those times
dwelling in. They held the same house and lands that Richard KIRBY had,
both in the time of King Henry Vl, Henry Vll, Henry Vlll, Queen Mary and
Queen Elizabeth. And whereas one William VALE of Gumbley was seised
about 9 or 10 years since of one messuage and one yardland in Gumbley held
of the plaintiff's father as of his manor of Foxton, and which he and his ancestors before him had done suit at the court leet and court baron at Foxton, he,
the said VALE, and his ancestors and KIRBY and his ancestors have acknowledged in the court baron before the then steward within the time of our late
sovereign lord King James and of the late Queen Elizabeth and in the time of
the late King Henry Vll, that they hald their several lands of the lord of the
manor of Foxton. But in respect the plaintiff's father did in his lifetime lose
several court rools of the said manor, the plaintiff is unable to say by what
tenure the lands are now held, as otherwise he might, but he is able to prove
they are held by fealty in suit of court. Richard KIRBY and William VALE
being so severally seised of their houses and lands held of the plaintiff's
father's manor and other lands beside held of other lords, which have been
so occupied together for many years, so that the ILSTONS and VALES
ancient lands cannot be known from the other lands occupied therewith, he,
Richard KIRBY, in consideration of marriage, did convey the messuage and
other lands in Gumbley whereof he was seised to Richard KIRBY his eldest
son and heir apparent, or to the heirs of the said Richard lawfully begotton.
The elder Richard KIRBY died, and after his death the premises descended
to the said Richard KIRBY accordingly, and shortly after he purchased of
the said William VALE his premises which he held of the manor of Foxton.
He then became seised of it and demised back the house to William VALE
for his life or for some other term not yet expired, in which house William
VALE still dwells in that part of Gumbley which is within the manor of Foxton,
and in the house of the VALES which has always come to the leet of Foxton

119

and is a resident within the said leet and ought to appear at the leet court. Richard KIRBY, being so seised of both the messuage and all the said lands held of the plaintiff's father as of his manor of Foxton, and William VALE so possessed of the messuage of his ancestors, about 6 or 7 years since the plaintiff's father conveyed the manor of Foxton to the plaintiff and his heirs with remainder to his other sons and grandchildren. Both KIRBY and VALE promised to become tenants to him and appear in his court as they had formerly done before. The plaintiff further says that the rest of the tenants of the manor, after the conveyance made to him, attorned tenants to him and did their suit and service to his court, but Richard KIRBY and William VALE withhold and refuse to appear at the plaintiff's court to do their suit, they also refuse to attorn tenants to the plaintiff contrary to their promise, and persuade others to withhold their suit also and detaining from the court roll other evidences of the plaintiff.

4 May 1641

The Answer of Richard KIRBY to the
Bill of Complaint of Thomas CHAPMAN.

Richard KIRBY acknowledges that the plaintiff's father was seised of the Manor of Foxton, but does not know or believe that it includes the lands in Gomondly, als Gumly. He believes that his father Richard KIRBY deceased, was seised of the premises mentioned in the bill, and says that he is now seised of them and that they were once the lands of the ILSTONS and came by inheritance to his father. He denies that they were ever held of the Manor of Foxton, or that his father, or any of his ancestors appeared at the Court Leet of Foxton to perform service for them. In fact they are held of the Manor of Gumly in common socage by fealty at a rent of 2/-, and he does fealty to Sir Edward GRIFFIN Kt. the present Lord of the Manor for them. If any of his ancestors, or the ILSTONS, did appear at the Court Leet or any court of the Manor of Foxton, as is pretended, it was only to the Court Baron and not in respect of the lands in question, but for some other lands. The same applies to the premises formerly William VALE'S.

*****

62.   C5/426/28
                28 May 1650

        Bill of Complaint of Richard KIRBY of
        Gumly, Leicestershire, yeom, grandchild
        and heir of Richard KIRBY, late of Gt.
        Bowden, Leics., woolwinder, versus
        Edward KIRBY and Christopher KIRBY
        and others.

Richard KIRBY, the plaintiff's grandfather, about 60 years ago was seised in fee simple or fee tail of an estate of inheritance of a messuage in Gt. Bowden and ¼ yardland of arable, meadow and pasture, heretofore the land of one Thomas HARPER, deceased, and in ¼ yardland arable meadow and

pasture in Foxton, heretofore land of Richard ILSTON, and of other lands in
Foxton to the yearly value of £12. Richard KIRBY, the grandfather died 50
years ago leaving issue three sons lawfully begotten, viz; Richard KIRBY,
the eldest, Christopher and John younger sons. After his death the property
came to Richard KIRBY as eldest son and heir. Richard KIRBY was the plaintiff's father. He died twelve years ago (1638) seised of the property, which
descended as of right to the plaintiff as eldest son and heir of his father, and
he ought to enjoy the benefits and profits of it. But one Edward KIRBY of Gt.
Bowden, yeoman being son of Christopher KIRBY and Christopher KIRBY of
Gt. Bowden, son of Edward KIRBY, and Livewell CHAPMAN of London,
stationer, and Joseph CHAPMAN of Foxton, yeoman, since the plaintiff's
father's death, have taken advantage of the late troublesome times and have
got possession of the messuage, lands etc. and taken all the profits thereof
for above 10 years. Although the plaintiff has often asked Edward KIRBY and
others to deliver up possession and to account for the rents and profits, they
have by some means during the late wars got possession of the ancient deeds
and evidences of the premises which would clearly set forth the plaintiff's title
to the property. They refuse to give them up or give them up or give him possession. They have contrived amongst themselves divers secret deeds to create
a title to themselves and have given out that Christopher KIRBY, father of
Edward, now deceased was son and heir to Richard the grandfather and had
right and title to the property, and that Edward, as son and heir of Christopher
ought to enjoy the same. At other times they say that John KIRBY, being now
deceased, was son and heir of Richard the grandfather, and that they have a
good title by some deeds or grant from John KIRBY. At other times they pretend that the grandfather and father of the plaintiff had no good right and title
so that it ought not to descend to him, whereas in truth the grandfather and
father were lawfully seised and Christopher and John were younger sons and
could not claim inheritance, which would be plain if the deeds were produced.

C 5/426/28
1 October 1650

The Answer of Edward KIRBY and
Christopher KIRBY to the Bill of
Complaint of Richard KIRBY.

They believe that Richard KIRBY, the grandfather, was seised of the lands
in Gt. Bowden, sometimes Harpers land, and off the ILSTON land in Foxton,
all of which were ancient demesne lands and heretofore part of the possessions
of the late Crown of England and ought to descend by gavelkynd as they are
informed. Richard, the grandfather, died on 10 Feb 36 Elizabeth (1593) at
Gt. Bowden, leaving issue Richard, the plaintiff's father, Christopher and
John KIRBY as the plaintiff says. However they absolutely deny that after the
grandfather's death any greater part came to Richard that his proportionable
third part as coheir with his brothers in gavelkynd, and that Richard, the
father, died possessed of any more than a hird part of the grandfather's lands,
although the plaintiff and his father were eldest sons. Shortly after the grandfather's death, Richard, Christopher and John made a tripartite indenture dated
20 Feb 36 Elizabeth between them which said, "whereas all the cottages land
and premises in Gt. Bowden and Foxton by course of lineal descent and inheritance did lawfully come unto them, the said Richard, Christopher and John
KIRBY, sons of Richard KIRBY the grandfather as his sons and co-heirs in
gavelkynd", they made division of the property whereby was allotted to Richard
the plaintiff's father and his heirs the two cottages and lands late ILSTONS;

121

to Christopher and his heirs the messuage and lands late HARPERS; and to John the lands in Foxton. According to the indenture aforesaid the defendants claim that the lands have been so held ever since. Edward KIRBY says that immediately after the making of the indenture of partition, his father Christopher took possession of the HARPER'S land and died 18 years ago, leaving this defendant Edward, his only son and heir. Immediately after his father's death, he took possession and has enjoyed the land ever since. He therefore refused to yield possession to the plaintiff. They deny ever having claimed the Foxton land. If however their title is found to be deficient they rely on an Article of Quiet Possession made nearly 60 years ago and on the Act for the Limitation of Actions. They deny all charges of conspiracy.

The Answer of Joseph CHAPMAN to the
Bill of Complaint of Richard KIRBY.

(Basically the same as the above so far as the claim to descent by gavelkynd is concerned.)

The defendant says he has never claimed title to the land in Gt. Bowden, but as far as the land in Foxton goes it has been quietly held for 60 years and more by John KIRBY to whom it was allotted and by those claiming title under him. He has been a tenant for 2 years under John at a rent of £3 per annum and is now a tenant to John LEWIS, gent, to whom the title was conveyed by John KIRBY. He denies all charges of conspiracy.

*****

5.   C.7/417/37 and 200/60
            Feb 1652/3 - May 1653

            Bill of Complaint of William KIRBY of
            Wooton, Northants, yeoman, versus
            Christopher CROUCH the elder of Cotten
            End. Hardingston, Northants, yeoman
            and Christopher CROUCH the younger,
            his son and heir apparent.

In January 1651/2 a marriage treaty was negotiated between the plaintiff and Christopher CROUCH, the father and the son, touching the marriage of Mary KIRBY, the plaintiff's daughter to Christopher CROUCH, the son. £280 was to be paid in instalments of £50 and £80 within a year after the death of the survivor of the plaintiff and his wife Dorothy, and £200 in goods within a month after the marriage. CROUCH senior was to settle on his son and Mary and their issue lands in Westoning and Tingrith, Bedfordshire, in the tenure of William BERNARD als CRISPE, Bushy Close in East End als East Town of Fleetwick, Beds. and in Fleetwick, in the tenure of Thomas BAYLY. CROUCH junior was to settle lands at Hill End als Sampshill in Westoning, then in the tenure of Thomas VAUX. The marriage took place and the plaintiff fulfilled his part of the treaty, but the CROUCHES have failed to sign the covenants settling the lands on Mary for her jointure.

122

Answer

The lands turn out to be incumbered with mortgages.

*****

C 5/512/10
27 October 1660

Bill of Complaint of Edward KIRBY of
Sileby, Leics., gent., versus Thomas
CHURCH and others.

Thomas CHURCH, son of Thomas CHURCH of Sileby, mercer, and Bridget,
his wife, was seised of a messuage, tenement and land in Sileby after the
life of his father, Thomas CHURCH and of Bridget, his mother, with remainder to the heirs of Bridget, by Thomas, and remainder over to the heirs
of Bridget and remainder over to the right heirs of Thomas THORPE. Thomas
CHURCH, junior, was heir apparent to Bridget who was one of the daughters
and coheirs of Thomas THORPE. Thomas CHURCH entered into a treaty with
Edward KIRBY concerning the sale of property to him after the death of Thomas
CHURCH the elder and Bridget. In Trinity Term 1659, Thomas CHURCH junior
levied a fine on the premises to Thomas DAWSON and William HALL to the use
of such persons as Thomas CHURCH should nominate. Shortly after it was
finally agreed that Thomas CHURCH should convey the premises to Edward
KIRBY, who was to pay £40 10s. 0d. for it. Edward KIRBY paid 30/- to
Ralph DIXON, on the instructions of Thomas CHURCH as part of the purchase
money, and £20 more to various other persons also on Thomas CHURCH'S
instructions. Edward KIRBY drew up a conveyance to be sealed by Thomas
CHURCH, but the latter, in combination with his father and Ralph DIXON
refuse to sign it. Edward KIRBY'S witnesses are absent overseas and he
cannot bring testimony to bear on his case.

9 January 1660/1

Answer of Thomas CHURCH sr to the
Bill of Complaint of Edward KIRBY.

He acknowledges that he and his wife, Bridget are seised of the premises
with remainder to Thomas CHURCH junior, their son. He told his son not
to proceed in any sale of the reversion of the property and informed Edward
KIRBY and his Attorney, John HOUGH, that they would not give their consent
to such a sale. He was advised that Robert BARNARD and Theophilus GREENE
would buy the property in trust for his son, and they have now done so.

*****

65.   C.10/79/55
                     May 1666

                     Bill of Complaint of Richard KIRBY senior
                     of Gumley, Leicestershire and Richard
                     KIRBY junior his son, versus Thomas
                     SPRIGGE of London, merchant and
                     John ONEBY of Grays Inn, Esq.

In 1655 Richard KIRBY senior borrowed £150 from Thomas SPRIGGE of
London. A fine was acknowledged before Oliver ST. JOHN, Lord Chief
Justice of the Common Bench on 8 Feb 1656/7. Richard junior was married
in 1658 or 59 and the property which secured the loan was transferred to
him. Thomas SPRIGGE gave Richard junior instructions to pay £120 to
Richard SPRIGGE of Scaldwell. About the same time Richard junior sold
the premises for £60 to John ONEBY of Grays Inn, Esq. and is thus able to
pay the balance of the debt, although he has not received full satisfaction for
the sale of the land to ONEBY. He has offered Thomas SPRIGGE to come to
a settlement and to pay the rest of the debt, but the latter and ONEBY have
refused.

*****

66.   C.10/250/46
                     21 July 1698

                     Bill of Complaint of Mary KIRBY, widow,
                     of Lutterworth, Leicestershire, Mary,
                     Anne and Joseph KIRBY, her children,
                     versus Thomas KIRBY and William ILIFFE.

The plaintiffs are Mary KIRBY, widow and relict of Joseph KIRBY, deceased,
late of Lutterworth, Leicestershire, malster, and Mary KIRBY, Anne KIRBY
and Joseph KIRBY their children. Joseph KIRBY in his lifetime was seised in
reversion in fee expectant on the death of Sarah FREER, widow, of half a
messuage and lands etc. in Castle Bromwich, Warwickshire, worth £25 a year.
Thomas KIRBY, of Lutterworth, yeoman, brother of Joseph KIRBY, the father,
was seised of the other half of the messuage on similar terms. Joseph KIRBY
made a will on 10 October 1690 by which he devised the moiety of the property
to William ILIFFE, Apothecary, of Lutterworth, and to Thomas KIRBY, his
brother in trust to sell the property and out of the money raised to pay his
widow Mary £30 and his daughters Mary, Anne and Elizabeth (since deceased)
£30 each within twelve months after the sale of the premises. If any of the
legatees should die before the premises were sold the share of her so dying
to be divided among the survivors. Any surplus from the sale money remaining
after the above legacies had been paid to be given to Joseph KIRBY the son.
Mary was appointed executrix, and proved the will after her husband's death.
Sarah FREER died three years ago, having had an estate for life in the premises
Before her death one John SADLER, the tenant of the premises, was in occupation, and the plaintiffs expected the trustees to proceed with the sale of the
property. But Thomas KIRBY, the testators's brother now claims ownership
of all the property, and persuaded John SADLER to attorne tenant to him on

124

the death of Sarah FREER, and has taken the rents and profits from the whole ever since. This prevents any purchaser from buying the property and the plaintiffs from receiving their legacies.

28 October 1698 at Birmingham

Answer of Thomas KIRBY and John SADLER
to the Bill of Complaint of Mary KIRBY.

They do not believe that Joseph KIRBY, the father was seised in fee expectant upon the death of Sarah FREER of half the premises. They know nothing about Joseph KIRBY'S will, neither of them ever having seen it. If Joseph did leave his half of the premises in the will, it is null and void, for he never had any power to devise it. The lands belonged to John Frederick FREER of Birmingham, Warwicks. gent, who settled them on Sarah, his late wife, for her life, and, failing any other settlement by John Frederick FREER, they ought to come to the defendant Thomas KIRBY as next of kin of John Frederick FREER. He therefore claims the whole estate, although he has heard that John FREER devised it half and half in his will to this defendant and the late Joseph KIRBY, though he has never been able to see the will. If the plaintiffs have any title, it arises under the will of John FREER, and if they can produce it he will concede their title to the same. Sarah FREER died about a fortnight before Lady Day last past. Thomas has received half the rents since her death and the other half is in the hands of John SADLER, who is ready to give it to the plaintiffs if they can prove title. The yearly rent is £20 per annum.

10 November 1698 at Lutterworth

Answer of William ILIFFE to the Bill of
Complaint of Mary KIRBY.

He believes Joseph enjoyed the reversionary interest in half the premises, and thinks the annual value was £10 or £12. He thinks Joseph did give his half to Thomas in trust to sell for the benefit of his wife and children. He thinks Sarah FREER died about 3 years ago. John SADLER was the tenant at the time of Sarah's death and since, but what he has done with the rent, he does not know. He has never received any of it. He is prepared to fulfil the trust, but is hindered from doing so by the other defendants who make frivolous excuses and refuse to come to terms.

*****

C.22/109/13   See C10/250/46

Interrogatories to be administered to
witnesses on behalf of Thomas KERBY
and other defendants, versus Mary
KERBY, widow.

1. Do you know the parties to the suit, did you know
    John Frederick FREER and Sarah FREER, his late
    wife, both deceased, and what relation was Thomas
    KERBY to John Frederick FREER ?

2. Do you know a certain messuage and lands in Castle
    Bromwich in the tenure of the defendant SADLER,
    and what is its yearly value ?

3. Do you know that the defendant Thomas KIRBY was
    ever tendered a copy of the will of Joseph KIRBY,
    the plaintiff Mary's late husband; did he ever see
    the original will or hear its contents, if so where,
    when and before whom, who was present ?

4. Did you ever search for the original will of John
    Frederick FREER and could you obtain a sight
    of it ?

5. Do you know of any offers Thomas KIRBY has made
    and when to the plaintiffs in case they should produce
    the will of John Frederick FREER to be perused by
    the defendant's counsel ? What answer was given ?
    Did the defendant offer to refer the matter to plain-
    tiff's Counsel ?

Depositions taken at the house of Francis
POTTER in Birmingham on 21 April 1699
before Edward HARE, Joseph COX and
Christopher HOCKE.

Moreton SLANEY of Birmingham,
gent, aged 43. Ex parte defendant.

4. About Easter Term a year ago he was employed to
    draw a conveyance of some lands near Birmingham
    agreed to be sold by John KIRBY, the defendant's
    brother to John LOUENS Esq. which were formerly
    the lands of John Frederick FREER and devised by
    him in his will to the said John KIRBY. In order to
    make clear the title, he was ordered by John KIRBY
    to search in the Registers of the Prerogative Court
    of Canterbury, where he was informed the will was
    proved in order to take a copy of it, but he diligently
    searched and could find no such will.

Elizabeth HUNT wife of William HUNT
of Aston, Warwickshire, aged 50.

5. One Mr. NELSON, the plaintiff Mary KIRBY'S brother
    at his sister's request came to Birmingham with the
    defendant Thomas KIRBY in order to put an end to the
    matter in question and Thomas KIRBY, in her presence,
    offered to produce FREER'S will to prove his title.
    Mr. NELSON said the will was in the Prerogative Court
    of Canterbury, but Thomas said his attorney had searched
    for it there without success.

John SADLER of Castle Bromwich,
husbandman, aged 40.

5. Last Lady Day he paid Thomas KERBY some rent
    for the lands he then held of him, who said that if
    Mary KIRBY could show a copy of John Frederick
    FREER'S will to prove her title he would not
    obstruct her. He therefore told Mary what Thomas
    had said, but she said Thomas had been cross with
    her and that she would not produce it.

Thomas BAREBONE of Castle Bromwich,
nailer, aged 45.

5. Corroborates the last deponent.

William HIGGISON als COOPER of Frankley,
Worcestershire, husbandman, aged 56.

1. He knows all the parties except William ILIFFE.
    Thomas KIRBY is second cousin to John Frederick
    FREER.

Joseph COOPER of Birmingham,
whitesmith, aged 70.

1. Confirms the last deponent and says Thomas is
    first or second cousin to FREER and his heir
    at law.

Interrogatories on behalf of Mary KIRBY, widow,
Mary, Anne and Joseph KIRBY, her children,
infants, plaintiffs.

1. Do you know that the defendant John SADLER has
    attorned tenant to the defendant Thomas KIRBY for
    the lands in question; what security has Thomas
    given SADLER to indemnify him from all damage
    that may arise from such attornment ?

2. Did you ever see the probate of the will of John
    Frederick FREER, when and where ?

3. What other thing have you seen or heard relative
    to this cause ?

Moreton SLANEY

1. He does not know that SADLER attorned tenant to
    Thomas, or that Thomas gave him any security.

2. Having unsuccessfully searched in the Prerogative
    Court of Canterbury for the will he was afterwards
    told it was in the custody of one Ambrose FOXALL
    of Birmingham to whom one Mr. VAUGHTON (a
    servant to Mr. JENNINGS) applied himself that this

deponent might have a look at it. He was ultimately
allowed to see that part of the will which concerned
John KIRBY and the lands in question. Mr. FOXALL
refused to let him have a copy of the will, and told
him it had been proved in the Prerogative Court of
Canterbury.

*****

58.   C.9/472/40
                12 January 1711/12

                Bill of Complaint of Valentine BREWIS of
                Aldgate, London, distiller, versus Thomas
                KIRBY, yeoman.

In February 1707/8 the plaintiff purchased a messuage and lands in Claycoten,
Northants, then in the possession of the defendant as tenant at will, who had
married the plaintiff's sister. On 24 February 1708/9 the plaintiff agreed to
let the defendant continue tenant at the rent of £22 p.a. for one year. Rent
to be paid half-yearly and if the midsummer instalment were unpaid by Christmas the defendant was to pay in addition one pot of butter weighing 12 lb. to
be delivered to the plaintiff in London. The defendant was to keep the property
in repair and not to plough up pasture or fell timber. No agreement in writing.
The defendant has felled timber, spoiled hedges and walls and threatens to
plough meadow and pasture. He asked for an injunction restraining the defendant from committing waste and that he be subpoenaed.

*****

59.   REQ 2/181/21
                1594

                Bill of Complaint of William BEYNHAM of
                Boxley, Kent, Esq., versus Robert LANE,
                Humfrey KIRBY and George WINCOTE.

Whereas the Burgesses of the Borough of Warwick were and yet are seised in
their demeasne as of fee of and in the Rectory and Parsonage of Budbrocke in
Budbrooke, Hampton Curlewe and Norton Curlewe in the County of Warwick
with appurtenances etc. etc., they did by their indenture dated 10 July 25
Elizabeth (1582) grant it to Your Highness' subject (the plaintiff) for the term
of 20 years for the rents and dues specified in the said indenture. Whereupon
Your Highness' subject entered into possession and enjoyed it until by casual
means the indenture of lease came into the hands of Richard BROOKE, Thomas
BROOKE, Robert LANE, Thomas OLDNEY, Humfrey KIRBEY, George
WINCOTE, William COMMANDER and Walter BAKER, who by colour of having
the indenture of lease, wrongfully, and without any other title, about Barthol-

omewtide next ensuing the date of the indenture, entered upon possession, and took the rents and profits for the next ten years in such a cunning manner that he is unable to discover who took them. He is remediless and craves for an action of trespass to be brought against the aforesaid.

27 Jan 37 Elizabeth

Answers of Robert LANE, Humfrey KIRBY
and George WINCOTE.

They do not believe the Burgesses of Warwick were seised of the Rectory of Budbrooke. They say that to their knowledge the plaintiff never was possess-ed of the Rectory nor had ever any such lease made to him, and they certainly have not in their possession any such indenture of lease as is surmised in the bill. They say the whole bill is false and untrue and pray to be excused of giving further answer to it.

*****

REQ 2/99/4
1 November 1564

Bill of Complaint of Thomas COGAN,
versus John KIRBY and Marcus DINGLEY.

Letter from Mayor and Aldermen of Oxford

They request that the suit between their neighbour Thomas COGGEN and Markes DINGLIE and John KYRBYE, Citizen of London be deferred until next term since Thomas COGGEN is sick.

Bill of Complaint of Thomas COGAN

The plaintiff lent Christopher CARY, late of London, Bachelor of Physick, deceased, the brother of Alice, the plaintiff's wife, £15, and sold him certain silks linen cloth and other wares and victuals for £10 15s. 0d. The plaintiff further lent him certain plate, goods, chattels and utensils (viz. one dozen silver spoons and one salt gilt, with a cover, weighing 29 oz. 3 quarters and a half, two feather beds with bolsters, furniture and apparel and other house-hold goods, such as brass, pewter and napery) which were worth at least £30, of all which an inventory was made. Christopher CARY died and, as if aff-irmed by John KIRBY and Marcus DINGLEY, he made his will, appointing them executors, by which means they obtained possession of the goods above. Christopher CARY'S proper goods were worth £200, which is sufficient to discharge all his debts. The plaintiff has lost his part of the inventory, and has requested the repayment of the £15 15s. 0d. and the return of his goods, but they refuse. The plaintiff has no specialty for the £15 15s. 0d. and therefore has no remedy at the common law.

22 November 1564

Answer of John KIRBYE and Markes DINGLEY
to the Bill of Complaint of Thomas COGAN.

The bill is untrue, uncertain and insufficient in law. Christopher CARY made his will on 31 August 1563, appointing defendants his executors. After his death KIRBY refused to act as executor, so Markes DINGLEY proved the will. He has not had any of Christopher CARY'S goods in his possession other than one dozen silver spoons, the gilt silver salt with a cover and certain old brass and pewter, which Christopher CARY showed to John KIRBY on his death bed and willed that the executors should return them to the plaintiff. Markes DINGLEY has been willing to return them upon any sufficient discharge. He denies knowledge of other loans, and denies that he has the inventory.

25 November 1564

Replication of Thomas COGAN to the
Answer of the defendants.

The goods of Christopher CARY came into the hands of the said KIRBY after his death and remain in his possession and in the possession of Marcus DINGLEY, wherefore KIRBY is also chargeable. The defendants had goods of Christopher CARY to the value of £230. Marcus DINGLEY would not deliver the items mentioned in the answer without a general acquittance from the plaintiff.

31 January 1564/5

Rejoinder of John KIRBY and Marcus DINGLEY
to the Replication of the plaintiff.

They offer to prove the statements made in their answer and deny the allegations in the replication.

.. February 1564/5

Surrejoinder of Thomas COGAN

Avers and maintains that the statements in the bill of complaint and replication are just and true.

13 February 1564/5

Writ of Privy Seal appointing John KENNELL D.C.L,
Richard ATKINSON, and John WAIGHT gent,
Commissioners to take depositions on behalf of
Thomas COGAN.

Undated

Interrogatories to witnesses on behalf of
Thomas COGAN

1.   Did you know Christopher CARY ?

2.   Were you familiarly acquainted with him ?

3.   When did he die; what goods had he ?

4.   Do you know John KIRBY and Marcus DINGLEY;
     were they executors of Christopher CARY ?

5. Did they make an inventory of Christopher CARY'S goods; were any goods omitted ?

6. What was omitted ?

7. Was there omitted :- one chain of gold, a silver pot, certain rings (viz.) a ring with a diamond stone, a gold ring with a Topasyne stone, a gold ring with a Turkes (turquoise), a gold ring with a square seal graven with a bird called a signett, a gold ring called a Cornelles graven with a pold head called a Signet, a gold ring enamelled, a gold ring with hand in hand, a precious stone called an Agatt, a pair of virginals, a great crystal glass, two new Spanish leather jerkins, a great chest wherein linen did lie, a new rapier with a scabbard of velvet, a scots dagger gilt with a dudgyn handle, all the wainscot in the chambers, hall and portholes ?

8. Did Christopher CARY possess a lease of the house in which he lived for a term of years yet enduring ?

9. Is the house sold; to whom; for how much; when ?

10. What goods, as wainscot, books, hangings, mats and globes, were sold with the house ?

11. Was it sold to satisfy the debts of Christopher CARY ?

12. Was Christopher CARY indebted to you at the time of his death ?

13. Was any of the debt repaid by Christopher CARY in his lifetime; did Christopher CARY pawn one chain or any other thing for the said debt ?

14. If any goods were delivered to you in person, how much did they weigh; have you sold them ?

15. Was Christopher CARY indebted to you at the time of his death; for how much ?

16. What have you received for the same debt since Christopher CARY'S death, in money or in goods; from whom ?

17. What parcels of the goods of Christopher CARY were undervalued in the inventory ?

26 March 1565

Depositions of witnesses on behalf of Thomas COGAN, plaintiff taken at Westminster.

131

William WANTON, St. Mary Woolchurch, London,
grocer, aged 26.

1. Knew Christopher CARY about 1 year.

2. Was well acquainted; they met together as occasion
   of business required.

3. Christopher CARY died in the plague time about
   two years ago; does not know the value of his
   goods.

4. Has known John KIRBY and Marcus DINGLEY for
   3 or 4 years; knows only by report that they were
   executors of Christopher CARY;

5. Knows of the inventory only by report.

6. Nothing.

7. Deponent had a gold chain of Christopher CARY for
   £8; has seen Christopher CARY wear a ring with a
   topaz, but does not know what became of it.

8. Christopher CARY possessed a lease of his house;
   deponent lent him money to buy it.

9. Deponent bought the lease from DINGLEY and allowed
   him £60 for it.

10. Deponent had all the wainscot about the house and
    has paid for it, but the landlord said that he should
    not remove it at the end of the lease, so deponent
    intends to have his money allowed again for it;
    deponent bought Christopher CARY'S books, hang-
    ings, mats and one globe, paying 20 marks for the
    books and globe, and 40s. for the hangings and mats.

11. Christopher CARY owed the deponent about £93; all
    the goods which deponent received from DINGLEY
    were to satisfy the debt; the debts were all owed
    for money lent.

12. Christopher CARY laid the lease of the house in this
    deponent's hand when he borrowed the money; deponent
    returned the lease to Christopher CARY when he demand-
    ed it.

13. Christopher CARY delivered the chain to deponent for
    a debt of £8; executors allowed deponent to keep it.

14. Deponent sold the chain to one PIGOTT a goldsmith
    for £8.

Christopher VITTALL, St. Martin-Orgar,
joiner, aged 50.

15. Christopher CARY owed deponent £3 14s. 4d. for
    one long drawing table price 50s; one joined chair,
    6s. 8d; one court cupboard, 6s. 8d; one long
    form, 4s certain old work, 3s; one frame for a
    fold table, 4s. 4d.

16. He received the goods again after the death of
    Christopher CARY from Marcus DINGLEY, except
    the old work; deponent gave Marcus DINGLEY 8s.
    for returning them.

17. Deponent saw an inventory of Christopher CARY'S
    goods in which the goods he had sold to Christopher
    CARY were under valued by 19s.

William BROKER, St. Saviours, Southwark,
tailer, aged 62.

1. Knew Christopher CARY for two years.

2. Christopher CARY was at this deponent's house once
    a week or once a fortnight since deponent made his
    clothes.

3. Christopher CARY died in the plague two years ago.

4. Christopher CARY made John KIRBY and Marcus
    DINGLEY his executors.

5. John KIRBY and Marcus DINGLEY made an inventory
    of Christopher CARY'S goods, certain rings were
    left out.

8. Christopher CARY had the lease of a house in which
    he lived in Colman St. London; deponent was present
    when £60 was paid for the lease; lease was for 21
    years.

9. Lease was appraised in money at £40, and allowed
    to one WANTON for debts due to him.

10. All the books were sold to WANTON for 20 marks.

11. Christopher CARY owed this deponent £9 9s. 0d;
    when deponent went to DINGLEY for payment,
    DINGLEY said that Christopher CARY'S goods
    should be appraised again since they were appraised
    under value; deponent has not yet been paid.

12. The debt grew for making certain garments for
    Christopher CARY as for certain linen cloth del-
    ivered to him for shirts and sheets.

17. One gown in the inventory which deponent made not
    one half year before Christopher CARY'S death,
    which had 4 yards of black puck cloth at 20s. the
    yard, and the same gown was faced with pampillion

and lined through with black cotton; it was worth
£5, but was appraised at 40s. And another gown
of black puck faced with satin and lined with bayes,
worth £4 was appraised at 40s; and a carpet which
Christopher CARY bought for 17s. not half a year
before was appraised at 5s. If the goods had been
appraised at their true value there would have been
enough to satisfy the debts.

Undated

Further interrogatories on behalf of Thomas
COGAN plaintiff.

1. Do you know the parties ?

2. Did you know Christopher CARY ?

3. Do you know of any wares sold by Thomas COGAN
   to Christopher CARY ?

4. How much did Christopher CARY owe the plaintiff ?

5. Do you know of goods of Thomas COGAN which
   remained in the house of Christopher CARY at
   his death, viz., two featherbeds, 2 bolsters, 2
   down pillows, one counterpoint or arras coverlet lined with canvass, one spanish cloak of french
   cloth faced with sarcenet, one spanish cloak of
   frisendowe faced with sarcenet, one spanish frized
   leather jerkin cut guarded with velvet, one black
   cloak, a desk ('dext') with a lock, 44 pieces of
   pewter weighing $\frac{3}{4}$ cwt. and 4 lb.; 11 pieces of
   brass and one tinned water laver weighing $1\frac{1}{2}$ cwt.
   and 7 lb ?

6. Whose goods were these ?

7. Did the plaintiff lend these to Christopher CARY of
   good will only ?

8. Were goods in Christopher CARY'S house at his death;
   to whom did they come after his death ?

9. Did the goods come to John KIRBY and Marcus DINGLEY ?

10. Did John KIRBY render to Thomas ROWE to the use of
    the plaintiff the frisindowe cloak above; what other
    goods did Thomas ROWE see in the house ?

11. Did you see a leather jerkin, a coverlet, two feather
    beds, 2 bolsters, 2 pillows and desk, and are these
    the goods of the plaintiff, your master ?

12. Were any of the plaintiff's goods put in Christopher
    CARY'S inventory as part of testator's property ?

134

13. Did KIRBY and DINGLEY know that these goods were the plaintiff's ?

14. Did you demand the goods of KIRBY and DINGLEY in the name of the plaintiff ?

15. How much money did Christopher CARY confess on his death bed that he owed the plaintiff for proceeding Bachelor of Physick at Balliol College, Oxford ?

16. How much money did Christopher CARY say on his death bed that he had left to the executors to pay his legacies and debts ?

17. Did you hear the plaintiff say that he had left in goods only to the value of £20C to discharge his debts and legacies ?

18. Was Christopher CARY possessed of one gold chain etc. (gocds as listed in interr. 7 of first set), including wainscot in hall, parlour, portals and chambers, and one hundred foot of glass ?

19. How much money did Christopher CARY have at his death ?

20. What money of Christopher CARY'S did you have at his death and to whom did you deliver it ?

21. Did Christopher CARY have a lease of his house ?

22. To whom was lease, chain of gold, silver pot, wainscot, portals of wainscot and glass sold ?

23. Were any gocds omitted from the inventory ?

24. Is the will now produced the will of Christopher CARY ?

25. What goods of Christopher CARY were given away after his death but before the will was proved ?

26. What goods were undervalued ?

27. How much did Christopher CARY owe you at his death ?

28. What goods, books, household stuff, apparel, implements of household and implements of astronomy were sold or delivered as payment of debt to you ?

29. Were you paid anything in part payment for debts in the life time of Christopher CARY, what have you received since his death ?

27 March and 2 April 1565

Further depositions of witnesses taken
at Oxford by John KENALL D.C.L.,
Richard ATKYNSON and John WAYTE,
gent, on behalf of Thomas COGAN of
Oxford, plaintiff.

Anne GRESSHAM, Ascot in Great Milton,
Oxon., before that in London for 14 years
and born at Basseldon, Berks., widow,
aged 40.

1. Knows parties.

2. Knew Christopher CARY; lived with him in London
   as his servant from Easter last until his death,
   which was about Bartholomew tide.

3. Nothing.

4. Heard Christopher CARY say divers times that he
   was much in debt to Thomas COGAN.

5. 6. Knew all the goods to be the goods of the plaintiff,
   at the time of the death of Christopher CARY,
   except the black cloak last mentioned.

8. 9. The goods were in Christopher CARY'S house at
   his death; the keys of the street door were delivered to KIRBY and DINGLEY before Christopher
   CARY'S death, the goods being then in the house;
   the day after Christopher CARY'S death, KIRBY
   and DINGLEY had the rest of the keys.

12. Inventory was made; knows nothing of the contents.

13. KIRBY and DINGLEY knew before probate of the will
    that the said goods were the goods of the plaintiff.

14. She did not.

16. Christopher CARY said to her on his death bed that
    he had left to his executors goods to the value of
    £200, saying that by that time that they have done
    that that I have appointed them they shall not have
    much left for themselves.

18. Christopher CARY was possessed of the goods ment-
    ioned; in the chest were: 6 pair of holland sheets;
    3 pair of canvass sheets; 12 diaper napkins; a
    diaper table cloth 4 ells long, all new; 2 towels of
    diaper 4 ells long; 2 table cloths of canvass, 2 towels
    of normandy canvass, 6 canvass napkins; a pair of
    new pillow beers; 8 'shourtes' worth 10s. apiece,
    which all came into the hands of KIRBY and DINGLEY.

20. Had no money in her hands, otherwise knows nothing
    except John JENNYNGES had any.

136

21. He had a lease for 30 years.

22. Has heard that the wainscot and glass and the
     lease were sold to Mr. WANTON by the executors.

26. All things in the inventory are far under-appraised.

27. Christopher CARY owed deponent 16s. 8d. at his
     death for her wages, which she received from
     DINGLEY.

John HODGESSON, M.A. one of King Edward IV's
chaplains at Windsor College, having been there
7 years and before that at Oxford University,
aged 40.

1. Has known Thomas COGAN for 16 years and KIRBY
    and DINGLEY for 2 years.

2. Knew Christopher CARY for 20 years; they were
    students and fellows together in Brasenose for about
    10 years and afterwards were chamber fellows in
    White Hall, Oxford about 1½ years.

4. Christopher CARY while his chamber fellow at White
    Hall in private communication had between them did
    often and sundry times declare to him that he had no
    help to find him in Oxford but his brother-in-law,
    Thomas COGAN, and that he owed Thomas COGAN
    £10 at least. Since deponent has been at Windsor,
    Christopher CARY visiting him while travelling
    between London and Oxford, often said that Thomas
    COGAN did continue still his chief friend in Oxford
    and without his help he had not been able to tarry in
    Oxford and that he did grow daily more and more into
    his debt.

5. At Easter, 12 months ago, deponent came to Christopher
    CARY'S London house and said to him 'You have a tryme
    house & well stuffed with implements', and Christopher
    CARY said 'yt is soo, for I thanke my brother COGAN
    muche of this stuffe and implementes be his & I borowed
    yt of hym'.

John JENNYNGES, aged 30, dwelling in London
for two years and somewhat more and before that
in Oxford for 14 years.

1. Has known Thomas COGAN for 14 years in Oxford
    and KIRBY and DINGLEY for 2 years in London.

2. Was Christopher CARY'S servant for one year in
    London.

4. Talking to Christopher CARY a little before his death, Christopher CARY gave him a ring to deliver to his sister HARPER and confessed that he owed Thomas COGAN a certain sum of money.

5. Deponent fetched from Thomas COGAN'S house in Oxford to house of Christopher CARY about 2 years ago, 2 feather beds, 2 bolsters, 2 pillows, a coverlet; other goods listed in this interrogatory were in Christopher CARY'S house at his death, with a locked desk.

7. Goods mentioned in answer to interrogatory 5 were lent to Christopher CARY.

16. Christopher CARY confessed that it was not so well with him in goods as some did think and that he had put KIRBY and DINGLEY in trust and that they had promised that they would disburse £10 apiece rather than he would be evil spoken of.

18. Knows of the goods specified - the chain of gold and silver pot were said by KIRBY to have been mortgaged; Christopher CARY had given him the dagger with a doygin shaft long before his death.

19. Christopher CARY had not above £3 in ready money of which KIRBY left part with Christopher CARY, being sick.

22. Has heard that William WANTON of London apothecary had the lease etc.

23. Deponent gave away 2 gold rings by command of executors (?), a piece of unicorn horn, a stone called aggott, a satin doublet, a coat, a pair of hose, a pair of virginals, a black velvet waist girdle, 2 English ribbons, girdle and waistcoat and glass, boots, spurs, 3 mats, a globe, a washing bowl.

25. Christopher CARY gave him two rings, one for his sister HARPER and one for Elizabeth AUSTIN, which were delivered by consent of the executors, with a felt hat which they gave to this deponent.

26. Certain articles are undervalued.

27. Christopher CARY owed BRUKER the tailor in Southwark £8 4s. 2d., to HARRISON in Cheapside mercer for wares, £5; and to this deponent 10s. for money paid; knows of no other debts.

29. Christopher CARY gave this deponent a ring of gold worth 14s., which deponent kept for his debt.

George HILLIARD, mercer, dwelling in Oxford
10 years, aged 24.

1. Has known the plaintiff for about 11 years, since
    he was his apprentice for 9 years, ending at Mid-
    summer 1563; knows KIRBY and DINGLEY by
    sight for 3 years.

2. Has known Christopher CARY as long as he has
    known the plaintiff.

3. Christopher CARY when at Brasenose about 7 years
    ago admitted £10 debt to the plaintiff; deponent
    delivered to Christopher CARY at his proceeding
    Bachelor of Physick certain goods of the plaintiff's.

5. Remembers that these goods came from the plaintiff's
    house, except the cloak of French cloth.

William NOBLE, citizen and mercer of Oxford
aged 30, dwelling in Oxford 20 years.

1. Knew the plaintiff for 18 years, knew DINGLEY
    about 12 years.

2. Knew Christopher CARY for 18 years.

3. Knew of goods to the value of £10 lent or sold to
    Christopher CARY.

Thomas ROWE, aged 21, dwelling at Oxford
8 years.

1. Knew the plaintiff since he has dwelt with him 8
    years; knew KIRBY and DINGLEY about 3 years.

2. Knew Christopher CARY for about 8 years.

3. Knows that Christopher CARY had goods of the
    plaintiff's shop when he proceeded Bachelor of
    Physick at Balliol, has heard that these were
    worth £8.

5. Knows the goods listed to be the goods of the
    plaintiff.

13. Before probate of will this deponent demanded the
    goods listed in 5th article on behalf of his master.

Thomas WANTON, M.A., Fellow of Merton
College, aged 26.

1. Has known the plaintiff for 7 years in Oxford; has known KIRBY and DINGLEY 9 years in London.

18. His brother William WANTON bought the lease from Marcus DINGLEY.

22. Lease was sold for £60.

28. William WANTON bought 14 score books of Christopher CARY'S and one globe along with the lease etc. for £96 and this deponent bought the lease, wainscot and glass for £6 and 20 marks for the books and globe; also bought other goods to the value of £13 18s. 4d.

*****

71.   C.21/A 17/28
         10 and 11 Charles I 1634-5

         The Attorney General, versus Humfry KIRBY, gent., Edward BEST and George WATT.

         (Brief summary only)

The Corporation of Warwick's claim against that of the King to present to the Rectory of Rushock.

         Witnesses
              Thos. HEATH, Borough of Warwick, gent. 86
              Wm. SPICER, of Stone, Worcs., clerk, 48
              George WEALE, Borough of Warwick, gent, 48 yrs.
              Gerrard SAUNDERS, Borough of Warwick, mercer, 68 yrs.
              Richard YARDLEY, Borough of Warwick, gent., 71
              Roger ECLES, Borough of Warwick, apothecary, 35

*****

72.   C 2 Chas. I K 20/50
         November 1638

         Bill of Complaint of John KERBY of Rivenhall, Essex, versus, Richard BROCK and Elizabeth, his wife.

John KERBY of Rivenhall, Essex, son and heir of John KERBY, deceased, and of Elizabeth, his wife, is the plaintiff. Humfrey KERBY, the plaintiff's grandfather, was in his lifetime lawfully seised of lands etc. known as New

Lesues in the parish of Tanworth, Warwickshire and also of a messuage
known as "The Sign of the Angel" in Juristreet, in the Borough of Warwick,
and also of a barn standing over against Saint Mary's Buttes in Warwick.
Being so seised, in consideration of a marriage to be solemnised between
John KERBY,.his son and heir apparent (the plaintiff's father) and one
Elizabeth ROE, by a deed dated 31 January 2 Jas. I (1604) he granted and
consigned to one Richard YARDLEY of Warwick, yeoman, and one Richard
ROE, also of Warwick, butcher, all the above recited premises for the
several purposes shown in the deed to the use of the said Humfrey KERBY
during his lifetime, and after his decease to the use of the said John KERBY,
the plaintiff's father and the heirs of his body lawfully begotten on the body
of Elizabeth with remainder to the right heirs of the said John for ever. As
for the messuage known as the Angel and the barn similar provisions and
conditions were made as above. There was a proviso that if John senior
should die before Elizabeth, then the feoffees (Richard YARDLEY and Richard
ROE) should stand seised of the Angel and the barn to the use of Elizabeth
during her natural life, provided she paid the heirs of the said John KERBY
an annual sum of 40/- and kept the Angel and the barn in good repair. Shortly
after making the deed Humfrey KERBY, the grandfather died. After his death
John KERBY, his son, entered into possession of all the aforesaid premises
by force of the deed of feoffment. He died in May 1617 so seised, and Elizabeth the plaintiff's mother survived him. The land and tenement in Tanworth
did and ought to descend to the plaintiff and he ought to have had the yearly
sum of 40/- apid to him out of the Angel and the barn in Warwick. But shortly
after the death of John KERBY senior (the plaintiff then being an infant of
tender years) Elizabeth, his widow, married one Richard BROOKE. After
the marriage BROCKE got into his hands all the aforesaid deeds and writings
and withheld the payment of the annuity of 40/- a year, entered upon the land
at Tanworth and felled, sold and carried away above 100 trees. He also devised various secret and fraudulent leases thereof with others in order to defeat the plaintiff of his just and lawful title, and moreover they, Richard
BROOKE and Elizabeth his wife, have suffered the Angel and the barn to fall
into great ruin and decay.

He asks the Court to restore the Tanworth land and the annuity to him.

Sworn 9 January 1638/9 at Warwick

Answer of Richard BROOKE and Elizabeth,
his wife, to the Bill of Complaint of John KERBY.

Richard BROOKE says it is true that Humfrey KERBY was seised of the
closes or lessows in Tanworth, and of the "Sign of the Angel" in Warwick
and of the barn over against St. Mary's Butts, and that he made over these
premises in the manner set out in the bill and died shortly afterwards. He
married Elizabeth some twenty years since. When, about 6 months ago, the
plaintiff claimed the rents and profits of the Tanworth land and an annuity of
40/- out of the messuage and barn in Warwick, he admitted that Elizabeth had
a life interest in the property. Richard BROOKE then examined the deeds in
question and found that the Tanworth lands were not assured upon Elizabeth
for her life, but descended to the plaintiff as heir at law to John KERBY, son
of Humfrey KERBY begotton of the body of Elizabeth. But he goes on to say
that until that time, which is but half a year since, he always conceived that
the Tanworth lands, as well as the messuage and barn, were estated upon
Elizabeth for her life, nor did he know till then that the messuage and barn
were charged with such an annuity of 40/- payable to the plaintiff since the

death of his father, for that Elizabeth at the time when he was a suitor to her, and since they married, said that all the premises concerned were settled upon her by Humfrey KERBY for the term of her life. He believes that Elizabeth herself thought so too. He was also ignorant of the annuity of 40/- payable to the plaintiff for he had never perused the jointure deed until half a year ago. He says that if he had known of the annuity, he would have long since claimed it (as he now does by this his answer) towards part payment for the great expense he was put to for the diet, eduction and clothing of the plaintiff, which he was in no way bound to provide. He says that the estate which he had in marriage with Elizabeth, the plaintiff's mother, has not by much counterbalanced the charges which he has been put to in eduction and bringing up and placing forth of the plaintiff and three of his younger brothers. John KERBY died intestate about 22 years since of mean and weak estate and endebted much more than all his personal estate was able to satisfy. He left Elizabeth and her four young children with no other means to support them but the benefit of the said messuage, barn and lands at Tanworth, which do in all amount to a matter of but 20 marks per annum.

The Tanworth lands were, by the advice of her friends long before Elizabeth married him, let out for eleven years without rent for the consideration of £22, which sum went towards the satisfaction of some part of the debts of her first husband, John KERBIE. Consequently for the space of eleven years after the death of John KERBIE, no rent was received from the Tanworth lands, but since the end of the term of 11 years he, Richard BROOKE, has received a rent of 40/- a year and no more. The plaintiff was the eldest of the children of John KERBIE, and was aged about 9 years and the others much younger, so that the cost of bringing them up in a decent manner amounted to £20 and more, which he paid. The plaintiff himself, ever since his father's death until about 4 years since, did every year, even when he spent least, stand him and Elizabeth in much more than 40/-, the amount received from the rent of the Tanworth land. Considering how well the defendant dealt with the plaintiff and his three brothers, who were left without any portion or provision at all, he conceives it somewhat hard that his love and respect towards the plaintiff and his brothers should receive no other acceptance with him but to be required with this unkind suite. If the plaintiff were answered with all the Tanworth rent since his father's death (which is more than he, the defendant, has received) and also the arrears of the annuity (but discounting the cost the defendant has been put to in bringing up the four children) it would appear that the plaintiff was indebted to the defendant, and not the other way.

Elizabeth, for her part, says that she always thought until lately that the Tanworth lands were estated upon her for her life as well as the "Angel" and the barn, for that both her late husband, John KERBIE, and the late Humfrey KERBIE, his father, had affirmed so much to her; nor did she take any notice of the annuity of 40/- claimed by the plaintiff, since until lately no one had ever asked for it to be paid. Her first husband died of very weak estate and left four sons, whose education, and especially the plaintiff's education, until of late years, was chargeable to her, and out of her love to her son, the plaintiff, for five years she was a good to him as 40/- per annum over and above the expense and allowance made by her second husband. She therefore can see no reason why the plaintiff should claim arrears of the annuity in view of what he has already received. They both deny they have felled any trees or sold timber from the Tanworth land.

Richard BROOKE says that about nine years since (1629 or 1630), the plaintiff being moved to give way to the sale of some underwood birch, shallowes, alders and such like then growing on the Tanworth land, and some roots of

some old decayed oaks that were fit only for firewood in order to raise
some money for the placing forth of two of the plaintiff's brothers as app-
rentices, he, the plaintiff, willingly gave his consent thereunto. Thereupon the underwood and roots were cut down, but no timber, and the plaintiff, then being about 21 years old, was on the land when the wood was felled
and then took no exception to what was done. He further says that upon the
sale of the said wood there was raised the sum of 20 marks which was disbursed for the advancement and benefit of the plaintiff's two brothers, William
KERBY and Humphrey KERBY. Richard BROOKES maintains his right to
hold the deeds in question so long as his wife shall live so that he may establish his title to the premises, and he denies any fraudulent intentions. As
for the barn, they say an exchange was made for a more commodious one with
one Timothy WAGSTAFFE, deceased, but that the exchange was done inform-
ally and there was no transfer deed. They deny the other charges, but say
that for the sake of peace they will be content to remit the surplus of what
they consider the plaintiff owes them for his education etc., they will yield
up the Tanworth land and pay henceforth the annuity of 40/- if the plaintiff
will drop his other claims.

*****

C.7/201/21
20 January 1653

Bill missing

Damaged.   The Answer of Margaret HEYNES,
                widow, and of Enoch HEYNES, an
                infant, her son, to the Bill of Complaint
                of William KIRBY.

They say it may be true that Edward KIRBY, father of the plaintiff, and the
plaintiff were seised of the messuage mentioned in the bill at the time stated,
and that they may, for £100, have conveyed it to Alexander EDWARDS and
Robert MORRELL, They say the plaintiff and his father continued in possession without paying rent for four years, and that they were put into possession by the sheriff on a Writ of Habeas Facias Possessionem. But whether
EDWARDS and MORRELL were given liberty to redeem the principal at any
time they do not know. However, William EDWARDS, son and heir of Alexander EDWARDS, then deceased, and MORRELL sold the property to Robert
HEYNES, deceased, late husband of the defendant for £160. They do not
know what profit EDWARDS and MORRELL made out of the property when it
was in their hands, but believe it was not above 20 marks a year, for shortly
before Robert HEYNES bought it, it was let to three successive tenants one
after another at £5 a year. EDWARDS and MORRELL had tried to let it for
21 years at a rent of £5 per annum without success, because it was in such
a ruinous state. When Robert HEYNES bought it, he had to spend £60 in
repairs to make it sound. Robert HEYNES on his deathbed appointed Margaret
MEYNES to hold the premises until Enoch HEYNES reached the age of 21, he
being now about 17 years old. Robert HEYNES fell violently sick, and did not
have time to make a formal will, consequently, although he intended to leave
the premises to Enoch, yet they descended in law to William HEYNES, his
eldest son and heir. William HEYNES conveyed it in trust for Enoch to John

143

PARSONS of Spernall, Warwickshire, Esq., and William HEYNES, the elder of London, citizen and baker, Enoch to have the use and enjoyment of it for life . . . . indenture of 27th . . . . 1650.

The rest of this document is too fragmentary to allow an accurate summary to be made of it.

*****

74.   C 2 Jas. I K4/59
14 June 1624

Bill of Complaint of Richard KIRBY, Robert KIRBY, Edward KIRBY, Thomas FREEMAN and Alice his wife, Anne KIRBY and Jane KIRBY, all children of the late Edward KIRBY, versus Margaret MASON, widow.

Thomas KIRBIE, uncle of the plaintiffs, died intestate about 13 years since (1611) leaving goods etc. to the value of £1,000. John MYLLER, another of the plaintiffs' uncles, obtained stock from Thomas KIRBY to the value of £57 as a portion for the plaintiffs about 12 years ago, the plaintiffs then being under age, which he put out to interest to be paid to the plaintiffs part and part alike as they reached the age of 21. In order to secure this sum, John MYLLER, about 11 years ago became bound to one John MASON, another of the plaintiffs' uncles, in the sum of £200 and to Gyles HARDING, yet another of the plaintiffs' uncles, either singly or together in trust for the plaintiffs with interest at the rate of 2/- in the pound. MASON and HARDING became bound by another obligation of £200 to MYLLER for the true answering of such part of the stock as should come to his hands. MYLLER, with the consent of MASON and HARDING put forth the money at interest for about 6 years, when the stock was recovered and accounted to amount to about £14 13s. 11d. MYLLER took some new bonds for the same either to himself or HARDINGE, in trust for the plaintiffs. Shortly after MYLLER made his will appointing his wife Mary executrix, and died about 6 years ago (1618) and Mary, his wife, took his place as trustee. She afterwards married one John PRIDDIE, gentleman, who undertook to perform the trust.

MASON, likewise, about 2 years ago (1622) made his will and died leaving Margaret, his wife, as executrix of his will. Margaret proved her husband's will and took upon herself the execution of it and possessed herself of all his goods and chattels, which amounted to much more than his debts and legacies. John PRIDDIE and Mary, his wife, Margaret MASON, widow and Gyles HARDINGE took the bonds, and especially the bonds made to MASON and HARDINGE, the bond made to MYLLER and the stock and became accountable to the plaintiffs for the interest etc.

All the plaintiffs are now over the age of 21 and have asked for the bonds and stock, but have not seen them or received them. The trustees each say that the other has them, and they are unable to get any satisfaction.

Further, one John MYLLER (senior), the plaintiffs' grandfather, made his will about 8 years since (1616) and by it devised £20 to John MYLLER junior,

144

his son, to be used for the benefit of Alice, the plaintiffs' mother, who was the daughter of John MYLLER senior. John MYLLER, junior, proved his father's will, lived for a year and then himself died, and his wife Mary took upon herself the execution of her father-in-law's will.

Alice, the plaintiffs' mother died about 6 years since (1618) and left ten living children, of which the plaintiffs are six. The plaintiffs claim that their share amounts to £30 each at least and ask the trustees to give it to them.

1 October 1624

Answer of Margaret MASON, widow,
to the Bill of Complaint of Richard
KIRBY and others.

Thomas KIRBY had no issue, apart from one brother, Edward KIRBY, now deceased, father of the plaintiffs, and also three sisters, namely Margaret this defendant, Joan, wife of Gyles HARDINGE, and Agnes, late wife of Hugh RATCLIFFE, by whom she had one son, Thomas RATCLIFFE, and two daughters, one of whom was married to John ROSE and one to Matthew ROSE. He lived about the time mentioned in the bill (1611) with his nephew, Thomas RATCLIFFE, and died there possessed of goods amounting to £400 not £1,000 as stated in the bill. Thomas RATCLIFFE took possession of the greater part of Thomas KIRBY'S goods and estate, and in order to avoid legal complications and lawsuits it was agreed between John MASON, Gyles HARDINGS and John MYLLER on the plaintiffs' behalf, and between John and Matthew ROSE, that Letters of Administration should be granted to the sisters of Thomas KIRBY then living, namely Margaret MASON and Joan HARDINGE, and John MASON and Gyles HARDING had the administration in the right of their wives. It was agreed that they should pay one quarter of the goods and debts of Thomas KIRBY to the use of the plaintiffs and the wives of John and Matthew ROSE, one quarter to Thomas RATCLIFFE alone, one quarter to Margaret MASON and one quarter to Joan HARDINGE. John MASON and Gyles HARDINGE became duly bound in various obligations for the perform-ance of the administration and division of the estate. MASON and HARDINGE exhibited an inventory of Thomas KIRBY'S goods amounting to £400 in the Prerogative Court of Canterbury. Accordingly by order of the Prerogative Court of Canterbury two quarters were to be paid to the plaintiffs, as child-ren of Edward KIRBY and to the children of Agnes RATCLIFFE. Accordingly about 10 years ago, John MASON and Gyles HARDINGE paid one quarter to Thomas RATCLIFFE and another quarter to John MYLLER amounting to £74 5s. 2d. to the use of the plaintiffs and of John and Matthew ROSE in right of their wives.

About 12 years since (1612) at the time of the agreement and about the time of the making of the bond of £400 entered into by MASON and HARDINGE to John MYLLER and John ROSE, MYLLER became bound on 29 September 1612 to MASON and HARDINGE in the sum of £200 for the true performance and use of goods to the use of the children of Edward KIRBY, deceased. Upon the payment of the £74 5s. 2d. to John MYLLER and John ROSE to bond entered into by John MASON and Gyles HARDINGE for £400 was cancelled. MASON and HARDINGE gave several new bonds of £50 apiece to pay to John MYLLER for the use of the plaintiffs, and to John amd Matthew ROSE a fourth part of such goods as afterwards should come to them by virtue of the Letters of Administration. The defendant knows of no other bonds concerned with the case. She thinks that upon payment of £74 5s. 2d. which was a full fourth part, it was intended that the fourth part be divided into eight equal parts

and that the plaintiffs being the children of Edward KIRBY were to have six
parts thereof for their several portions. She does not know how John MYLLER
has since disposed of it or what profit he has made. She says that since the
payment of the £74 5s. 2d., 25/- more has been paid to John MYLLER for the
use of the plaintiffs, and to John amd Matthew ROSE, and also £6 14s. 0d.
paid to John PRIDDY (after John MYLLER'S death) being a fourth part of such
goods and debts as have come into the hands of MASON and HARDINGE by
virtue of the Letters of Administration. Thomas KIRBY also had a number
of bad debts which the defendant believes will never now be settled or paid.

*****

75.

C.22/563/41
16 1601-2

Depositions taken at Sturton, Notts. by
.... THORNEHAIGHE and Robert
EYRE, Esqs., on part of the plaintiff,
Robert KIRKBIE, versus John CUTLER,
defendant.

(much damaged)

Nicholas HAMERTON, R.........., Lincs.,
gent, aged 40.

7. Knows that he, having an interest in the lands thereunto
belonging in Southleverton, Notts from William KEYNWORTH
.... John KYRBYE being in possession of part thereof
did by his deed release to ...... (his interest) in the same
about 14 April 1599, to which the deponent agreed that the
said John KIRKBIE should sow the ..... upon the same in
the following year ...... that deponent would either
answer and allow to John KIRKBIE ...... about the same
or take the crop of corn and give to John KIRKBIE the
overplus ...... more than such sums of money due to
deponent by John KIRKBIE, viz £25 ...... the price of
7 quarters of barley at 16s. a quarter. Deponent allowed
John KIRKBIE 14 or .... in consideration of the overplus of the crop.

Last interrogatory :

John KIRKBIE before sowing the crop (sent) ..... SAWER
then servant to this deponent to make known to his master
that ...... the said crop, whereupon deponent appointed
SAWER to deliver to John KIRKBIE ...... seed in need
of for that purpose, which he delivered accordingly.

9. Deponent did now owe John KIRKBIE ..... other than he
has already deposed.

146

Richard HUNT, Southleverton, Notts.,
clerk, aged 65.

1. Knows the parties.

2. Knows of making of the deed of gift, which he wrote.
    It was a conveyance of all the goods and chattels of
    John KIRKBIE. The deed was made between the
    Purification of the Blessed Virgin Mary and the ....
    day of Arpil 1599, delivered by John KIRKBIE to
    John CUTLER the defendant ..... and one Nicholas
    ASTON and others. A groat was paid in name of
    seisin.

3. Knows that John CUTLER, the defendant .... sealed
    and delivered his deed to .... a letter of attorney
    to dispose and sell to his use all the goods and chattels
    given him by the said (John KIRKBIE) by the deed of
    gift.

Alexander CURRIOR, Southleverton,
husbandman.

1. Knows the parties.

3. Knows of the letter of attorney (as a witness) by John
    CUTLER to Thomas SMITH and John ......

5. .... 2 horses and a mare of the said John KIRKBIE'S
    part of the goods and chattels ...... after the letter of
    attorney to Thomas SMITH and John KIRBIE .... also
    knows that one bay stoned horse which was sold by ....
    five pounds was taken by the defendant from the said
    MAWER.

William B(ATER)BIE of Reempton, Notts.,
yeoman.

(End of membrane, what follows is probably his deposition.)

1. Knows parties.

2. About February 2 years past he was requested by
    Robert KIRKBIE plaintiff to go with him to South-
    leverton to John ...... goods of the said John KIRKBIE,
    whither they went. And being ..... the said Robert
    KIRKBIE certaine of the goods and chattels of the said
    John ..... this manner (viz) horses and mares £30,
    kyne (£)8, ... wheat upon the ground £20, pease Garth
    and barley ..... in Southleverton, £15, amounting in
    all to four score pounds .... him for the residue of a
    bond wherein the said John KIRKBY and Robert KIRKBIE
    (as sureties) ..... to the said John CUTLER in £200
    for payment of £100 ..... for £8 which he would have
    for the interest and use of the said four score pounds
    ..... pounds he said he would have away with him.

Upon ..... said John CUTLER, he the said Robert
KIRKBY was willing to accept .... the said CUTLER
the residue of his said debt; CUTLER refused .....
said offer, upon which Robert KIRKBY instantly desired .... the said goods and discharge him of his said
bond, and he the said ...... 20 marks more of his own
goods, or else permit him the said Robert (KIRKBY)
all the residue of his principal debt. But the said
CUTLER accepted ...... goods rise to such a value
did presently after ...... of gift of the said John
KIRKBY of all his said goods and chattels and that ....
the said deed of gift away with him. And he also saith
that it was spoken at ..... John KIRKBY had three bonds
of the sum of £30 of principal debt due ......

6. Being at Southleverton for the purpose abovesaid he
    this (deponent) .... said John CUTLER confess and
    say to the said Robert KIRKBY 'content thy selfe (for
    here is) Goodes inoughe to satisfie me and discharge
    thee. But thy brother ....(that thou shouldest) have
    them. But I can have a deed of Gifte of them and I will
    have it (ere I go)'.

William PORTER, Truswell, Notts.,
yeoman, aged 3..

1. Knows parties.

4. Went with Robert KIRKBY to Southleverton to price
    certain goods of John KIRKBIE'S .... the said John
    CUTLER offered to Robert KIRKBY certain of the
    goods of (John) KIRKBIE'S and valued them himself
    in this manner (viz.) horses and mares, £30; ......
    foals and calves, £7; wheat upon the ground, £20,
    pease .... Garth of the said John KIRKBIE'S farm
    in Southleverton, £15; .... £80 which he said would
    satisfy him for the residue of a bond wherein ......
    and Robert KIRKBY (as surety for the said John) stood
    bound to John CUTLER. Robert KIRKBY was willing
    to accept but John CUTLER refused to proceed. Robert
    KIRKBY then desired him to take the said goods and
    discharge him of the bond and he would give him 20
    marks more of his own goods.

6. As above (missing parts of John CUTLER'S speech
    supplied from this text.)

William BOOTHBIE, Southleverton,
husbandman, ...

5. Knows that 2 mares sold to him by Thomas ...... by
    virtue of letters of attorney from John CUTLER made
    unto them, price £7 ..... sold to William MAWER,
    price £5, 1 cow sold to Christopher WHITEHORNE
    for ...... 4d., 1 bald horse sold to Matthew SCARLET

for 46s. 8d.,...... sold to Robert COTTAM for
20 nobles, 1 gray ...... nobles, 3 foals sold to
the said Robert COTTAM .... were all part of
the goods of John KIRKBY.

7, 8. In February ..... he went with John KIRKBY to
the house of Nicholas HAMERTON ..... Lincs.
to buy seed corn of him, and there this deponent
bargained ..... for some 14 quarters ....
whereof the price was £16. HAMERTON demanded
that he should be paid in money for the corn, to
which John KIRKBY answered .... the crop which
he should reap of the same seed, which the said
Mr. HAMERTON did admit ..... deponent knows
that the said seed corn so bought by John KIRKBY
was afterwards ..... SAWER the man of Mr.
HAMERTON. Also knows that the said John KIRKBY
...... charges sow the wheat crop of the said farm,
which was reaped in harvest time, the .... 10 acres
whereof he sold divers parcels to several men to be
reaped .... barley crop and pease crop the said
Nicholas HAMERTON had ..... £25, which John
KIRKBY owed to him .... and the rest of the said
crop (was sold) to other men.

William BROWNE, Cottam, Notts.
yeoman, aged 32.

Adds nothing.

Rowland BUXSTON, Truswell, Notts.,
yeoman, ...

Adds nothing.

*****

C.8/7/80
May 1604

Bill of Complaint of William KIRKBYE of
Beeston, Notts., husbandman, versus
Thomas CHARLTON of Sandyacre,
Derbyshire, gent. and Richard EATON
of Dreycott, Derbyshire, yeoman.

Aleys ADENBOROUGH of Beeston, Notts., spinster, took a lease in Nov.
37 Elizabeth for 60 years at the cost of £5 from Sir Francis WILLOUGHBY,
late of Woollaston, Notts, Bridget WILLOUGHBY and Dorothy HASTINGS,
his daughters. Sir Francis died shortly after making the lease and the
plaintiff married Alice ADENBOROUGH. The plaintiff went to Thomas

CHARLTON (probably a lawyer) to ask him to buy the freehold of the land from Edmund PIERSALL of London, grocer, who had bought the inheritance of it from Sir Francis WILLOUGHBY in the right of Lady Bridget, his wife. CHARLTON bought the freehold for himself, and not for the plaintiff as he had promised, and made a fresh lease to Richard EATON, who has issued a writ to eject the plaintiff, his wife and children.

*****

77.   C.9/2/84
        11 June 1649

        Bill of Complaint of Francis ELDERSHAWE
        of Kegworth, Notts., yeoman, versus Nicholas
        STREY, Robert KIRKBY and Elizabeth his
        wife.

Francis ELDERSHAWE, the plaintiff's great-grandfather, was seised of one messuage, one cottage and 8 oxgangs of land in Kegworth and of two messuages, 2 cottages, one windmill and 15 oxgangs of land in Normanton, near Plumptree, Notts. By feoffment of 4 December 1574 he conveyed to Gabriel GREAVES and Nicholas HOWLETT all his lands in Kegworth and Normanton to the use of himself for life, then to the use of John ELDER-SHAWE, his eldest son, and his heirs male, with divers remainders over to the sons of Francis, and Francis afterwards died. John ELDERSHAWE, late of Normanton, brother of the plaintiff, was by virtue of the said deed seised of the lands as heir male to John ELDERSHAWE, his grandfather. In May 1636 falling dangerously ill of a sickness whereof he shortly after died and being very mcuh indebted to the value of £1,320, and having no issue male and but one daughter called Elizabeth ELDERSHAWE, now wife of Robert KIRKBY gent., he, the said John ELDERSHAWE, knowing that his lands would descend to the plaintiff, sent for some of his neighbours, to consult with them how he might provide for his daughter. Whereupon, John ELDERSHAWE was advised to send for the plaintiff and persuade him to give security for the payment of £300 to the use of his daughter. The plaintiff agreed and became bound to Nicholas STREY of Beeston, Notts., gent, uncle of Elizabeth, in £600 for the payment of £300. It was expressly agreed that the bond should be cancelled if Elizabeth obtained any part of her father's lands. John ELDERSHAWE shortly after died, having drawn the plaintiff into several obligations with his creditors to the value of £1,200 over and above the bond above. The plaintiff entered his brother's lands but shortly after upon an inquisition taken before the escheator by the procurement of Elizabeth and others it was found that Francis ELDER-SHAWE, father of the plaintiff, by indenture of 6 April 1611 had demised to one Thomas ELDERSHAWE a messuage and 7½ oxgangs of land, part of the lands in Normanton, for 80 years if Thomas ELDERSHAWE, Elizabeth his wife and one Laurence ELDERSHAWE should so long live, at the yearly rent of 26s. 8d. and in the same indenture covenanted to levy a fine to one John BALDOCKE, so that the latter might stand seised to the use of Francis ELDERSHAWE. This was intended to enable Francis to make the said lease and not to bar the entail. It is now pretended that these lands, which are worth £60 p.a. should descend to Elizabeth. Elizabeth has now married Robert KIRKBY, and they and Nicholas STREY have combined to ruin and

150

defraud the plaintiff, and have entered the messuages and lands and notwithstanding they demand the £300 of the plaintiff, and have caused him to be
arrested.

Answers of Nicholas STREY, Robert
KIRKBY and his wife Elizabeth to the
Bill of Complaint of Francis ELDERSHAWE.

Nicholas STREY admits possession by Francis ELDERSHAWE; does not
know of the settlement. Believes he died seised but does not know what
estate he had in it. The property passed to his son, John, and to John's
son, Francis. By indenture of 6 April 1611 Francis demised to Thomas
ELDERSHAWE the messuage and 7½ oxgangs and covenanted to levy a fine.
Thomas still holds the property. Francis died seised in September 1619,
and the property descended to his son and heir, John, who married Dorothy
STREY a sister of the defendant. John died of the sickness. The defendant
knew John to be indebted to the amount of £600, but not £1,300 as alleged.
John, considering that his daughter Elizabeth would only receive the 26s. 8d.
p.a. rent from the property demised to Thomas, induced the defendant and
the plaintiff to enter bond for payment of £300 to Elizabeth at the age of 14;
the bond was dated 19 April 1636. Recites condition of the bond. About 9
May next John ELDERSHAWE died. The plaintiff entered John's property,
including his personal estate to the value of £1,230 and within a week of his
entry he sent Elizabeth, then aged 11, to the defendant to be brought up,
allowing her nothing except the 26s. 8d. rent. He denies that there was any
agreement for cancelling the bond if any lands came to Elizabeth. The plaintiff obtained a Writ of Diem Clausit Extremum for holding the Inquisition
Post Mortem; the defendant produced the demise to Thomas before a jury to
prevent the plaintiff getting possession of all the lands. Elizabeth at her
father's death was aged 11 years, one month and 11 days. The bond should
have been paid at her age of 14, which is about ten years past.

*****

C.3/450/51
23 May 1653

Bill of Complaint of Richard KIRKBY of
Haggonfield by Worksop, Nottingham,
yeoman, versus William TURNER and
Joan his wife, and Ralph WESTBY.

On 23 August 1627 the plaintiff acknowledged by bond that he was bound to
George WESTBY in the penal sum of £22 for the payment £11 17s. 7d. on
23 August next following at the house of George WESTBY in Birks in the
county of Nottingham. The plaintiff discharged this debt on 23 August according to the condition of the bond, and demanded to have the bond delivered
to him for cancellation. George WESTBY promised to do this, but said it

could not be found, and asked him to call for it some other time, but acknowledged himself to be fully paid and satisfied. The plaintiff did not call any witnesses to attest the same between them but shortly afterwards George WESTBY died, and William TURNER and Joan, his wife, and one Ralph WESTBY, claiming to be executors of George WESTBY'S will, have got the bond into their custody uncancelled and caused the plaintiff to be arrested on it in Hilary Term last past, notwithstanding they know that George WESTBY had been satisfied for the bill. He craves the court to compel TURNER and Ralph WESTBY to prove the debt has not been paid or else to show cause why it should not be cancelled.

*****

79.   C.8/816/62
                  24 October 1678

                  Bill of Complaint of Robert KIRBY, of
                  Ashby Puerorum, Lincs., yeoman, and
                  Mary his wife, one of the daughters of
                  Henry PIERSON, who was brother of
                  Thomas PIERSON, late of the parish of
                  St. Olaves, Southwark, Surrey, feltmaker,
                  deceased, versus Elizabeth PIERSON.

Thomas PIERSON died seised of property in Southwark. By his will, dated December 1668, he appointed his wife Elizabeth executrix and left her a tenement in Bermondsey St. and Legg Alley to his wife for life out of which she was to pay an annuity of £3 to the two daughters of his brother Henry. The plaintiff married Mary, one of the daughters of Henry PIERSON. The defendant has not paid the annuity for the last two years.

                  Answer of Elizabeth PIERSON

She says that Henry PIERSON only had two daughters, Alice and Katherine, to whom she paid the annuity until they died. She denies Henry PIERSON ever had a daughter called Mary, and does not know the plaintiff. She paid the annuity to Mary in error, and has since discovered her mistake.

*****

80.   C 2 Jas. I K7/26
                  30 May 1614

                  Bill of Complaint of Marmaduke KIRKBY of
                  Richmond, Yorks., versus Thomas BELL.

About 7 or 8 years ago, Marmaduke KIRKBIE bought from Thomas BELL, of Felixkirke, Yorks, clerk, the inheritance in fee simple of a tenement, or burgage, with a little close at the back of it in Bargate Street, Richmond, Yorks, which he already occupied and was hereof lawfully seised as of fee. At the request of Thomas BELL he conveyed it about Lent 1606 or 1607 to one George KEYE of Richmond, glover and three other feoffees whose names he does not certainly remember, in trust to him for his life, and to his own lawful heirs male, and in default to the heirs male of his body, and in default of heirs female then to divers other of the kindred and blood of Thomas BELL in remainder. Since making this deed of feoffment, due to the evil dealings of Thomas BELL, he has fallen into great want and poverty and is unable to maintain himself, his wife and poor children without the sale of the premises. And because the deed in trust concerning the tenement etc. is in the hands of Thomas BELL, being vendor of the premises, he fears that Thomas BELL, in order to secure his own heirs, will convey the premises to his friends unknown to Marmaduke KIRKBY, to his and his children's utter impoverishment. He asks Thomas BELL to let him sell the property, or else agree to have the deeds transferred to feoffees known to him. Thomas BELL is uncle to some of his children, and having great malice and intending utterly to overthrow and undo him, refuses to let him sell the tenement, or to let it, or to yield the deeds to anyone out of his possession. Consequently no one can buy the inheritance, or any other estate in the premises without the consent of Thomas BELL, who is known as a contentious man and troublesome, most of his neighbours fearing to deal with him.

Thomas BELL is also endebted by his obligation in trust to Marmaduke KIRKBY and George KEYE for £6 10s. 0d. but he says he refuses to pay him till Domesday if at all.

About 12 years ago, Thomas BELL, unknown to Marmaduke KIRKBIE, borrowed a gold ring with a toad stone engraved valued at £3 from Katherine KIRKBIE, his then wife, which he refuses to give back. Also about 7 years ago in the 3rd or 4th week of Lent, one William BELL, of Thirsk, merchant, did by the persuasion of Thomas BELL and for his only use and benefit, demise to KIRKBIE and his assigns the parsonage of Birton-en-le-Coggles in the county of Lincoln, with closes, appurtenances, tythes etc. from Lady Day 1606 for 3 years, and for the performance of the said demise William BELL covenanted that KIRKBIE should quietly without any interference of Henry BELL, his brother then and now parson of Birton Coggles, occupy the parsonage house and enjoy it and the tythes etc. at a rent of £80 a year. After the deeds were sealed William BELL departed forth and Thomas BELL, by whose means KIRKBIE took the parsonage, persuaded him to accept for his benefit the sum of £10 yearly for 3 years, and for that purpose did enjoin him to enter a great bond to him, Thomas BELL that he, KIRKBIE, should for the £10 a year ride to Birton yearly and collect the rents tythes, dues and pay the rent of £80. The £10 was to be for KIRBIE'S pains and charges therein. And for better security of KIRKBIE for his payment of the £10 Thomas BELL sealed articles of agreement and a bond for £40 to him for its true payment. In the last week of Lent 1606 or 1607 KIRKBIE, at his own expense, went to Birton nearly 120 miles away. On the way during the first day's journey his mare took a halt and fell lame so that he was forced to buy another horse. At last by costly means he came to Birton about Thursday before Easter 1607. When he arrived he desired Henry BELL, then and now parson of Birton-en-le-Coggles that he might according to his brother William BELL'S bond of £300, receive to his own use the profit of the Easter books and the rest of the commodities belonging to the parish of the parishioners. When the parson heard this he fell into a great rate, and absolutely desired KIRKBIE not to meddle or deal with any manner of tythes or other profits belonging to the parsonage, and violently thrust him and his horse out of the house and stables. By this means William BELL forfeited his bond of £300 to KIRKBIE, who was forced to return home again without receiving any benefit for his loss in charges and spoiled mare, besides his great pains and loss by his absence from home, to the value of £10 at least. About Easter or Trinity Term following Thomas BELL sued William BELL on the bond of £300 in the name of KIRKBY and upon the said suite got £40 from William BELL, as William BELL himself has reported. Thomas BELL refuses to pay KIRKBY the £40 or any part of it, and also to recompense him for the loss of his mare.

> 27 June 1614
>
> The Answer of Thomas BELL to the Bill of Complaint of Marmaduke KIRKBIE of Richmond, Yorks.

Thomas BELL says he is an aged and sick man and unfit to be sued, and that the bill has been issued out of malice. Nevertheless he says that Marmaduke KIRKBIE married Katherine BELL, daughter of Henry BELL, who was his brother, by whom he had issue divers children. At the time of the marriage Marmaduke was very much in debt, and so far decayed in his estate that shortly afterwards all or a great part of his goods were seised by some of his creditors towards the satisfaction of their debts, insomuch as he was like to have been utterly overthrown if he had not been helped by his friends and kinsmen of his wife Katherine, especially by the defendant Thomas BELL. Besides the competent portion he received on his marriage to Katherine, he, Thomas BELL has from time to time supplied his wants and given or lent him money, none of which he has repaid. He says that Marmaduke forfeited to him £400, for breach of covenant made for the good of his (KIRKBIE'S) children. He also says he bought the house in Richmond for the benefit of his niece, Katherine, and freely gave Marmaduke the inheritance of it. But Katherine died leaving divers children who were like to be undone by the evil and prodigal courses of the plaintiff. For this reason he admits it to be true that he and several of the children's kinsmen persuaded the plaintiff to settle the property on the children and that KIRKBIE did assure it upon the children in such manner that he (KIRKBIE) may not make a lawful sale of it. He admits that he will not give his consent to Marmaduke to sell the property because of his unthrifty way of living. He denies the allegations of malice contained in the bill.

He says he is not endebted to Marmaduke for £6 10s. 0d. or any other sum, nor is it material to the case, since the plaintiff is endebted to him for £400 at least. He denies borrowing the gold ring and says he has not got it, though he admits he did give Katherine a gold ring.

Concerning the parsonage of Birton-en-le-Coggles and the profits and tythes thereof, he says that it appears from the bill that if any such lease were made it was in trust for his, Thomas BELL'S use and that therefore KIRKBIE ought not to expect any benefit from it. He denies agreeing to give Marmaduke £10 a year for collecting the tythes etc. He hopes to prove that he has helped the defendant and even helped to redeem him when he was imprisoned for debt in London and has also given him another house which he did not mention in his bill.

*****

81.   C.3/355/47
            25 June 1622

Bill of Complaint of Peter HALL of
Hovingham, Yorks., yeoman, versus
Thomas KIRBY of the same.

William KIRKEBIE, late of Hovingham, Yorks., deceased, made his will,
appointing Elisabeth, his wife, executrix, and about 6 or 7 years ago, having
issue four children, viz. Helen, Elizabeth, Agnes and Cicilie, he died, the
children being yet very young; Helen, the eldest is not about 12 or 13. The
will was proved at York and the plaintiff was bound for true administration of
the will. Not long after Elizabeth married one Thomas KIRKEBIE of Hovingham,
nephew of William, after which the plaintiff, doubting Thomas's good dealing
towards the children, put the bond in court against Thomas and Elizabeth,
whereupon Thomas delivered to the plaintiff certain goods at a very dear rate
to pay to Helen and Agnes KIRBY £32 7s. 0d. apiece at their ages of 12 years,
for which the plaintiff became bound to Thomas KIRBY. Thomas and Elizabeth
are now divorced for affinity, so that now Thomas seems not to take any care
or regard either of the said Elizabeth or any of her children, but seeks to get
and hold from them what he may. Now that Helen is 12 years old Thomas has
put the plaintiff's bond into suit. The plaintiff has offered to pay the principal
due, provided Thomas gives security to convert the same to the use of the children, but he refuses. Asks that Thomas KIRBY be subpoenaed.

Undated

Answer of Thomas KIRKEBIE to the
Bill of Complaint of Peter HALL.

After his marriage to Elizabeth they were willing to settle portions on the
children, and the plaintiff owing Elizabeth £13 for money borrowed, and also
59s. 4d. more for two mares which the plaintiff had bought of Elizabeth, being
much better worth, and Thomas LEAFE owing Elizabeth £22, and the plaintiff
wishing to borrow more of the defendant to make up £64 14s. 0d., the defendant lent them the money out of his own estate. Whereupon the plaintiff, with
Thomas LEAFE and Thomas HUTCHINSON on 19 November 1618 became bound
in £64 14s. 0d. apiece, with condition that they should pay £32 7s. 0d. to the
tutor or administrator of Helen on 7 November 1620 and the same to the tutor
or administrator of Agnes at a day yet to come. The money has not been paid.
After his divorce, the defendant made letter of attorney to Elizabeth to commence a suit against the plaintiff and the two others for the recovery of the debt.
Denies other allegations.

*****

C2 Chas. I K 20/37, 13/45 and 26/65
20 June 1629

NOTES

Note: This Bill of Complaint by William KIRBY of Hatfield, Yorks., against
John CONSTABLE of Waffham, Yorks., Esq., Mary his wife and
Robert MORE of Hornsey, is basically the same as that against
Marmaduke CONSTABLE (C2 Chas. I K 13/45, 17th January 1635/6),
and accuses the defendants of wrongful possession of a tenement,
lands and premises to Goxhill.

C2 Chas. I K 13/45, 16/65
17 January 1635/6

Bill of Complaint of William KIRKBYE
of East Hatfield, in Holderness, Yorks.,
yeoman, versus Marmaduke CONSTABLE.

Roger KIRKBYE, late of East Hatfield, father of the plaintiff, was in his
lifetime seised of a tenement with divers houses and buildings and one close
adjoinging it known as Heden Close, and 2½ oxgangs of land and of divers
other lands situated in the townfields of Goxhill in the county of York.
Roger KIRKBYE died many years since and after his death the lands descended to the plaintiff, William KIRKBYE, as eldest son and next heir. But
Marmaduke CONSTABLE of (?Waffen) Yorks., Esq., Thomas WALKER of
Goxhill, yeoman, and Jennett, his wife, having by some indirect means obtained the deeds of the land, have by false pretences pretended to have bought the
premises from Roger KIRKBYE or from Thomas KIRKBYE, William KIRKBY'S
guardian, he being an infant and under age at the death of his father. They
have for many years past and still do keep possession of the lands and take
the rents and profits thereof to their own use. They will not suffer William
to have the same according to his just right and title, although they have no
right since Roger KIRKBYE never sold the premises nor received any money
for them. CONSTABLE and WALKER have made several leases of the land
between themselves and others and connittee great waste and spoils on it
having cut down trees etc. William KIRKBYE asked the Court in the absence
of the deeds to uphold his right and inheritance against CONSTABLE and
WALKER.

C2 Chas. I K 20/37
Ca 1630

Answer of John CONSTABLE, Mary his
wife, and Robert MORE to the Bill of
Complaint of William KIRKBYE of
Hatfield.

Marmaduke CONSTABLE, late of Waffham, Yorks., Esq., deceased, was
seised for many years before his death of the premises mentioned in the bill.
He died 22 October 1603. After his death the premises descended to his
eldest son and heir, Philip CONSTABLE, by force whereof Philip CONSTABLE
entered the premises and became thereof lawfully seised until his death on 15
May 1618, during all which time Marmaduke CONSTABLE and Philip, his son,
did respectively continue in peaceful occupation without any suit or demand to
enter the premises by Roger KIRKBY Esq., or his heirs. On the death of
Philip the premises descended to Marmaduke CONSTABLE, his eldest son and
heir who was at the death of his father a child of 18 months old, and shortly
after, by reason of some other lands descended upon him from his father, held
of the King, he was found to be His Majesty's ward, and His Majesty did by
his letters patent dated 24 February in the 16th year of his reign grant the
custody of Marmaduke during his minority to Robert MORE and Mary CONST-
ABLE, two of the defendants, who by reason of this grant entered the premises
as of right. About Easter 1628 the plaintiff, having by some means got some
material evidences of the premises belonging to Marmaduke, and being a contentious man did enter the same, claiming them to be his inheritance and brought
an action at Common Law against these defendants. The defendant John CON-
STABLE who has since the death of Philip married Mary CONSTABLE and the

156

defendant Mary CONSTABLE and Robert MORE severally further answer that since Easter and the plaintiff's entry they have continued in possession in right of their ward and claimed the premises. They admit that they have no other right or interest in the property but as in their ward's inheritance. They do not claim any of it for themselves.

5 March 1638/9

Answer of Marmaduke CONSTABLE.

Marmaduke CONSTABLE says that Roger KIRKBYE was not to his knowledge lawfully seised in his lifetime of the estate of inheritance of the said close and 2½ oxgangs of land mentioned in the bill, nor did he die thereof so seised, nor did they descend to the plaint iff as eldest son and next heir, nor did the plaintiff become thereof lawfully seised, nor hath he had the rents, issues and profits of the same (as claimed in the bill) for this defendant says that over fifty years since, in the lifetime of Roger KIRKBYE and long before his death, Marmaduke CONSTABLE Esq. deceased, this defendant's late grandfather, was lawfully seised in fee in all the premises and being thereof seised, died thereof so seised. After his death they came to Philip CONSTABLE, Esq. deceased, eldest son and next heir of the said Marmaduke. Howbeit Philip CONSTABLE being then thereof so seised William MALTBYE, gent, and Anne, his wife, and John ROCHE, gent, having good right and title to all the aforesaid premises (as they made it appear) did thereupon threaten to sue Philip for them, yet afterwards they did convey all the aforesaid premises and all their estate, right, title and claim of and in the same to Philip CONSTABLE and his heirs, which this defendant does not doubt but that he shall very well prove. On the death of Philip, the premises descended to this defendant, Marmaduke CONSTABLE, his eldest son and next heir, by force of which he entered and became lawfully seised thereof and still is so seised. He denies all the charges in the bill on the ground that the plaintiff has no estate in the property.

K 26/65
29 May 1638

Further Bill of Complaint of William KIRKBYE, versus Marmaduke CONSTABLE and others.

The plaintiff declares that the defendants upon false pretences have had possession for divers years past of one tenement with a garth and close belonging to it and 2½ oxgangs of arable land and a close, called Heden Close in Goxhill, Yorks., all which Roger KIRKBYE, the plaintiff's father was lawfully seised of, and did buy the same of Robert SHIPPABOTTOM of Bridlington, and the same descended to the plaintiff as eldest son and next heir to his father. To which the said defendant Marmaduke CONSTABLE does frivolously and not fully answer, for he says that Philip CONSTABLE his father bought Heden Close and the two oxgangs of land from William MALTBYE and Anne his wife and John RICH, but neither shows where they dwell or dwelt nor what Philip the defendant's father gave them for the same nor what right MALTBYE, his wife and RICH had in it, nor what deeds he has to show for the same as by the bill he is required, neither has the defendant CONSTABLE answered at all to the half oxgang of land as likewise by the bill he is required.

157

The further Answer of Marmaduke CONSTABLE
Esq., to the Bill of Complaint of William KIRKBYE.

Marmaduke CONSTABLE recites the descent of the land from his grandfather
and says that his father Philip CONSTABLE being seised of the land, one
William MALTBY and Anne his wife, in the right of his wife and William
ROCHE pretending to have right and title to all the premises threatened to
sue Philip for them and arising from this Philip came to an agreement with
them, details of which appear in articles of indenture dated 25 August 7 Jas I
(1609), by which it was agreed that MALTBY and ROCHE within the space of
two years then next after should acknowledge all acts for the better assuring
of the premises to Philip, his heirs and assigns for ever by fine or otherwise
and did likewise by their release of the same date they did release and for
ever acquit claim to Philip all their right, title and interest in the premises
as by the said articles and release may appear. He further says that in
Easter Term 9 Jas I (1611) William MALTBY and Anne, his wife, according
to the agreement in the aforesaid articles of indenture, did levy a fine of all
the premises to Philip CONSTABLE, by virtue whereof he became lawfully
seised, and was so seised at his death when the premises descended to the
defendant as eldest son and next heir. He confesses that the articles and the
release and the exemplification of the fine are in his custody but denies that
he has any deeds which manifest the plaintiff's title to the premises.

*****

83.   C.22/663/45
             1632

             William KIRKEBY, plaintiff, versus
             John CONSTABLE, Esq., Mary CONSTABLE,
             his wife, and Robert MOORE of Hornsey,
             defendants.

             Interrogatories to witnesses on behalf of plaintiff.

             1.   Do you know the parties; do you know Roger
                  KIRKEBY, father of the plaintiff?

             2.   Did you know that Roger KIRKEBY was seised
                  of a tenement and one close and two oxgangs and
                  a half of lands in Goxhill in Holderness, Yorks.;
                  what was its clear yearly value?

             3.   Did Roger KIRKEBY die seised of it; when did he
                  die; ought the premises to descend to the plaintiff,
                  who is the eldest son and heir of Roger KIRKEBY;
                  did he enter it; what have you heard Marmaduke
                  CONSTABLE, late of Waffham, deceased, say
                  concerning the said lands?

             4.   What deeds of the premises have you seen?

5. How long is it since the defendant took the profits
   of the premises; what interest have they in it ?

19 January 1631/2

Depositions taken at Albroughe in Holderness
before Thomas DAKINS gent. and Francis
ELLIS clerk on behalf of the plaintiff.

James PECK, Kingston-upon-Hull,
aged 45.

1. Knows the plaintiff and Robert MORE.

3. He has heard Marmaduke CONSTABLE say that
   there were lands in Goxhill which were KIRKEBIES
   and wished that the right owners had the same.

Thomas WALKER, Gonsell,
husbandman, aged 60.

1. Knows parties.

2. Never knew that Roger KIRKEBY possessed the
   tenement, close of 2½ oxgangs; he has deeds
   mentioning the bargain and sale of a house and
   close in Gonsell from one Roger KIRKEBIE late
   of Great Hatfield, to one Richard WOOD, late of
   Gonsell deceased, which he thinks is worth 20s.
   by year.

5. Knows Mary CONSTABLE and Philip CONSTABLE,
   her former husband, and Marmaduke CONSTABLE,
   father of Philip, have had the profits of the premises
   these 30 years.

William WILLAN, Gonsell,
husbandman, aged 40.

2. He and his father before him occupied land in Gonsell
   until these 12 years, which is called KIRKEBIES
   land, then worth 20s. a year.

5. Knows that the CONSTABLES have received the
   profits for the past 30 years.

Jennet WALKER, wife of Thomas WALKER above,
aged 40.

1. Knows the parties and knew Roger KIRKEBY.

2. Never knew Roger KIRKEBY possessed of any
   tenement or lands in Gonsell, but has heard
   Richard WOOD which was her first husband say
   that he bought the house wherein she now dwells
   of Roger KIRKEBY of Gt. Hatfield, father of the
   plaintiff, for £20.

159

3.   Roger KIRKEBIE died about 40 years ago.

Bridget MAXWELL, wife of John MAXWELL
of Gonsell, husbandman, aged 60.

Adds nothing.

*****

84.   C2 Chas. I K 27/7
         damaged
         undated

         Bill of Complaint of Christopher KIRKEBY
         of Huggett, Yorks., versus William KIRKEBY.

Whereas his father (no name) left the plaintiff a portion of £42, his uncle
and tutor, William KIRKEBY, very cunningly and by fair speeches has detained the money. Asks that the defendant be subpoenaed to answer.

*****

85.   C2 Chas. I W/47/35
         20 May 1631

         Bill of Complaint of Nicholas WALLIS
         and Phyllis his wife, versus Thomas
         KIRBY and William CONSETT.

Phyllis, wife of Nicholas WALLIS, is one of the daughters and co-heirs of
Thomas CUNDALL, late of Hovingham, Yorks. deceased. William CHENY-
SON, alias JENYSON, by his deed of feoffment dated 10 April 14 Elizabeth,
granted to Thomas CUNDALL, his heirs and assigns, a messuage, or cottage,
with barn and garth in Hovingham, now in the tenure of Thomas KIRBY worth
£5 a year to be let and £100 to be sold, and for the lawful executing of estate
by livery and seisin, William JENYSON did by his deed of attorney dated 18
April in the year aforesaid ordain Ralph KIRBY to have full power of livery
of the premises to Thomas CUNDALL. Thomas CUNDALL therefore became
seised and so for many years he, and one, Ellen KIRBY, and others, his
tenants and farmers thereof under him, held the possession of it. He received
the yearly rent until he died about 15 years since. After his death it came to
the plaintiff Phyllis and Elizabeth his two daughters and co-heirs. Elizabeth
married Thomas BOAKE, who about 10 or 11 years since conveyed the cottage
etc. to the plaintiffs and their heirs for ever, by virtue whereof they are now
entitled to enjoy the whole to their own use. Thomas KIRBY and William
CONSETT have combined to defeat the plaintiff of the premises and to divide
it amongst themselves. For this purpose they have got the deeds into their
custody with the intention of disinheriting the plaintiffs, and they and William

SMALLWOOD are the more emboldened in respect that they have got some deeds which within the last 7 or 8 years were unsealed which now they pretend are sealed, whereby they claim that one John WRIGHT should make some conveyance of the cottage to Thomas KIRBY. They ask for the return of the deeds.

17 June 1631

The Answer of Thomas KIRBY to the
Bill of Complaint of Nicholas WALLIS.

Some two years ago this matter was brought to trial in York and the plaintiffs failed to prove their title and were forced to let the action fall. At another time they sued these defendants before the Lord President of the Council and they were dismissed. Notwithstanding all this the plaintiffs will not rest satisfied, but are still clamouring against these defendants in every court and place where they can without any just cause at all. The defendants say it is true that William JENYSON was seised of the lands and conveyed them to Thomas CUNDALL, who sold them to John WRIGHT, who in his turn sold the cottage to Ellen KIRBY, widow, for ever. She held the premises during all her life and died seised of them. After her death they came to William KIRBY her son and heir, who likewise held them all his life, and after his death they came to Ellen and Cicely KIRBY, his daughters and co-heirs who now hold them so that by computation the possession of the premises has continued in line and descent for 50 years in those that have been owners and seised thereof. The defendant is only tenant of the property, and pays rent for it, and for more certain proof of the case they to whom the inheritance and estate of the land now are, are ready to show forth their deeds. William CONSETT for himself says that Thomas CUNDALL was seised of a messuage at Hovingham and that for a good consideration granted and sold to his father William CON-SETT the elder the said messuage by virtue of which they were jointly seised to them and their heirs and William CONSETT the father being since dead, the whole is descended to this defendant by right of survivorship and has been for 25 years. They deny all the other charges.

*****

C.9/8/147
24 May 1650

Bill of Complaint of Frances WALKER, of
Wandermarshe, Yorks., widow, executrix
of Francis WALKER, versus George KIRKEBY,
formerly of Kirkby Malzeard, now of Wensley,
Yorks.

William LEATHLEY, late of Grewelthorpe, Yorks., many years ago borrowed of George KIRKBY, the defendant, £20 and for security Francis WALKER and William LEATHLEY were bound to the defendant in £40 for repayment of £21 12s. 0d. The debt was not repaid on the day appointed. About 11 years ago, the defendant put the bond in suit versus William LEATHLEY and Francis WALKER in the Council of the North. William LEATHLEY for fear of other debts due to others did fly away and leave the country. Francis WALKER was forced to compound with the defendant. It was agreed that Francis WALKER should pay £15, provided that the bond remained with the defendant. The £15 was paid. Afterwards William LEATHLEY returned and lived divers years at or about Kirkby Malzeard. The plaintiff does not know whether he paid anything to the defendant, but no further demand was made of him. William LEATHLEY died about 7 years ago and now Francis WALKER is dead also. Now the defendant demands the full debt of the plaintiff. Asks that he be subpoenaed to answer.

Ripon
20 June 1650

Answer of George KIRKEBY to the
Bill of Complaint of Frances WALKER.

Admits that on 11 November 1636 William LEATHLEY and Francis WALKER became bound to him in £42 12s. 0d. for repayment of £20 16s. 0d. within 6 months, and that Francis WALKER paid £15. Denies that Francis WALKER was thereby discharged; denies that any payment was made by William LEATHLEY. The defendant demanded payment of the plaintiff about 4 years ago. Remembers that he was solicited to discharge Francis WALKER at the time of the payment of the £15, but he refused.

*****

87.   C5/K 512/14
            15 July 1671

            Bill of Complaint of Thomas KIRKBY, of
            Thirsk, Yorks., fellmonger, versus
            William and Henry GILLING, of Dishforth.

There was great familiarity between the plaintiff and one William GILLING, of Dishforth, yeoman, the cousin of the plaintiff. William GILLING procured for the plaintiff £50 which he alleged he had borrowed of George LOWSON a person unknown to the plaintiff. About June 1670, the plaintiff was lawfully seised of lands in South Kilvington, Yorks., worth £43 p.a. He then agreed with William GILLING and his son Henry GILLING that the plaintiff would convey the said lands to them and they would pay him £50 and discharge his debts, viz. £200 to Margaret ATKINSON, of York, widow, £50 to George LOWSON, £52 to Timothy KITCHINGMAN, of Balke, yeoman, £24 to Robert DOWKER, of Salton gent., £20 to George STUBLEY, of York. The conveyance was to be a security for payment by the plaintiff within two years. It it were not paid to them in two years the property was to be conveyed to the plaintiff (sic.). The conveyance was sealed without payment of the £50 and the plaintiff took no copy of the conveyance, refusing to take the bond they offered. Now the defendants refuse to pay the £50, or the debts, and they claim an absolute estate in the premises, and they refuse to deliver it unless the plaintiff pays them £450. The defendants have caused declarations in ejectment to be delivered to the plaintiff. The plaintiff has no remedy at common law. Asks that they be subpoenaed to answer etc.

At Thirsk
18 October 1671

Answer of William and Henry GILLING,
and George NORTON, William DALE and
John SMITH, to the Bill of Complaint of
Thomas KIRKBY.

About nine years ago the plaintiff stood in great need of money and desired
William and Henry GILLING to procure £50 for him, which William borrowed
from Francis LOWSON. The plaintiff failed to repay this and William
GILLING paid LOWSON £50 and £15 interest. He did not borrow from George
LOWSON, as is alleged in the bill. Afterwards William WILLING and the
plaintiff became bound in £400 to John DODSWORTH Esq., Philip PRINCE,
gent, Winifred ATKINSON and Mary ATKINSON for payment of £200 due to
Margaret ATKINSON of Towthorpe widow, on 1 November 1666. The plaintiff failed to pay and it was paid by William GILLING with interest, in all
£240. William GILLING and Henry GILLING have also paid the following
debts of the plaintiff (as in bill). They pressed the plaintiff to give them
security for the above, and in May 1670 account was made. By lease and
release of 27/28 May 1670, the plaintiff conveyed to George NORTON of
Dishforth gent. and William DALE yeoman all his lands in South Kilvington,
which lands do not amount to the yearly value of £30. It is true that there is
a covenant for re-entry by the plaintiff if he pays £450 by 20 May 1672.
Deny suit against the plaintiff by Robert DOWKER with their knowledge,
since the defendants paid him in June 1670. They deny that they have claimed
to have an absolute estate in the property, but they conceive that the plaintiff
ought not to retain possession of it while he is not paying interest for the £450.
They admit the issue of declarations of ejectment. They admit that the plaintiff delivered to them the title deeds of the property, viz., 7 deeds between
Richard DANBY and his wife Elizabeth and the plaintiff, and an exemplification of a fine between the same, and other deeds.

*****

C.5/511/62
16 October 1675

Bill of Complaint of Rowland KIRBY of
York, goldsmith, versus Henry RODWELL
of York, pewterer.

The defendant is indebted to the plaintiff for £25, secured in December 1673
by bond in £50, for payment in November next. One Christopher DAWSON,
then servant of the plaintiff, delivered the bond to the defendant. The
defendant refuses to pay.

18 January 1675/6

Answer of Henry RODWELL to the
Bill of Complaint of Rowland KIRBY.

163

Admits to former debt to the plaintiff of £25 and security for £50 under
bond of 23 December 1673 for payment on 11 November next. On 17 April
last, the plaintiff being in the house of William BELWOOD in York, the
defendant asked the plaintiff to make a reckoning of all debts due. By this
it appeared that the plaintiff owed him £16 for work done, and also for three
cheeses, one pair of brass candlesticks and a close stook pan, and one
charcoal pan. The defendant paid £9 to the plaintiff for balance of principal
due under the bond and it was agreed that the goods should cover the interest.
Denies that he obtained the bond through Christopher DAWSON.

*****

89.

C.5/512/12 and 13
Undated (ca 1675 or 76)

Bill of Complaint of John KIRBY of
Conyston Hall, Lancs., gent, versus
Thomas HILTON.

Robert HILTON of Whirtan, Westmorland, Esq., in the year 1673, needing
£300, hearing that the plaintiff had money to put out at interest, he asked
him to lend him that sum, telling him that he was lawfully siesed of an absolute
estate and inheritance in the manors of Hilton and Allerton in Westmorland,
and that they were not entailed either before his marriage by himself or any
other person, or since. He proposed to the plaintiff that if he would lend
him the £300, he and John HILTON, his son and heir, (since deceased) would
secure the repayment thereof by a statute merchant. It was agreed that the
plaintiff should lend the £300 on payment of £45 per annum during the plaintiff's life by way of instalments to sink the principal sum of £300 and interest.
It was to be secured by such statute as aforesaid. The statute was dated 15
February 25 Chas. II (1674) and acknowledged before Stephen BIRKETT Esq.,
Mayor of Kirby Kendal, and Alan PRICKETT, clerk. Robert HILTON became
bound in the sum of £600 the £45 to be paid in half-yearly payments on 2 August
and 2 February during the life of the plaintiff, the first payment of £22 10s. 0d.
to be made on 2 August then next ensuing. Robert HILTON and his brother
George HILTON, and Matthew RICHARDSON of Bonehead likewise standing
bound as securities for him. In January 1675/6, Robert HILTON asked the
plaintiff to give him and his brother a meeting in order to agree the quantum
of the debts and what did rest due for the proper debts of George HILTON,
for which Robert HILTON was surety for his brother who was likewise in the
plaintiff's debt. Robert HILTON likewise asked the plaintiff to persuade George
HILTON to make him a counter security. On February 7 1675/6 the various
debts having been cast up, it was discovered that Robert HILTON stood bound
with George HILTON to the plaintiff in the sum of £248 2s. 0d. and these
debts were acknowledged by George HILTON to be his own proper debts and
that Robert HILTON stood bound only as surety for him. At the importunity
of the plaintiff, George HILTON agreed to settle several messuages, of which
he was then seised in fee upon Robert HILTON and his heirs, in Appleby in
Westmorland for a counter security to Robert HILTON against the bonds wherein he stood bound to the plaintiff for the proper debts of George HILTON, and
for the payment of the moneys thereby secured to the plaintiff. Robert HILTON
has made over his estate to Thomas, and gone to live in the college of the

164

Cathedral of Durham, which is a place privileged from arrest, and Thomas
HILTON refuses to pay the plaintiff his yearly sum of £45.

        The Answer of Thomas HILTON to the
        Bill of Complaint of John KIRBY.

He acknowledges the debt. Thomas HILTON of Hilton, the defendant's
great-grandfather, in the 2nd and 3rd year of Philip and Mary, conveyed
to Thomas BLENKINSOP of Hellbeck, Westmorland, Esq., Thomas, his
son and heir, John CRACKENTHORPE of .... in Cumberland and
John MACHELL of Crackenthorpe, the elder, his manor of Hilton and all
his other lands in Hilton, Duffton, Murton, Sandforth and Bondgate in
Westmorland, and all his burgages in Allleby, to the use of Thomas HILTON
the grantor, for his life, and after his death, to the use of Thomas HILTON,
his heir apparent, and of his lawful heirs, and in default of such heirs, to
the use of Robert HILTON, his son and his heirs, and in default to Nicholas
HILTON, his son and his heirs, and in default to James HILTON, his son
and his heirs, and in default to John HILTON, his son and his heirs, and in
default of all such heirs, to the right heirs of Thomas HILTON the grantor.
The defendant says that he is not threatening the plaintiff with the terms of
this entail and has offered to repay the £300 with interest. He does not
know that his father, Robert HILTON, stands bound as security for George
HILTON with Matthew RICHARDSON as alleged, and he does not know if
his father guaranteed the debts of his uncle, as is suggested, for he was in
no way privy to any such transactions. He denies that his father has conveyed to him, or to any other person, in trust for him, any lands whatsoever,
and he himself has not taken upon him the payment of his uncle's debts.

                        *****

        C.5/512/11
        28 November 1681

        Bill of Complaint of Henry KIRKBY of
        Blawith-in-Furness Lancs., yeoman,
        executor of Isabel FELL, late of
        Milthorpe, Westm., widow, versus
        Jeffrey RUSSELL of Cartmell, Lancs.

Whereas Richard FELL of Woodbroughton, Lancs., yeoman, was seised of
a considerable estate and intended to leave a great part of it to his wife
Isabel, who was infirm and incapable of acting as his executrix, he appointed
his kinsman, Jeffrey RUSSELL, of Cartmell, as executor in trust for his
wife. Richard FELL made his will on 19 August 1670 and shortly after died.
Isabel distrusted Jeffrey RUSSELL, and on 24 November 1670 she and
RUSSELL agreed that in consideration of £15, RUSSELL would disclaim
the executorship to her. Administration was entrusted to William KNIPE.
He administered the estate faithfully and no claim was made by RUSSELL.
Isabel made her will 28 August last, appointing the plaintiff, her nephew,
as executor, and shortly after died. The defendant has now revived his
claims, having got possession of the release of his executorship. He claims

the whole personal estate of Isable FELL, under an agreement obtained
from her by fraud in April 1671.

*****

91.   C.3/461/1
               Undated
               (damaged)

               Bill of Complaint of Christopher SHOTBLOCKE
               of .... in the suburbs of Durham and his
               wife Elizabeth, versus George KIRBY of Durham,
               gent.

Whereas Christopher HUTCHINSON, late of Elvett co. Durham, yeoman,
deceased, father of the plaintiff and Elizabeth .... were seised of
messuages, shops etc. in the barony of Elvett, one William FARROW of
Elvett ...... married and taken to wife the plaintiff Elizabeth, and being
so seised the said Christopher HUTCHINSON some years since in consideration of love and affection to his daughter Elizabeth, settled on her and
William FARROW a moiety of his messuages in the East End of Elvett Bridge
in the parish of St. Oswalds, a messuage in the barony of Elvett occupied by
John HODSHON, lands in Bellasis in St. Oswalds and other lands. FARROW
delivered the writings and the bond to George KIRBY. Two years since
FARROW died, leaving Elizabeth and three children. Letters of Administration were granted to Elizabeth who then married the plaintiff. The defendant George KIRBY has the deeds and other evidences and refuses to deliver
them.

*****

92.   C.22/388/63   1656
               Interrogatories to be administered to witnesses
               produced by Roger KIRBY, John MORLAND and
               John JOPLING, versus John and Thomas
               FETHERSTONHALGH.

       1.   (partly damaged) Did you know the defendants,
               Thomas and John FETHERSTONHALGH, Ralph
               FETHERSTONHALGH, Esq., deceased, (late
               grandfather of defendants) .... and John
               FETHERSTONHALGH, Esq., late great-grand-
               father of defendant Thomas FETHERSTONHALGH,
               and Isabel MAN deceased, of York, widow ....
               Thomas FETHERSTONHALGH and Robert BELL,
               late of York, counsellor at law, John BROWNE,
               late of Flasse, Co. Durham, clerk and Katherine,
               his mother (?) .... George COURTPENNY,
               and .... of Wiserly, Co. Durham, gents.,

166

Robert BROMWELL of Hanging Wells, Co. Durham
.... Do you know the messuage ....
called Braidlaw with the lands belonging ? Did you
know one Thomas DARCY, late of York, Esq., and
do you know Thomas APPLEYARD of ....
Austwicke Garth in York esq. ?

2. Is the messuage above parcel of the manor of Stanhope
    Co. Durham, does it lie in Racopside in the parish of
    Stanhope ?

3. Do you know that John FETHERSTONHALGH, great-
    grandfather of the defendant, Thomas, on marriage
    of his son Ralph FETHERSTONHALGH, or later,
    settled the said messuage on his son and heir, Ralph,
    and his heirs in tail male; have you seen the deed,
    and if so, in whose possession was it, what was the
    date ?

4. Do you know that Ralph FETHERSTONHALGH, after
    the death of his father, became seised of a great
    estate of inheritance in Stanhope-in-Weardale and
    elsewhere in Durham; what was its clear annual
    value; was treaty made 38 or 39 years since concer-
    ning the marriage of the defendant John FETHERSTON-
    HALGH, son and heir of Ralph FETHERSTONHALGH,
    and the aforesaid Alice MAN; were articles drawn
    up by Robert BELL, counsellor at law, between Ralph
    FETHERSTONHALGH and Isable MAN, mentioning
    what portion John and Alice were to expect and what
    lands were settled, to what uses; was the messuage
    called Braidlaw included or expressly excepted; by
    the agreement to have all the lands so that he might
    have an estate in tail after his father's death or was
    he only a life tenant; is the copy shown you a true
    copy ?

5. Did the marriage take effect; how much did Ralph
    receive as portion with Alice; did he not delay
    settling the estate; were not John and Alice forced
    to begin a suit at York before the Council of the North
    to compel settlement; did Ralph answer that there was
    a second agreement and that according to the same by
    deeds dated 19, 20, 22 or 23 October 1621, he conv-
    eyed certain manors to Thomas APPLEYEARD and
    Thomas DARCY, part of them to the use of John and
    Alice for their lives, part to himself for life with re-
    version to John for life with remainder to sons of
    John and Alice; was Braidlaw included; were you
    a party to any of these deeds; are the deeds shown
    true copies; did John complain and hold himself
    wronged by his father in that he was life tenant only;
    what were the terms of the York decree; were the
    deeds mentioned by Ralph in his answer ordered to
    be suppressed because John was not made tenant in
    tail; was Ralph ordered to make new assurances
    giving John an estate in tail; did Ralph then fly into

167

Scotland or some other remote place and remain
there a long time to avoid being served with process ?

6. Are these true copies of the bill, answer and interr-
    ogatories at York ?

7. Was there later an agreement between John and his
    father, Ralph, about 1634 or 1635 whereby Ralph
    was to grant the messuage called Braidlaw to John
    and his heirs, so that it might be sold to pay John's
    debts; did John then choose George COURTPENNY
    and Robert BROMWELL as trustees; did Ralph by
    deed or 23 March 1635/6 and 15 August 1636 convey
    the property to these trustees; are these the deeds ?

8. Did George COURTPENNY and Robert BROMWELL
    in consideration of a competent sum paid to John by
    John BROWNE of Flashe by deed dated 15 August
    1636 convey Braidlaw to John BROWNE; for how
    much; did you see the deeds; did John BROWNE
    enjoy the property for his life ?

9. Did John BROWNE by his will devise Braidlaw to
    his wife Katherine; did she enter and enjoy the same;
    did she by will or otherwise devise the same to the
    plaintiff Roger KIRBY and his heirs; did John
    FETHERSTONHALGH assure the same to KIRBY;
    for what consideration; has the plaintiff subsequently
    conveyed the same to the other plaintiffs, John MOR-
    LAND and John JOPLING; for what consideration;
    did you see the deeds ?

10. Has Thomas FETHERSTONHALGH since the plaintiffs
    entered their bill produced indenture of .... October
    1621 between Ralph FETHERSTONHALGH on the one
    part and Thomas APPLEYEARD and Thomas DARCY
    on the other, in which Ralph covenants to stand seised
    of Braidlaw for life, remainder to the sons of John
    FETHERSTONHALGH and their heirs male; does he
    also covenant to made feoffment to the same uses;
    have you seen the defendant produce the alleged feo-
    ffment dated 23 October 1621; of whom did Thomas
    FETHERSTONHALGH say that he had the deeds; did
    he say from Thomas APPLEYEARD ?

11. Did you handle the wax wherewith the alleged deeds
    were sealed; was it soft ?

12. When you last saw the said writings, was a letter
    produced in which Thomas APPLEYEARD denied
    that he delivered the deeds of 22 or 23 October to
    the plaintiff, or that he ever knew of such deeds ?

13. Have you seen drafts of deeds like those mentioned
    above; where did you see them; how did the def-
    endant come by them; has the hand and seal of Ralph

FETHERSTONHALGH been added to them since
you saw them; did you lend the seal of Ralph
FETHERSTONHALGH to the defendant about
two years past; did the defendant confess to
you that he had sealed the deeds ?

9 January 1656/7

Depositions of witnesses on behalf of the plaintiffs
taken at Durham before Robert NEWHOUSE and
Ralph TAYLOR, gent.

(Only answers relating to KIRBY have been noted below.)

William CHURCH, Durham, gent, one of
the Commissioners, aged 45.

-   Last June was employed by Roger KIRBY to go to
    York to make search there for writings as to
    proceedings at the court at York in the suit bet-
    ween John and Ralph FETHERSTONHALGH; the
    depositions of witnesses on behalf of Ralph FETH-
    ERSTONHALGH 1633, a copy of the decree made
    25 July 1633 and other writings now shown to him
    are true copies; was present when John FETHER-
    STONHALGH delivered to Roger KIRBY the indent-
    ure dated 9 February 1651, now also shown to him.

Robert THOMSON, Gateside, Durham,
clerk, aged 67.

-   Nothing relevant

Ralph FETHERSTONHALGH, Durham,
gent, aged 28.

-   Is half-brother of the defendant, John FETHERSTON-
    HALGH; Braidlaw was conveyed to George COURT-
    PENNY and Robert BROMWELL in trust for the
    satisfying of the debts of John FETHERSTONHALGH.

Henry JOHNSON, Hanybanck, Co. Durham,
aged 43.

-   Was present when COURTPENNY and BROMWELL
    delivered indenture dated 15 August 1636 to John
    BROWNE.

Peter BAINBRIGG, Ludwell, Co. Durham,
aged 50.

-   Knew John BROWNE and Katherine his wife, mother
    of the plaintiff, Roger KIRBY; has been farmer of
    part of Braidlaw for 20 years past; was present at
    the conveyance to John BROWNE.

169

William EMERSON, Billingshield, Co. Durham,
yeoman, aged 53.

- Albeit he was not present as a witness to the
feoffment by Katherine BROWNE to the plaintiff,
Roger KIRBY dated 25 September 1649, he was
there when livery of seisin was made.

William BROCKETT, Durham,
gent., aged 39.

- Was present when John FETHERSTONHALGH
delivered the indenture dated 9 February 1651/2
and the deed of 25 March 1656.

Arthur PHILLIPPS, Durham,
gent., aged 51.

- damaged, nothing relevant.

Alice, wife of Matthew COOPER, Dalton, Co. Durham,
clerk, aged 55.

- Knew John BROWNE and his wife Katherine, late
stepfather and mother of Roger KIRBY; Roger
KIRBY has enjoyed the property since her father's
death.

John JACKSON, a soldier of Tynemouth Castle,
Northumberland, aged 28.

- nothing relevant.

Ralph TAYLOR of Flass, Co. Durham,
gent., aged 31.

- Was present when Katherine BROWNE, then a
widow sealed and delivered to Roger KIRBY the
feoffment dated 25 September 1649.

John KIRBY of Broome, Co. Durham,
gent., aged 44.

- Roger KIRBY is his brother, John BROWNE and
Katherine his stepfather and mother; John BROWNE
held Braidlaw for life, then devised it to his wife
who held it for her life and after her death Roger
KIRBY held it. Was present when Roger KIRBY
conveyed it to John MORLAND and John JOPLIN by
deed of ...... October 1655.

John TEMPEST, Old Durham, Esq.,
aged 33.

- nothing relevant.

.... Co. Durham,
Dr. of Law, aged 51.

-    nothing relevant.

Philip COLVILL, Snowhope Close, Co. Durham,
gent., aged 38.

-    nothing relevant.

Henry JACKSON, Whicklaw, Co. Durham,
yeoman, aged 56.

-    nothing relevant.

...... ELVELL, Co. Durham,
pewterer aged 52.

    nothing relevant.

...... APPLEYARD, Burstwick, York, esq.

-    Is brother to the mother of John FETHERSTONHALGH.

*****

93.
C.3/352/8 (see also C.3/301/8)
20 June 1622

Bill of Complaint of George GARDNER of
Wenneston, Suffolk, versus William LYNN,
Daniel RUSHMERE and Richard ARNOLD.

About 1618, Thomas WATTS late of Hockwold, Norfolk, conveyed to the
plaintiff, George GARDNER, the Manor of Ellingham, alias Allens, in
Hockwold, with all lands, tenements etc. The property was valued at £3,000,
of which John WATTS, gent., the father of Thomas, had granted two yearly
rent charges of £20 each to Daniel RUSHMERE of Norwich, scrivenor, and
another similar annuity of £30 a year to William LYNN of Norwich, grocer.
William LYNN, in consideration of a marriage of one of his daughters to
William PORTER, granted his annuity of £30 to them. The plaintiff, as owner
of the Manor, which is encumbered as stated above with these and other rent
charges, was forced to sell it in February 1618/9 to Francis BAXTER of
Fainthorp, Norfolk, gent., in exchange for an estate of BAXTER'S in the
parish of St. Michael, South Elmeham, Suffolk, and in Wenneston, Suffolk,
and the sum of £1,000. The plaintiff was to unencumber the estate in Hockwold. When the conveyance was made, the following money transactions were
to be undertaken :-

£491 to Daniel RUSHMERE of which the plaintiff paid £191.

£400 to William LYNN and William PORTER of which the
plaintiff paid £100.

In order to secure the £300 to RUSHMERE and the £300 to LYNN and PORTER
the plaintiff assigned in trust the estate at Wenneston, RUSHMERE to receive
one half of the revenue and LYNN and PORTER the other half. The plaintiff
arranged for Francis BAXTER to become bound to RUSHMERE, PORTER and
LYNN in the sum of £1,000 on condition that BAXTER'S wife released in trust
.... (damaged passage.)

William PORTER has since died, but LYNN and RUSHMERE have put a tenant,
one Richard ARNOLD, into the lands at Wenneston with the intention of trying
their title at Common Law and to expel the plaintiff.

*****

94.
C2 Chas. I P29/17
...... November 1625

Bill of Complaint of Derrick POPLEY of
Bristol, merchant, versus John FOORD
and George FLOWER.

Whereas John FOORD, late of Pucklechurch, in December 1623 was possessed
for the life of himself, William FLOWER, his brother, and Elinor, his sister,
of four parcels of ground in Pucklechurch for the term of 28 years, and of a
messuage and lands in Pucklechurch, being desirous to settle the premises,

by the motion of George FLOWER, brother-in-law of John FOORD, who persuaded the plaintiff that they were of greater value than they were. The
plaintiff agreed to take an assignment of the property for £1,370. Although
the plaintiff has spent large sums in repairs, he cannot let the property for
above £108 per annum. The plaintiff paid £900 of the purchase money. Before
the assignment was completed, in January 1623/4, Elinor FOORD died, whereby only two lives were left, John FOORD being very sick and ready to die.
The plaintiff demanded reduction in the purchase price (in accordance with
the terms of their agreement.) John and William agreed to a reduction on
terms to be fixed by arbitrators. The plaintiff also found that the lease had
only 27 years to run. The plaintiff made full payment, except £400 which he
agreed to pay on 25 March. George FLOWER persuaded the plaintiff to pay
him part of the £400 before 25 March, then refused to nominate an arbitrator.
The plaintiff is unable to recover his money.

*****

C2 Chas. I P63/61
28 May 1628

Bill of Complaint of Francis POPLEY
of the Inner Temple, gent., versus
Richard TAILBOYS, gent., and
Rowland BAUGH.

The plaintiff, about the end of 1606, being then very young, was brought to
London, and by the persuasion of Richard TAILBOYS, citizen and draper of
London, was left by his father Roger POPLEY to the care of Richard TAIL-
BOYS, that he might be well educated at some school in the city. Roger
POPLEY then delivered to Richard TAILBOYS 20s. to buy necessaries.
The plaintiff has heard Richard TAILBOYS say that he never desired anything
for diet and lodging in consideration of kindnesses received by Richard TAIL-
BOYS and his sister and his parents. His parents were poor and had obtained
wealth through the assistance of Roger POPLEY and Richard TAILBOYS and
his sister had received free board and lodging from Roger POPLEY. Afterwards Richard TAILBOYS employed the plaintiff as his servant about affairs
of merchandise and did not put him to school. The plaintiff's father wished
to place the plaintiff with some merchant in London of good worth and fashion,
but Richard TAILBOYS sent the plaintiff to France to live with one William
ENGLISHE, a poor man who kept a victualling house for the entertainment of
Englishmen only in Rouen, not so much to learn the language, but to be the
servant, or factor, of Richard TAILBOYS. Not long after when the plaintiff's
father understood by letters that the plaintiff was sent to France without his
privity of consent and that he vainly consumed his youthful days there, he was
exceedingly displeased and directed the plaintiff to move to a French house to
learn the language. For this purpose, the plaintiff received by his father's
direction certain sums of money from an English merchant in Rouen, with
which he paid for his 3 or 4 weeks stay in the English house, and moved to a
French house, where he was taught to read and write French. Richard
TAILBOYS paid nothing for his keep. Richard TAILBOYS also detained
moneys sent by the plaintiff's father and the plaintiff was forced to borrow
from an English knight, who knew him and his friends in England. In 1607
the plaintiff returned to England and came to London, where his kinsman Sir

Edward PARHAM kept him until he wnet to his father's house in Somerset, where he remained for a long time. Richard TAILBOYS has received sums amounting to £60 and upwards for the maintenance of the plaintiff. Before the plaintiff's father's death he had settled accounts with Richard TAILBOYS up to the end of the year 1611 (details of receipts given, one of the payments was made at Chilton Cantelow, Somerset; recites receipt - board of the plaintiff in England and France from 10 May 1606 to August 1610.) The plaintiff and his father have also paid divers sums to Simon TAILBOIS, Richard TAILBOYS' father for which they are not fully satisfied (details given, relating to a lawsuit versus Robert BARNERS, the executor of William BARNERS of London). On his father's death the plaintiff became his executor; the plaintiff's mother was called Bridget. In January 1614/5, Richard TAIL-BOYS being indebted and full of troubles he asked the plaintiff to allow him lodging in his chambers in the Inner Temple. The plaintiff agreed on condition that Richard TAILBOYS paid half the cost of the chambers. Richard TAILBOYS was unable to pay but agreed to give household goods in lieu, but secretly carried them away. Richard TAILBOYS again asked to have lodging, to which the plaintiff was willing because he wished to leave his chambers and betake himself to travel. It was agreed that Richard TAILBOYS should rent the chambers except for a little study, at 40s. per annum. Richard TAILBOYS entered in September 1517 and remained there until 4 February 1621, paying no rent. Richard TAILBOYS used the chambers for the study and practice of the law and for teaching music and let part of it to Mr. RAYNOLDS for £4 per annum; he broke into the study and stole divers things inclduing acquittances given to the plaintiff by Richard TAILBOYS. In the plaintiff's absence abroad, Richard TAILBOYS became suitor to the Treasurer and Benchers of the Inner Temple to be admitted into their society and secured admittance to the plaintiff's chambers (plaintiff recites his bill for building the chambers). Richard TAILBOYS having studied Machiavell (like the Snake in Aesop) endeavoured to undooe and hurte your said Orator bot h in estate and good name'; he informed the Benchers that the plaintiff was a popish recusant, whereas the plaintiff has from his infancy conformed to the Church of England. Richard TAILBOYS has taken a cloak of the plaintiff's, and has pawned it for £4; the plaintiff alleges combination between Richard TAILBOYS and Rowland BAUGH arbitrator in King's Bench concerning a bond relating to this debt. All suits between the plaintiff and Richard TAILBOYS were heard before two Benchers of the Inner Temple in Easter Term 1627, but Richard TAILBOYS refused to abide by their decision Asks that Richard TAILBOYS and Rowland BAUGH be subpoenaed to answer.

8 June 1628

Answer of Richard TAILBOYS gent., to the
Bill of Complaint of Francis POPLEY.

The bill is too long and is frivolous (Otherwise adds nothing.)

7 June 1628

Answer of Rowland BAUGH Esq., to the
Bill of Complaint of Francis POPLEY.

His case is under the value of £10 and ought to be dismissed.

*****

174

C2 Chas. I P70/51
26 June 1628

Bill of Complaint of John PARHAM of Mile End
Green, Middx., Esq., versus Francis POPLEY,
Maurice COTTINGTON and James COTTINGTON.

The plaintiff is aged and of an imperfect body and has been so these ten years.
Whereas he has been unable to solicit his law causes himself he has employed
Francis POPLEY of London, gent., his kinsman in suits in Chancery and
Court of Common Pleas versus Maurice COTTINGTON of Godmanston, Somerset
gent., and James COTTINGTON of Discoe, Somerset, gent., for the recovery
of money. In June 1625 the plaintiff delivered to Francis POPLEY divers bills,
bonds, books of account and other notes, including bond of June 1623 whereby
James COTTINGTON stood bound to the plaintiff for £10, and another of Sept.
1623 whereby James COTTINGTON stood bound to the plaintiff for £7, and an
account book with entry of 9 Oct. 1618 relating to loan of £130 to Maurice and
James COTTINGTON. Francis POPLEY now refuses to deliver the records
and has delivered them over to the other defendants. Asks that they be subpoenaed to answer what records they hold.

*****

C2 Chas. I P31/3
22 February 1633/4

(Bill missing)

Answer of Sir Gervase CUTLER to the
Bill of Complaint of Francis POPELEY
gent.

It is true that Robert POPELEY married Martha sister of the defendant and
daughter of Thomas CUTLER Esq., and that Robert POPELEY conveyed his
estate to the defendant, as alleged in the bill, which the defendant delivered
to Martha at Easter last. Robert POPELEY first died then John POPELEY
died, both dying about March last. The plaintiff was brother of Robert and
next cousin and heir by the father side to John POPELY deceased. Martha
has no other children living by Robert POPELEY. Martha freely became
bound in £1,000 as stated in the bill. A bond was taken for the sole benefit
of the POPELEYS. The true intention of all parties was that if the issue of
Robert and Martha should fail, then all the estate of inheritance should be
settled as is stated in the condition to the bond, and the next heir of the
POPELEYS should be appointed to be settled in the estate. Robert POPELEY
was secretly much indebted. Martha was willing before her husband's death
and her remarriage to have settled the estate according to the bond, but now
she refuses.

*****

C2 Chas. I P91/55
1 June 1633

Bill of Complaint of John LANGTON, senior,
Alderman of Bristol, and John LANGTON,
junior, merchant, his son, administrators
of Derrick POPLEY of same, merchant,
during the minority of Derrick POPLEY his
son, versus William WYNTER and Mary POPLEY,
widow.

Whereas Derrick POPLEY, senior, in November 1629, became suitor in the
way of marriage to Mary, daughter of William WYNTER, WYNTER promised
to give Derrick POPLEY £1,000, and Derrick POPLEY agreed to settle on
Mary his house in Bristol called the "Red Lodge", of the annual value of £30.
Whereas Derrick POPLEY possessed a tenement and lands in Pucklechurch,
being the inheritance of Mr. DENNYS, of the annual value of £60, and held
for his life and the life of Edward POPLEY, and a tenement and lands in the
same, being the inheritance of Edward HUNGERFORD, he agreed to assign
the rents of these properties to Mary for life. He also agreed that on receipt
of the £1,000 he would purchase land to the value of £100 p.a. to be settled
on himself and his wife in tail. When Derrick POPLEY came to marry Mary,
William WYNTER refused to assure lands as security for payment of the £1,000
and Derrick POPLEY was forced to accept new articles, whereby he was to
purchase the lands of £100 annual value from William WYNTER. William
WYNTER asked double the price the land was worth and Derrick POPLEY
looked for lands elsewhere. William WYNTER told him he could not pay the
£1,000 until he had married off his son or sold lands. Derrick POPLEY grew
discontented especially as William WYNTER was much in debt and had drawn
Derrick POPLEY into bonds as a surety for debts amounting to £500, or £600.
Derrick POPLEY being unwilling to keep his money lying dead which he had
provided for the purchase, which was about £1,300 or £1,400, therefore resolved to employ the said moneys in merchandise. He adventured the money with
other moneys to the seas by way of merchandise in two ships called the "Bon-
adventure" and the "St. John Baptist" of Bristol. Both ships were captured
by Turks and he lost all his money. On 24 June 1630 he executed a settlement
of his Bristol and Pucklechurch estate according to the terms of the marriage
articles. Nothing was paid by William WYNTER despite please by Mary who
kneeled on her knees to her father and promised to pay him £300 out of her
husband's estate without his knowledge. Derrick POPLEY fell into a consumption and died about Michaelmas last. He had three or four £1,000's of desperate debts due to him. By his will he left to his daughter Anne by his first wife
(the daughter of John LANGTON sen) £625 and household goods, and to his
daughter Mary (by his second wife) £350 and household goods, and to his wife
Mary £100, the Red Lodge and lands in Pucklechurch, and to his son Derrick
plate and household goods. The overseers of his will refused to act and his
wife refused to accept administration. The plaintiffs accepted administration,
as father of Derrick POPLEY'S first wife. Mary POPLEY widow and her
brother William WYNTER are charging Derrick POPLEY'S estates with the
debts for which he stood bound to William WYNTER senior. Mary POPLEY
carried off plate, jewels, etc., of Derrick POPLEY in a trunk in the night
after his death. They have brought suit in Chancery against the plaintiff,
claiming the purchase of lands of £100 annual value for the use of Mary POPLEY

22 June 1633

Answer of William WINTER, Esq., to the
Bill of Complaint of John LANGTON.

176

Recites agreement of November 1629 whereby William WINTER agreed to give £1,000 to Derrick POPLEY before 24 June next, and that Derrick POPLEY would purchase lands of £100 annual value of William WINTER and settle them on his wife before that date, and if not he would pay Mary £2,000. It was subsequently agreed that Derrick POPLEY should purchase of William WINTER the manor of North Weston, Somerset worth £100 p.a. in demesne and £6 10s. 0d. p.a. in rents and services, for £2,400. Derrick POPLEY would not give any security for the £1,000 owing on the purchase money. The defendant is willing to pay the £1,000 due under the articles if Mary is provided with the lands.

22 June 1633

Answer of Mary POPLEY widow, to the
Bill of Complaint of John LANGTON.

As in answer of William WINTER. Derrick POPLEY sustained little or no loss with the ships as they were both insured. The "St. John Baptist" was freighted and ready to go to sea when her husband first became acquainted with her, so it was unlikely that his trading ventures had anything to do with her father's failure to pay the £1,000. Derrick POPLEY was sickly and inclining towards consumption for many years before he died. Denies that his estate was wasted at the time of his death. Derrick POPLEY desired on his deathbed that the plaintiffs should have nothing to do with his estate. The plaintiffs persuaded the original overseers not to act and persuaded this defendant to do the same. Lists the household goods which she took to the "Red Lodge" after her husband's funeral; she took no jewels other than her own.

*****

C2 Chas. I P80/5
22 June 1633

(Bill missing)

Answer of William WYNTER Esq., one of the
defendants to the Bill of Complaint of Mary
POPLEY widow.

It is true that about the time stated in the bill, a treaty was made between William WYNTER Esq., father of the defendant, and Derrick POPLEY concerning the marriage of Derrick POPLEY and the plaintiff. The defendant's father agreed to pay Derrick POPLEY £1,000, being a greater sum than his estate could admit. Articles to this effect were signed and sealed. It was agreed, though not inserted in the articles, that the £1,000 was to be allowed to Derrick POPLEY out of the purchase price of lands worth £100 p.a. which the defendant's father was to convey to Derrick POPLEY in tail. The defendant's father became bound to Derrick POPLEY in the sum of £2,000 for the performance of the articles and Derrick POPLEY became bound to the defendant's father in £4,000. The marriage shortly after took effect. On the death of his father, the defendant offered to agree with Derrick POPLEY touching the bonds and articles; Derrick POPLEY promised to accept such money as the defendant was to pay him, in such manner as might be best for the defendant. The defendant is willing to settle on the terms agreed by his father. On the death of his father, lands to the value of £150 p.a. descended to him; as executor the defendant must pay his father's debts of £1,800; the lands are incumbered with an annuity of £30. The defendant has one brother and two sisters to be maintained. He does not know of what estate Derrick POPLEY died possessed. He denies combination with the other defendants, John LANGTON, the father, and John LANGTON, the son, to defraud the plaintiff of her jointure. Asks that the plaintiff be paid rateably out of his father's estate.

Undated

Replication of Mary POPLEY widow to the
Answers of William WYNTER Esq., John
LANGTON senior, and John LANGTON junior.

Derrick POPLEY deceased her late husband died possessed of a very great personal estate, sufficient to satisfy all debts and legacies with a great overplus.

*****

100.

C 9/152/1
27 January 1697/8

Bill of Complaint of Anne MOONE of St. Paul's,
Shadwell, widow and executrix of George MOONE,
mariner, versus her son William MOONE.

George MOONE, being captain of the ship called the "St. George", and being also possessed of one eighth of the ship and having bred up his son William a mariner and the said George being willing to prefer his son as captain of the said ship, he prevailed on the other owners to appoint him captain. In December 1690, William was made captain. George MOONE'S share was then worth £150 and his goods there were worth £40. William agreed to pay £30 for the goods. George MOONE lent William £77 for an adventure and for William to traffic with on his own account, and also lent him £30 more to buy wine, bacon and other food for his intended voyage to Alicante and Barcelona, to be repaid on his return. Before George MOONE had quitted the captaincy, the owners had left with him £172 7s. 5d. to fit out the ship, but as a longer voyage was intended, George MOONE laid out the several sums following, (details from accounts, totalling £314 4s. 10d. Details of further sums supplied by George MOONE given). William returned to England in May or June following having made a very profitable voyage. George MOONE paid the pilot's fees, customs fees, etc. totalling £60. William refused to come to account with his father until after the latter's death, which happened in October 1691. George MOONE had made his will, 10 October 1681, bequeathing to William and George MOONE, his sons, £120 each. The will was proved in the Prerogative Court of Canterbury. On 16 January 1692 William took another voyage to Alicante and borrowed money from the plaintiff to pay debts (specified, including £26 10s. 0d. to Mr. KIRBY). The plaintiff was entitled to one

178

eighth of the ship as executrix, whi ch William insured for £200. The ship was cast away near Malaga and William received the £200 from the insurers, which he kept. William came and loved with the plaintiff and in June and July 1692 he borrowed more money (specified) from her, with 7 months board and lodging at 8s. a week. Further details of loans and debts to the plaintiff. In February 1696 William was arrested for debt by Mr. WILLMOTT. The plaintiff had a daughter Mary by George MOONE who died after a long illness aged 15; by deed of 13 January 1696 she assigned her legacy under the will of George MOONE to the plaintiff. The legacy was spent on doctor's bills and funeral. In March last William caused the plaintiff to be arrested for debt of £200 and threatens to sue the plaintiff in Chancery for £120 legacy left by George MOONE and for a share of his sister's legacy. Asks that William be subpoenaed to answer for debts in detail.

.... March 1697

Answer of William MOONE, mariner, to the
Bill of Complaint of Anne MOONE.

In 1689 after the proclamation of the war with France, George MOONE told the defendant that if he should be taken prisoner it would go near to kill him, but the defendant, being young, he could better endure it, so he would get the owners of the ship to make William master thereof. His father gave him the money at setting out the ship, but lent nothing. On his return, the defendant paid his father what was owing, with £37 10s. 0d. for his share in the ship. He had no other money from his father, who often came on board the ship and was allowed to take what quantity of wine, brandy, fruit etc. he wished. About 6 months later his father became ill and the defendant was advised by his friends to speak to his father about settling his estate which was locked upon to be worth 6 or 7 thousand pounds. The father refused to alter his will, made 10 years before, leaving only £120 to the defendant, whilst the father had got the greatest part of his estate in the last 10 years of his life. The defendant had reason to believe that this was not his last will. On his second voyage the defendant insured his own share for £200 and wrote from Falmouth advising his mother to do the same with her share. After escaping from the French fleet at night, the defendant sunk his ship in the Road of Fangarolla, hoping to preserve the cargo, but the French weighed her up, took the goods and set the ship on fire, along with two men of war and 17 merchant ships. The defendant got credit for £120 4s. 9d. to get him to England on security of a bill on his mother, which she refused to pay. On his return he lived with his mother, but made no bargain to pay for his keep. He supplied more food than his mother. When she complained of ill health he took her to Epsom where he spent £20 on her. He lent her various sums of money. A gentleman who was courting her offered the defendant £500 to release his claims on the estate, (which his mother would forfeit under the terms of the will is she remarried); the defendant refused. He believes this to be a great occasion of the present suit. She has persuaded creditors to have him arrested; four actions were laid against him; he was imprisoned for 10 months in the Poultry and is reduced to extremity and dare not appear in public.

*****

C 9/47/45
17 February 1669/70

Bill of Complaint of Anne MOONE, Scarborough,
Yorks., widow of David MOONE of the same,
mariner, versus Joshua MOONE, London gent.,
and Peter WILSON.

One David MOONE was heretofore seised of two messuages in Scarborough
and made his will in 1669, devising the same to the plaintiff, and died not
long after. The plaintiff entered, but Joshua MOONE of London, gent.,
and one Peter WILSON pretend a mortgage of the property to Joshua MOONE
for £212, which was not paid. They have brought an action of ejectment at
common law. The plaintiff denies mortgage or that David MOONE was indebted to Joshua MOONE. Asks that they be subpoenaed to answer.

16 (sic) February 1669/70

Answer of Joshua MOONE gent., to the
Bill of Complaint of Anne MOONE.

On 16 January 1668/9 David MOONE mortgaged the defendant for £200 a
messuage in Long Gate, Scarborough, formerly a malt kiln, called the
Lower House, late occupied by Jonathan MOONE and others, devised to
David MOONE by Thomas MOONE late of Scarborough gent., his father
and father of the defendant, and a mansion house in Albrough St., lately
purchased by David MOONE. Repayment to be made at Grays Inn. On 20
November 1666 the defendant accounted with David MOONE for £60 which
David MOONE owed him for the 8th part of a ship called the "Leviathan",
of which William NEFFIELD was master, and for other moneys lent by the
defendant and received from their brother Jonathan. On the same day the
defendant took a bond of £200 of David MOONE for the payment of £100 to
the defendant. On 8 January 1667/8, David MOONE again accounted with
the defendant for debts amounting to £67 6s. 4d., for which the defendant
took a bill obligatory. All these debts are still owing. The debts were
made up to £200, secured by the mortgage. David MOONE pretended that
he had delivered the deeds to Cornelius or Jonathan MOONE his brothers
living in Scarborough.

*****

180

PART III

C 2 Jas. I/c.5/50
24 October 1613

Bill of Complaint of Edward CHADWELL
of Chipping Norton, Esq., only son of
Michael CHADWELL, dec'd, and Anne
CHADWELL, and Joyce CHADWELL,
daughters of Edward CHADWELL,
versus George WIRRALL

During the lifetime of the late Michael CHADWELL, a marriage was
arranged and solemnized between one William WIRRALL, gent., son and
heir of George WIRRALL, gent., dec'd, and Katherine CHADWELL,
dec'd, daughter of Michael CHADWELL and sister of Edward CHADWELL.
It was then concluded that Michael should give £725 in marriage with
Katherine and that the lands of inheritance of George WIRRALL, the
father, descendable to William should be settled on some of the friends of
Katherine for a jointure to her. The said lands were conveyed to Michael
and Edward CHADWELL and others accordingly. The conveyance always
remained in the custody of Michael during his lifetime. At the time of the
marriage, Michael paid £200, part of the agreed £725 and entered into a
recognizance together with Edward CHADWELL for the sum of £1,000 for
the payment of £525, the residue, which sum not being paid, George
WIRRALL, the father, did therefore exact of Michael £100 more, which
he assented to pay, and thereupon gave a new defeazance upon the statute
for the payment of the said £100 over and above the £525 at a day then
following. £520 of the above was paid to George WIRRALL, the father,
during his lifetime, so that at the time of his death only £175 at the most
was outstanding. By his will, George, the father, made his younger son,
George WIRRALL, his executor. George, the son, after the death of
his father finding the recognizance unsatisfied and albeit there was only
£175 unpaid, yet extended the lands of the plaintiff Edward CHADWELL,
and having the same delivered to him in extent would not be persuaded to
depart with the possession thereof until the plaintiff agreed to pay him
£420 in full satisfaction, and in discharge of a debt to one WINTER that
the plaintiff stood bounden to with George, the father. To free himself
from further trouble (not then indeed knowing how much there was behind
on the recognizance) Edward CHADWELL agreed. At the making of the
said last agreement of the sum of £420 (the same being about August 1611)
Edward CHADWELL paid £220 to George, the executor, and agreed to
pay the other £200 in two separate payments, viz. £100 at Michaelmas
1612 and £100 at Lady Day last past (1612/3). And for security it was
agreed that the recognizance should remain in force. Thereupon the
extended lands were handed back to Edward CHADWELL. According to
the last agreement he was willing to pay the £200 and has in fact paid
£80 of it and until lately George the younger has foreborn to intermeddle
with the extended lands or their profits. However William and his brother
re-entered the land in August last (1613), the lands being then sown with
corn, of which some are the proper and personal lands of Edward CHAD-
WELL and others the lands of Anne and Joyce, which were settled on them
by their grandfather, Michael, after the making of the recognizance for
their further advancement and preferment. George WIRRALL entitled
himself to all the corn growing on the land worth about £400 notwithstanding

that only £120 was owing to him. William, having got Edward to become his surety to several persons for sundry sums of money, has caused Edward to be compelled to pay the same out of his own money viz; to Edward PANNISSER and Wm. WINTER Esqs., Captain BAKER and Erasmus RECORD, of London, sums amounting to a good value of money. Edward also says William WIRRALL is also privately indebted to him and refuses repayment. William by indirect means possessed himself of the conveyance mentioned above whereby his lands were settled on his children and is now endeavouring to suppress the same, having lately sold a great part of the land. Since Edward cannot tell what the terms of the covenant are, he is altogether remediless.

23 November 1613 and 1 December 1613

The Plea and demurrer of George WIRRALL,
Gent, to the Bill of Complaint of Edward
CHADWELL Esq., and Anne CHADWELL
and Joyce CHADWELL, daughters of the
said Edward.

Sir George SANDYS, Knight, issued a writ for debt against Edward CHADWELL in the High Court of Chancery for a debt of £40 which Edward owed to Sir George SANDYS. As Edward did not appear to answer the writ a further Writ of Exigi Facias dated 12 Feb. 1610 was issued against him. Upon this and other writs Edward CHADWELL was summoned to appear at five several County Courts, and because he did not appear, he was outlawed on 21 June 1611 by the judgement of Robert SOUTHROPP, Nicholas WALKER, George AMENEY and Robert BRUSTER, the Coroners of the said County of Oxon. Therefore, the defendant demurrs in law and prays the Court whether Edward, standing outlawed shall be answered. The outlawry was pronounced since the King's Majesty's last gracious pardon and before the preferring of the bill. He further pleads that Edward CHADWELL on 4 Nov. 1610 exhibited his bill in the Court of Chancery against WIRRALL comprehending the whole matter and substance of the present bill, to which he, WIRRALL answered. Further on 15 May last past (1613) the first bill was dismissed with costs to be paid by CHADWELL to him, the defendant. When CHADWELL failed to pay the costs, George WIRRALL issued a writ for payment, but CHADWELL still refuses to pay and has not yet done so, therefore this is another reason why he George WIRRALL demurrs in law to answer the bill. The other plaintiffs, Anne and Joyce, are only infants under ten years old, and can have no interest at all in the lands in question and are only joined in the bill to make colour and pretence to force him to answer the second bill.

Writs addressed to the Sheriff of Oxfordshire
15 November 1613, for the appearance of
Edward CHADWELL, Gent., lately of Chipping
Norton, to appear at Westminster of 3 February
1613/4

1. On a plea of debt at the suit of Joan FOSTER, widow
    in London 8 May 1609.

upon the sum of £800 and now is in extent to Thomas AYLWORTH upon a
security of £1,200 for which reason the plaintiff is forced to rely on
Gibbs Leasowe and Hassette Meadow for the means of maintenance and
living for himself, his children and family. For that reason the plaintiff
exhibited a bill of complaint against Thomas AYLWORTH that had the pasture and meadow delivered to him in extent upon the said security of £1,200.
Whereupon the said pasture and meadow were by order of the Court dated
1 Dec. 15 Jas. I devised to the plaintiff and his wife for their sustenance
and maintenance during their joint lives, free from all charge and encumbra-
rance whatsoever. Thereupon one Simon CHADWELL of .... in the
County of Gloucester, claiming the said pasture and meadow ground by
virtue of a lease long since made to him by Edward AYLWORTH, and whereas the said Simon has received the rent amounting to £90 a year for the
space of two whole years now last past, exhibited a bill of complaint last
Michaelmas and therein set forth that he was engaged in great sums of
money for the debts of Edward AYLWORTH (1 word missing) and was (1
word missing) by one Robert ROGERS of £200 for the debt of Edward
AYLWORTH, and that Edward AYLWORTH for security had long before
acknowledging of the £1,200 unto Thomas AYLWORTH, determined that
the said lease of the said pasture and meadow within his occupation should
end in May next come twelve month or thereabout. Simon CHADWELL in
his bill asked to be allowed to enjoy the said pasture and meadow and the
rights and profits thereof until the end of the lease towards the satisfaction
of the debt of £1,200 and his other engagements for Edward AYLWORTH.
Simon CHADWELL obtained an order of the Court for his enjoying of the
pastures and meadows during the said term pretending he was deeply
engaged for the said Edward AYLWORTH. Simon CHADWELL, together
with one John TIMBRELL stood jointly bound as sureties for the sum of
£200 for the payment of £100 to Robert ROGERS, whereof John TIMBRELL
has since paid £70 unto Robert ROGERS and Simon CHADWELL paid the
residue. Simon CHADWELL stood bound also as surety for Edward
AYLWORTH for the payment of £200 (?) or thereabouts to one William
SLAUGHTER of which sum Simon CHADWELL has not paid any part,
AYLWORTH having taken order with William SLAUGHTER for the payment
thereof and for freeing Simon CHADWELL from it, which said several
sums above mentioned are the only debts for which Simon CHADWELL
stood engaged for Edward AYLWORTH. Edward AYLWORTH has paid
and disbursed for Simon CHADWELL (several words missing) several
sums of money to several other persons and has not been repaid by him.
(damaged passage) still due to Edward from Simon CHADWELL to one
.... BIRD, late Under-Sheriff of the County of Gloucester, the sum
of £10 for the fees of the said Sheriff for certain .... extended by the
said Sheriff for the debt due by Simon CHADWELL unto one ....
SPOTTELL, Gentleman, for which Edward AYLWORTH was bound as
surety .... unto one .... SEALE the sum of £183 6s. 4d. for
which Edward AYLWORTH stood engaged as surety for Simon CHADWELL
by several obligations entered into by Edward AYLWORTH to the said
SEALE, and also has paid Elizabeth CHADWELL, daughter of Simon
CHADWELL, the sum of £3 .... for the debt of the said Simon, and
likewise also unto one John CHADWELL, brother of Simon CHADWELL,
the sum of £30 and likewise unto one .... BRAY the sum of £16, to
one Edward CHADWELL, another son of Simon the sum of £16, all which
money was paid by Edward AYLWORTH for the debts of Simon, together
with the rents received by Simon for the pasture and meadow for two
years now past amounting to £100, which, being cast up amounts to much

more than the engagements of Simon CHADWELL for Edward AYLWORTH whereby Simon CHADWELL stands apparently indebted to Edward AYLWORTH and not the other way about. In consideration whereof and forasmuch as Simon CHADWELL claims title unto Gibbs Leasowe and Hassetts Meadow by virtue of the lease for the satisfaction of such debts as Simon CHADWELL stands engaged for the debt of Edward AYLWORTH ,and for no other cause, and as Simon CHADWELL obtained the pasture and meadow upon his sureties, and for as much as CHADWELL being indebted to Edward AYLWORTH and not AYLWORTH to CHADWELL as aforesaid it is therefore clear that the plaintiff ought to enjoy the pasture and meadow notwithstanding the two years rent received by Simon CHAD-WELL; and for as much as the truth and certainty concerning the premises cannot be made justly and truly to appear so that this Court but by the several and particular answers of Simon CHADWELL and Edward AYLWORTH and the accounts of all debts and engagements by both of them for the other, and as Simon CHADWELL has got into his hands the counter-part of the lease, may a writ of Subpoena be directed to Simon CHADWELL and Edward AYLWORTH commanding them to appear to answer the premises.

The Answer of Simon CHADWELL and AYLWORTH missing.

Replication of Bray AYLWORTH to the Answer
of Simon CHADWELL, defendant.

The defendant's answer is very uncertain and insufficient. The plaintiff maintains that every thing in the bill of complaint is true, but says further that Edward AYLWORTH, his father, was possessed of Gibbs Leasowe and Hassetts Meadow for a term of many years and intending to purchase the reversion of it to him and his heirs in fee simple, assigned the lease of the pasture and meadow to the said defendant upon trust and confidence only to the intent the same might not be extinguished by the purchase of the fee simple thereof, and thereupon Edward AYLWORTH purchased the reversion to him and his heirs forever. And by the indenture tripartite mentioned in the bill, he appointed Gibbs Leasowe and Hassetts Meadow to and for the maintenance and livelihood of the plaintiff, his wife, children and family, and the said pasture and meadow are accordingly ordered adjudged and decreed to and for the plaintiff in such manner as in the bill of complaint is set forth. The trust and confidence reposed in the defendant concerning the term of years was assigned by Edward AYLWORTH to the defendant for his behoof and he ought therefore to enjoy the possession and occupation of the pasture and meadow, notwithstanding his engagements for Edward AYLWORTH. The defendant has others bound with him as sureties for Edward AYLWORTH who are to be charged for the engagement and he ought not in equity to receive and take the profits of the pasture and meadow as his own behoof contrary to the trust reposed in him. The plaintiff will prove to the Court that Edward AYLWORTH has paid John WILLEY, John COXWELL and William BANISTER and all his other creditors all the money due to them and also has paid all other sums of money mentioned in the bill. And as touching the £400 mentioned in the defendant's answer which the said defendant pretends himself to be bound for Edward AYLWORTH, or to have lent the said Edward, the plaintiff says that there are three sureties for the payment of the £400, and that for all he knows the sum is paid. The lease was not assigned for any security against the £400

*****

104.   C2 Jas.I/A 49/34
          No date (See No. 103)

          The Replication of Edward AYLEWORTH
          to the Answer of Symon CHADWELL.

AYLWORTH says CHADWELL's answer is very uncertain and insufficient
in law.   He maintains everything he said in his original bill of complaint.
He further says he can prove to the Court that he has paid Robert ROGERS,
Walter JONES, John MILLER, John COXWELL, William BANISTER and
.... BANISTER all the sums of money due to them, and all the
other sums of money for which Symon CHADWELL stood bound for him,
or at least taken such order for all the debts for which he was bound to
CHADWELL by giving new security for the same, wherein CHADWELL
is not bound.   He has paid the other sums mentioned in the bill to the
various parties named therein ....   As to the £400 mentioned by
CHADWELL in his answer, which CHADWELL alleges he lent to
AYLEWORTH, he replies that there are three sureties bound for this
sum and that it has been paid for anything he knows to the contrary. The
lease mentioned in the bill was assigned to CHADWELL as security for
the £400, and that CHADWELL has received rent and profit for the meadow
and pasture to at least £300, for which he ought to be accountable to
AYLEWORTH.   All the debts for which CHADWELL claims to be engaged
are either paid for by AYLEWORTH, or secured on his behalf.

*****

105.   C2/Jas.I/C.2/59
          26 January 1620/21

          Bill of Complaint of Simon CHADWELL of
          Taynton, Oxon., versus Sir Paul TRACEY, Bt.,
          and Richard VASTON.

About ten years ago (i.e. 1610 or 1611) Simon CHADWELL was lawfully
seised of divers messuages and tenements in Gt. Rissington, Glos., and
of lands thereto belonging in Rissington amounting to about 16 yard lands
(approx. 640 acres) as well as about 20 years then to come of a lease of
a capital messuage or farm house in Gt. Rissington with about 8 yardlands belonging thereto (approx 320 acres).   Being so seised and being
also possessed of the said lease, the plaintiff had speech with Sir Paul

TRACY, of Stanway, Bart.* concerning the purchase to be made from
the plaintiff of his messuage, to say that an agreement was reached to
transfer the property and whereby it was agreed to get one Richard
VASTON of the Middle Temple Counsellor at Law to draw up the several
assurances from CHADWELL to TRACY; viz. one indenture of bargain
and sale and one indenture of assignment of the said lease, the same
indentures to be made of two parts to be interchangeably sealed and
delivered between Simon CHADWELL and Sir Paul TRACY. VASTON
also agreed to undertake to make the conveyance and assignment. Several
drafts were left with VASTON to be engrossed and a time was agreed upon
for the ensealing and delivery thereof. At which time Simon CHADWELL
met Sir Paul TRACY and Mr. VASTON who tendered him two indentures
ready engrossed to be sealed by him, the one containing the bargain and
sale from Simon CHADWELL of the messuage and lands of inheritance
and the other containing an assignment of lease. But CHADWELL not
finding any counterpart thereof, ... and being told by Sir Paul TRACY
and Mr. VASTON they they were not yet engrossed, he refused to seal
the indentures, until the counterpart should be engrossed to be sealed
by him also. TRACY and VASTON excused themselves by saying that
because of the shortness of time, and Sir Paul being in a hurry to get
home it had been impossible to engross the counterparts, and earnestly
entreated Simon CHADWELL to sign and seal, promising that there should
be counterparts engrossed very shortly after and the same should be
sealed and delivered to him (CHADWELL). Thereupon CHADWELL signed
on the strength of these promises. However no counterparts were forth-
coming and Simon has many times spoken to Sir Paul TRACY and Richard
VASTON for them to be made to him, and has many times desired Sir Paul
TRACY both in the city of London and in the country to let him have the
counterparts, and upon the requests so made, Sir Paul TRACY has from
time to time promised that the same should be made and sent to the plaintiff. But at such times as the requests were made in London, Sir Paul
has pretended that the original indentures sealed by him (Simon CHAD-
WELL) were at his house in the country, and upon the same requests
being made to him in the country, then that the said indentures were in
London. This delay has now being going on for ten years, and they now
refuse to give him any counterparts contrary to their agreements and
promises. Sir Paul TRACY, knowing him to have no counterparts and
thus being unable to check the terms of the indentures is saying that
Simon CHADWELL has broken their covenant, and that he, Sir Paul will
sue him for breach of covenant at Common Law. Since he cannot by the
course of the Common Law compel Sir Paul TRACY to made, seal and
deliver to him the counterparts nor compel Mr. VASTON to procure the
same to be made and delivered ... may Sir Paul TRACY and Richard
VASTON be commanded to answer and to abide such order and decree
as the Court shall decree.

*Sir Paul TRACY was a cousin of Elizabeth BRAY, wife of Simon
  CHADWELL.

*****

106.   C2/Jas.I/c 11/68
          1 February 1620

          Bill of Complaint of Edward CHADWELL
          of Chipping Norton, Co. Oxon., Gent.,
          versus William LEIGH and Jane CARRICK

The Cathedral Church of the Holy and Indivisible Trinity in Gloucester
granted long since a lease of their Rectory of Chipping Norton to .....
which lawfully came into the possion of one Richard CARRICK, Gent.
About 11 years since (1609) he demised to the plaintiff Edward CHADWELL
for a term of 21 years all the tythes and rent charges of one ground
commonly known as Prinsden, or Princedown in the parish of Chipping
Norton. The agreed rent was £10 to be paid in two equal portions at
Michaelmas and Lady Day during the time the grounds were to be sown
with corn and grain but £6 per annum during the residue of the term when
the grounds should lye ley and unsown. If however CHADWELL should
fall behind in his payment of the rent by seven days after the dates specified, CARRICK had the right to re-enter and re-occupy the ground and
to retain the tythes and profits. Since the lease was made between
CHADWELL and CARRICK, CARRICK has made over his interest and
title in the rectory to William LEIGH of Addlestrop in the County of
Gloucester, Gent., who upon some conceived malice against CHADWELL
without just cause, upon the supposition that some of the rent is yet unpaid, has caused the plaintiff to be sued at the Common Law for the
arrears of rent which he pleads in £60 behind. Edward CHADWELL
claims that he has from time to time duly paid his rent and that he has
notes and acquittances for it signed by LEIGH, or his assigns, but
without seals or witnesses. Some of the rent was paid to William
TURNER, the assignee or farmer of Wm. LEIGH, and some to one
Middlemore WADE, the servant of Wm. LEIGH. Edward CHADWELL
goes on to shew that "Richard FITZALAN, Earl of ARUNDEL and sometime Lord of the Manor of Chipping Norton, conveyed the Rectory with
4 yardlands (160 acres approx.) to the Cathedral Church of Gloucester
on condition that the said Church, their farmers or lessees should every
year yearly for ever in seed-time find and keep one customary plough
and do one day's ploughing within the demesne lands of the said Manor
of Chipping Norton which the farmers and tenants of the said rectory or
parsonage have from time to time duly performed till now of late one Jane
CARRICK, widow, undertenant of some part of the said parsonage and
living in the parsonage house through the persuasion and procurement
of the said Wm. LEIGH doth deny the finding and usage of the said
custom plough and the doing of one such day's service with plough ...
to the great prejudice of your said Orator and other your Orator's
tenants." Not being able to discover whether Jane CARRICK or Wm.
LEIGH is truly responsible, and not knowing against whom to bring his
action at Common Law, Edward CHADWELL asks the Court for a Writ
of Subpoena to be issued against Jane CARRICK and Wm. LEIGH to
desist from further prosecution at Common Law for the rent and arrears
till the case shall be heard and judgement given.

          C2/Jas.I C.11/68
          31 March 1621

                                188

Answer of Wm. LEIGH, Esq., one of
the defendants to the Bill of Complaint
of Edward CHADWELL.

William LEIGH says he believes it to be true that the Dean and Chapter
of Gloucester Cathedral owned the rights tythes and dues of the Rectory
of Chipping Norton as stated in the bill of complaint, and that on 29
August in the first year of the reign of Queen Mary (1553) they granted
John APPRICHARDS, of the city of Gloucester, Gent., for many years
to come the rectory with one annual pension of 10s. to the Warden and
Scholars of Kings College Brasenose in Oxford for the tythes in Cold
Norton, and their messuages and cottages etc. in Chipping Norton,
Over Norton, Cold Norton and Salford which belong to the said parsonage
(the patronage of advowson and presentation of the living there only to
the Dean and Chapter and their successors always reserved).   APP-
RICHARDS lease, which was for 90 years, was to start at the end of the
term, or forfeiture of the lease of Richard CARRICK, and at a rent of
£18 a year payable at Lady Day and Michaelmas.   LEIGH believes that
the unexpired term of the lease granted to APPRICHARDS afterwards
came to Richard CARRICK and that by force of this transfer CARRICK
was lawfully possessed of the lease for more than the 21 years.   Edward
CHADWELL was then seised of the grounds lying in Chipping Norton
called Princedown which were in his own occupation and tenure.   On
4 Aug. 1610 Richard CARRICK granted a lease of all the tythes of corn
and grain, hay, wool and lambs issuing from Princedown to Edward
CHADWELL for 21 years on the terms stated in the bill.   If the yearly
rent of £10 or £6 is unpaid in whole or in part for more than seven days
after Lady Day or Michaelmas, and no sufficient distress for the discharge of it be had, then Richard CARRICK was free to re-enter and re-
occupy the property.   He believes that CHADWELL is still lawfully
possessed of Princedown by virtue of this lease and that he, CHADWELL
has paid CARRICK rent at the rate of £10 a year for 5 years out of his
term of 21 years.   Edward CHADWELL is possessed of the tythes and
Richard CARRICK being possessed of the residue of the years granted
to APPRICHARDS he, CARRICK, in June 1615 sold his right and title
of about 60 years to come in the rectory to him William LEIGH, including
his right to the rent of £10 for Princedown.   He further says that
CHADWELL has sown corn and tilled the land yearly from the time he
bought the lease from CARRICK till the issuing of the bill of complaint,
unless he or his tenants have at some time suffered the same or some
part thereof to lye fallow for the getting heart and gathering of strength
for the bettering of the crops in the next sowing thereof as in the course
of the best husbandry is sometime used, and then has sown the same with
corn and grain again to his better profit and benefit.   Letting the land
lye fallow is no cause for paying the reduced rent of £6 mentioned in the
lease and in this he is supported by Counsel's opinion.   He goes on to
say that since he took over the head lease from CARRICK, and before
the bill of complaint was issued against him, 6½ years rent have accrued
to him from CHADWELL, and that some part of these rents have been
paid and recovered by himself, or by Middlemore WADE, or TURNER,
mentioned in the bill, and that he, LEIGH, has given acquittances for
such sums as he has received from CHADWELL.   Much of the rents
as the plaintiff has paid since he (LEIGH) bought the lease of the rectory
have been paid very slackly and uncertainly.

He goes on to accuse CHADWELL of trying to avoid the terms of the lease and of having raised and altered the term of years in the indenture of lease and other material particulars, and of challenging him to sue for the payment of the rent at Common Law. LEIGH thereupon began proceedings to recover the rent amounting to £60, but later these were dropped and new proceedings were begun for the recover of £40 only in Michaelmas Term 1619. This action was sent down to the Oxford Assizes for trial on 27 Feb 1619/20 where CHADWELL's Attorney served an injunction for a stay of proceedings issued by the Court of Chancery. At the time of the issuing of the bill of complaint (1 Feb. 1620/21) £26 only was outstanding and LEIGH says that he has attempted to come to an amicable agreement with CHADWELL out of Court, which he repeated after the issue of the Writ of Subpoena, but CHADWELL has refused to account to him or to pay him his rent.

LEIGH next deals with the pretended gift of the rectory of Chipping Norton and 4 yardlands allegedly made by Richard, Earl of ARUNDEL, to the Cathedral Church of Gloucester, conditionally for the keeping and finding of a custom plough for doing one day's work a year within the demesne lands of the Manor. He says he neither knows nor believes that the Earl of ARUNDEL made the gift upon any such conditions or otherwise, but on the contrary the late Abbot and Convent of the lately dissolved Monastery of St. Peter in Gloucester were seised of the rectory of Chipping Norton and that afterward the monastery and all the lands thereof in the 31st year of Henry VIII (1540) did come to King Henry VIII either by surrender of the then Abbot, or by force of Act of Parliament. King Henry VIII was then seised of the rectory in the right of his Crown of England. After the dissolution of the said monastery the King established in the same church a Dean and Chapter by the name of the Dean and Chapter of the Collegiate Church of the Holy and Indivisible Trinity of Gloucester and endowed them with divers Manors and Lands ... and amongst other things the rectory of Chipping Norton. By force of this, and not by a grant of the Earl of ARUNDEL, the Dean and Chapter are the true owners of the rectory. LEIGH goes on to deny all knowledge of the provision of the customary plough or that any tenants have been in the habit of performing this service. He also denies that he has brought pressure to bear on Jane CARRICK to deny the finding of the customary plough; but, he adds, if any such custom or service were due or to be done which he does not believe, it would be nothing material to CHADWELL nor ought he (Edward CHADWELL) to have any benefit thereof for he (LEIGH) has heard that one Michael CHADWELL, gent., the plaintiff's father, and the plaintiff himself, did many years since convey the Manor of Chipping Norton and all the wastes, rents, customs, services, liberties, privileges, profits, etc. unto one John THROCKMORTON, Esq., now deceased and his heirs saving only to themselves the ancient site and now capital messuage and demesne lands of the said manor with some other small tenements in and about Chipping Norton. The CHADWELLS also retained grazing rights on the Manor wastes and Commons. Turning to the rectory once more, William LEIGH goes on to state that the remainder of the lease granted to APPRICHARD is vested in him saying that Jane CARRICK has some interest in the dwelling house and 4 yardlands of the glebe. He concludes that he is prepared to prove all the foregoing and asks for the case to be dismissed with costs.

Witnessed: George GREENWAY
John TYDMARSH

*****

C.2/Chas.I/C. 75/54
29 October 1624

Bill of Complaint of Richard CHADWELL
of Taynton, Oxon., Gent., versus
Oliver STEPHENS

About ten years ago (1614) John CHADWELL, one of the brothers of
Richard CHADWELL, became endebted to Oliver STEPHENS, mercer,
of Northampton, for £20, for the payment of which, with Richard as his
surety, he became bound to STEPHENS for £40, to pay £20 within three
weeks. John CHADWELL paid STEPHENS £14 within the stipulated
time and the other £6 was with STEPHENS' agreement foreborne until it
amounted with interest to £10. However during the time of the forebearance of the £6, the obligation of £40 continued in STEPHENS' hands
as security.

Richard CHADWELL, however, being unwilling to suffer a forfeited
bond to remain in STEPHENS' hands, wished STEPHENS to call in the
money due to him, and told him that he (Richard) would not continue to
stand bounden for his brother. At this STEPHENS, who was endebted
to Symon CHADWELL, another brother of Richard CHADWELL, to the
tune of £80, asked Richard to pay the £10 in part payment to Symon, and
upon such payment, he (STEPHENS) would surrender the bond to Richard.
Richard to avoid the hazard of a forfeited bond and to get it out of the
hands of STEPHENS paid out of his own pocket £10 to his brother Symon,
which Symon accepted and discharged STEPHENS so much out of the
gross sum he owed him. STEPHENS, however, having thus achieved
satisfaction on his bond, kept making excuses to Richard, until such
time that Richard removed his dwelling out of those parts (Northampton)
about 60 to 80 miles distant, (to Taynton, Oxon). By that means he,
Richard, forebore a great while to make any demand for the delivery of
the bond, until now of late he has again desired STEPHENS to deliver it
up to him for cancellation. But now STEPHENS refuses and gives out
that there is a debt of £40, or some such sum, due to him by John CHAD-
WELL on his shop books, saying he will retain the bond until this debt
is settled, and failing settlement he threatens to sue Richard for it.

22 February 1624/5

Answer of Oliver STEPHENS to the
Bill of Complaint of Richard CHADWELL

STEPHENS says that about eleven years since he lent John CHADWELL
£20 for the space of a month, and for security John and his brother,
Richard, jointly and severally became bound to him in the penal sum of
£40, on condition the £20 was repayed at the end of a month. The £20
was not paid by the date it was due. At this time, STEPHENS was a
tradesman and kept a mercers shop. John CHADWELL before and after
borrowing the £20 was endebted for wares to the tune of £5 12s. 4d.,
so that then he was endebted for a total sum of £25 12s. 4d. At this
point, John determined to go and live in Ireland, whereupon STEPHENS
sued him for payment, however Richard refused to acknowledge the book
debts, but only the money he owed upon bond as surety. However it
was agreed that Richard should pay £10, out of the £20 due on the bond

but no more of the debt of £25 12s. 4d. STEPHENS accepted this as payment of part of a debt he and one Thomas BERRISSE, dec'd owed to Symon CHADWELL, another brother of Richard CHADWELL. STEPHENS hoped this would settle the matter and he was willing to surrender the bond, but as this was not done to the satisfaction of Richard and Symon, they obtained an extent on STEPHENS' land, (two pieces in his own possession to the annual value of £6 and some other land) against the debt he, STEPHENS, owed Symon. For this reason STEPHENS is unable to sell a small parcel of land as yet unsold to pay his debts which are many, and he is every day expecting to be cast into prison on the strength of these bonds, to the utter undoing of his wife and children, and he pleads to detain the bond mentioned in the bill of complaint until he be paid the money justly due to him.

The Replication of Richard CHADWELL to the Answer of Oliver STEPHENS.

Richard CHADWELL reaffirms the truth of his bill of complaint and states that STEPHENS' answer contains a number of inaccuracies and uncertainties. Firstly, the £20 was not paid in the first instance, but £14 was paid to STEPHENS on the day specified, and the residue with interest was paid in such manner as is shown in the bill of complaint. Regarding the alleged debt of £5 12s. 4d. for wares, which STEPHENS says he was owed by John CHADWELL, this has nothing to do with him, Richard, and as regards the alleged full debt of £25 12s. 4d. which John owed before he went to Ireland, this is not true, because John did not go to Ireland until 9 or 10 years after the £20 was lent to him, so he could not be endebted for this amount at the time of his going to Ireland, since £14 had already been paid on the date it was due. Regarding the £6 outstanding, Richard paid £10 to settle this and to be rid of it, and he paid it to his brother Symon to whom STEPHENS was in debt. With regard to the extent placed upon STEPHENS' lands for the debt due to Symon, Richard says he has often heard Symon say he is owed a great sum by STEPHENS and it was for the debt of £80 which STEPHENS owed Symon that the lands were extended, and not for want of payment of £10 paid by Richard to Symon.

*****

108.   C2/Chas.I/S 69/59
         22 June 1625

         Bill of Complaint of Oliver STEPHENS of
         Northampton, Mercer, versus Symon
         CHADWELL

About 12 years ago (1613) STEPHENS and one Thomas BERISSE, late of Brington, Hunts., yeoman, dec'd, jointly borrowed at interest £40 on two separate occasions from Anne CHADWELL, then of Molesworth, in the County of Huntingdon, widow, and since deceased. BERISSE received one half of the £40, which he disposed of to his own particular use and benefit, the other half STEPHENS had, and for the payment of the debt and interest at 10%, STEPHENS and BERISSE became jointly bound in two several obligations with the penalty of £40 apiece. The date of repayment was agreed, but has long since past. The money continued on loan during Anne's life for several years, and the obligations were never renewed, howbeit the interest due on it was duly paid. BERISSE and STEPHENS were surety for each other. As each of them had reaped an equal benefit from the loans it was agreed between them that each should pay his respective half without prejudice to the other. This reflected the trust that STEPHENS reposed in BERISSE, who was his father-in-law. He therefore did not renew the bond during Anne's lifetime trusting to BERISSE to pay his share according to their agreement. Meanwhile Anne CHADWELL, falling dangerously sick, made her will and appointed her son, Symon CHADWELL, then of Molesworth, executor. Anne CHADWELL died in 1615. After her death Symon CHADWELL took upon him the probate and execution of his mother's will and so became interested in the obligations and debts due on them. With Symon's approbation the bonds continued unrenewed until such time as Symon purposed to leave his then habitation in Huntingdonshire, where he then lived, and to make his abode where his mother had in her lifetime resided in the County of Oxford. Without STEPHENS' knowledge Symon CHADWELL removed, and brought a lawsuit at Common Law against BERISSE, thereby intending underhand and cunningly to obtain judgement not only against BERISSE, but also against STEPHENS. For this purpose Symon CHADWELL combined with one William THURLBY, an attorney, as also with BERISSE who dealt so cunningly together to circumvent STEPHENS as that without any warrant from STEPHENS, who was named principal in both bonds, several judgements were obtained against both him and BERISSE. When all this came to STEPHENS' notice long after the judgement had been obtained against him, he perceiving an inclination in Symon CHADWELL and BERISSE wholly to charge him with the several debts, and by this time understanding the condition of CHADWELL to be avaricious, he repaired to Symon CHADWELL, who accepted £14, which he, STEPHENS, paid in part satisfaction, and £8 more, and by deducting £4 8s. 11d., which CHADWELL owed STEPHENS at that time for wares and commodities, they agreed to accept a debt of £17, then owing to him, STEPHENS, by John CHADWELL and Richard CHADWELL, brothers of Symon, in further payment for so much as concerned him, STEPHENS. Symon CHADWELL accordingly accepted this and agreed not to trouble STEPHENS any further. STEPHENS paid as above £43 and upwards. Howbeit all this while Symon CHADWELL never took out any execution against BERISSE or troubled him, although he had had one half of the money originally lent. BERISSE, in an underhand way, let Symon CHADWELL have £20 towards the payment of his debt which Symon accepted accordingly and promised to discharge and free him from it and yet to keep the judgement on foot against STEPHENS. Since then Thomas BERISSE has died, leaving Edmund BERISSE, his son and heir, a real estate in lands. Since his father's death he was forced for his own safeguard to pay £13 or thereabouts to Symon CHADWELL in full discharge of the debt, on the receipt of which Symon CHADWELL acknowledged satisfaction. Edmund BERISSE told STEPHENS about this, and he, STEPHENS, not seeking to enforce CHADWELL further, declared himself satisfied. Symon CHADWELL received out of the whole affair £80 plus interest, which STEPHENS and Thomas BERISSE had from

time to time paid. He refuses to acknowledge the receipt of any of the
sums of money paid to him by STEPHENS, and is now reviving the
judgement against him, which has lain dormant for nearly 8 years. Now,
however, Symon CHADWELL has moved against him and has taken out an
elegit on the judgement against a small parcel of land to the value of £6
per annum, and also against other lands of which STEPHENS was seised
in the right of his wife at the time of the judgement, but which he has
since sold for the better enabling of him to pay his debts. But CHADWELL
has lately extended not only the lands in STEPHENS' possession but also
the said bargained premises and has lately sealed one or more leases on
some part of the latter with the purpose to try the title and turn the purch-
asers or their undertenants out of possession. By this means STEPHENS
is not only deprived of the means to sell the land in his own possession to
enable him to pay his debts, but also is left upon the extremity of the law
touching the forfeiture and penalties of the several bonds which he entered
into by way of collateral security for the peaceable enjoyment of the land
he sold, and for this he is daily subject to arrest and imprisonment.
STEPHENS asks that Symon CHADWELL be required to declare how
much he has received and to answer the other charges contained herein.

*****

109.   C.2 Chas.I/C.111/41
            12 February 1625/6

            Bill of Complaint of Edward CHADWELL
            of Chipping Norton, versus Robert
            VEYSEY and John COLLIER

In the 11th year of King James (1613) having issue two daughters (Anne
and Joyce CHADWELL), and not then being likely to have any more
children (in respect he had then been long beforehand without any more
children) and purposing to settle his while inheritance upon Anne
CHADWELL, his eldest daughter, after his then wife's death, and to
provide a large portion of money for Joyce, his second daughter, for
her advancement in marriage, and whereas Robert VEYSEY, of Chimney,
in the County of Oxon, gent., being a man of good estate and having no
children, and intending to make one Robert VEYSEY, his brother's son,
his heir, and to confer upon him his whole estate, Edward CHADWELL
and Robert VEYSEY of Chimney made about this time an agreement for
the marriage of Robert VEYSEY, the nephew, and Anne, the eldest
daughter. The terms of the agreement were (if the marriage had taken
effect) that Edward CHADWELL should have assured after his and his
wife's deaths, all his lands to Robert VEYSEY, the nephew, and Anne
and their heirs. In return, Robert VEYSEY, the uncle, should have
given Edward CHADWELL £1,500 for the advancement of the marriage.
However, Edward CHADWELL's lands were held In Capite, and his
then wife had the greatest part of them for her jointure, so that if
Edward died during the nonage of Anne, all his lands in that event would
have been in ward to the King, and therefore very small or no livelihood

194

would have been left for Anne and Joyce. For that reason Edward
CHADWELL, at the persuasion of Robert VEYSEY, the uncle, made a
lease of all his land in the County of Oxford to VEYSEY at a rent and
for a term of years set out in the lease, in trust, for the use and behoof
of Edward CHADWELL, who should continue in possession of it, and
should himself receive the rents and profits of it for his own use during
his lifetime, and after his death the lease should be maintained for the
preservation of the estate against the foregoing purpose and intent. This
agreement subsisted for some time, and many mutual courtesies and kindnesses afterwards passing between Edward CHADWELL and Robert
VEYSEY the uncle, Edward CHADWELL borrowed several sums of money
from Robert VEYSEY amounting to about £80 over and above the sum of
£50 which he owed for some sheep he had bought from him; these sums
were, according to Edward CHADWELL to be repaid at such time as was
reasonable and convenient to him and no interest was charged. There was
no agreement to say that VEYSEY held the lease as a security for such
debts, but only that CHADWELL would repay the money when VEYSEY
asked for it, and VEYSEY was to hold the lease until asked to surrender
it by CHADWELL. Edward CHADWELL, by the hands of Thomas STONE,
William BELCHER, Brian PORTER, William LINDERS and his (CHAD-
WELL's) then wife, having not only paid the several sums of money he had
borrowed from Robert VEYSEY, the uncle, yet having afterwards issue
a son, the marriage did not take effect. Robert VEYSEY, taking exception thereat endeavoured to exact several sums of money again, and now
demands the sum of £600. Now after 13 years VEYSEY is trying to set
on foot the lease which was made to him on trust for the marriage and not
as security for any moneys, claiming it to be his own lease, and as forfeited to him for non-payment of the moneys and interest thereon, when
little or none of the money is due to him and no time limit was placed upon
the loan. VEYSEY, intending to hold the lease and expel Edward CHAD-
WELL from his lands under the pretence that the lease was a security for
debts, has now lately signed a lease upon part of the lands to one John
COLLIER. Having done this, VEYSEY procured one James TROUT, one
of CHADWELL's tenants to eject John COLLIER, promising him (TROUT)
a great reward for his secrecy. CHADWELL fears that by confederation
between VEYSEY, COLLIER and TROUT, TROUT will either confess a
judgement to be had against him be default in the said action to the intent
that the possession of the said lands may be thereby had against him by a
writ of Habere Facias Possessionem upon such judgement, by which means
he, CHADWELL, is likely to loose possession of the lands. CHADWELL
asks that VEYSEY produce the counterpart of the agreement which he
holds so that he can defend his title.

      The joint and several plea and demurrer
      of Robert VEYSEY and John COLLIER,
      Co-defendants to the Bill of Complaint
      of Edward CHADWELL.

They say that as Edward CHADWELL is at present an outlaw and thereby
is disabled by the laws of England to commence and execute any suite in
this Court or any other until the outlawry be voided. These defendants
say that in Michaelmas Term last in the second year of the reign of the
King's Most Excellent Majesty that now is of England in one suite or
action of debt brought against the Complainant in His Majesty's Court
of Common Pleas (See C.2 Jas.1/C5/50, No. 102), he, the plaintiff, was

outlawed at the suite of the defendant Robert VEYSEY. The defendants say that the outlawry still stands.

*****

110.   C2. Chas.I/C.94/38
          24 January 1628/9

          Bill of Complaint of Edward CHADWELL
          of Chipping Norton, versus Robert
          VEYSEY and Christopher BLORE.

About 14 years ago (1614 or 1615) Edward CHADWELL, being seised in tail in the Manor of Chipping Norton made a lease for 21 years to Robert VEYSEY of Chimney, Oxon, being sick and pretending great care for him, but to be to the private behoof of CHADWELL. Whereupon CHADWELL trusting to VEYSEY made a lease for 21 years of the Manor, for £2,000 which was done to appear as a consideration to make the lease more forcible and effectual in law, and it was never intended the lease should be enjoyed against CHADWELL otherwise than for his good, and to be revoked at his will and pleasure. Meanwhile some reckonings growing up between CHADWELL and VEYSEY, and wishing to find out how they stood, they both agreed to get William BATSON of Burford, who was allied to them both, to cast up all the reckonings between them and that CHADWELL should pay or secure all such moneys as should appear to BATSON to be due to VEYSEY by CHADWELL. After the enquiry, CHADWELL delivered two obligations for £600 each to VEYSEY at BATSON's house for the payment of some sums of money which VEYSEY then claimed due to him. Upon these obligations it was endorsed that mis-reckonings should be no prejudice to either of them. It was a condition of the obligation that VEYSEY should hand over the lease to CHADWELL at the ensealing of the agreement for cancellation. However, when the time came VEYSEY hedged, saying he had not the lease about him, but that he would send the lease shortly afterwards. VEYSEY was only a surety for the plaintiff to one widow DIGER alias HERES for the payment of certain money for him, and VEYSEY, supposing the money not to have been paid put one obligation in suite at Common Law against him. When this came to trial CHADWELL proved payment, and VEYSEY proceeded no further in the cause and the obligation was taken as collateral security for such money as VEYSEY had undertaken to pay for CHADWELL. CHADWELL, himself paid all these sums of money and not VEYSEY. Then the marriage question arose (See C.2 Chas I/111/41, No. 109). One of the articles in the agreement was that if the marriage did not take place CHADWELL would repay to VEYSEY the money VEYSEY had made over to CHADWELL in anticipation of the marriage taking place. As the marriage did not come off, CHADWELL repaid the money due and expected VEYSEY to give back the lease. Robert VEYSEY further persuaded him to make over some estate in fee of the manor to have been kept secret to have settled on a wife in case CHADWELL, who was then a widower, should remarry. CHADWELL delivered to VEYSEY an ancient deed of

196

entail to one Christopher BLORE, VEYSEY's attorney, concerning the manor, to his own use and behoof, all which leases, bonds, deeds of entail belong to him and nothing being due from him to Robert VEYSEY upon the same, he having no right to retain them. Yet now, CHADWELL having several times asked for them back, Robert VEYSEY and Christopher BLORE set them on foot against him to get possession of the manor, and have refused to give them up, by means whereof he is now a prisoner in the Fleet Prison for some small debts, and not able to relieve himself out of his own estate. He therefore asks for writs to obtain the documents from VEYSEY and BLORE.

*****

C.2/Chas.1./C.23/21
26 January 1630/1

Bill of Complaint of Edward CHADWELL,
Chipping Norton, Oxon, Esq., versus
Robert VESEY, Walter VESEY sen.,
Walter VESEY jnr. and William BATSON

Edward CHADWELL for many years put great trust in one Robert VESEY of Chimney, Oxon, Gent., his kinsman, concerning the management of part of his estate, he having then only two daughters and no son. About 17 or 18 years since he delivered to Robert VESEY divers horses, mares, oxen, kine and milch cows worth about £100 and upwards for which Robert VESEY never gave any account nor made him any satisfaction, although he, Edward CHADWELL, often required him so to do, having been inform- ed by divers persons of good credit that Robert VESEY dealt very unjustly and hardly with divers men to attain his own ends, which by woeful exp- erience is found to be true.

Amongst other things Edward CHADWELL delivered to Robert VESEY a statute of £800, wherein Edward CHADWELL was bound to Sir Edward STANHOPE, Knight, deceased, at a day long since past, and divers other statutes and deeds of great value, which Robert VESEY now refuses to deliver to Edward CHADWELL, or to any other to his use, although he has been often required to do so. About that time he made a lease to Robert VESEY for 21 years for the better advantage of his two daughters wherein mention is made of a consideration of £2,000 to be paid to Edward CHADWELL, who well knows that he will confess that he never paid one penny to him for it, for he doubts not but that Robert VESEY will also confess that it was made in trust for the benefit of Anne CHADWELL and Joyce CHADWELL, Edward's two daughters. At the time of the delivery of these writings, CHADWELL was very sick and likely to die, and about the same time there was speech between Edward CHADWELL and Robert VESEY touching a marriage to be made between VESEY's brother's son and CHADWELL's daughter, Anne, upon which marriage, if it had taken effect, Robert VESEY was to pay to Joyce CHADWELL, the other daugh- ter, £1,500, so that the said lease was not made for any manner of security at all for any of the debts of Edward CHADWELL, but only in trust for the good of the daughters. If VESEY did undertake for any of CHADWELL's debts, it was not at his entreaty, but done for his own benefit to creep into and to work some advantage upon Edward CHADWELL, having got the said statutes, deeds and lease into his custody. CHADWELL asserts that he never borrowed a penny from VESEY at all.

CHADWELL's late wife delivered, in trust, several sums of money to Robert VESEY privily, the exact amount of which he does not know because VESEY took the bonds and securities in his own name. After her death the securities being taken in his name as aforesaid, but to her only use and behoof, VESEY received the same to his own use, utterly refusing to disclose to whom they were lent or their value, all which he has converted to his own use. Edward CHADWELL says that he lent him at one time £5, and paid £10 for him to one Thomas VOIEDON, from whom he received a note for the receipt thereof under VOIEDON's hand, as VESEY well knows. This was by Robert VESEY, Walter VESEY, or William BATSON, his kinsman, or one of them, embezzled, and he denies to acknowledge the same or the lending of the said £5. Edward CHADWELL shows that BATSON, having been for many years employed by him as his attorney at law, he, Edward CHADWELL, being in question in the Exchequer Court upon a ... (several words missing) ... he, Edward CHADWELL, delivered to BATSON divers writings and evidences to manifest the title and to plead in Court. BATSON combined with his uncle, Robert VESEY, to detain CHADWELL's evidence, denying to deliver them, though requests have been made to them. Robert VESEY, William BATSON and Walter VESEY, the younger, theretofore have and still do labour to undermine CHADWELL's whole estate and supplant him thereof and work him out of the same.

The plaintiff shows that he was indebted to several men for the sum of which Robert VESEY stood engaged for him, viz; one bond for the payment of £52 to Gabriel MATHEWS (VESEY having a counter-bond which being put in suite in the law and judgement obtained upon the same, the plaintiff was thereupon charged in execution in the Prison of the Fleet, where he now lies, although VESEY never paid any sum of money to MATHEWS, or if he did would never tell the plaintiff how much he paid him, but charged him on execution for £200 with costs of suite). Further Robert VESEY by practice with his attorney, Walter VESEY, his brother's son, got judgement upon a bond of £600 to which CHADWELL never pleaded, though he had got matter to plead, whereupon he was compelled to move the Judges of the Common Pleas to overrule the cause, thereby putting him, Edward CHADWELL, to 20 nobles charges. Walter VESEY, the father, being arrested at Chipping Norton, Edward CHADWELL was driven to pay the money (£5 or £6) which Walter, the father, refused to pay to him Edward CHADWELL, but neither of them ever did nor would account with him for any sums of money delivered to them, for if they had Robert VESEY would be found to be in Edward CHADWELL's debt.

(The following membrane is damaged)

CHADWELL was bound to Thomas BROWN for about £60 ... VESEY and BATSON cast that £60 into the account pretending that he had paid BROWN, but he is able to prove that he paid it himself with his own money, and that BROWN gave him a receipt sealed and delivered in the presence of Robert VESEY and he was a witness to it. Edward CHADWELL and Robert VESEY stood bound to one Widow DIGGES for

CHADWELL's debt for the payment of £55. Edward CHADWELL paid
Widow DIGGES and she cancelled the same and delivered it to Robert
VESEY, yet by combination with BATSON, he ... did by stealth and
cunning sue CHADWELL to an outlawry and returned him outlawed.
Edward CHADWELL never heard of any such action being connenced
against him, neither did BATSON ever deliver any proclamation of outlawry to the Sheriff of Oxfordshire, which outlawry CHADWELL was
compelled by writ of error to reverse. Edward CHADWELL believes
that if the reckonings and accounts between him and VESEY were truly
cast up, VESEY would stand indebted to him for great sums of money
which ought and should be re-satisfied to him with a great surplus.
He asks that Robert VESEY, Walter VESEY, the father, Walter VESEY,
the son and William BATSON, be commanded to appear in answer.

Answer missing.

                    *****

        C.2 Chas.I/F6/60
        1633

        Damaged Bill of Complaint of Anthony
        FREEMAN and William FREEMAN,
        versus John SHAYLER and William
        CHADWELL

Details illegible.

        22 June 1633

        The Answer of John SHAYLER, one of
        the defendants to the Bill of Complaint
        of Anthony FREEMAN and William
        FREEMAN.

SHAYLER says he believes that the FREEMANS were at the time
mentioned in the bill jointly seised of the Manor of Hidcot Barthrim,
and of all the other lands mentioned in the bill. He does not know for
what rent the manor and lands are now let. He also believes that at
about this time the plaintiff, Anthony FREEMAN, was endebted to William
CHADWELL, Anthony HODGES and Michael FREEMAN for several large
sums of money, the amount of which he does not know. He has, however,
seen a bond of the penal sum of £220 dated 1 May 7 Jas.I (1609), in which
Anthony and Michael FREEMAN stood bound to William CHADWELL,
dec'd., father of the defendant William CHADWELL, for the payment of
the sum of £110 to William CHADWELL, dec'd on 3 May 1610, which bond
was afterwards put into suite by the defendant, William CHADWELL, and
his brother, Thomas CHADWELL, the executors of their father's will.
A judgement was obtained against Anthony and Michael FREEMAN. At

about the same time Anthony FREEMAN being endebted to Anthony
HODGES, and for security, demised by an indenture dated 13 August
1614, his half of the said manor to Anthony HODGES for the term of 21
years and the other half he granted on 17 Feb. 1614 to Michael FREE-
MAN in reversion for 99 years after the expiry of the term of 21 years
to Anthony HODGES. On 21 Sept. 1618 Anthony HODGES made over to
John SHAYLER his half of the manor for the remainder of the term of
years then to come. Michael FREEMAN, for the better satisfaction of
the judgement of £220 obtained against him by William and Thomas CHAD-
WELL, and for the securing of a debt of £56 then said to be due him from
Anthony FREEMAN, made over his reversionary interest to SHAYLER at
the same time, in trust for the use and benefit of William CHADWELL.
Shortly after, a quadripartite agreement was made between John SHAYLER,
William CHADWELL, Anthony HODGES and Michael FREEMAN dated 23
Sept. 1618 as follows: first SHAYLER acknowledged that the lease was
only assigned to him in trust for the use and benefit of William CHADWELL,
and therefore he, SHAYLER, covenanted to let William CHADWELL enjoy
the rents and profits of this half of the manor for such uses as were stated
in the agreement. It was also agreed that William CHADWELL should
take £100 paid by SHAYLER to Anthony HODGES for the said lease with
the allowance of forbearance at the rate of 10% until the £100 with charges
in that behalf be laid out and sustained should be fully paid.

It was next agreed that after the £100, with allowances for forebearance,
charges and damages should be levied, then William CHADWELL should
take the rents and profits outright for 2 years for raising the sum of £100
for his own use in payment for the judgement of £220 aforementioned.

SHAYLER asks for the case to be dismissed.

20 May 1634

The Answer of William CHADWELL to the
Bill of Complaint of Anthony and William
FREEMAN.

This is almost exactly the same as SHAYLER's answer, the only difference being in the wording, and the emphasis of William CHADWELL's
part in the affair.

*****

113.   C.2 Chas.1/A.47/35
         22 November 1637

         Bill of Complaint of Edmund ANSLEY, the
         elder, of Brookend in the parish of
         Chastleton in the County of Oxon, gent.,
         versus Edmund ANSLEY, junr., William

CHADWELL, sen., and William CHADWELL, junr.

In about 1625 Edmund ANSLEY was seised among other things of the
Manor House of Brookend, together with the following land; Elme Close,
the Pigge Close, the Way Close, Broad Close, West Close, one meadow
called the Over Duxnest, Longhill, Hogg Ground, West Furlong, the
Heath adjoining the Manor House; three several closes of tillage adjoining the Heath on the west side. This was held as a jointure for his then
wife Mary ANSLEY, since deceased, and conveyed to Edward FREEMAN
and John BARNARD in trust to provide for her in the event of her widowhood, and after her death to the use and behoof of Edmund ANSLEY, the
younger, son and heir of Edmund ANSLEY. About 3 years ago (i.e. 1634)
Edmund ANSLEY, the younger, then aged twenty, without his father's
knowledge, proposed to marry Hannah, the daughter of William CHADWELL
of Broadwell, but with the knowledge of William CHADWELL. When
Edmund, the father, discovered that William CHADWELL was not prepared to give a marriage portion with his daughter answerable to the
estate he had settled on Edmund ANSLEY, his son, he objected to the
match, it having meanwhile come to his notice. However at the entreaty
of William CHADWELL and Edmund, the son, Edmund ANSLEY did at
last consent to a treaty of marriage, and William CHADWELL agreed to
give £800 as a marriage portion with his daughter. Edmund ANSLEY,
for his part consented to confirm the settlement of the above lands, ex-
cluding the Heath, when the marriage should take place , Edmund the
father, having the use of them during his life, the entail passing to
Edmund, the son. As Edmund, the son, was only 20 years old, and therefore a minor, the land was not assigned over to him, and the jointure
agreement stated that Edmund, the elder, should continue to enjoy the
use of the land during his lifetime.

Edmund ANSLEY, the elder, also had other land in Brookend known as
Lower Heath, Decayed Piece, The Mill Piece, and the Heath adjoining
it, Ox Leasowe, Mill Pound, Over and Lower Whitehall Meadows, Longe
Meade, Jacksonslade, The Lower Ducksnest. This land was given as
security for the jointure that Edmund, the son, should have for his wife
Hannah when he reached the age of 21, and a tripartite lease between
himself, William CHADWELL, the elder William CHADWELL, of Lincolns
Inn, and Edmund ANSLEY, the younger, was signed, giving half the manor
and the last mentioned land in trust to the CHADWELLS after the death of
Edmund ANSLEY, the elder, for the use of the heirs of Edmund, the
younger, and Hannah. After Edmund and Hannah married, the son took
his father to court and extracted a fine for £200 from the court for non-
fulfilment of the above agreements, the CHADWELLS holding on to the
lease agreement, and claiming the money on it. Edmund, the father,
complains that as he has two daughters on whom he must make settlements,
and without the title to his land he is unable to do so, he asks for the
CHADWELLS and his son to make answer and produce the agreements
before the Court.

The Answer of Edmund ANSLEY, the younger,
gent, one of the defendants to the Bill of
Complaint of Edmund ANSLEY, the elder.

Edmund ANSLEY agrees that at the time mentioned in the bill his father seised of the Manor of Brookend and of the other lands mentioned. He also agrees that his father, for £700 conveyed for the marriage portion of Mary, his wife, this defendant's mother, the Manor and lands in trust to Edward FREEMAN and John BARNARD. Touching the marriage treaty between himself and Hannah CHADWELL, he says that his was not made without his father's knowledge as his father alleges in the bill, nor did William CHADWELL, the elder, persuade him to it against the elder ANSLEY's wish. He hopes to prove that the first marriage treaty was made with the free consent of his father, and was concluded between him and William CHADWELL senior, without him, Edmund ANSLEY junr., being a party to it. Regarding the land which was entailed on him, and regarding the fact that he was then only 19 years old, Edmund ANSLEY, the father, made an agreement with William CHADWELL, senior, on 7 Dec. 1635 for the necessary provision and maintenance of Edmund junr., and Hannah, his then intended wife, whereby he demised half the manor of Brookend and all the land mentioend in the bill to his son for 80 years at a peppercorn rent. At the same time he also made an agreement by tri-partite indenture between Edmund ANSLEY senior, William CHADWELL senior and junior, and Edmund ANSLEY, junior, whereby he granted half the manor and some land to William CHADWELL, senior and junior, in trust for the young couple, and in return William CHADWELL agreed to pay the young couple £200 after conveyance of half of the manor. But Edmund ANSLEY denies that he promised to pay the £200 to his father, or that the lease made to the CHADWELLS was made only for securing the jointure of Hannah, but that it was made for the necessary maint-enance and living of himself and of Hannah, his now wife, if she should survive him; and for some provision to be had for their heirs. Though his father asked him for assurances before he reached the age of 21, he then refused, in order not to prejudice himself, but that since he has reached the age of 21, he still refuses to give any promise that would tend to jeopardise his position in regard to his coming into the full use of the lands that are already entailed to him and his heirs. If he did give the assurances asked for by his father he would be debarred from giving a jointure to any second wife he might wish to marry should Hannah predecease him. He denies all knowledge of the Oxford Assize incident, but says he believes a paper was sent by his father to William CHADWELL, senior, but does not know if William CHADWELL consented to it. He believes that the lease granted to the CHADWELLS is still kept on foot against his father and he hopes it will be, as his father has sold lands to the value of £200 per annum, which he promised he would not sell; also his father has much encumbered the rest of the estate and has allowed divers persons to reside in the house at Brookend, who lop trees and commit wastes and spoils on the land and suffer the house to fall into decay, whereas his father had promised him the free use of the house if he should no inhabit it himself. Besides his father has in such wasteful and ill manner demeaned himself and his estate not only to the disinherison of his son, but also to the manifest disgrace and obloquy of himself and of his posterity, so that he, the son (albeit he yet forebeareth to express the same upon record against a father) yet in case he shall be by the causeless suite of his father forced to it, then for the safeguard of the residue of his inheritance out of the hands of his father to sell away and consume, he hopes he will be admitted to make proof to the Court. He also denies that his father has made him any lease of any lands mentioned in the bill other than the lease for his maintenance. He denies that he has give out in speeches that he has any writings whereby

he has any claim to the land known as the Homeward Heath, and he does
not challenge any present possession of it otherwise than as tenant intail
by virtue of the first recited deeds and conveyances. He denies that he
has borrowed £100 from his father, or any other money or chattels, or
that he has made any promise to repay such money or chattels. He says
he went to his father's house and there found the counterpart of the aforesaid lease and some other of his father's writings which were negligently
and carelessly left there and took them into his own custody, well knowing
that his father often absented himself from home, however he is ready to
give them back if his father takes care of them and provided his father
agrees not to trouble him further.

> The Answer of William CHADWELL, the
> elder, one of the defendants to the Bill
> of Complaint of Edmund ANSLEY, the elder.

William CHADWELL says he believes it to be true that Edmund ANSLEY
senior was seised at the time mentioned in the bill of the manor and lands
mentioned. He also confirms the conveyance to Edward FREEMAN and
John BARNARD. He says that Edmund ANSLEY, the father, made the
first move in the marriage question and had several meetings with him.
After divers offers and propositions it was in about November 1635 agreed
that the marriage should take effect, and that William CHADWELL, the
elder, should give £500 portion with his daughter, Hannah, whereof £300
was to be paid to Edmund. ANSLEY, senior, and the residue to Edmund
junior, and by the same agreement he was to entertain Edmund, the son,
and his wife, with one man-servant and one maid-servant, with meat
drink and lodging for the space of the first year after their marriage;
and likewise to provide apparel and other goods for Hannah to the sum
of £50, so that in all he was to give Edmund ANSLEY about £600 on the
marriage. In consideration of this, Edmund, senior, was to settle lands
to the value of £100 per annum at least for the maintenance of Edmund,
junior, and his wife and family. It was also agreed that he should settle
other lands as a jointure on Hannah and Edmund and their heirs. In part
performance of this agreement, Edmund, the father, let to farm half of
the manor aforesaid in Brookend as well as the Elme Close, Pigge Close
etc. mentioned in the bill, for 80 years. He confirms that these lands
were entailed on Edmund, junior, and his heirs, and that he was 19 at
the time, and that the tripartite agreement was made to secure the payment of £200 to Edmund, junior. To further the marriage, Edmund,
senior, promised not to sell any lands of inheritance from his son, and
that the son should have the other half of the house at Brookend if he
did not inhabit it himself. And yet, since the marriage Edmund ANSLEY,
senior, has much wasted his estate and sold away lands of inheritance
whereof he was then seised to the yearly value of £200, and has put divers
persons to dwell in the house and suffers it to fall into decay. He says
he knows of no agreement made between the father and son before or
since the marriage, or of any promise by the son to assure the lands.
However a deed was drawn up to this purpose and sent to him CHADWELL,
to peruse. But afterwards it was sent back, and it was not engrossed
with his consent, or with Edmund ANSLEY, junior's consent. Nor was
any date fixed for the signing of any such deed, or for the levying of a
fine, or that Edmund, senior, went to Oxford Assizes to acknowledge a
fine. He also denies persuading the son not to meet his father and not

to sign the assurance. He says it is true that the lease was kept on foot and is now in the custody of Hannah for whose benefit it was made.

He also denies he has casually, or otherwise, got the counterpart of the leases made by Edmund, senior, or any other deeds, nor does he know of any money borrowed by the son from his father. He concludes by saying that what Edmund ANSLEY, senior, did regarding the marriage, he did of his own free will and without any persuasion or force applied by him, William CHADWELL, the younger, or Edmund ANSLEY, the younger.

> The Answer of William CHADWELL, the younger, one of the defendants to the Bill of Complaint of Edmund ANSLEY, the elder.

William CHADWELL, the younger, repeats the statements concerning the Manor of Brookend and its conveyance to Edmund FREEMAN and John BARNARD. He says he was not a party to the marriage agreement, but afterwards he was made a party to the tripartite agreement as a trustee. The rest of this document is largely a repetition of the answer given by William CHADWELL, the elder.

*****

114. C.2 Chas.I/C.98/36 & C.93/34.
14 Feb. 1650/1

> Bill of Complaint of Michael CHADWELL of Chipping Norton, Oxon, Gent., versus William VEYSEY and Robert VEYSEY

Whereas Edward CHADWELL, late of Chipping Norton, deceased, the plaintiff's father, in his lifetime became indebted to one Robert VESEY, of Taynton, in the County of Oxford, Gent., for the payment whereof gave several securities by lease, bonds and other security, by force of which Robert VESEY raised great sums of money out of the land of Edward CHADWELL during his life, and also received many great sums of money from Edward CHADWELL in satisfaction of the debt or the greatest part of it. About the year 1630 Edward CHADWELL died leaving the plaintiff his only son and heir, then an infant aged 15 years or thereabouts. Shortly afterwards, Robert VESEY died and made William VESEY of Taynton, Oxon, Gent., his executor. About 1640 William VESEY, his executor, claimed that great sums of money were due to him as executor upon the bonds and other securities given by Edward CHADWELL to Robert VESEY and brought several actions against the plaintiff as heir of Edward CHADWELL, and the tenants and occupier of the lands, the plaintiff then being nearly 21 years of age, whereas in truth the plaintiff was not liable either in law or equity to pay the debts of his father, Edward CHADWELL, as heir to him, for he had no lands by descent from Edward CHADWELL. Nevertheless,

the plaintiff, being then young and ignorant was wrought upon by William
VESEY to come to an agreement with him. Accordingly the plaintiff,
trusting to the honesty of William VESEY, who protested that there was
about £600 due to him, asserted that he would favourably treat him if
he would come to terms with him, or otherwise if he did not he would
prosecute him to the extremity of the law. Michael CHADWELL, in
order to purchase his "quiet" agreed to pay William VESEY £500, or
£100 per annum for 7 years immediately following in full satisfaction of
all the debts of Edward CHADWELL, his father to Robert VESEY,
father of William VESEY, and that all bonds and securities and assurances made by Edward CHADWELL to Robert VESEY should be vacated
and made void and the satisfaction acknowledged, and for the security of
the performance of this agreement, Michael CHADWELL agreed, in
1640, to grant William VESEY four closes of pasture land and all the
premises belonging to them called the Grove, one meadow called Longe-
ham, one close called Harper's Leyes, one close called Pool Close,
and Foxholes, and one further close (name illegible) all in Chipping
Norton, to the yearly value of £100 for a term of 21 years at the yearly
rent of 1d, with a proviso that if Michael CHADWELL or his heirs, or
executors paid William VESEY £100 per annum for 7 years, that then
the lease should be void and that during the term of 7 years Michael
CHADWELL should continue the possession and receive the rents and
profits of the siad lands to his own use, or to such purposes as was laid
down in the indenture of lease. By force of this Michael CHADWELL
continued in possession of the lands for the space of two years, or
thereabouts, and paid William VESEY £100. He sowed the great part
of the land the third year with corn and intended to pay the £200 for the
second and third year according to the agreement, but by the unhappy
distractions of these times, he is much impoverished and for that cause
failed to pay £100 which should have been paid the second year. William
VESEY taking advantage of the breach of the conditions according to the
strict rules of the law, and desiring to possess himself of the plaintiff's
lands and crops of corn growing upon them, about six years since entered upon the lands and took the crops of corn growing upon other of
Michael's lands to the value of £400 at the least. He, and others under
him, have ever since taken the rents and profits of the lands, and of
divers other of the plaintiff's messuages, lands and tenements in Chipping
Norton. By these means William VESEY not only received his just and
due debts according to the agreement but has received further sums, and
now refuses to restore the surplus to Michael CHADWELL, or to restore
the lands, or to give an account of his receipts from the crops, rents
and profits, whereby it might appear what he has received, but on the
contrary he combined and confederated with Robert VESEY, his son,
and Robert VESEY of Chimney, Oxon, his cousin, to keep the lands
during the term of 21 years, although the debts be satisfied, and for
that end William VESEY granted his estate thereon to Robert VESEY
his son, and Robert VESEY, his cousin, to their own use, but for what
consideration Michael CHADWELL is unable to find out, which is contrary to law and equity. He has no remedy by the strict rules of common
law to avoid the lease and the entry to William VESEY to gain possession of the lands and discover what estate both Robert VESEYS have in
the lands nor by whom and for what consideration the VESSEYS account
for the twon rents and profits received against the premises, but only
by enquiry in this Court. He requests that William VESEY be required
to set forth the agreement and the truth and need thereof, and what, and

how much money was justly due to him at the time of the agreement, and
likewise to show forth the indenture of lease with its particular grants
and conditions, and further that William VESEY and both the Robert
VESEYS to set forth what title they have for the claim to the lands
contained in the lease and the other messuages and lands of Michael
CHADWELL which they hold in Chipping Norton or elsewhere; and to
set forth which sums of money they have raised by corn growing upon the
lands at the time of their entry and by the profits and rents they have
received from the other lands. Michael CHADWELL also asks that they
make a true account to the Court of what they have received, and if the
debts have been satisfied, and in which case that the lease should be
made void, since it was only made in satisfaction for the debt of £500,
also that the bonds be delivered up, and that any surplus of rents or
profits should be returned to Michael CHADWELL to go with all bonds,
judgement and other securities given by Edward CHADWELL to Robert
VESEY in his lifetime.

> The Joint and several Answers of
> William VESEY and Robert VESEY,
> his son, to the Bill of Michael
> CHADWELL, gent., complainant.

William VESEY says that Edward CHADWELL in his lifetime was endebted to Robert VESEY, decd. to the tune of £1,500 and upwards and he
gave Robert VESEY securities for a great part of this debt. Robert
VESEY paid several large sums of money for Edward CHADWELL during
his lifetime to several persons to whom CHADWELL was endebted, to
the value of £150. William VESEY became possessed of a bond dated
29 November 18 Jas.I (1620) for the penal sum of £600 conditioned to pay
£305, and upon this bond Robert VESEY obtained a judgement in Trinity
Term 1631 in the Court of Common Pleas. He also became possessed of
another bond of about £600 dated in September 1620 conditioned for the
repayment of £325 on 29 Sept. 1621. He also has various notes and
endorsements under the hand of the late Robert VESEY, which intimate
that Edward CHADWELL was endebted to him for several other sums of
money, and that Robert VESEY paid Edward CHADWELL's debts after
his death to one BROWNE for £100 and some other debts, the particulars
of which William VESEY does not know. He also says he can prove that
the late Robert VESEY paid £400 to Edward STANHOPE, Doctor at Law,
which Edward CHADWELL owed STANHOPE, sometime one of the
Masters of this Hon. Court. William VESEY also believes that Edward
CHADWELL at the time of his death was endebted to the late Robert
VESEY for at least £1,500. The defendants deny that they know of any
money raised by the late Robert VESEY out of the lands of the late
Edward CHADWELL, or of any money received from Edward CHADWELL
during his lifetime in settlement of his debts. Robert VESEY died on
11 July 1635, and by his will made William VESEY his executor. Robert
VESEY at his death was engaged for others for nearly £1,000 and giving
many charges and annuities by his will amounting to £3,000, and left
many desperate debts at his death. He William VESEY, being importuned
by creditors and legatees for their moneys and finding that Edward
CHADWELL was endebted in his lifetime to the late Robert VESEY for
upwards of £1,500, and being informed that Michael CHADWELL had now
attained the age of 21 years, and that he had inherited an estate in lands

from his father to the value of £400 per annum, he asked Michael for
satisfaction of what was due from him as heir to his father, Edward
CHADWELL, as executor of the late Robert VESEY. Finding Michael
CHADWELL unwilling to satisfy his father's creditors, William VESEY
instituted proceedings for the recovery of £600, but did not push the
thing to trial as he hoped to settle amicably. He denies that he prosecuted the suite with violence on purpose to vex Michael CHADWELL,
but only for the remedy of his just debts. On the contrary, being earnestly solicited by friends to come to a composition with Michael CHAD-
WELL, and bearing in mind that he was owed £1,500, he did agree to
accept £750 which was due to him, and for security Michael CHADWELL
gave him a bond on about 27 January 1641 or 1642 of the penal sum of
£1,500 on condition that Michael CHADWELL should procure one Henry
BEAUFOY, Gent., to join with him; and that they before 1 April then
next following did deliver a lease to William VESEY to farm let so much
arable, pasture and meadow at a rent of £100 per annum for 21 years free
from all encumbrances, with a promise contained in the lease that if
Michael CHADWELL should pay William VESEY £750 in seven years
then the obligation and lease to be void. There was an endorsement in
the agreement that all former judgements and securities should remain
in force against CHADWELL's land until performance of the conditions
contained in the bond. In the event of breach of the agreement, William
VESEY was at liberty to take any course on his securities. William
VESEY further says that CHADWELL and BEAUFOY by their indenture
dated 1 April 18 Chas.I (1642) devised the several parcels of ground
mentioned in the agreement, but did not give a bond of £1,000 for performance of the covenant in the lease as they ought to have done. VESEY
confesses that there is a clause in the indenture of lease which says that
if he pays £750 in the following manner, i.e. £100 in September next
following, £100 on 24 June next following and £100 per annum on 24 June
for 5 years and £50 in June the 6th year, then the indenture be void, but
he does not remember if there was any clause permitting Michael CHAD-
WELL to retain possession during these seven years, for the lease has
been long out of his possession and custody. He denies that the grounds
were worth £100 a year to him as is alleged in the bill, and he also denies
that CHADWELL paid him £100 as alleged in the bill. CHADWELL failing
for two years to pay the money due, and having left his estates and betaken
himself to the service of the late King in his war against Parliament, he,
VESEY, is desirous to have what is due to him. Accordingly towards the
latter end of March 1644 he entered the grounds in question and possessed
himself of them, and did for some time by the direction of one BROWNE,
formerly CHADWELL's bailiff or agent, dispose and let the land at the
best rate they would yield, it being in the midst and heart of these dist-
racted times of war. CHADWELL received £55 10s. 0d. rent for that
part of 1644 before VESEY took possession. For the year 1645 VESEY
says he did not receive more than £20 in rent and profits from the land,
for John BROWNE, CHADWELL's agent had received the profits of most
of the land from the tenants, and for aught he knows BROWNE handed
them on to CHADWELL. For 1646, he made £64 11s. 0d, for the year
1647 he received £32 for the Committe of Sequestrations for Oxfordshire
entered upon the premises in about April 1648 and received the last half
year's rent for 1647, so VESEY was informed by William THOMAS,
gent., then tenant. About May 1648 he, VESEY, was ousted of possession of the land by the Committee of Sequestrations, and the rents have
been kept from him ever since either by the Committee or CHADWELL,

so that he made only £176 1s. 0d. during the whole time he had possession of the land, and that he disposed out of the rent he received from the land the following sums; To the soldiers of the King part for contribution purposes upon the grounds and for mounding the grounds and particular disbursements and occasions for the use of the Complainant, the sum of £14 4s. 0d. To the Parliament's Garrison of (? Gai ...ts House) near Cxon in the year 1645 for ... of contribution imposed upon the grounds and all the rest of CHADWELL's estate in Chipping Norton towards maintenance of the garrison £32 5s. 0d. For contribution and other payments for that part of the year 1647 which he held the land £5 at the least, and some other disbursements.

CHADWELL having another ground called Princesdown, part of which was tillage fit to be sown with corn, and as he went in sowing time in 1645 into the service of the late King, he entreated VESEY to look after the managing or sowing of it and the disposing of the corn that should grow on it. CHADWELL also asked VESEY to overlook BROWNE in the husbanding and managing of it, which VESEY did out of the love and respect he had for Michael CHADWELL. He also suffered BROWNE to receive most of the rents due for the leased grounds to buy seed barley and pay for ploughing and other things necessary, and likewise spent much of his own time overseeing the same; but when the corn that was sowed was inned, one Mr. WHARTON and one HANWELL, who married one of Michael CHADWELL's sisters, pretending that CHADWELL was dead, did violently enter and possess themselves of a great part of the corn, and hurt one of VESEY's servants for defending it, and sold it for how much he does not know. In all VESEY only made about £50 out of it. WHARTON, HANWELL and BROWNE with part of the corn they had taken sowed the ground again the second year, and Michael CHAD-WELL coming home before it was inned, entered and possessed himself of it, but the Committee of Sequestrations seized it and sold it for the benefit of Parliament for some misdemeanour of CHADWELL's. WHARTON and HANWELL discharged some of the people to whom VESEY (? had sold) part of the corn growing in the year 1645 from paying for it, that is to say John OSBALDSTON, Esq., who still owes £ ? 16 or thereabouts as OSBALDSTON has informed William VESEY's son, and several other people who keep the money in their hands due for such corn as VESEY sold to them. He also paid out of the corn money £20 tythe, and for a room to lay the thrashed corn in for his own diet and his men's diet. He also says that on CHADWELL's authority he received £5 12s. 6d. from CHADWELL's tenants in Chipping Norton and Over Norton, but he denies that he received £100 for the crop of corn as is alleged in the bill. William VESEY further says that being endebted to one of the other defendants, Robert VESEY of Chirney, on 8 June 1648 he demised all the land he had leased from Michael CHAD-WELL and Henry BEAUFOY to Robert VESEY, but as CHADWELL knows, Robert VESEY never took possession of the land as one Thomas CHADWELL, who pretended to act for Michael CHADWELL and on his behalf, misinformed the Committee of Sequestrations and by this means, for aught he, VESEY, knows, intending to decieve him and Robert VESEY, procured an order from the Committee to put out the VESEYS.

Robert VESEY the other defendant says that at the death of Robert VESEY, the testator, he was a child of about 8 years old. By his father's order, being the sole executor of the late Robert VESEY he

received some small sums of money out of rents from Chipping Norton,
but how much he does not know as he did not keep accounts. William
VESEY says that allowing for all the disbursements mentioned above,
the net amount he received from the land was £144 12s. 0d; after due
allowance he is still owed nearly £700 by Michael CHADWELL, which
he hopes the Court will order CHADWELL to pay.

*****

C.9/17/58
26 Jan 1654/5

Bill of Complaint of Thomas HOLFORD,
baker, of London, versus Michael
CHADWELL, John CRISPE, John
JORDAN, Robert BRIDGEMAN and
others.

On 6 May 1652 Thomas HOLFORD, being possessed of 20 acres of
pasture ground called The Grove, lying in Chipping Norton in the County
of Oxon, and also, among other lands etc. of a close of meadow called
Longham, in the occupation of John PHILIPS; one close of pasture
called Harpers Leyes, in the possession of Wm. DISTON; one close
of pasture called Clay Lane Close, in the possession of John DISTON;
certain enclosed grounds called Princesdown Meadow, Lower or Little
Princesdown, Middle Princesdown being two grounds now, or late, in
the possession of Wm. DISTON, John SMITH and Philip CAVE, all in
Chipping Norton by virtue of a Statute Staple of £1,000 dated 30 November 1650, and by a writ of Extent and Writ of Liberate upon the said
Statute lawfully executed by Robert LOGGIN, Esq., then Sheriff of
Oxon. On 6 May 1652 he was put into possession of these premises by
the Sheriff and the Statute filed and Writs returned in the Office of the
Petty Bag in this Court. In about February 1652 (1652/3) he let one
Robert BRIDGEMAN of Chipping Norton, yeoman, the 20 acres of
pasture until 1 August next following at a rent of £12. BRIDGEMAN
entered into possession of the pasture ground called the Grove and
took the profits thereof during the term above mentioned, and paid to
HOLFORD the rent, excepting deductions according to Acts of Parliament
amounting to about £10 received by him. On 30 March 1653 Robert
BRIDGEMAN was persuaded by one John CRISPE of Chipping Norton,
gent., an attorney at law, to become his tenant. CRISPE would purchase
a 21 year lease of all the premises formerly granted to Michael CHAD-
WELL, then of Chipping Norton, gent., but now of Dailsford in the
County of Worcester (now Glos.) and one Henry BEAFOY of Warwick,
in the County of Warwick, Esq., on purpose to deceive and defraud the
creditors of the said Michael and his father, Edward CHADWELL decd.,
to William VESEY, executor of the will of Robert VESEY, the elder
decd. about 1641 and afterwards came by means of assignments or otherwise to Robert VESEY the younger of Chimney in the County of Oxon,
gent; (sic) all which CRISPE purchased accordingly and not only had

the premises assigned to him during the remainder of the term ... but also bought of Robert VESEY, the younger, one judgement of £600 entered into by Edward CHADWELL unto Robert VESEY, the elder, in the 6th year of the late King Charles (1630) and £9 damages in Trinity Term. He likewise bought from Robert VESEY, the younger, or William VESEY divers other judgements entered into by Edward CHADWELL and Michael CHADWELL to Robert VESEY, the elder, William VESEY and Robert VESEY, the younger, amounting to great sums of money. William VESEY has taken forth a Writ of Sciri Facias upon the judgement of £600 as executor of the will of Robert VESEY, the elder, and John CARTWRIGHT, Esq., now High Sheriff of Oxon has summoned Michael CHADWELL, as son and heir of Edward CHADWELL, and also HOLFORD's tenants in possession, to wit; William THOMAS, gent, Thomas LODGE, John WILDEGOOSE, John PHILIPS, Robert BRIDGEMAN, Thomas HUGGINS, the elder, William DISTON, Richard DANCE, Hugh FISHER, Ellis LYNDERS, John DISTON, Samuel FARMER, Mark RADBURNE, Thomas REEVE, John BENNET, Robert BEAMONT, John SHEPHEARD, Edward KITE, Thomas MARGETT, Thomas HUGGINS, the younger, James TROWTE, John GOODRIDGE, Robert CHORLEY, Joyce WILDEGOOSE, John SMITH and Philip CAVE to answer it.

All these judgements were long since paid by Edward CHADWELL in his lifetime, or by his son Michael after his death ... John CRISPE, Robert and William VESEY have so continued the matter amongst themselves together with Michael CHADWELL and Robert BRIDGEMAN, that Robert VESEY on 18 April 1653 entered the premises and demised them to a person unknown in these parts of Oxfordshire as his lessee, by name Thomas STAMPE, and they made their own Ejector one Thomas TOMLIN and took the case out of the Court of Upper Bench to the Assizes at Oxford on 18 July 1653. A verdict was passed for STAMP against TOMLIN without any notice or knowledge thereof given to HOLFORD. Thereupon a Writ of Habere Facias Possessionem was issued whereby BRIDGEMAN was with the agreement of Robert VESEY and Michael CHADWELL, Robert BRIDGEMAN, John CRISPE and Thomas STAMP put out of possession of the 20 acres known as the Grove. He was then HOLFORD's tenant by virtue of the Statute Writ of Extent and Writ of Liberate. Robert BRIDGEMAN is now in possession of the Grove under STAMPE or CRISPE by ... right and interest from Robert and William VESEY.

In August 1653 John CRISPE contrived to obtain a promise from Robert VESEY that CRISPE would have all the benefit of the lease of ejectment made to STAMP. CRISPE, BRIDGEMAN and one John JORDAN, gent., attorney at law retained by CRISPE for STAMP, or Michael CHADWELL and Robert VESEY caused an action for trespass to be brought in the Court of Upper Bench in the name of STAMP against BRIDGEMAN, who caused CRISPE to appear for him and to plead not guilty. But no defence being made, HOLFORD not having any notice thereof, was deceived and circumvented by CRISPE and BRIDGEMAN that a trial and verdict passed at Oxford in July last against BRIDGEMAN whereby HOLFORD is likely to suffer to above the sum of £20, CRISPE and BRIDGEMAN not content with doing HOLFORD these wrongs, have combined with John JORDAN to sue BRIDGEMAN again as a trespasser on the said lease for recovery of more damages, notwithstanding that they themselves receive the rents and profits of the 20 acres and other premises under the interest of

Robert VESEY as aforesaid.

Further, Robert BRIDGEMAN has lately sued HOLFORD in the Sheriff's Court of London for £100 damages, claiming that HOLFORD was to save him harmless from the aforesaid trial and verdict; whereas in truth the same was unduly obtained by STAMP, CRISPE, CHADWELL and BRIDGEMAN without any notice thereof given to HOLFORD. HOLFORD has been at apins to remove this action to the Court of Upper Bench.

Further Robert VESEY, John CRISPE and STAMP together with TOMLIN have outed the plaintiff's tenants John PHILLIPS, William DISTON and John DISTON from Longham, Harpers Leyes and Clayland Close. They have caused them to become tenants to CRISPE, Michael CHADWELL, STAMPE and Robert VESEY, the rents being £21 13s. 4d. a year. The plaintiff, living at London far distant from the said parties, having no notice of these proceedings, both to maintain his title to the premises and make his defence against them is enforced to complain in this Court to be relieved against all their frauds and decepts. In pursuance of their dealings CRISPE and JORDAN proceeded as if BRIDGEMAN had never appeared, and amerced the Sheriff, and BRIDGEMAN, Ellis LYNDERS and John HOLFORD were afterwards put to great charges and expenses without any just cause.

On 10 November 1654, CRISPE, Michael CHADWELL, Robert VESEY and William VESEY at Chipping Norton demised to Henry CHAMBERS the farm called Six Yardelands and other land and tenements now in the occupation of William THOMAS, viz; 140 acres of land, 20 acres of meadow and 20 acres of pasture in Chipping Norton, for 4 years from 8 Nov. 1654. They have made one Henry HANDS an ejector of their own choosing a: person unknown to HOLFCRD. CRISPE, as attorney in the Court of Common Bench and attorney in the same cause has delivered a declaration in ejectment to William THOMAS, HOLFORD's tenant in possession, by reason whereof HOLFORD is to answer for William THOMAS to maintain his title and interest and his lease.

Now BRIDGEMAN has quietly enjoyed the Grove during this time from 2 Feb. 1652/3 to 1 August next following, and in all that time he was not troubled for his rent by any person or persons; and being sued upon the trespass at the suite of STAMPE and damages of £9 recovered against him, yet he, HOLFORD, knew nothing of all this. CRISPE, CHADWELL, Robert VESEY, BRIDGEMAN, STAMPE and TOMLIN have combined together to deceive and defraud him.

> The Demurrer of Michael CHADWELL, Esq.,
> John CRISPE, gent., John JORDAN, gent.,
> Robert BRIDGEMAN, William VESEY, Robert
> VESEY, Thomas STAMPE and Thomas TOMLIN,
> defendants to the Bill of Complaint of Thomas
> HOLFORD.

The defendants refuse to acknowledge any of the matters contained in the bill, and say they are not compelled to answer by reason of uncertainties and impertinences contained therein. They therefore demur. Their reasons for demurring are that the plaintiff says he has a right to certain lands by virtue of a Statute Staple of £1,000, but does not say by whom

it was acknowledged to him, whether by the defendants or any person
under whom the defendants claim, or that they are in any way concerned,
or for what moneys it was entered into, or by whom, or where it was
acknowledged. Further the plaintiff does not establish his title to the
lands in question or that they are liable to the Statute ... The plaintiff
has a remedy at Common Law by the examination of the pretended mis-
carriages in the Courts, and can there obtain redress and be restored
again to his possessions if there be cause, and therefore the defendants
ought not to be questioned, or molested in this Court. CRISPE and
JORDAN further say that being attorneys-at-law many of the matters in
the bill scandalously tend to slander them with foul practices in their
profession and they are not compellable to make any answer. BRIDGE-
MAN says that by the plaintiff's own showing, HOLFORD let the lands
named in the bill to him from February 1652 till 1 August next following,
and no longer and received all the rent for it; as the plaintiff does not
instance any other lease, BRIDGEMAN is not obliged to make any answer.

*****

116.　　　C/9/16/65
　　　　　2ό Jan. 1654/5

　　　　　Bill of Complaint of Thomas HOLFORD
　　　　　of London, White baker, versus Michael
　　　　　CHADWELL and John CRISPE.

Michael CHADWELL, late of Chipping Norton, gent., decd., and Edward
CHADWELL of Chipping Norton, son and heir of Michael CHADWELL
being seised in fee or fee tail of divers lands etc. in Chipping Norton
and Over Norton hereafter mentioned, on 26 Nov. 2 Jas.I (1604) in consideration of the sum of £500 granted Edward GAGE Esq., and Francis
EYRMAN alias FRONMAN gent. and their heirs an annuity or rent charge
of £50 to be issuing out of the farm, 6 yardlands and other lands now in
the occupation of William THOMAS, gent;

　　　　　Long Close & Masharells Close now occupied by Thomas
　　　　　LODGE, gent and John WILDEGOOSE;

　　　　　The Overmill, Longham New Close, and Berrie Piece,
　　　　　now occupied by John PHILLIPPS;

　　　　　20 acres of pasture called the Grove, now occupied by
　　　　　Robert BRIDGEMAN;

　　　　　Little Fords Yardeland and the Sydelongs, now occupied
　　　　　by Thos. HUGGINS, the elder;

　　　　　Harpers Leyes, now occupied by Wm. DISTON;

　　　　　Brade Close, now occupied by Richard DANCE;

　　　　　A yardland and Westend Close, now occupied by Hugh
　　　　　FISHER and Ellis LYNDERS;

212

Shering Close now occupied by Ellis LYNDERS;

Clayelands Close now occupied by John DISTON;

One tenement now occupied by Samuel FARMER
One tenement now occupied by Marke RADBURNE;
One tenement now occupied by Thos. REEVE;
One tenement now occupied by John BENNETT;
One tenement now occupied by Robert BRANCOME (?);
One tenement now occupied by Thos. HUGGINS;
One tenement now occupied by John SHEPHEARD;
One tenement now occupied by Edward KYTE;
The Farm tenement now occupied by John CRISPE, gent;
One tenement now occupied by Thos. MARGETTS;
One copyhold tenement & 2½ yardlands now occupied by
Thos. HUGGINS and Thos. HUGGINS;
One copyhold tenement & 3 yardlands now occupied by
James TROUTE;
One copyhold tenement & 2 yardlands now occupied by
John GOODRIDGE;

One messuage & ½ yardland now occupied by Robert
SHERLEY;

One cottage now occupied by John and Joyce WILDEGOOSE;

Certain enclosed grounds called Prinsdown or Princesdown,
now occupied by Wm. DISTON, John SMITH and Philip
CAVE, gent.

All of which are in the parishes of Chipping Norton and Over Norton, in
the County of Oxon.

On 29 Nov, 2 Jas.I, Michael and Edward CHADWELL acknowledged one
Statute Staple to Edward GAGE of £1,000 defeazanced for the performance of covenants etc. comprised in the deed. After the annuity was
granted to Edward GAGE and Francis EYRMAN and the Statute acknowledged to GAGE by Michael and Edward CHADWELL, they in due form
levied a fine upon recognizance of right in the Court of Common Pleas,
and suffered a recovery with double vouchers in the same Court. By an
indenture leading to the use of the said fine and recovery they settled
the fee simple and all the premises on themselves, and thereby made good
and annuity or Statute Staple. Shortly after Michael died, and Edward
GAGE took the rents and profits for about ten years, and being a recusant
he also died beyond the seas, having by his will made Sir John SHELLEY,
Bart and John THATCHER his executors. For non-payment of some of the
yearly payments out of the annuity Sir John SHELLEY and John THAT-
CHER extended all the premises by virtue of the Statute Staple, as certified to this Court about the thrid year of the late King (ca 1627) in the
lifetime of Edward CHADWELL, and a Writ of Liberate thereupon was
issued. The Sheriff of Oxfordshire was directed to put Sir John
SHELLEY and John THATCHER into possession of the premises. Edward
CHADWELL died in the sixth year of the late King (1630) leaving issue
Michael CHADWELL, one of the defendants hereafter named, his only son
and heir. Michael, after the death of his father, being seised in fee of
all the premises, became a delinquent for many years by taking up arms
against Parliament and Commonwealth of England, and all the premises
were seised and sequestrated to use of the Commonwealth for his

delinquency. In September 1650, Michael CHADWELL came privily and
secretly to London and addressed himself to the plaintiff (Thomas HOLFORD)
to seek his advice about how to regain his estate, and to free himself of his
delinquencies, he then having neither money nor friends to trust unto.
HOLFORD, being persuaded by Michael CHADWELL, and being his country-
man and near neighbour, to be compassionate towards him and being willing
to assist him to make his peace with Parliament, was drawn on by many fair
promises and protestations to believe that all the estate of inheritance was
free from all entails and other encumbrances; and that the beforementioned
Statute of £1,000 to Edward GAGE had been paid and satisfied long before.
By this means HOLFORD was inveigled to hazard all his estate, and thereupon procured £500 for Michael CHADWELL. For security Michael
CHADWELL acknowledged a Statute Staple for £1,000 dated 30 November
1650 before Henry ROLL, Chief Justice of the Upper Bench. Thomas
HOLFORD also lent Michael CHADWELL £200 more to furnish him with
apparel and divers other necessaries and accoutrements, taking his bare
promise without witness to make him satisfaction within six months. He
also used all his best endeavours in helping Michael CHADWELL to his
composition for his delinquency. The £500 not being paid, Thomas
HOLFORD caused the premises to be extended on 26 Feb. 1651/2 by Robert
LOGGIN, Esq., Sheriff of Oxon, and a Writ of Liberate issued thereon,
dated 5 May 1652 directed the sheriff to give Thomas HOLFORD possession of all the premises. This was done on 6 May 1652, as freehold until
such time as he be satisfied of his debt of £1,000 plus costs and damages.

John THATCHER died and Sir John SHELLEY surviving him as executor
received the rents and profits of the premises in the lifetime of THATCHER,
and Sir John SHELLEY after his death until about the 12th year of the
late King's reign (1636). They were recusants, and one Christopher
LEWIS, of London, gent., and one SKYNNER, dec'd., being in all the
time of the reign of the late King Charles (I) especially employed as agents
for the executors or assigns of Sir John SHELLEY, for receiving rents
etc. from the premises in satisfaction of the said £1,000 amounting to
£177 16s. 4d. the year, from 1604. The £1,000 with rights and interest
therein is by conveyance come to Christopher LEWIS, and he on about 16
June 1648 demised all the premises to Thomas CHADWELL of Chipping
Norton, gent from the Feast of St. John Baptist for one year at a yearly
rent which, 'for want of the said lease, Thomas HOLFORD is unable to
state exactly. Shortly afterwards, in the same month (i.e. June), LEWIS
and SKYNNER were found to be delinquents by the Committee of Sequestrations then sitting at Banbury, and then and there their estates, whereof
the premises were a part, were sequestrated for recusancy, and part of
the premises were then let to Thomas CHADWELL by the Committee for
which they received a rent of £198. SKINNER is since deceased.

Notwithstanding the annuity has ever since the granting thereof been duly
paid, and notwithstanding the Statute of £1,0CC has many years since been
satisfied; yet lately Christopher LEWIS has combined with Augustine
BELSON and William ROOPER ... to defeat the plaintiff of his just debt
and made some assignment to one Thos. BOWLE, dated 24 Feb. 1652/3,
and Thos. BOWLE has by the aforesaid confederacy made an (? evictor)
of his own one Thos. ROWLAND, and has proceeded in law in the Court
of Common Bench both in Easter and Trinity Term 1653 unknown to the
plaintiff.

Further Christopher LEWIS on 1 Oct. 1653 has sealed a lease of ejectment to one George VAUGHAN, who has likewise made an ejector of his
own, one John DAYE. The plaintiff is in great danger to be outed of his
possession and he is therein altogether without remedy. All this is well
known to LEWIS, BELSON, ROOPER, BOWLE, ROWLAND, VAUGHAN
and DAYE, and they have combined with Michael CHADWELL and William
HASTINGS of Dalesford, in the county of Worcester, gent., and John
CRISPE of Chipping Norton to the end and purpose that the Statute of
£1,000 and Writ of Liberate may be fraudulently and deceitfully kept upon
record without acknowledgement of satisfaction on purpose to defraud the
plaintiff and to out him of possession.

Further, John CRISPE has for a like purpose agreed with Michael
CHADWELL to purchase all the premises, and has possessed himself
of the same and paid thereupon several sums of money to Michael
CHADWELL and fraudulently agreed with him to keep on foot the extent
of £1,000 of Edward GAGE purposely to defraud him (HOLFORD).

About two years since, LEWIS confederated with Michael CHADWELL,
BELSON, ROOPER, ROWLAND, BOWLE, VAUGHAN, DAYE and
CRISPE and agreed that his extent of £1,000 may be continued and kept
on foot in the interest of LEWIS, for the benefit of Michael CHADWELL
and John CRISPE, or such other purchaser as CRISPE shall appoint,
to bar HOLFORD from all benefit of his Statute of £1,000. He requests
that all the said confederates be required to answer these charges.

       The Demurrers of Michael CHADWELL, Esq.,
       and John CRISPE, gent., two of the defendants
       to the Bill of Complaint of Thomas HOLFORD.

The defendants say they are not obliged to make any answers at all to
the bill by reason of the manifest insufficiencies and imperfections
contained in it. Therefore they demur. They further say that the bill
consists of several particulars which do in nowise concern the defendants,
but relate to other persons, and that therefore the said matters having
no dependency the one upon the other they ought not to have joined together in one suite but in several distinct suites. Michael CHADWELL
further says that the bill alleges that he became a delinquent for many
years together by taking up arms against the Parliament and Commonwealth of England which is so great and (? heinous) a crime and of so
dangerous a consequence to him that he humbly conceives that he is not
bound to give any answer at all to the same upon oath lest thereby he
should accuse himself.

John CRISPE says that many of the matters do not conern him, but only
in his practice as attorney.

117.   C.9/157/3
        28 Nov. 1699 (damaged)

        Bill of Complaint of Robert and John
        ADAMS of Westminster, Cordwainers,
        versus Edmund CHADWELL and
        Deborah, his wife.

One John PALMER of Childerditch in the County of Essex, yeoman, grandfather of the plaintiff was seised of certain houses and lands in Essex and
elsewhere, and also possessed of a considerable estate, made his will
dated 17 October 1677. Amongst other legacies and bequests he left to
his two daughters, Deborah and Rebecca PALMER, and their heirs, all
his houses and lands in Essex, but that if either of the said two daughters
should die without issue, then that daughter which survived to enjoy her
sister's share as well. If both the daughters died without issue, then the
property to descend to his three grandchildren Samuel BRETT, Robert
ADAMS and John ADAMS. If Samuel BRETT and the ADAMS brothers
should die without issue then the property to descend to the survivor.
If anyone tried to avoid the entail from the daughters by making a lease,
or sueing a fine of recovery on the lands, or in any way doing anything
that would deprive the three grandchildren of the benefit of the entail,
then the daughters were to give the grandchildren £600. John PALMER
also left £100 each to his three grandsons when they attained the age of
24, and in default of payment at the respective times, the grandsons were
empowered to enter certain lands at Hornchurch in the County of Essex.
He also instructed his executors to provide for the education of his grandsons until they were 24 and to take care to put them apprentice to some
honest calling. He made his daughters Deborah and Rebecca executrixes
of his will and left a considerable estate in houses lands and money.
Robert and John ADAMS say that they received what they were entitled
to under their grandfather's will until they reached their respective ages
of 24. Rebecca PALMER died and Deborah PALMER married one,
Edmund CHADWELL of St. Martins in the Fields, London, gent. After
the marriage Edmund CHADWELL and the ADAMS brothers drew up an
account of the money disbursed, and several sums were charged against
them which ought not to have been charges. It appears that Edmund
CHADWELL and his wife tried to defraud the ADAMS brothers of their
rights under their grandfather's will by pretending that the legacy of
£100 was to pay for their education and not in addition to the cost of their
education. They say that Edmund and Deborah sold or otherwise alien-
ated the Essex property, and as Samuel BRETT is since dead, they are
entitled to the £600 mentioned above. They say they have tried in fair
and friendly manner to arrive at a settlement with Edmund and Deborah,
but that now they combine with one Oliver MARTIN of the Middle Temple
to avoid coming to an account.

        13 Jan. 1699/1700

        The joint and several Answers of Edmund
        CHADWELL and Deborah his wife, defendants
        to the Bill of Complaint of Robert and John
        ADAMS.

                            216

About 20 years since (i.e. 1680) they married and believe that John PALMER was seised of lands in Essex, and did make his will to such effect as is mentioned in the bill. Rebecca died much about the same time as her father, and Deborah was left to prove the will. John PALMER's estate so far from being considerable as is alleged, did not amount to more than £41 per annum, plus a small copyhold tenement let at about £4 per annum, of which only a third part descended to Deborah. The estate let at £41 per annum was charged by John PALMER with the payment of £8 per annum to Ann, his wife, during her life over and above the sum of £12 per annum which he settled on her before, and £3 a year to his sister during her life. Ann PALMER survived her husband 15 or 16 years, and the sister about 2 years. Besides the £100 apiece he left to the ADAMS brothers, he also left £100 to his widow to be paid within three months after his death. He also left other legacies amounting to about £129. She says that his son-in-law Samuel BRETT prevailed upon him to make his will in favour of his, BRETT's, son although PALMER was a very old and infirm man of over 80. In his last sickness he declared that BRETT had prevailed upon him to benefit BRETT's family at the expense of his own, and declared his intention of altering his will, but died before he was able to do so. However Deborah, before and after her marriage to Edmund CHADWELL, took pains to educate the ADAMS brothers and put Robert ADAMS apprentice to one ROLT, a house joiner, and John to one STEPHENSON, a shoemaker, both very honest men well skilled in their respective trades. When the ADAMS brothers reached the age of 24 Edmund CHADWELL told them that the legacies of £100 became payable and reminded them of the great burden John PALMER had placed on his estate by virtue of his will, and reminded them of the great expense he and his wife had been at to educate them in compliance with the terms of the will for nearly 20 years, and of several charges they had been put to as the result of the imprudences and extravagance of the ADAMS brothers. Edmund CHADWELL said that he would nevertheless pay them their legacies and signed a note for £100 each, but kept it back until they made some amends for the charges they had put him to. In view of the great charges on the estate, Edmund and Deborah got the ADAMS brothers to agree to cut the entail without invoking the penalty of £600, and to agree, as their uncle and aunt had been as father and mother to them, not to insist on the receipt of the £600 if the CHADWELLS should dispose of the property. They agreed freely to go with Edmund CHADWELL to counsel to find out how they might best cut the entail. The ADAMS brothers signed a deed dated 18 September 1698 acknowledging receipt of £100 and thereby acquitted and released the house and land of the late John PALMER in Northend in the parish of Hornchurch, Essex, made liable to the payment of the legacy and also relinquished their rights to all other legacies under the will of John PALMER ... These deeds were severally and distinctly read over to the plaintiffs and they freely and voluntarily acquiesced thereon, and understood that they would thereby be debarred from the receipt of the £600, or any other money by reason of the cutting of the entail. They flatly deny any suggestion of fraud on their part. At this time they had free use of their uncle's house and table, and Robert had continued to live with his uncle and aunt for a considerable time after he was 24, for which no charge was made. If as they allege, they had been in such poverty and need, they could have entered the property at Northend and taken possession before they received the notes for £100, but they did not do so, nor did they appear to require ready money for a considerable time since they did not take up the notes for some time after they had been issued to them. In view of the foregoing Edmund and Deborah CHADWELL ask the Court to uphold them in their refusal to give the ADAMS brothers £600 with interest as they ask in the bill. Edmund and Deborah deny the various charges made against them, and Edmund says that he paid a fine for Robert to his admission to a copyhold estate held of the Manor of Childerditch in the County of Essex, amounting to £4 which he deducted from his account, and when he made up his accounts with the plaintiffs he furnished them with all the vouchers and receipts for the sums he had disbursed on their behalf.

*****

ROYALIST COMPOSITION PAPERS

118.   SP 23/195

William Chadwell, the younger, of Broadwell in the county of Gloucester, Gent., was a member of the House. His delinquency that he deserted his dwelling and went to Oxford and lived there whilst it was a garrison holden for the King against the Parliament and was there in the time of the surrender. To have the benefits of those articles by Sir Thomas Fairfax's certificate of 26 June 1646 he doth appear. He had neither taken the negative oath nor the national covenant but prays to be spared on these articles and the vote of the House of Commons pursuant. He compounds upon a particular delivered in under his hand by which he doth submit to such fines etc., by which it doth appear that he is the owner of goods and chattels, and hath owing to him in good debts in all to the value of £300. Other estates he hath none.

Fine at a tenth £30   16 Dec 1646

To the Honorable Committee at Goldsmith's Hall for compounding with delinquents. The humble petition of William Chadwell, the younger, of Broadwell in the county of Gloucester showeth that he did adhere unto the King in this present war against the Parliament; by reason of which delinquency he, being a person comprised within the articles of Oxford, desires to be admitted to compound according to them for his estates and though very small, his father, living, and in displeasure with him for his said adhering.

William Chadwell
Accepted: 17 Nov 1646

218

SP 23/195

A particular of what William Chadwell, the younger, of Broadwell in the
county of Glos desires to compound for according to the Articles of
Oxford. The remainder of his books £80, horses £60, some other small
goods in his possession £70, a debt owing to him from one Mr. Kilburn
£40, a moiety of a chamber in Lincoln's Inn £50. A total of £300.

(s) William Chadwell.

SP 23/195

Sir Thomas Fairfax Knight General of the forces raised by the Parliament:
Suffer the bearer hereof, William Chadwell, Esq., with two men who was
in the city and garrison of Oxford at the surrender thereof and is to have
full benefit of the articles agreed unto upon the surrender, quietly and
without let or interruption, to pass your guards with his servants, horses,
arms, goods and all other necessaries and to repair unto London or elsewhere upon his necessary occasions. And in all places where he shall
reside or whereto he shall remove, to be protected from any violence to
his person, goods or estate according to the siad articles, and to have
full liberty at any time within six months to go to any convenient port and
to transport himself with his servants, goods and necessaries beyond the
seas and in all other things to enjoy the benefit of the said articles.
Hereunto due obedience is to be given by all persons whom it may concern
as they will answer to the contrary. Given under our hand and seal 6
day of June 1646. To all officers and soldiers under my command and to
all others whom it may concern.

(s) Sir Thomas Fairfax.

SP 23/214

Michael Chadwell of Chipping Norton in the county of Oxon, Gent., His
delinquency that he was in arms against the Parliament. He petitioned
here the first of May 1649. He compounds upon a particular delivered
in under his hand by which he submits, etc., and by which it appears that
he is seised in fee to him and his heirs in certain messuages, lands and
tenements in Chipping Norton aforesaid and Over Norton in the said
county of Cxon of the yearly value before the war of £167, and of certain
old rents there to the value of £2 11s. 4d., out of which he craves
allowance of one thousand pounds debt due by statute in 2 Jas. I (1604)
to Sir John Shelly and long since extended and assigned over to William
Skinner and Christopher Lewis in whose right it is still enjoyed. £100
debt to William Vesey, for which the said Vesey had an old judgement
against the compounder's father. And the compounder by his deed
bearing date 1st of April 18 Caroli (1642) leased divers parcels of the
premises to the said William Vesey for 21 years redeemable upon payment
of £750 by equal instalments (?) for 7 years, and the last £50 the 24th
June 1649 which deed is not produced but appears only by the affidavit
of William Thomas, Gent., who engrossed the lease and William Batson,
Gent., who drew it. £110 debt due to Christopher Kendall by judgement

in the Common Pleas in Easter Term 1642 and for which the moiety of the premises were extended by the Sheriff of Oxon upon an edict dated the 20 March 1642/3.

Fine at 1/6 £505 15s 4d.   (s) 19 June 1649

SP 23/214

William Thomas of Chipping Norton in the county of Oxon, Gent., age 46 yrs. of thereabouts, makes oath that a lease being the date of 1st day of April in the 18th year of Charles the King, from Michael Chadwell of Chipping Norton in the county of Oxon, Gent., and Henry Beaufoy of Warwick in the county of Warwick, Esq., was granted unto William Vesey of Taynton in the county of Oxon, Gent., for the consideration of £1,200 of those several grounds of pasture land hereafter mentioned, to wit: Prince Down Meadow, Lower or Little Prince Down, Middle Prince Down, being two grounds of pasture, The Grove, Longham, Pools Close, Harpers Lees, and Clay Lane Close from the date of the said lease for 21 years at 12 pence a year rent, and with a proviso herein contained that for the use of Michael Chadwell did pay the sum of £750 in manner following, that is to say a £100, 29 September next following the date of the said indenture and £100 more the 24 June which was in the year of our Lord 1643; £100 more the 24th of June 1644; a £100 more the 24th of June 1645; £100 more on the 24th of June 1646, also 1647 and 1648 and £50 more the residue 24 June 1649 then the lease to be void. Which lease was drawn in paper by William Batson, Gent., and his dep-onent did engross the same and was sealed by Mr. Chadwell, Mr. Beaufoy, and Mr. Veysey in the presence of the said Mr. Batson and others who subscribed their names thereunto, as witnesses. And for non-payment of the said moneys the said Mr. Wm. Veysey hath entered upon the premises and doth enjoy the same.

Sworn 31 May 1647

John Page.

Wm. Batson of Staple Inn, Gent., aged 56 years or thereabouts maketh oath that he did draw the foresaid lease in paper and desired the foresaid Mr. Thomas to engross the same and was present at the ensealing and delivery thereof in form aforesaid.

Sworn 31 May 1647

John Page.

SP 23/214

To the Right Honorable Commissioners for Compositions sitting at Goldsmith's Hall. The humble petition of Michael Chadwell of Chipping Norton in the county of Oxon, Gent., now living in Durham, showeth that your petitioner was in arms against Parliament in these late wars and humbly moves to be admitted to compound for his said delinquency and for his estate, both real and personal

(s) Michael Chadwell
Received: 10 May 1649

A true particular of my estate in the county of Oxford. I have a house called "the Farm" in Chipping Norton with certain closes and tenements belonging to it held in fee, valued in the best times at the yearly value of £50. I have in Chipping Norton, a mill with two closes belonging to it valued at £16 a year; one pasture called Prince Down near the town of Chipping Norton, £80 a year. I have in Over Norton land to the value of £21 a year. In old rents £2 11s. 4d. All this land is extended for my father's debts viz William Veysey, clothier, hath an extent for £800. Also extended by Sir John Shelley and assigned over to William Skinner and Christopher Lewis £1,000 and Christopher Kendall hath an extent for £110.

(s) Michael Chadwell.

SP 23/73

To the Honorable Commissioners for the Compounding with Delinquents. The humble petitions of Michael Chadwell of Chipping Norton in the county of Oxon showeth, that your petitioner being siesed in fee simple of the Manor of Chipping Norton and divers land thereto belonging, and having had a fine imposed on him for his delinquency, which fine he is not able to raise by reason of his imprisonment at Oxford, by reason whereof his whole estate is under sequestration still. He humbly prayeth Your Honor's order to the Commissioners of the county of Oxon where your petitioners estate lieth, to allow unto him a full 1/5 part of the profits of his lands for the sustenance of his wife and children and he shall pray your humble indulgence, etc.

Michael Chadwell
24 Oct 1650

SP 23/73

The Right Honorable Commissioners for Compounding with Delinquents, etc. The humble petition of Michael Chadwell showeth that your humble petitioner being in town in prosecution of his composition cannot by reason of the late Act of Parliament stay in town to effect the same without power from your Honors. He therefore humbly prayeth your Honorable Honors will be pleased to grant your humble petitioner liberty to continue in the town to perfect his composition.

Michael Chadwell
undated.

SP 23/73

To the Right Honorable Commissioners for Compounding with Delinquents. The humble petition of Michael Chadwell of Chipping Norton showeth your petitioner was fined the 25th of June last in the sum of £505 15s. 0d. for his delinquency by the Committee for Compounding, when he, coming up to London in prosecution of the said composition and to pay in the moiety of his said fine, and to have it reviewed by reason of divers extents and engagements that were upon his estate, and not allowed upon his

composition, was by the undue practise of some who sought your petitioner's ruin, arrested upon suspicion of murder and carried to the Common
Gaol of Oxford, where he hath lain in prison until the last Assizes held
for the said County of Oxon where your petitioner was tried for the said
supposed murder and acquitted of the same. By reason of which restraint
he hath been disabled to pay the said fine and prosecute his (?) review
within the times limited for the same. Now in regard your petitioner hath
not wilfully neglected the payment in of his moneys nor the prosecution
of his review, it please the Honorable Committee to accept of the moiety
of his said fine and grant him the favour to have it reviewed by reason
his whole estate is in extend and liable to many other engagements.

26 April 1650

The penalty imposed makes the fine in the whole £632 3s. 9d., which is
to be paid.

By the Committee for Compounding, 6 June 1651.

Upon reading the petition of Thomas Holeford in behalf of Michael Chadwell,
Gent., alleging that he hath paid in full the fine for his delinquency and had
a full discharge from us and yet notwithstanding possession for the lands
for which he hath compounded is denied to be delivered to him and upon
reading our order of the 13th of May 1651 whereby we ordered the said
Mr. Chadwell should be restored unto the possession of the said lands
whereof he was seised at the time of the sequestration and for which he
hath compounded mentioned in his particular, sent down with the aforesaid discharge of the Committee of Sequestrations in Oxfordshire, who
were to see the petitioner put into the quiet possession of the said estate,
and in case of resistance to use the power given them by the ordinances
for Sequestrations; and for that it appears to us by the affidavit of
William Prickett that the said Commissioners of Oxfordshire having
refused to yield obedience to our said order; it is therefore ordered
that the said Commissioners for Sequestrations in Oxfordshire do forthwith pursue the directions of our former order of 13 May aforesaid and
that they see the said Mr. Chadwell put into the quiet possession of the
aforesaid premises accordingly whereof he was possessed at the time of
sequestration.

SP 23/73

Mr. Thomas Holeford of London, baker, maketh call that he did about
the 10th of June 1651, serve an order made by the Commissioners for
the Compounding of Estates dated 6 June 1651 upon Mr. Appletree and
Mr. Draper and others of the Commissioners of Sequestrations in the
county of Oxford at the Sign of the Star in Oxford, being the meeting
place of the said Commissioners for Oxford, by which orders the Commissioners were directed to pursue the former order of the said Committee
for Compounding of the 13th of May 1651 to see Mr. Chadwell in the
order mentioned to be put into the quiet possession of the lands for which
he had compounded, but a parcel of enclosed lands called Prince Down
to the value of £90 a year or thereabouts is still detained from this
deponent, and also from the said Mr. Chadwell, upon pretence of a

statute acknowledged to Mr. Nicolson above 40 years since.

(s) Thomas Holeford.

To the Worshipful Committee for Sequestrations.

The case of Michael Chadwell humbly presented. Showeth that Michael Chadwell of Chipping Norton in the county of Oxford, Gent., heretofore delinquent, did compound with the Commissioners for Compositions for his estate in Chipping Norton and there being some statutes or judgements not vacated, prayed allowance of them, but was denied it by the Committee in regard they were very old and presumed satisfied. The Committee set his fine as for land clear of them and he paid it, and had their order of the Committee of Sequestrations in the county of Oxon for his discharge and restitution to possession. The Committee of Oxfordshire allowed it, but one Mr. Dyson and Lt. Smith of the county Troop, his son-in-law, and Philip Lane having formerly possessed themselves of a ground called Prince Down, a parcel of the said sequestrated estate, under some estate or title derived from the Committee of Sequestrations of the said county, do now confederate themselves with one Michael Overblow of Southwaite, who pretend a statute of about 40 years old, and the said Dyson, Smith and Lane, being in possession as aforesaid will and now, notwithstanding the said Committee's order for discharge, hold over, pretending some title from the said Nicholson, and plow up the lands of the said Michael Chadwell, and hold him out of them by strong hands. Our humble request therefore is that you would grant your order for quiet possession, and if they have any title for the said land, to prosecute of their remedy for the recovery thereof at law. Mr. Chadwell paid £548 7s. 6d. for his fine and was forced to mortgage his land to procure the money. The time of the mortgage being even now expired and he not yet in possession of his land.

SP 23/73

The Committee for Compounding. The humble petition of Thomas Holeford on behalf of Michael Chadwell, showeth that your petitioner having paid in full of his delinquency, and for which he has the full discharges and acquittances from this Honorable Board, yet notwithstanding, one William Thomas, William Dyson, Philip Lane, and others do deny to deliver possession of the said lands to the said Thomas Holeford or to Michael Chadwell. Therefore they humbly pray your Honorable Board to grant an order that they may have possession of the said lands for which they have compounded, and if there by any other things (damaged passage) the said estate that they may have their course in law there being one Gabriel Nicholson and Nicholas Chomley who pretent a title to the said estate.

Thomas Holford.

SP 23/73

Haberdasher's Hall, London.

By the Committee for Compounding. 9 November 1650.

223

Whereas Michael Chadwell of Chipping Norton in the county of Oxon hath accordingly satisfied the whole fine which was imposed on him, and hath applied himself to this Committee for a full discharge thereupon: It is therefore ordered that the estate of the said Michael Chadwell according to the particular hereunto annexed shall be, and is hereby, clearly freed and discharged from sequestration (with an exception to the right or estate of the said Michael Chadwell in, or to all advowsons, presentations and right of patronage to any church or chapel and the said Michael Chadwell permitted to·dispose of it, or any part thereof, as freely and fully as at any time before the said delinquency he might or could have done; And that he be not further troubled molested or proceeded against in the way of sequestration for any delinquency charged upon him for anything said or done against the Parliament; But if there shall be any further estate discovered belonging to the said Michael Chadwell not mentioned in the said Particular or that the estate therein specified were before these troubles of greater value than by the said Particular is given in, the profits of such estate so omitted, as also the surplusage of what is specified, is not hereby to be discharged but to be sequestrated and so to continue until further order. And if the said estate, or any part thereof, be leased out to any person by such who have power to let the same, the Compounder is to satisfy himself with the rent for which the same is so let during such time or the remainder of such time for which the same is leased as aforesaid. And hereof all Commissioners for Sequestrations and other officers whatsoever are to take notice and observe the same and yield obedience hereunto notwithstanding the said Michael Chadwell shall (damaged passage) or any particular ordinance or act for his discharge) as they will answer the contrary at their peril.

Signed: Edward Winslow
William Molins
Richard Moores

Received by us Richard Waring and Michael Waring, treasurers of the moneys to be paid into Goldsmith's Hall of Michael Chadwell of Chipping Norton in the county of Oxon, Gent., the fine of £505 15s. 4d. the full of his £505 15s. 4d. fine and for one year for 4 months interest of his first moiety £26 19s. 2d. and also for 9 months at 10% interest of the latter moiety, £15 13s. 0d. imposed on him by the Parliament of England as a fine for his delinquency to the Commonwealth which we have received this 9th day November 1650 in full for principle and interest.

(s) Richard Waring
£548 7s. d.

I have taken note of this acquittance, 26 Nov 1650

(s) R. Sherwyn, auditor.

SP 23/73
7 Jan 1650/51

By the Commissioners for the Sequestration for the county of Oxon.

Whereas there was produced unto us this present day an order from the Commissioners for Compounding with Delinquents dated 9 November 1650 whereby it is expressed that Michael Chadwell of Chipping Norton, Gent., hath satisfied and paid the whole fine which was laid upon him for his delinquency, whereupon it is ordered by the said Committee for Compounding with Delinquents that the estate of the said Michael Chadwell shall be and is hereby discharged from sequestration (with an exception of the right or estate of the said Michael Chadwell in or to all advowsons presentations and right of patronage to any church or chapel). And the said Michael Chadwell permitted to dispose of it or any part thereof as freely and fully as at any time before his delinquency he might or could have done; and that he be no further molested, troubled, or proceeded against for anything said or done against the Parliament but if the said estate or any part thereof were leased out to any person by such who had power to let the same the compounder is to satisfy himself with the rent for which the same is so let during such time or the remainder of such time for which the same was so leased as aforesaid. It is hereupon ordered by this Committee that the said estate of the said Michael Chadwell be discharged from sequestration accordingly and he be permitted to dispose thereof freely and fully as he might or would have done at any time before his delinquency. That the said order of the said Commissioners for Compounding be in all things fully and punctually observed and all sequestors and other officers and persons whatsoever are to take notice and observe the same and yield obediance hereunto as they will answer the contrary at their peril.

(s)   Wm. Dray
Thos. Apletree

SP 23/107

To the Honorable Commissioners for Compounding with Delinquents:
The humble petitions of Gabriel Nicholson, sheweth that your petitioner hath extended certain lands and tenements in Chipping Norton and the county of Oxon for a just debt of £500 due unto your petitioner upon a statute staple long since acknowledged by one Edward Chadwell who died divers years since, and the land so extended descended upon Michael Chadwell as son and heir to the said Edward, and the premises so extended are in the hands of the Commonwealth under separate sequestration for delinquency of the said Michael Chadwell, and your petitioner cannot have benefit of the said extent without your honor's order. Therefore your petitioner humbly prayeth his extent that it may be allowed of. That he may hold the premises until he be satisfied his said debt or that you would be pleased to admit him to compound for the said estate so extended according to your new act having regard to the said debt for such interest rate and fine as you shall think meet.

(s)   Gabriel Nicholson
29 August 1650

Rejected.

SP 23/165

The estate of Michael Chadwell.

The estate of Michael Chadwell of Chipping Norton posted at £124 clear rent set to Mr. Thomas Chadwell for £126 from the 18 January 1650 payable at Lady Day and Michaelmas, out of which estate one Thomas Coleman of Chipping Norton claimeth an annuity of £14 for the term of his life so that the improvement is 40s.

PART IV

C.2 Chas.I C 100/9
13 Feb 1614/5   (Very mutilated)

Bill of Complaint of Arthur CURRER
of West Morton, Yorks, yeoman.

The gist of the beginning seems to be that about 15 December 1613 a
marriage was arranged between Samuel WADDINGTON of Horsforth
and Jane, daughter of Arthur CURRER, part of the terms of the agreement being that WADDINGTON should buy some land with the £60 dowry
Arthur was giving with Jane and that Mr. ...... CURRER of Farnhill
Esq., Arthur's brother, should be a trustee. It is impossible to read
the Christian name, but of Arthur's three brothers, Henry and William
are the most likely in that order. Abraham BYNNS is the other trustee.

*****

C.2 Chas.I C 65/60
7 Feb 1624/5

Bill of Complaint of William CURRER
of Marley, Esq., John RAWSON of
Greenhill, Yorks, John BYNNES of
Bingley, yeoman, versus Henry
GAMBLE and William GAMBLE.

John RAWSON and John BYNNES are the administrators of the goods and
chattels of John OLDFIELD, late of Calfend, Yorks, decd. yeoman.
William CURRER about 25 September 11 Jas.I, then standing in need of
some money and understanding that one Richard SUNDERLAND of Coley,
Yorks, Esq., had had committed to his charge the portions of Ann and
Elizabeth SALTONSTALL, daughters of one Samuel SALTONSTALL,
of Kingston-upon-Hull, merchant, then lately deceased, which Richard
SUNDERLAND intended to put forth for the use of the two sisters at
interest without exacting the full rate of 10%, which then was the usual
rate for money so lent, William CURRER understanding thereof took
steps to borrow £100 from SUNDERLAND at the rate of 9% for one whole
year. William CURRER and Arthur CURRER, his brother, and John
OLDFIELD, on his sureties did become bound to Sir Richard BEAMOND
(BEAUMONT) Kt., and to William RAMSDEN Esq., two gentlemen who
were likewise trusted by SALTONSTALL to the use of the children in
the sum of £100, with condition for the payment of £104 10s. 0d.

William CURRER kept the £100 many years and he paid to the use of Anne
and Elizabeth SALTONSTALL the consideration thereof after the rate
of 9% until about Michaelmas 19 Jas. I (1621) when one Henry GAMBLE
of Doncaster, gent, having married Elizabeth, one of the daughters of

227

Samuel SALTONSTALL, did by licence of Sir Richard BEAUMONT and
Mr. RAMSDEN, in whose names the bond was taken, put the bond in suite
at Common Law against William CURRER. Whereupon William CURRER
on 12 May next following (1622) did compound with Henry GAMBLE and
did pay him £100, being the principal debt due by the bond, by the appointment and direction of Sir Richard BEAUMONT and Mr. RAMSDEN, at
which time Henry GAMBLE demanded of the plaintiff £25 more which he
then alleged was due to him for 8½ years' interest at 10% per annum.
William CURRER refused to pay for he had borrowed the money and had
agreed with Mr. SUNDERLAND to pay at the rate of 9% and no more.
GAMBLE further demanded the sum of £3 10s. 0d. which he (GAMBLE)
then alleged had been disbursed for costs and charges in suite and for
interest of arrears at the rate of 10%. GAMBLE reckoned William
CURRER owed him in all the sum of £27 10s. 0d. for which sum he agreed
with GAMBLE and one William GAMBLE, his father, on his behalf in
manner and form following:- William CURRER, with John OLDFIELD as
his surety should enter into a bond of the sum of £60 with condition for
the payment of £28 10s. 0d. to Henry GAMBLE at a day then shortly to
come yet upon this further condition between William GAMBLE, the father,
and Henry GAMBLE, the son, that if Richard SUNDERLAND should affirm
and make it known to Sir Richard BEAUMONT that the £100 was lent to
William CURRER by Mr. SUNDERLAND at the rate of 9% that then Henry
GAMBLE would abate £8 10s. 0d. of the said £25 claimed by him, and
that William CURRER should but only pay £16 10s. 0d. thereof which was
the rate of 9%.

Yet notwithstanding William CURRER's offer, Henry GAMBLE has put
the bond in suite about a year since, but not liking the proof, the hearing
was discontinued at GAMBLE's instigation. But now divers of the plaintiff's witnesses are dead and he is unable to prove the verbal agreement
except only William GAMBLE, the father of Henry GAMBLE, and
GAMBLE has taken advantage of that fact to put the bond in suite again
at Common Law at Westminster.

         The joint Answer of Henry GAMBLE and
         William GAMBLE to the Bill of Complaint
         of William CURRER and others.

They admit that Richard SUNDERLAND was entrusted by Samuel
SALTONSTALL with the portions of his daughters, Anne and Elizabeth,
to be put forth for their use and benefit. They believe it true that
Richard SUNDERLAND was restrained from taking after the rate
normally given, but they think that it was left to his discretion. They
agree that William CURRER did borrow from SUNDERLAND £100 for
six months, and that he was to pay interest at the rate of 9% for that
one half year. They agree that William CURRER, together with his
brother Arthur CURRER and John OLDFIELD became bound to Sir Richard
BEAUMONT and Mr. RAMSDEN in the sum of £200 for the payment of
£100 within six months.

They hope to prove that William CURRER did not pay £104 10s. 0d. to
Mr. SUNDERLAND nor to the SALTONSTALL sisters according to the
agreement, but desired that the money might remain in his hands for a
longer time, and that he was contented to pay at the rate of 10% per annum

for it so long as he should have it. They agree that Sir Richard BEAU-
MONT and Mr. SUNDERLAND agreed to let William CURRER have the
money remain in his hands, but that the rate of 9% was for the first half
year only.

Henry GAMBLE agrees that he married Elizabeth SALTONSTALL to
whom the money was owing; because he could not get the money which
was due to him in right of his wife, Sir Richard BEAUMONT and William
RAMSDEN Esq., trustees for his wife put the bond in suite and proceeded so far therein that William CURRER and two of his sureties were
outlawed. After they were outlawed, William GAMBLE, on behalf of
Henry GAMBLE, his son, went to William CURRER's house and took
with him a Writ of Capias Obligat against him and his sureties, and showed
him how far the Law had proceeded against him. William CURRER earnestly importuned him (Wm GAMBLE) that the £100 might remain in his
hands for ... ... (2 words) William CURRER said that he and his sureties would presently appear to the said Action and that they would confess
the debt. William CURRER at that time gave warrant under his own hand
and seal to one Thomas RENTON, an attorney in the Court of Common
Pleas, to confess the debt and judgement against him and Arthur CURRER,
one of his sureties upon the bond of £200. After this William CURRER
earnestly entreated William GAMBLE that the £100 might remain in his
hands for six months longer, and he admitted that he owed Henry GAMBLE
£20 for interest for 2 years which he attempted to pay to William GAMBLE
for his son's use, but William GAMBLE not knowing how much was then
due, nor for how long, refused to accept it, deferring the same until about
six months after being that they had appointed to meet at Mr. RAMSDEN's.
At the meeting at Mr. RAMSDEN's, William CURRER and Henry GAMBLE
came to a reckoning at which time William confessed that he was 2½ years
behindhand with the interest for the £100, amounting to £25, and although
Henry GAMBLE conceived that he was behindhand for much more, yet for
quietness sake he now consented to allow William CURRER's own reckoning, but he demanded a further £3 10s. 0d. for charges in connection with
the aforesaid proceedings in getting his two judgements against William
CURRER, who thought that the charges could not amount to so much as
that. Henry GAMBLE agreed that if he could not bring written proof of
the costs under his attorney's hand and seal that so much had been disbursed, he would restore the difference when the £28 10s. 0d. was paid.
William CURRER, not having the money to pay the £28 10s. 0d. then,
together with John OLDFIELD, now deceased, became bound to Henry
GAMBLE in the sum of £60 for the payment of the £28 10s. 0d. They
both absolutely deny that there was any agreement amongst them then or
at any other time that if Richard SUNDERLAND should declare to Sir
Richard BEAUMONT that the £100 was lent at the rate of 9%, that then
Henry GAMBLE would abate £8 10s. 0d. of the £25 claimed by him for
8½ years interest, nor that William CURRER should pay but £16 10s. 0d.
as is declared in the bill of complaint. But Henry GAMBLE does admit
that he agreed that he would obtain a written account of his costs and
charges from his attorney to show that this amounted to £3 10s. 0d. and
no less and that he would abate so much as might be less than £3 10s. 0d.
when the bond of £60 was honoured. As the second bond has not been
paid, nor any tender of payment made, Henry GAMBLE has put the bond
in suite for non-payment thereof and he intended to proceed in the cause,
but in obedience to the order of this Hon. Court he has forborne to proceed until he has put in this answer to the bill of complaint. Whereas

William CURRER by his bill pretends that Henry GAMBLE put the bond for £60 in suite before H.M. Council for the Northern Parts against him and John OLDFIELD and the cause after answer and replication came to issue and was down for hearing, and that (Henry GAMBLE), not liking the way things were going, proceeded not to the hearing so that it was discontinued, William and Henry GAMBLE say that after Henry GAMBLE had forborne the money due to him by the last mentioned bond for two years or thereabouts, and neither William CURRER nor his sureties had attempted to pay it to him, he did commence suite against William CURRER and John OLDFIELD, and the cause did come up for hearing. Henry GAMBLE retained counsel, but the attorney of William CURRER and John OLDFIELD in open court spoke to William GAMBLE, who was there attending on behalf of his son, and entreated him that the hearing of the cause might be stayed, that there might be a reference to Sir Richard BEAUMONT for the ending of it. The attorney at the same time showed William GAMBLE a letter that Sir Richard BEAUMONT had written to William CURRER to that effect. After perusal of this letter William GAMBLE agreed on behalf of his son to stay the proceedings and to refer the ending and determining thereof to Sir Richard and undertook that Henry GAMBLE would be contented with what end or order Sir Richard should make.

William GAMBLE says that Sir Richard BEAUMONT appointed a day that William CURRER and Henry GAMBLE should meet him at his house at which time he would, as he said, order the difference. Henry GAMBLE attended at the appointed time in expectation of an end being made, but neither William CURRER nor any of his sureties turned up, though he had promised he would attend for that purpose. Henry GAMBLE having long waited and hoped that William CURRER would come and being desirous of having an end to the business, desired Sir Richard to make an end in his absence and undertook to abide by that decision; but William CURRER having gained his own end, by putting off the hearing at York, neglected to come to Sir Richard to speak to him as Sir Richard affirmed, and Sir Richard, perceiving William CURRER's dishonest dealing therein, did disengage Henry GAMBLE of his willingness to refer the ending of the difference to him, and gave him liberty to take his cause against William CURRER as before he has set forth. Henry GAMBLE thereupon proceeded at Common Law against William CURRER.

Nevertheless if William CURRER can show that the £100 was lent at 9% he will abate the £8 10s. 0d. of the money due, but Mr. SUNDERLAND must certify that the rate of 9% was to continue for longer than six months and that he did not state that he lent it to William CURRER at 10% for any period after the original six months had expired. He begs the Court if this is done to order William CURRER to pay the £60 into Court and Henry GAMBLE will then stop proceedings.

Sworn: 18 June 1625 at Doncaster.

*****

125.   C2. Chas.I C 129/57
        5 May 1627

        Bill of Complaint of William CURRER

of Marley, Esq., versus John LOVEDEN.

On 18 March 12 Jas. I (1614) John LOVEDEN, late of Lions Inn, Middlesex, gent, together with William CURRER at his request and for his debts became bound by obligation to one Francis MARTYN of Lions Inn, gent for £100, with condition that William CURRER should pay MARTYN £52 10s. 0d. on 21 September then next following at the Dining Hall of Lions Inn. After making and sealing this obligation William CURRER, at the request of John LOVEDEN, and for security to save him harmless from any damage which might happen by entering the obligation, then became bound by obligation to John LOVEDEN for £150, with condition that if William CURRER should pay Francis MARTYN the sum of £52 10s. 0d. at the day and place mentioned in the former obligation in full discharge of the same, then the said obligation to be void or else to stand in full force. According to the true meaning of which obligation William CURRER has hitherto saved harmless and kept LOVEDEN indemnified for all suits and charges which might happen to him by reason of the entering of the former obligation to MARTYN. Further although William CURRER did not pay the £52 10s. 0d. to MARTYN at the precise time and place appointed, yet he did about the same time agree and compound with MARTYN for the payment of it and obtained further time yet to come, and so has hitherto discharged LOVEDEN from the penalty of the obligation. But now LOVEDEN, although he is not in any way demnified by reason of the said obligation made to MARTYN, yet he has most unconscionably commenced suite against William CURRER intending thereby to enrich himself by William CURRER's great loss and damage.

(Answer missing)

*****

C2. Chas. I C. 97/36
2 Feb 1627/8

Bill of Complaint of William CURRER
of Marley, Yorks., Gent., versus
Thomas CAVE.

About 21 June Jas. I (1623) William CURRER borrowed £60 at 10% from Peter LUPTON, yeoman, for the repayment whereof he, together with Thomas CAVE, Gent., gave security of £126 to Peter LUPTON, conditioned for repayment of the principal sum of £60 and £3 interest on 15 December next following. William CURRER, for the indemnity of Thomas CAVE likewise became bound to him (CAVE) for the sum of £200 conditioned for the payment of Peter LUPTON according to which CAVE was kept free of any obligation to LUPTON. Nevertheless William CURRER was not prepared to pay the £63 at the very day mentioned in the condition of the first obligation, but he did pay LUPTON a consideration for forbearance and interest insomuch that Peter LUPTON was well pleased and satisfied that the money should remain in William CURRER's hands a longer time. Later William CURRER paid LUPTON £20 in part satisfaction, and LUPTON agreed to forgo repayment of the rest until William CURRER was better able to pay it, but he still continued to pay interest on it. Thomas CAVE was acquainted with all this, and he expressed himself content so long as William CURRER kept him indemnified. Since this time William CURRER has fully contented and paid Peter LUPTON all the residue of the principal with full consideration for forbearance. The bond is to be delivered to William CURRER to be cancelled, but Thomas CAVE seeking to take advantage and forfeiture of the obligation and counterbond of £20, he not being demnified to the value of one penny, and also being freed of all future charge by taking in of the said bond first entered into by William CURRER and Thomas CAVE with Peter LUPTON, has put the counterbond in suite at Common Law saying he will have the uttermost penny of the forfeiture, since William CURRER did not pay Peter LUPTON the £63 on the day mentioned in either bond, the counterbond being only to save Thomas CAVE harmless from LUPTON. William CURRER has in fact paid LUPTON all and interest and given him full satisfaction.

(Answer missing)

*****

27. C2. Chas. I T 6/46
19 Oct 1631

Bill of Complaint of Edward THEAKER,
son and heir of William THEAKER,
brother of John THEAKER, the elder,
dec'd., versus Anthony LUTHER,
Henry CURRER and William WATSON.

Whereas Diana Posthuma THEAKER, daughter and heir of John THEAKER, the younger, deceased, being seised of one third part of the rectory of Gargrave in the County of York, and of one third part of all the tythes and wool thereunto belonging died in the month of June 1630. After her decease the premises descended and came as of right to the plaintiff Edward THEAKER as cousin and heir of the said Diana and of her father, and the plaintiff is or ought to be seised thereof accordingly. Whereas Anthony LUTHER of the Middle Temple, London, Esq., being seised of some other estate in the other two parts of the said rectory and tythes, and Henry CURRER of Kildwick in the County of York, and William WATSON of Silsden Moor in the said County, yeoman, (husband of Henry's daughter, Anne) holding in farm the said two parts of the rectory and tythes of Anthony LUTHER and the third part of Diana Posthuma THEAKER or her guardians at a yearly rent of £140 or thereabouts or some other rent, they, Henry CURRER and William WATSON presently after the death of Diana to wit in August then following did atturne tenants to the plaintiff for his third part of the rectory and tythes and

232

promised to pay him his third part of the rent at Michaelmas last, there
being then due to him one whole year's rent amounting to £46 13s. 4d.
The plaintiff accepted Henry CURRER and William WATSON as his tenants and expected payment of his rent of them according to their promise.
But Henry CURRER and William WATSON did not pay the rent to the
plaintiff at any time, but contrariwise paid the whole year's rent of £140
to Anthony LUTHER, to whom, as they pretend, the two parts are due.
Anthony LUTHER has given an acquittance and discharge to Henry
CURRER and William WATSON for the same and promise to save them
harmless against the plaintiff concerning the payment of the rent, pretending the whole rent be due to him, whereas in truth one third part is
due to the plaintiff. Anthony LUTHER, Henry CURRER and William
WATSON know the same to be true, yet Anthony LUTHER pretending
the whole rent to be due to him having gotten the whole rent into his
hands and also having gotten both parts of the lease of the said third
part made unto him doth detain the plaintiff's third part of the rent in
his hands and refuses to pay the same to the plaintiff.

> The joint Answer of Henry CURRER and
> William WATSON to the Bill of Complaint
> of Edward THEAKER.

The defendants agree that Diana Posthuma THEAKER, daughter and heir
of John THEAKER, the younger, deceased, was in her lifetime seised of
one third of the rectory of Gargrave, and of the tythes and rents belonging to it and that being so seised she died, and that the premises descended to the plaintiff as cousin and heir of Diana and her father, but they say
all the same that they cannot conceive or understand how the plaintiff as
yet ought to receive any present profit of the premises, for they have
credibly heard and believe it to be true that the said third part of the
rectory of Gargrave and of the tythes was and is by order of the Rt. Hon.
Sir Robert NAUNTON, Kt., Master of H.M. Court of Wards and Liveries
adjudged and decreed to Edmund DUNCOMBE Esq., and Hester his wife,
mother of the late Diana Posthuma THEAKER as the dower and third
belonging to the said Hester, and happening to her forth of the lands of
John THEAKER, the younger, her late husband deceased; and that
Edmund DUNCOMBE and Hester, his wife, may and shall in right of the
said Hester at all times after the said decree and during the life of
Hester have, hold and quietly enjoy the said third part of the rectory
etc. as assigned to her for her dowry. They say that they believe it be
lawful for Edmund DUNCOMBE and Hester to receive to their own use
the rents and profits thereof during Hester's life without the let or inter-
vention of the plaintiff. The defendants are informed by their counsel
the plaintiff cannot, and ought not during the life of Hester, to entitle
himself thereunto more than to the reversion after her death. The defendants further answer that they think that Anthony LUTHER Esq.,
deceased and late uncle of Anthony LUTHER named in the bill was in his
lifetime seised of the other two parts of the rectory of Gargrave, but
who is heir and right owner of the inheritance of the said two parts since
the death of Anthony LUTHER, deceased, they do not certainly know.
They further say that they hold in farm the said two parts of the rectory
by virtue of a lease made to them by Anthony LUTHER in his lifetime as
also from Thomas LUTHER, brother of Anthony LUTHER named in the
bill for a term of years not yet determined. They also hold in farm the

other third part of the rectory etc. by the demise of Anthony LUTHER, under the yearly rent of £46 13s. 4d. but they both deny that they ever held in farm the said third part of or from Diana Posthuma THEAKER, or her guardians, either at the rent mentioned in the bill, or at any other rent. They confess that they have paid Anthony LUTHER Esq. the yearly rent of £140 for all three parts, viz; for two parts first demised to them by Anthony LUTHER dec'd and Thomas LUTHER, his nephew, £93 6s. 8d. and for the other third part £46 13s. 4d. according to their several and respective agreements. They further answer and deny that either of them at any time had any intention to atturn tenants to the plaintiff for the third part of the rectory, but they confess that they did give the plaintiff six pence but did not give it him with any (? records) of atturnment nor had they any purpose so to do for the reasons hereafter set forth. They further absolutely deny that they did promise to pay the plaintiff a third part of the rent, or any rent at all, either in respect of the rectory, or any other respect although the plaintiff in his bill has untruly surmised and charged them with such a promise. But it is true that after the death of Diana Posthuma THEAKER, the plaintiff came to them and would have had them pay him rent, and offered to bargain with them for a longer term affirming that the same had come to him as heir of Diana, whereupon they did return him answer that they durst not as yet adventure to make any bargain with him at all, neither durst they pay him any rent for they were neither of them ever tenants to him, or to Diana Posthuma, or to her late father, neither had they at any time paid any rent to them, but to Master LUTHER named in the bill, or to Master LUTHER, his late uncle, dec'd, or to Thomas LUTHER. They were immediate tenants to Master LUTHER for the third part of the rectory etc. and felt themselves bound and tied to him to pay the rent to him. When the plaintiff had received this answer and could get no better from them, he seemed to be well satisfied and replied that it would serve his turn as well if they paid the same to Master LUTHER, as if they paid it to himself, or words to that effect. They accordingly paid the £46 13s. 4d. for the third part of the rent to LUTHER for that year. They utterly deny that any part of the £140 paid to Anthony LUTHER was due to the plaintiff.

They further answer that it is true that Anthony LUTHER Esq. named in the bill upon payment of the said £140 did give acquittance and discharge to them and did promise to keep them harmless against the plaintiff, which they hope Master LUTHER will do, for they are persuaded that Edmund DUNCOMBE and Hester his wife, have sufficiently and lawfully authorised Master LUTHER to demise and let the said third part of the rectory to the defendants and to receive the yearly rent for the same.

Taken at Skipton in Craven 12 January 7 Chas. I (1631/2) before us,

William CURRER
William BAWDWEN
Thos. ELLIS

*****

128.   C2. Chas. I C.3/27
26 Oct 1632

Bill of Complaint of Henry CURRER of
Stainton, yeoman, and Robert BAILYE
of West Bradford, yeoman, versus Sir
Robert BANISTER and William LOW.

Whereas John BANISTER, late of Waddington, Yorks., gent, dec'd.,
became endebted in his lifetime to one Sir Robert BANISTER of Passenham,
alias Passingham, Northamptonshire, Kt., in divers sums of money upon
what occasion is unknown, and having given divers bills and bonds under
his hand and seal for payment of the moneys to Sir Robert BANISTER, he,
during his lifetime, but long ago, did afterwards make payment of all or
most of the said sums to Sir Robert BANISTER so that upon account had
between them there remained for consideration moneys and some small
remainder of the principal debt £60, which Sir Robert BANISTER was
contented to accept of at two several days for payment by £30 so as John
BANISTER would become bound with two sufficient securities in two
several bonds for payment at such times as agreed between them. John
BANISTER being well acquainted with Henry CURRER, and being his
neighbour, did entreat him to become bound with him as surety in two
several obligations of £60 apiece for the payment of the two sums of £30
to Sir Robert BANISTER, and to this Henry CURRER agreed.

In December 1625, Henry CURRER at John BANISTER's request therefore
entered into two several obligations for £60 apiece conditioned severally
for the payment of £30 apiece to Sir Robert BANISTER at a time and
place which Henry CURRER cannot now remember. John BANISTER and
the plaintiff have long since paid Sir Robert BANISTER or William LOW,
his agent, the two several sums of £30 amounting in all to £60 in full
discharge of the two obligations.

In respect that Sir Robert BANISTER and William LOW, his agent, whom
he appointed to receive the money, had not the obligations about them at
the time of the payment of the sum mentioned ready to be cancelled, they
promised faithfully to John BANISTER or Henry CURRER and Robert
BAILYE that they would assuredly cancel the bonds whensoever the same
should next come to hand, and would deliver them to Henry CURRER or
Robert BAILYE or John BANISTER for cancellation. But Sir Robert
BANISTER has lately put either one or both the bonds in suit at the
Common Law against Henry CURRER and Robert BAILYE seemingly to
have himself double paid.

Answer of Sir Robert BANISTER and William
LOW to the Bill of Complaint of Henry CURRER
and Robert BAILYE.

Sir Robert BANISTER says it is true that John BANISTER became during
his lifetime endebted for divers sums of money amounting to £262 10s. 0d.
part whereof was due to Sir Robert for money he lent to him or for moneys
received by John BANISTER of four of Sir Robert BANISTER's tenants,
and part for the yearly rent of a certain messuage called Plumpton Hall
and for three watermills called Plumpton Mill, the New Mill and Holeforth
Mill in Plumpton and Newsham in the County of Lancs., and the windmill
called Plumpton Windmill and certain other things demised by Sir Robert
BANISTER to John BANISTER for the yearly rent of £45 to be paid twice

a year, i.e. on 2 Feb and 24 Aug. On 24 July 19 Jas. (1621) John BANI-STER, for securing part of the aforesaid, i.e. £202 10s. 0d., became bound to Sir Robert BANISTER in 9 several bonds, eight being of the penal sum of £45 apiece and one of £50 all conditioned for the several payment of £22 10s. 0d. at several days then to come and now long since past. For securing the other part, i.e. £60, John BANISTER, together with Henry CURRER and Robert BAILYE, became jointly bounden to Sir Robert BANISTER in two bonds of £60 apiece conditioned to pay £30 at a day then to come, but now long since past.

Sir Robert BANISTER denies that John BANISTER at any time during his life paid him all, or the most part of the sums in the 9 obligations, or any part thereof, and likewise denies that upon account being taken between them there remained some small sum or remainder of the principal debt £60. He says that he, finding the remissness of John BANISTER in not making payment of the sums formerly due to him, and John BANISTER being endebted to him for £60 over and besides the same sum amounting to £202 10s. 0d. contained in the nine obligations, he begged John BANI-STER to secure the £60 by his own bond and two sureties; whereupon John BANISTER, Henry CURRER and Robert BAILYE, they being then sons-in-law of John BANISTER, by marriage with two of his daughters, did about the time mentioned in the bill become bound to Sir Robert BANISTER in two several bonds of the penal sum of £60 apiece. Sir Robert denies that John BANISTER in his lifetime, or either of the plain-tiffs, have at any time paid him the sum of £60 for which they became boudn. Howbeit he confesses that Robert BAILYE did pay him £29 19s. 6d. which he, Sir Robert BANISTER, did account of in full discharge of one of the sums of £30 which is all he has received of the sum due to him.

Sir Robert says it is true he did at the time of the receipt of the £29 19s. 6d. promise to deliver to Robert BAILYE one of the two bonds, which he is still willing to do. He confesses he has long since put one of the bonds in suite against the plaintiffs and has obtained judgement thereupon endeavouring thereby to get his due debt and damage. He further says that often in the lifetime of John BANISTER he called upon him for the moneys due, and John BANISTER told him he could not pay as he had bestowed his daughters in marriage, with whom he had disbursed moneys, meaning as Sir Robert believes that daughters the plaintiffs married. Whereupon Sir Robert BANISTER told him that he must not dower his daughters with his (Sir Robert's) money or words to that effect, and that was the last time he saw John BANISTER.

William LOW, agent of Sir Robert BANISTER, says he was willed by his master to call upon John BANISTER for moneys due to Sir Robert on bond often. At length John BANISTER on or about 8 June 1626 paid him part of the sums due, to wit £30 and that this £30 is all he ever received for his master from John BANISTER.

*****

236

C. 22/214/43
1653/4

Interrogatories to be administered to
witnesses produced on the part and
behalf of the Rt. Hon Philip LORD
WHARTON, Sir John DANVERS, Kt.,
Sir Gervase CLIFTON, Kt. & Bart.,
The Rt. Hon. James, EARL OF
NORTHAMPTON and the Lady Isabella,
his wife*, versus Henry CURRER, Esq.

(Bill and Answer missing.)

1. Do you know the parties, plaintiff and defendant,
   and which of them ? Do you know Philip, late
   Earl of PEMBROKE and MONTGOMERY, dec'd ?
   Do you know the Lady Anne, his wife, and how
   long have you known them or any of them, and
   which ?

2. Did you see the deed now showed unto you bearing
   the date (5 June 1645) ... by the said Earl of
   PEMBROKE and MONTGOMERY and the Lady
   Anne, his wife; and were you not a witness thereunto and is not your name endorsed thereupon as
   a witness of your proper hand written ?

3. Do you know that the defendant, Henry CURRER,
   by himself alone, or together with any other person,
   and with whom, was receiver of any rents, profits
   and other sums of money of the plaintiffs, and which
   of them, and for what time, out of any castle, manor,
   messuage, lands, tenements, woods, lead or other
   materials in or about Skipton-in-Craven, Barden or
   elsewhere in the county of York, now belonging to
   the Countess of PEMBROKE and MONTGOMERY;
   of what yearly value are the said rents and profits,
   and how received ? Which did the said sum, or
   sums of money, which the defendant by himself, or
   his agent, raised out of the said castle etc., amount
   to; and for whose use were the same received ?
   Declare what you know, and how ? Any by what
   authority did ...... in collecting the said rents ?

4. Do you know, or have you heard, that the defendant
   Henry CURRER, has authority from the plaintiffs,
   and from which of them, to receive and raise the
   sum of £5,000 out of the said castle and premises ?

*Anne CLIFFORD, Countess of DORSET, PEMBROKE and MONTGOMERY,
1590-1676 married the Earl of PEMBROKE on 3 June, 1630. He died
23 Jan 1649/50. Isabella, Countess of NORTHAMPTON, was the
daughter of Lady Anne CLIFFORD by her first husband, the Earl of
DORSET.

237

Was he not to be accountable therefore to the
plaintiffs, and which ? When and where was
such authority given and upon what occasion ?
Have you heard the defendant confess that he
was but only entrusted by the plaintiffs and
was to be accountable to the Earl of NORTH-
AMPTON and his Lady, or the other plaintiffs,
or which of them ? Declare what you know and
have credibly heard in this behalf.

Depositions of witnesses on the plaintiffs'
behalf taken at the house of Robert
FORESTONE in Settle in the County of
York 20 January 1653/4, before William
WATSON, Thomas LISTER and Robert
HEBLETHWAITE, gents, by virtue of a
Commission forth of the High Court of
Chancery to them and Thomas HEBER
Esq., directed in a Cause there depending
between the Rt. Hon. Philip Lord
WHARTON, Sir John DANVERS, Sir
Jarvis CLIFTON, the Rt. Hon. James,
Earl of NORTHAMPTON and the Lady
Isabella, his wife., versus Henry
CURRER Esq.

Elizabeth KITCHIN, wife of William KITCHIN of
Skipton, aged 50 or thereabouts.

1. To the first interrogatory, she says she knows
    Sir Jarvis CLIFTON and James Earl of NORTH-
    AMPTON.

3. She says that her husband farmed the Milnes of
    Skipton, part of the lands mentioned in the inter-
    rogatory, of the defendant and one Mr. KENT for
    one year about five years since, and paid for the
    same £85 to Mr. KENT, and did likewise farm the
    said Milnes the next year after of the defendant
    and paid him the sum of £100 for the same.

Ingram BRONDEN of Thorleby in the County of
York, yeoman, aged 57 years.

1. He says he knows only James, Earl of NORTHAMPTON.

3. He says that he was authorised and appointed by the
    defendant to collect and receive the rents due from
    the tenants of Sturton and Thorleby, part of the
    Manor and lands mentioned in the interrogatory,
    and he did accordingly receive of rents £12 2s. 4d.
    which he paid to the defendant and his servant by
    his appointment in the year 1649. He also says that

he was able to collect the same by the writing
now showed to him purporting a deputation from
the defendant under his hand bearing the date
1 November 1649.

Peter HORNE, of Silsden in the County of York,
yeoman, aged 74 years.

1. He says he only knows Sir Jarvis CLIFTON, James,
    Earl of NORTHAMPTON, and the defendant, and
    also the Countess of PEMBROKE.

3. He says he was employed and authorised by the def-
    endant to receive the rents due from the tenants of
    Silsden, part of the manor and lands mentioned in
    the interrogatory, and he did accordingly receive
    out of the same £100 13s. 4d. which he paid to the
    defendant's own hands, the same being for the use
    of the Earl of NORTHAMPTON and the Lady Isabella,
    his wife, as the defendant himself confessed, which
    moneys were so collected and paid by him in the
    year 1649. He further says that he was enabled
    thereunto by a writing under the defendant's hand,
    which writing is now showed unto him, bearing the
    date 1 November 1649.

John EASTBURNE of Silsden, Yorks, yeoman,
aged 50 years.

1. He says that he only knows James, Earl of
    NORTHAMPTON, the Countess of PEMBROKE
    and the defendant.

3. He says that he and one Arthur CRYER did about
    five years since farm of the Countess of PEMBROKE
    a certain coalpit within the Manor of Silsden, part
    of the premises named in the interrogatory, and paid
    £20 to the defendant for the same.

William WADSWORTH of Embsay in the County of
York, mason, aged 36 years.

1. He says that he only knows the Lord WHARTON,
    the .... the Countess of PEMBROKE and the
    defendant.

3. He says that about five years since he was the
    servant of one Mr. SMITHSON, and received at
    the hands of one John BAXTER, the defendant's
    then servant, by the defendant's appointment as
    he truly believes for that he conceived that
    BAXTER would not have done the same without

the defendant's consent, forty four tons of lead which
belonged to Skipton Castle at £9 a ton. And he further
says that BAXTER, as the defendant's servant, did
deliver unto one Thomas ODDY stones out of Skipton
Castle which were valued by this deponent and the
said BAXTER at 17s.

John BAXTER of Carlton in the County of York,
clothier, aged 50 years.

1. He says that he knows only the Countess of PEMBROKE
   and the defendant.

3. He says that about the years 1648, 1649, and 1650, by
   the defendant's appointment and order, and oftentimes
   in his presence, he did receive of the tenants of the
   lands and premises mentioned in the interrogatory
   several rents and sums of money, but how much the
   same amounted to he does not now certainly remember.
   This money and the rents were paid by him to the
   defendant for the use of the Rt. Hon. James, Earl of
   NORTHAMPTON towards £5,000 for his wife's portion
   as he has heard. And he further says that by the defendant's order he did deliver to the carriers of Skipton
   about forty tons of lead which was taken of the Castle
   of Skipton, and he did also by the same order deliver
   certain quantities of wood, which belonged to the Castle
   of Skipton, in all amounting to the sum of three or four
   score pounds, to his now best remembrance, and stones
   of about the value of forty shillings unto several persons
   who had bought the same of the defendant, his then master.

Edward WATKINSON of Bradley in the County of
York, yeoman, aged 30 years.

1. He says that he knows only the Countess of PEMBROKE
   and the defendant.

3. He says that about five or six years since he farmed of
   the defendant one piece of ground called the New Park,
   part of the lands and premises named in the interrogatory, and paid unto him for the same the sum of £105.

Charles BRADFORD of Flasby in the County of
York, gent., aged 30 years.

1. He says that he knows only Anne, Countess of
   PEMBROKE, Sir Jarvis CLIFTON and the defendant.

3. He says that he knows that the defendant received in
   rents and otherwise out of the manor, lands and
   premises mentioned in the interrogatory in the years

1646, 1647, 1648 and 1649 the sum of three-hundred and odd pounds or thereabouts.

Thomas ATKINSON of Barden in the County of York, yeoman, aged 60 years.

1. He says that he knows only the Countess of PEM-BROKE and the defendant.

3. He says that he, John BAXTER and Roland TATHAM about five years since on the defendant's order sold and delivered from the Manor and Forest of Barden, part of the premises mentioned in the interrogatory, wood and bark to the value of £351 or thereabouts, and that BAXTER received the money for the defendant's use, which the defendant said was for the use of the Earl of NORTHAMPTON and Isabella, his wife, for part of the marriage portion of the said Lady Isabella. And he further says that the defendant likewise received out of the lands and premises for the use aforesaid several rents in all amounting to £31 10s. 0d. or thereabouts.

Thomas ODDY of Skipton, yeoman, aged 42 years.

1. He says that he knows only Sir Jarvis CLIFTON, Anne Countess of PEMBROKE and the defendant.

3. He says that about four or five years since he paid the defendant 30s. 8d. for rents of a house and lands which he, this deponent, held of the Manor of Skipton, part of the premises mentioned in the interrogatory. He further says that the defendant sold a certain quantity of lead out of the Castle of Skipton containing about forty tons as he believes and has heard from one Anthony JOHNSON, the carrier thereof, who had £53 for the carrying thereof as he told this deponent. And he, this deponent, also paid unto John BAXTER the sum of seventeen or twenty shillings, who received the same for the defendant's use for some stones and other things which belonged to the Castle of Skipton.

Thomas JACKMAN of Skipton, yeoman, aged 52 years.

1. He says that he knows only Sir Jarvis CLIFTON, Anne, Countess of PEMBROKE and the defendant.

3. He says that he and one John BRADFORD and Charles BRADFORD farmed of the defendant certain lands, part of the premises named in the interrogatory for three years together, viz; 1648, 1649, 1650, and paid him the sum of £105 for the first year and £110 for either

of the said latter years, the defendant discharging
all the assessments due for the same all the said
three years.

Peter ATKINSON, of Ilkley, Yorks, whitesmith,
aged 27.

1. He says that he knows only the Countess of
    PEMBROKE and the defendant.

3. He says that he was a soldier and was present when
    Skipton Castle was slighted. A great quantity of
    lead and certain wood, iron and stone which belonged
    to the said Castle (which were sold by the defendant
    and one John BAXTER by his order) were delivered
    to the persons who bought the same, but the certain
    particulars and value thereof he cannot set down.

Thomas MITCHELL of Skipton, carpenter, aged
50 years.

1. He says that he knows only Sir Jarvis CLIFTON,
    Anne, Countess of PEMBROKE and the defendant.

3. He says that, upon the slighting of Skipton Castle,
    he was with others appointed by the defendant to
    apprize the timber taken down therein, and they
    valued the same to £130. The same timber was
    afterwards sold or disposed of by one John BAXTER,
    by the defendant's order and appointment, and he says
    that the Countess of PEMBROKE herself bought 50s.
    worth thereof.

Edmund GREENWOOD of Skipton, blacksmith,
aged 47 years.

1. He says that he knows only Sir Jarvis CLIFTON,
    Anne, Countess of PEMBROKE and the defendant,
    and has seen the Earl of NORTHAMPTON.

3. He says that about seven or eight years since at
    the defendant's request, he valued and apprized
    several iron guns called sling-pieces, munitions,
    one half cannon and one murdering piece, anciently
    belonging to the Castle of Skipton to the value of
    £20 and upwards, some of which were sold by the
    defendant to him and others. Others of them were
    wrought by him for the defendant's use. He further
    says that there were also four field pieces of brass
    in the Castle which were also sold by the defendant
    unto Wigan in Lancashire, but for how much he knows
    not.

Thomas WILSON of Skipton, blacksmith, aged 35 years.

1.　He says that he knows only Sir Jarvis CLIFTON,
　　Anne, Countess of PEMBROKE and the defendant.

3.　He says that six years since he bought a great Iron
　　Gun called a demiculveringe of one John BAXTER
　　and paid him £3 for the same to the defendant's use,
　　and he also paid 12s. to BAXTER for the use afore-
　　said for a cow grass in the grounds mentioned in the
　　interrogatory. He further says that three great brass
　　field-pieces were sold by the defendant's appointment
　　to the town of Wigan in Lancashire as he verily believes.

Henry GOODGION of Skipton, gent, aged 39 years.

1.　He says that he knows only Sir Jarvis CLIFTON,
　　Anne, Countess of PEMBROKE and the defendant.

3.　He says that he did in the year 1647 farm of the
　　defendant two closes called Low Waltonwray and
　　Townley Close, part of the lands and premises
　　mentioned in the interrogatory, and paid him for
　　the same £9 10s. 0d. and did likewise pay to the
　　defendant, or his servant for his use £4 18s. 0d.
　　more for rent of certain lands. He also paid him,
　　or his servant, about 3/4 more for a door and
　　shelves belonging to the Castle of Skipton bought
　　by him, this deponent.

William WAINMAN of Embsay, Yorks., yeoman,
aged 40 years.

1.　He says that he knows only Anne, Countess of
　　PEMBROKE and the defendant.

3.　He says that he and others did farm of the defendant
　　certain lands called the Low Field, Tullan Close
　　and Elsay Crest, part of the lands named in the
　　interrogatory for three years 1647, 1648 and 1649,
　　and paid for the first and second years £48 10s 0d.
　　a year and for the third year £41.

Rowland TATHAM of Eshton, Yorks, milnewright,
aged 49 years.

1.　He says that he knows only the Countess of
　　PEMBROKE and the defendant.

3.　He says that about 7 years since he was employed
　　by the defendant together with one Thomas ATKINSON
　　and John BAXTER to sell certain wood and bark in

Barden, part of the lands named in the interrogatory,
which they did accordingly, and the same amounted to
£340 odd. The moneys were paid for the same to John
BAXTER for the defendant's use. And he further says
that he was also employed by the defendant (being this
deponent's Master) to value and apprize certain wood,
felling timber and wooden work in the Castle of Skipton,
and they valued the same to £130 and that the same was
afterwards sold by the defendant's appointment and
moneys paid for the same to his use, £60 whereof was
paid at several times to BAXTER as aforesaid in this
deponent's presence.

William GOODGION of Skipton, yeoman, aged 47 years.

1. He says that he knows Sir Jarvis CLIFTON, the
   Earl of NORTHAMPTON, Anne, Countess of
   PEMBROKE and the defendant.

3. He says that in the years 1647 and 1648 he farmed of
   the defendant certain grounds, part of the lands named
   in the interrogatory, and paid him for same £20 a year.

Robert COLLINGES of Skipton, gent., aged 50 years.

1. He says that he knows James, Earl of NORTHAMPTON
   the Lady Isabella, his wife, Anne, Countess of PEM-
   BROKE and the defendant, and did know Philip, the
   late Earl of PEMBROKE.

3. He says that the manor, messuages, lands, tenements
   and premises mentioned in the interrogatory, and the
   rents thereunto belonging, which now belong to the
   Countess of PEMBROKE, are of the full clear yearly
   value of (? £1,050) or thereabouts. He knows this
   because he is now the receiver thereof for the said
   Countess of PEMBROKE.

Thomas GABITES of Crosby Raven in the County of
Westmorland, gent., aged 38 years.

1. He says that he knows Philip, Lord WHARTON,
   James, Earl of NORTHAMPTON, the Lady Isabella,
   his wife, Anne, Countess of PEMBROKE and the
   defendant.

3. He says that the manor, messuages etc., and the rent
   thereunto belonging to the Countess of PEMBROKE
   are of the clear yearly rent of £950 or thereabouts.
   He knows this because he is now auditor for the yearly
   revenue of the Countess of PEMBROKE and has been

so deputed by her for that purpose for two years and
a half and more last past.

Signed: William WATSON
Thos. LISTER
Rob. HEBLETHWAITE

Interrogatories to be administered to
witnesses to be produced on behalf of
Henry CURRER, defendant to the Bill
of Complaint of Philip Lord WHARTON
and others.

1. Do you know the parties complainant and defendant
    in the suite and which of them ? Did you know Philip,
    late Earl of PEMBROKE and MONTGOMERY deceased,
    and how long have you known them or any and which of
    them ?

2. Do you know, or have your heard by whose authority
    and at whose command the defendant, Henry CURRER,
    became entrusted with the management of the affairs
    of the said late Earl of PEMBROKE in Craven, which
    came to ...... Ann, his Countess, and how do you
    know the same ?

3. Have you been, or are you acquainted with the hand-
    writing of the said Earl of PEMBROKE ? Is not the
    hand subscribed to the writing now shown to you
    purporting a commission and command from the said
    deceased Earl the subscription or proper handwriting
    of the said Earl ? Did you see the said Earl subscribe
    the same ?

4. Did not the defendant, Henry CURRER, enter upon
    the ordering of the estate when it lay unfenced, the
    pales burnt, the walls and fences thrown down; were
    not the milnes and other houses belonging to it quite
    spoiled and wasted ? Did he not manage the same, in
    your opinion to the best of his ability and to the said
    Earl's advantage ? To whom do you know he made
    his accounts or addresses during the Earl's life ?
    And whether to any other as you have heard, know
    or believe ?

5. Do you not know, or have your heard, that one Mr.
    KENT was sent down with commission or order from
    the Lord WHARTON and others of the plaintiffs to
    collect and receive the profits and rents due from the
    estate ? Did he not collect, gather and receive great
    sums of money upon their order ?

6. Do you not know, or have you heard, that by the Earl of PEMBROKE's order and said Henry CURRER was sent for to London, and by the said Earl's order, and at his appointment, did pay to the Earl of NORTHAMPTON, or to whom he appointed, the sum of £1,000 as by his acquittance will appear. Did not the said Henry CURRER procure part of the said £1,000 till it could be received out of the next rents and profits of the estate ? Have your not heard, or do you not know that a writing was sealed and published by the said Earl of NORTHAMPTON called a declaration to satisfy all whom it might concern that the power of managing that estate was solely in the said Earl of PEMBROKE by whose authority this defendant acted ?

7. Were you present when the plaintiffs, or their agent, did solicit and move the defendant to manage the said estate in Craven for them, and did the defendant accept thereof or did he undertake the same for them, and who was present beside yourself, and when was it ?

8. What other matter or thing do you know or can depose on the defendant's behalf touching the matters in difference ?

*****

130.

C. 22/831/19
-: Jan 1667/8

Interrogatories to be administered to witnesses to be produced and examined on behalf of Richard TENNANT, William CURRER and William CURRER.

(Bill and Answer missing.)

1. Do you know the parties complainant and defendant in this suit, and which of them ? Do you know, and how long have you known them ? Did you know Richard TENNANT, late of Burnsall, Yorks, clerk now deceased; and Anthony WALKER, late of Burnsall, Notary Public, and is the said plaintiff nephew and heir of the said Richard TENNANT, clerk, that is to say son and heir of Thomas TENNANT, brother and heir of the said Richard TENNANT, deceased ?

2.   Do you know or believe that Richard TENNANT, clerk,
     dec'd, was in his lifetime, and at the time of his death,
     seised of one moiety of the impropriate Rectory of
     Kettlewell, Yorks, and of the moiety of all glebelands,
     houses, tythes, profits etc. belonging to the said
     rectory ? And of what yearly value is the same moiety
     worth to be let at best advantage ?

3.   Have you at any time seen a writing bearing date 20
     June 1650, now in question in this suit purporting to
     be made between the said Richard TENNANT, clerk,
     of the one part and the said Anthony WALKER of the
     other, whereby it is mentioned that Richard TENNANT,
     clerk, in consideration that he stood indebted to Anthony
     WALKER for the sum of £69 did grant the same moiety
     of the Rectory of Kettlewell etc. to Anthony WALKER
     for the term of 99 years to commence after the deter-.
     mining of a former lease of the same premises mentioned
     to be made to one William CURRER and Hugh CURRER
     or to some such effect ? In whose handwriting is the
     same writing ? When did you first see the same ? Is
     the same now in all particulars as it was when you first
     saw it without any addition, interlineation, erasure or
     alteration either of any of the parties or witnesses'
     names, or of any other matter whatsoever ? And if
     not, then set forth the particulars as near as you can
     whereof such addition or alteration etc. is made, and
     by whom, and when it was so made and what you can
     further say concerning the same.

4.   Have you at any time seen any such account or any
     writing purporting such account as in the said writing
     is mentioned to be the consideration of making thereof ?
     And say when, and where, and in whose hands, did you
     see the same, of whose handwriting was such account ?
     Was Richard TENNANT's name subscribed or set there-
     unto ? Was his name so set in his own handwriting, as
     you know or believe ? What were the particulars whereof
     such account did or doth consist ? Was the same for money
     lent, or for any other matter ? And how much did the same
     in the whole amount to ? And what is become of this account ?
     Set forth the truth of the whole matter as near as you can
     concerning the same.

5.   Did you know or were you acquainted with Anthony
     WALKER in his lifetime, of what esteem and reputation
     was he as to his estate ? Was he reputed to be a moneyed
     man, or likely to furnish Richard TENNANT with the sum
     of £69 or any such sum of money ? Or was he not rather
     reputed to be a borrower ? Did he not for several years
     before the death of Richard TENNANT dwell in the house
     with Richard TENNANT, and had his diet and lodging
     with him ? Was it not the general reputation of the country
     that WALKER was maintained by him at his charge, and
     that he was not able to pay for the same ? Was not

WALKER at the time of Richard TENNANT's death rather a debtor to him than that Richard TENNANT a debtor to WALKER ? Do you believe that Richard TENNANT was at the time of the making of the said pretended account in any way endebted to WALKER, and how much ? What induces you so to believe ?

6. Were you acquainted with Richard WALKER, Richard NEWBY and Henry CURRER, whose names are subscribed as witnesses to the said writing mentioned in the third interrogatory ? Which of them could write and read ? Were you acquainted with the manner and character of the writing of their respective names or any of them at the time of the date of the said writing and how came you so to know this ? Do you believe that their respective names subscribed as witnesses to the said writing are of their own respective proper handwritings, yea or nay ? Of whose handwriting or engrossing is the said pretended lease or writing as you know or believe ? Is not the same all of it of the proper handwriting of Anthony WALKER ? And do you not believe in your conscience that the witnesses' names as well as the writing itself are in the handwriting of Anthony WALKER himself and not of the said respective witnesses ?

7. Of what relation or kindred was Richard WALKER, Richard NEWBY and Henry CURRER or any of them to Anthony WALKER ? Of what age were they respectively at the time of the date of the writing ? Were not Richard WALKER and Richard NEWBY, the pretended witnesses, or the one of them, then schoolboys ? And do you believe they could then write their names in so fair and legible and clerk-like character as the same are respectively written to the said writing ? Are not Richard WALKER, Richard NEWBY and Henry CURRER now dead ? And when did they respectively die ?

8. Were you acquainted with the handwriting of the late Richard TENNANT, clerk, dec'd., and do you believe that his name set to the said writing is in his own proper handwriting ? And if the fair deed or writing were really sealed and delivered by Richard TENNANT, do you not believe that the same was gained from him by some fraud or improper practice, or that it was made upon some trust, for the benefit of Richard TENNANT and his heirs and was intended not to be absolute, or for the benefit of Anthony WALKER ? And have you at any time heard Richard TENNANT or Anthony WALKER declare anything to any such purpose or effect ? Declare what you know, believe or have credibly heard concerning the matters of this interrogatory, and what you further can say concerning the same.

9. Were you acquainted with the handwriting of the said
    Anthony WALKER during his lifetime ? Do you believe
    that the writing showed you at the time of your examin-
    ation, bearding the date 20 June 1650 and signed by
    Anthony WALKER, and purporting to be a counterpart
    of the said pretended lease mentioned in the 3rd inter-
    rogatory, and now in question, and the name of Anthony
    WALKER put thereto, as well as the names of Richard
    WALKER, Richard NEWBY and Henry CURRER thereto
    subscribed as witnesses, are all of them in Anthony
    WALKER's handwriting and that the names of Richard
    WALKER, Richard NEWBY and Henry CURRER are not
    of their own proper handwriting ? Was that writing
    purporting to be a counterpart in your keeping, or how,
    or from whom did you receive the same ?

10. Do you know of any deeds, evidences or writings
    concerning the moiety of the rectory and promises
    which are come to the possession of the defendants ?
    If so set forth the particulars thereof and the dates
    and contents and the parties between whom they were
    made as near as you can, and if you can say anything
    further concerning them.

11. Did you believe that the names of Richard TENNANT,
    Anthony WALKER, Richard NEWBY, Richard WALKER
    and Henry CURRER respectively subscribed to the resp-
    ective writings now produced to you are in their own
    respective handwritings ? Whose names are so respect-
    ively subscribed ? And were you acquainted with the
    manner in which they wrote their respective names and
    do the same respectively agree therewith, and what are
    the reasons that induce you so to depose ?

12. What other matter or thing do you know material to this
    cause which may make for the plea against the defendants ?

13. Do you believe that these two letters now shewed to you
    which the Commissioners have endorsed, one bearing
    the date 5 August 1662 and the other dated 6 September
    1662, are in the proper handwriting of Richard NEWBY,
    one of the witnesses to the pretended lease, and whether
    do you believe that the name of Richard NEWBY to be in
    the same handwriting as the name on the lease or no ?

14. Do you know whether Richard TENNANT dec'd., made
    any will or no before he died ? What estates did he
    dispose of by virtue of that will and to whom ? What
    legacies were given by virtue of that will, and to whom,
    and how many legacies were paid and to whom ?

15. What discourse have your heard ? From whom ? To
    whom ? And when concerning the pretended lease from
    Richard TENNANT dec'd to Anthony WALKER ? Did

you hear say that the lease was torn, interlined and
so small written that it was scarce legible, and that
they were forced to write a new one ?

Signed: Jo. ASSHETON
T. HEBER.

Depositions of witnesses taken at Gisburne
in the West Riding of the County of York on
Thursday the 16th day of January in the 19th
year of King Charles II A.D. (1667/8) before
John ASHTON and Thomas HERBER Esqs.,
by virtue of a Commission out of the High
Court of Chancery to them and Robt. SAVILLE
and John JACKMAN, gentlemen, directed for
the examination of witnesses in a Cause there
depending between Richard TENNANT,
Complainant, and William CURRER and William
CURRER, defendants, as followeth:

Hugh CURRER of Kildwick, gent., aged near 60 years.

1. He knows the parties and likewise knew Richard
   TENNANT, clerk dec'd., and Anthony WALKER.

7. He knew Henry CURRER father to one of the defendants, (William). He was, as he believes, near cousin
   to Anthony WALKER, and son of William CURRER of
   Skipton, whose sister was Anthony WALKER's mother
   and wife to Richard TENNANT, Clerk, (Isabel
   CURRER). As to the paper writing purporting a
   counterpart of a lease made between Richard TENNANT
   and Anthony WALKER he knows nothing or can say anything as to the witnesses names, nor at present does he
   remember that he was a person interested or concerned
   in any lease or any other estate of Richard TENNANT,
   clerk, by any lease or other conveyance from him, the
   said Richard TENNANT.

Richard WADINGTON of Horton, gent aged 35 years
or thereabouts.

9. Concerning the paper writing now showed to him dated
   20 June 1650, this deponent, being at Wetherby about
   this time two years, William CURRER one of the defendants showed him this draft purporting to be a counterpart of a lease made between Richard TENNANT of
   Burnsall, clerk, and Anthony WALKER. This deponent
   was desired by William CURRER to give the writing to
   Richard TENNANT. To his knowledge no alteration
   appears unless the seal be torn off, and that the writing

is lined and something torn which when he retained
it, it was not.

James TENNANT of Burnsall, clerk, aged about
60 years.

1. He knows the complainant and has formerly known the
   defendants, also Richard TENNANT, late of Burnsall,
   clerk, brother of this deponent. He also knew Anthony
   WALKER, late of Burnsall, Notary Publique. The
   plaintiff is nephew and heir to Richard TENNANT
   dec'd., which Richard did marry Isabel, sister to
   William CURRER who was grandfather to William
   CURRER one of the defendants, and uncle to Anthony
   WALKER in the pleadings mentioned, and further to
   this interrogatory deposes not.

2. Richard TENNANT, his brother, dec'd., was in his
   lifetime seised of the moiety of the impropriate Rectory
   of Kettlewell with all profits and appurtenances.

7. Richard WALKER was nephew of Anthony WALKER,
   but that Richard NEWBY was of no relation to Anthony
   WALKER that he knows. WALKER and NEWBY were
   schoolfellows together taught by his brother Richard
   TENNANT, clerk, but Henry CURRER was nephew to
   Anthony WALKER* and he believes that Richard
   WALKER and Richard NEWBY were scholars to his
   late brother about the year 1650.

11. The letter now showed to him was the proper handwriting
    of his late brother, Richard TENNANT, clerk. He very
    well remembers and knows the character of his hand-
    writing.

John ELLIS of Burnsall, Yorks., yeoman aged
about 62 years.

1. He knew Richard TENNANT, the complainant and
   William CURRER, the younger, one of the defendants
   in this suit and has known them for some time. He
   also knew Richard TENNANT late of Burnsall, clerk,
   very well; so well that he was most in his company of
   any man in that parish. He also knew Anthony WALKER
   Notary Publique, and also knows that the complainant is
   cousin and heir to Richard TENNANT, dec'd.

Henry CURRER was not a nephew of Anthony WALKER; the deponent
is incorrect.

2. He knew Richard TENNANT, dec'd., was possessed of the moiety of the Rectory of Kettlewell a year or two before his death. He also says that the said moiety has to his knowledge been let for £26 a year for some years and for some ... £28 and other some years, but for £23 or £24 which he has had from Mr. Richard TENNANT's own mouth in his life-time.

7. About 16 or 17 years ago, or thereabouts, he remembers that Mr. Richard WALKER and Richard NEWBY were both scholars with Richard TENNANT dec'd. and they did learn with him in chambers.

12. He was once sent for by Richard TENANT, dec'd., when he was much troubled with head-ache, and at that time there was a paper lying before him and the deponent asked him what that paper was. Richard TENANT answered and said that he intended to make his will and this deponent further says that he then desired Mr. Richard TENANT to be kind to his nephew John TENANT, but he replied that he could not do as he would for fear of his wife, and Mr. Anthony WALKER, her son, and he was sorry for it, for they would never let him be quiet if they knew he did any-thing. And further this deponent says that Mr. Anthony WALKER was Publick Notary and had little or no estate at that time to the best of his knowledge, but he lived with Richard TENANT, his step-father, and was main-tained by him whilst that he lived and also he further deposed that Mr. WALKER was accounted neither a borrower nor a lender and cannot believe that he did ever give Mr. Richard TENANT any consideration in moneys for his making a lease to him.

Mrs. Elizabeth TENANT of Burnsall, Yorks, aged
? 40 years or thereabouts.

1. She knew Mr. Richard TENANT, late of Burnsall, clerk, her brother-in-law and knows Richard TENANT, his nephew, and she also knew Mr. Anthony WALKER. She, her husband and they did all live under one roof for five years or thereabouts. Mr. Anthony WALKER had no other dwelling place.

12. Her brother-in-law, Mr. Richard TENANT, had a very good estate (? in several places besides the) moiety of the Rectory of Kettlewell. Mr. WALKER lived with him and had his table and maintenance there, but she does not know, nor has heard that Mr. WALKER did pay for his table etc. Mr. WALKER was in a condition to lend money, but did much to impare his estate by helping Mr. Henry CURRER, father to William CURRER one of the defendants, in his troubles.

Francis CARTER of Horton, Yorks, yeoman, aged 40.

1. He knew Mr. Richard TENANT, late of Burnsall,
    clerk, and knows the complainant to be nephew and
    heir of said Richard TENANT, clerk, and son and
    heir of Thomas TENANT. He lived with Mr. Richard
    TENANT, dec'd as a servant for the space of twelve
    years before he died. Richard TENANT mentioned in
    the pleadings was his uncle.

2. He knew Mr. Richard TENANT, clerk, his uncle,
    to be owner of the half part of the Rectory of
    Kettlewell with all its profits etc., and as he was
    his servant, he was employed several years in
    gathering tythes there for him. He knew for what
    rent the premises were let, viz. £23 a year besides
    paying of all taxes that the farmer paid for it.

5. He was acquainted with Anthony WALKER in his
    lifetime, and he was not reputed to his knowledge
    to be a moneyed man or likely to furnish Mr.
    TENANT with the sum of £69 or any suchlike sum,
    but rather WALKER was helped by Mr. TENANT.
    In all the time he lived with Mr. TENANT he never
    heard of any such account as might amount to such
    a sum as £69 or any considerable sum between them.

7. He knew Richard WALKER to be cousin to Anthony
    WALKER, dec'd., but Richard NEWBY was no
    relation to Anthony WALKER, which he knows of.
    Richard WALKER and Richard NEWBY were school-
    boys together and learned and had their table with
    Mr. TENANT, dec'd. He believes he could write
    but how well he knows not, being but scholars.

14. He knows nothing of his own knowledge whether there
    was a will made by Mr. Richard TENANT or no, only
    his widow, this deponent's aunt, told him that there
    was something left to him which should be mended and
    not impaired, and so the discourse ceased betwixt them
    at that time till another time that his aunt was sick and
    laid on her deathbed, and when this information came
    to her there passes some speeches from her that she
    desired this deponent to pray for her and to forgive
    her, but what she meant by these speeches he knows
    not, she not speaking much more then.

John HEARTLEY of Weddiker, in the parish of
Gisburn, yeoman, aged 30 years.

14. He hath heard Isabel, widow to Richard TENANT, say
    three or four time that there was a note under her hus-
    bands own handwriting left, which was, as she said,

her husband's will, but was lost.

Mary HARGREAVES of Thorpe in the County of
Yorks., aged 37 years.

14. She lived with Richard TENANT dec'd., uncle to
this deponent, and at one time in his sickness
Richard TENANT, this deponent, and Richard
TENANT's wife being all together in his room
where he lay sick, he called for his papers and
took up one amongst the rest and said it was his
will, and read it to his wife, and by the reading
of it this deponent understands there was £10 given
for one Francis CARTER, and £5 to this deponent,
Mary, upon which this deponent left the room in
discontent that her fellow servant had more left
than she had, and so going away heard no more.

Thomas HOWSON of Cracoe, Yorks, yeoman,
aged 59 years and upwards.

2. He knew Richard TENANT late of Burnsall, clerk,
and that he was the owner of half the Rectory of
Kettlewell.

5. He knew Mr. Anthony WALKER and that as to his
reputation he never heard him so accounted of as
to be able to lend £60 or any such sum, but that he
did reside and dwell with the said Mr. Richard
TENANT, dec'd.

12. At the day of the marriage of Mr. Richard TENANT,
clerk, dec'd., he, Richard TENANT, came to his
house to meet his bride and there this deponent
asked him what estate he had settled upon his intended
wife, and Richard TENANT answered that he had
settled no estate upon her nor was never so desired to
do so by her relatives or friends and further to this he
cannot depose.

Thos. RIPLEY of Kettlewell, yeoman, aged 60
years or thereabouts.

2. He knew Richard TENNANT, late of Burnsall, and
that he was the owner of the moiety of the Rectory
of Kettlewell, and that since Mr. WALKER died he
has been a farmer of the premises, together with some
others, and that the yearly rent that he paid for it
upon the first lease for three years was £22 and discharged from all taxes to the King and Poor. Together
with (his) former partner, he took a new lease of Mrs.

TENANT which lease was ended at Midsummer last,
and for the said moiety be paid by the last lease £20
a year rent and discharged as in the former.

Roger GRYMSHAGH of Marton in the County of
York, gent., aged 38 years.

9. He believes the writing now showed to him dated
20 June 1650, signed Anthony WALKER, purporting
to be a counterpart of a lease which Richard NEWBY
and others have subscribed their names as witnesses
is not the proper handwriting of Richard NEWBY.
He is induced so to believe for he knew how Richard
NEWBY wrote his name, having had several letters
in his proper handwriting and has his name subscribed,
but neither with the same character nor spelling.

13. He verily believes that the two letters now showed to
him dated 5 August 1662 and 6 Sept 1662 are both the
proper handwriting of Richard NEWBY. Comparing
the two letters with the counterpart of the lease dated
20 June 1650 ... he believes not to be the handwriting
of Richard NEWBY, it being written with other characters
and other letters.

Depositions of witnesses taken at Gisburn
in the County of York on 1 April 20 Chas. II
(1668) before John ASHTON and Thomas
HEBER Esqs., and John JACKMAN and
Richard KING, gents by virtue of H.M.
Commission out of the High Court of
Chancery to them directed for examination
of witnesses in a Cause there depending in
variance between Richard TENNANT,
Complainant, and William CURRER and
William CURRER, defendants.

Abraham BINNS of Rushforth, Yorks., gent, aged
35 years formerly sworn and examined on the defendant's
behalf, and sworn and examined on the Complainant's
behalf.

11. He was school fellow with Richard NEWBY and did
know his handwriting. The letters now showed to him
he believes not to be in the proper handwriting of
Richard NEWBY, yet he will not deny that it may be
his own handwriting, but if it be, that it very much
differs from what his handwriting was when he was
a schoolboy.

Mrs. Elizabeth TENNANT, wife of James TENNANT,
of Burnsall, clerk, aged 40 years or thereabouts.

11. She verily believes that the letters now showed to
her are the proper handwriting of Richard TENNANT,
clerk, dec'd., for she was very well acquainted with
his handwriting and lived in the same house with him
some years before his death.

John HARTLEY of Weddiker, Yorks., yeoman,
aged 30.

12. He was with Mr. SUTTON and John DIXON in Skipton
about the latter end of February last past. He did
then hear John DIXON say to Mr. SUTTON that his
name, set to the lease which Mrs. FANNER had
formerly shown him was not his own handwriting but
counterfeited, and that Mrs. FANNER had also showed
him another writing whereunto he, John DIXON, did
acknowledge his own name was set as a witness,
written with his own hand, and Mrs. FANNER would
have persuaded him that both the names were alike
and written with his own hands, and that there was no
difference in any letter thereof but in the J.

Isabel, wife of John HARTLEY, the deponent above
names, aged 28 years.

12. She heard Mrs. Isabel TENNANT, the relict of
Richard TENNANT, clerk, dec'd., several times
express and declare after the death of her husband
that he had made his will in his lifetime or a paper
written with his own hand purporting to be the
declaration of his mind, which she, Isabel, his
relict had then in her custody, and she then told
this deponent that Richard TENNANT, her husband,
had thereby given her, this deponent, a legacy and
that she would make it better and no worse to this
deponent. She did further tell this deponent that
Richard TENNANT, her husband, did thereby intend
Mr. CLERKE, his cousin, to be heir to his estate at
Burnsall after his death and did deliver the deeds
which she had in her custody concerning his said
estate at Burnsall to this deponent to and for the use
of the said Mr. CLERKE, which she did afterwards
deliver accordingly.

Interrogatories to be administered to
witnesses to be produced, sworn and
examined upon the part of William
CURRER, the uncle and William CURRER,

the nephew, defendants at the suit of
Richard TENNANT, complainant.

1. Do you know the Complainant and Defendants in the
   suit ? Did you know Richard TENNANT, Clerk,
   Anthony WALKER, gent, deceased, in the pleadings
   named ?

2. Do you know, or have your heard of a marriage
   solemnized between Richard TENNANT, clerk, and
   Isabel WALKER, widow, relict of Nicholas WALKER ?
   Were you present and a witness to the deed now shown
   to you at the time of your examination purporting to be
   the lease of a moiety of the rectory, tythes etc. of
   Kettlewell ? Did you see the same sealed, signed and
   delivered on or about the time the same bears date, by
   the said Richard TENNANT to the use of the parites
   William CURRER and Hugh CURRER therein named ?
   Did you subscribe your names as witness thereunto ?
   Are the rest of the witnesses dead ? Of which of them
   were you acquainted with their handwriting and do you
   know or believe that the same are their own proper
   handwriting ? Did you see them subscribe their names
   thereunto ?

3. Do you know, or have you heard of a parchment deed
   or lease between the said Richard TENNANT, clerk,
   on the one part, and the said Anthony WALKER on the
   other part dated 20 June 1650, purporting to be a demise
   of the moiety of the rectory and tythes in question ?
   Did you know the parties and witnesses thereunto subscribed? Are they all, or which of them, dead ? Were
   or are you well acquainted with their handwriting ? Do
   you verily believe that the name Richard TENNANT
   mentioned to be lessor therein and the names Richard
   WALKER, Richard NEWBY and Henry CURRER subscribed thereto as witnesses were of their own handwriting ? Have you often seen them, or any and which
   of them, write their names ? Have you at any time, and
   when, heard the parties, or witnesses, acknowledge
   witnessing the said lease ? What are the motives and
   grounds which induce you to believe the same ?

4. Is the writing now shown to you containing eight sheets
   of paper purporting to be the last will and testament of
   Anthony WALKER a true copy of the original will ?
   Did you carefully examine the copy with the original ?
   Where did you so examine the same, or how do you
   know the same to be a true copy thereof ?

5. When did Richard TENNANT, clerk, die, and when
   Isabel, his late wife ? Did the said Isabel presently
   after the death of Richard TENNANT, her husband,
   enter upon and quietly enjoy the whole premises in

question during her life, or for what time enjoyed
she the same ? Were not Richard TENNANT and
Isabel, his wife, living since the year 1650, and
how long after died they ? And how do you know ?

6. Were you present, or a witness to any deed or
writing executed by Richard TENNANT and Anthony
WALKER, Notary Publick ? Were you present at any
agreement made between them, if so what was the content or purport of such deed or writing or agreement
and upon what cause or consideration were they executed ? When did such deed bear date ? Where was
the same executed and when and who else beside yourself was present or witness to the execution thereof ?

7. Were you at any time present upon any discourse bet-
wixt Richard TENNANT, clerk, and Anthony
WALKER ? What did you then hear Richard TENNANT
say concerning any sums of money which he had received of Anthony WALKER ? What did he express touching
the enjoyment of the rectory and tythes by WALKER
after his death ?

Depositions on behalf of the defendants.

John DIXON of Skipton, Yorks, woollen draper,
aged 76 years or thereabouts.

1. He knew the complainants and defendants, and did
know Richard TENNANT, clerk, and Anthony
WALKER, dec'd.

2. He has heard that there was heretofore a marriage
solemnized between Richard TENNANT and Isabel
WALKER, widow, but was not present at the marriage.
They lived together as husband and wife for many
years. He was present and a witness when Richard
TENNANT sealed and signed a deed to the use of
William CURRER of Skipton, gent, and Hugh CURRER,
son and heir of Henry CURRER of Kildwick, gent.,
dated 10 June 13 Chas. I (1635). He did not endorse
his name to any deed or instrument as witness of the
sealing and execution thereof unless he first saw the
same sealed and signed according to the purport thereof. He did very well know Thomas WALBAND, Henry
GOODGICN, John GREENE, and Henry CURRER whose
names are also endorsed onto the back of the said
indenture as witnesses, and says that they are all of
them dead, but believes their several names so endorsed
as witnesses are of their several and particular proper
handwritings, and that the name John DIXON endorsed
on the back of the said indenture is of his proper handwriting.

Agnes GREENE of Skipton-in-Craven, Yorks,
widow, aged 48 years.

1. She knows the defendants in this suit and did know
    Richard TENNANT, clerk, and Anthony WALKER,
    both since dead.

2. She was not present at the sealing, signing and
    execution of the indenture mentioned in the inter-
    rogatory. She knew Thomas WALBANK, Henry
    GOODGEON, John GREENE and Henry CURRER
    very well in their respective lifetimes. Their
    names are endorsed as witnesses and they are
    now all dead. John GREENE was this deponent's
    husband. She has very often seen him write his
    name upon divers occasions and she says that she
    faithfully believes that the name John GREENE
    endorsed as witness was is the proper handwriting
    of her husband. She further says she was well
    acquainted with the handwriting of Henry GOOD-
    GEON, whose name is also endorsed, as witness
    and she believes the same is his proper handwriting.

Henry MARSDEN of Gisburn, Yorks., Esq.,
aged 46 years.

2. He was not present at the sealing, signing and
    executing of the indenture mentioned in the inter-
    rogatory, but he was very well acquainted hereto-
    fore with Thomas WALBANK and Henry GOODGEON,
    whose names appear as witnesses, and also well
    acquainted with their several handwritings and
    believes that their names endorsed on the back of
    the said indenture are in their proper hands.

Abraham BINNS of Rushforth, Yorks, gent.,
aged 35 or thereabouts.

3. He knew Richard TENNANT, clerk, and Anthony
    WALKER well and was well acquainted with the hand-
    writing of Richard TENNANT, having seen him write
    his name upon divers occasions. He verily believes
    that the name Richard TENNANT subscribed to the
    bottom of the indenture of lease now showed to him
    dated 20 June 1650 ... was of the proper handwriting
    of Richard TENNANT. He was well acquainted with
    the handwritings of Richard WALKER and Richard
    NEWBY, whose names are subscribed as witnesses
    and he verily believes that their several names are
    in their own proper handwriting. The reasons that
    so induce him to believe are because he, this deponent,
    Richard WALKER and Richard NEWBY were for many

years together schoolfellows, and about the time
of the date of the said indenture they were all three
schoolfellows together under the teaching of Richard
TENNANT, clerk.

5.   Richard TENNANT, clerk, died in the year 1652 or
1653 to his best remembrance, and Isabel TENNANT,
the widow died about two or three years since. (i.e.
1665 or 1666)

Peter ALCOCKE of Burnsall, Yorks, husbandman
aged 52 years.

1.   He knows the defendants, the complainants, Richard
TENNANT and Anthony WALKER.

2.   He verily believes that Richard TENNANT and Isabel
WALKER were married.

3.   He was not present nor a witness of the signing and
execution of the indenture of lease between Richard
TENNANT and Anthony WALKER, but he was a near
neighbour of Mr. TENNANT in Burnsall for many
years and was intimately acquainted with him and has
very often seen him write his name. He believes the
name Richard TENNANT on the indenture was in his
proper handwriting, but knows not whose handwriting
the body of the indenture is.

5.   He believes that Richard TENNANT died about 14 or
15 years since.

William ALCOCKE of Embsay, Yorks, yeoman,
aged 30 years.

3.   He was not a witness to the indenture but he says he
was very well acquainted with Richard TENNANT
during his lifetime being a scholar to the said Mr.
TENNANT for several years. He has seen some
hundreds of times Mr. TENNANT write his name,
and he faithfully believes that the name Richard
TENNANT subscribed at the bottom of the indenture
was, and is, the proper handwriting of Richard
TENNANT, clerk. He further says that while he
was scholar to Richard TENNANT, Richard WALKER
and Richard NEWBY were likewise scholars to Mr.
TENNANT. He was therefore intimately acquainted
with them and he believes that the names Richard
WALKER and Richard NEWBY subscribed as witnesses are in their proper handwritings.

Timothy TOPHAM of Grassington, Yorks, Bachelor
of Arts, aged 30 years.

3. He was not present at the signing and execution of
    the indenture of lease but he was very well acquainted
    with the handwriting of Richard TENNANT, being a
    scholar to him at or near the time of his death and he
    believes the signature to be Richard TENNANT's.

Katherine,* the wife of Robert FANNER of Skipton,
Yorks, aged 47 years.

3. Immediately upon the making and sealing of the lease
    in question by Richard TENNANT, late of Burnsall,
    clerk, and Anthony WALKER, Notary Publique, of
    the moiety of the rectory and tythes in question,
    Henry CURRER, this deponent's late husband,
    coming home from Burnsall, told her that he had
    been stayed longer than he expected, for his uncle
    TENNANT had been sealing and executing a lease of
    one half of the Rectory of Kettlewell to his cousin,
    Anthony WALKER, which lease was to commence
    and take place immediately after Richard TENNANT's
    death, and Isabel, his wife, or the survivor of them.
    Her husband then also told her that he had subscribed
    his name as a witness of the sealing and delivery of
    the said lease. She verily believes in her conscience
    that the name Henry CURRER subscribed as witness
    to the bottom of the indenture of lease now showed to
    her dated 20 June 1650 is of his own proper handwriting.

5. Richard TENNANT, her late uncle, is dead, how long
    since he died, she now remembers not. Immediately
    after his death, Isabel, his widow, entered into the
    possession of the moiety of the Rectory of Kettlewell
    and received the rents and profits during her life.
    She died about 3 years 9 months since to her now best
    remembrance. After the time that this deponent's late
    husband had told her that Mr. Richard TENNANT had
    made the lease mentioned in the proceedings to Anthony
    WALKER, he lived several years and tabled at this
    deponent's house in Skipton and taught scholars there.

Edward MARSDEN of Gisburne, Yorks., gent.,
aged 33 years.

4. The paper writing now showed to him containing
    eight sheets of paper is a true copy of the last will
    and testament of Anthony WALKER, late of Skipton,

*Katherine, daughter of Ambrose LORAINE of Tynemouth,
 Northumberland, and widow of Henry CURRER.

dec'd., which remains in the Prerogative Office in London. He, this deponent, did in Michaelmas Term last diligently examine and compare the said paper draft with the original will and the same does accord and agree with it.

Ellen, wife of Thomas TOMLINSON of Skipton, grocer.

7. In the lifetime of Richard TENNANT, this deponent's late uncle, she was servant to him for the space of four years before his death. Not long before his death she was present at some conference between Richard TENNANT and Anthony WALKER, and Richard TENNANT said that he had received from Anthony WALKER a considerable sum of money for the one half of the tythes of the Rectory of Kettlewell, and that it came very seasonably to him, and did him, Richard TENNANT, a courtesy. Richard TENNANT then also said that you (meaning Anthony WALKER) are likely to have a very fine estate for your moneys after the death of me and my wife, meaning as she believes the moiety of the said tythes of the Rectory of Kettlewell, or words to that effect.

Robert FANNER of Skipton, Yorks, gent., aged 39 years.

5. He knew Isabel TENNANT, late widow of Richard TENNANT very will. She was buried at the Parish Church of Skipton upon the 21 June 1664. He was present at her burial. Isabel received the profits of one half the tythes of the Rectory of Kettlewell during her lifetime. He knows this because he wrote several acquittances on her behalf, whereby she did acquit and discharge the tenants or farmers of the tythes upon paying of their rents as the same became due or as she received them.

*****

131. C 22/816/31
1673

Interrogatories to be administered to witnesses to be produced and examined in a cause depending in Her Majesty's Court of Chancery wherein Christopher

PALEY is Complainant, and Henry
CURRER Defendant, on behalf of the
Complainant.

(Bill and Answer missing)

1. Do you know the parties, complainant and defendant,
   in the suite, and did you know Henry GARFORTH,
   late of Langerhouse, in the pleadings named, now
   deceased ? Do you know Jane, his relict, the defendant's now wife ?

2. Do you know a parcel of land situate at Belbush
   within the parish of Gargrave in the County of York
   in the pleadings mentioned, which the complainant
   did farm, wherein there is a limestone quarry ?
   And do you know that the complainant and his children, or servants, have been employed in getting
   and burning limestone there ? Have you been employed as a servant for the complainant about it, or
   have you been partner or sharer with the complainant about it or no ?

3. Do you know that the complainant did usually buy coals
   for burning the said limestone of Henry GARFORTH
   at the rate of 4d. the horse load, or at what other
   rate being gotten in a coalmine within the Lordship
   of Bordley in the pleadings mentioned; and that after
   the death of Henry GARFORTH the defendant marrying
   Jane, his relict, entered into the said coalmine and
   sold coals to the complainant ?

4. Do you know which oxen the complainant sold to the
   defendant and for what rate; whether for the sum of
   £12 10s. 0d. or what other sum; whether the said
   sum of £12 10s. 0d. mutually agreed between the
   complainant and defendant to be accepted and allowed
   in payment for the said coals.

5. What other sums of money have you seen paid to the
   defendant for coals by the complainant, and when and
   where ?

6. Do you know what corn, dust or other things the defendant had of the complainant in payment and satisfaction
   for coals or to be allowed for the same, and at what rate,
   and of what value ?

7. Do you know that £29 8s. 0d. was paid to the defendant
   and when by the complainant ?

8. Do you know of any account made between the complainant and defendant in about the beginning of March 1666,
   or at any other time and when ?

9. Do you know that the defendant did upon the said
    account ... acknowledge himself to have received
    of the complainant any sum of money or what oxen,
    corn, grain, dust or other things amounting in all
    to £29 8s. 0d ? Did not the defendant acknowledge
    that the money which the complainant had then paid
    him did extend to the worth of the coals which the
    complainant had then received, and to 48s. 4d.
    more ? Did not the defendant promise to deliver
    coals to the complainant for the said 48s. 4d. which
    the defendant was then found to be endebted to the
    complainant upon the said account ?

10. Were you present with the complainant and defendant
    at the time of the making of the said account, and at
    the making of the promise; were you a witness there-
    of and when was the same made ? What coals or other
    satisfaction had the complainant of the defendant after
    the time of the making of the said account for 48s. 4d ?
    If he had any more coals after, were they not of the
    worst which were then left unsold, and of what value
    were they ?

11. Do you know or believe that the defendant is still
    endebted to the complainant 35s. justly due to him
    upon account ?

12. What other matter or thing do you know material in
    this cause, which may make for the complainant
    against the defendant ?

The Deposition of Robert PALEY taken
at the house of Thomas ELLIS in Gargrave
in Craven in the County of York 27 August
25 Chas. II (1673) before Richard
WILKINSON, Samuel WADDINGTON,
Wilfred LAWSON and John DODSWORTH,
gent., by virtue of H.M. Commission out
of the High Court of Chancery to them
directed by special order of the said Hon.
Court in a cause there depending between
Christopher PALEY, Complainant, and
Henry CURRER, gent., Defendant.

Robert PALEY of Malham Moors within the Parish of
Kirkeby in Malham Dale, Yorks., husbandman, aged
36 years and upwards.

1. He says he knows the parties complainant and defendant
    and did know Henry GARFORTH, now dec'd., and also
    knows Jane, his relict, the defendant's now wife.

264

2. He knows the land situate at Belbush where the complainant burned limestone, and says he was employed as a servant for the complainant in burning limestone there, but was never a partner with the complainant in the work.

3. He says he did buy several horse-loads of coal of Henry GARFORTH in his lifetime at four pence the horse-load for burning limestone, and that after the death of Henry GARFORTH, the defendant marrying Jane, his relict, sold several loads of coal to the complainant.

4. He says the complainant delivered two oxen to the defendant about 14 May 1664 at the rate of £12 10s. 0d. in payment for coal, which the complainant had then received of the defendant and should afterwards be delivered by the defendant to the complainant, and that upon account there made between them about coals, it appeared that the price of the coals, which the complainant had fetched before that time came to £8 17s. 0d. which was then allowed by their account out of the said £12 10s. 0d. The complainant was by their then agreement to fetch as many more coals as would amount to the remainder of the said £12 10s. 0d. being the price of the said oxen.

5. He says that he paid £5 more to the defendant by the complainant's order for coals in the month of June 1665 at the then dwelling house of the defendant situate at Langerhouse. And that he was also a witness and present with the complainant and defendant at the dwelling house of the complainant at Belbush in the month of August 1665 when the complainant paid the defendant 20s. for coals. He also paid 20s. more to the defendant for the complainant for coals at Lane Head, Yorks, in the month of February 1665/6, and he was likewise present with the complainant and defendant in Gisburne in or about September 1666 when the complainant paid the defendant £3 for coals.

6. He says that the defendant had 20 bushels of girts of shilling delivered him by the complainant at the rate of £6, 10 bushels whereof were delivered in December 1666 and the other ten in February the same year (1666/7). The defendant had a quarter of oats delivered him at the rate of 15s. by the complainant in December the same year and 6 bushels of dust at 6d. per bushel in January the same year (1666/7). All which the defendant had from the complainant and by his appointment in payment and satisfaction for the coals, and he further says he himself was present at the delivery thereof.

7. He says that the price of the oxen, corn and grain and dust and the several sums of money paid to the defendant by the complainant for coals amounted to £29 8s. 0d.

8, 9, 10 & 11.

He was present with the complainant and defendant in the house of John SHUTT of Gargrave in about the month of March 1655 and that he was there a witness when the complainant and defendant accounted about coals. Upon their said account between themselves it then appeared that the complainant had then already truly paid the defendant with the oxen, corn and grain etc. and several sums of money amounting to £29 8s. 0d. for all the coals which the complainant had then received and 48s. 4d. more. The defendant did then promise the complainant that he should have coals for the said 48s. 4d. which the defendant was then found to be endebted to the complainant. The complainant had more coals after the time of the making of the said account between them in satisfaction of the 48s. 4d. save only forty loads of the outcast coals which were then left unsold, the best of the coals being but at four pence a horse load. He confidently believes that the defendant is still endebted to the complainant 35s. and the complainant had never any more satisfaction since the said account for the said 48s. 4d. than the said forty horse-loads of outcast coals.

*****

132. C 22/897/40
1686

Interrogatories to be administered to witnesses to be examined on behalf of Thomas CURRER and Henry CURRER complainants against James GREENE defendant.

(Bill and Answer missing)

1. Do you know the parties complainant and defendant; did you know Samuel GREENE and Mary, now deceased, and Mary and Ann, their daughters; do you know William SPENCER and how long have you known them ?

2. Do you know or have you heard of a bond wherein the
complainants stand bound to the defendant, James
GREENE; what sum of money is due by it, and to
whom was it properly due; to the defendant as in his
own right, or as trustee for the use of Mary and
Anne GREENE ?

3. Do you know when William SPENCER married Mary
GREENE; did he at the defendant's direction receive
£50 from Thomas CURRER in right of his wife, Mary;
was it not paid and received in part satisfaction of the
said bond; did not William SPENCER on receipt thereof give a discharge for it; did you subscribe your
name as a witness thereunto ?

4. Do you know what other sums of money the complainants
have paid to the defendant towards the discharge of this
bond; when was it paid ? What did the defendant James
GREENE confess touching the receipt thereof, or of
any other sums which Thomas CURRER paid him when
he went to London, or at any other time ? Do you believe that the complainants in the year 1681 owed the
defendant anything at all ?

5. Do you know that Thomas CURRER and James GREEN
had discourse concerning the delivery up of the said
bond to be cancelled and at what place was the said
discourse ? Did not the defendants declare at that
time that he had received £100 upon the bond besides
the money paid to William SPENCER and that it was
totally and fully satisfied ? Did he not then promise
to give the complainants a general and complete release and to deliver up the bond ? What was the reason
then given by him that he desired the bond might remain
in his keeping, did he not allege that if Samuel GREENE's
children knew that if he delivered up the bond they would
sue him for the money thereby due ?

6. Did James GREEN at any time ask Thomas CURRER to
become bound with him to Abraham BOULTON for a
certain sum of money, and what was that sum, and did
he not offer to give Thomas the bond to be cancelled
only on condition that he became so bound with him ?
Was not Thomas's refusal to become bound the reason
for the defendant putting the bond in suite ?

7. Were you and the defendant about two months ago at the
house of Robert TOWINES in Addingham ? Who were
then in company with you and what discourse had you,
or any other person, with the defendant concerning this
present suite ? Did not James GREEN then declare that
he would compel Thomas CURRER to pay him £100 over
again which h e had before that time paid, and make him
pay double duty ? Did James GREENE proffer to give

you a certain sum of money for being a witness for him
and swearing as he would direct ?

8.   Do you know any other matter or thing concerning this
     suite ?

Deposition of witnesses taken at the
house of Elizabeth FRANK in Addingham,
widow, 5 June Jas. II (1686) before Roger
COATES and Samuel WHITLEY, gents.,
Charles BULL and Robert PARKER,
gents., directed for the examination of
witnesses.

John Thornton of Burnsall, Malster, aged 30.

1.   He knows the complainant and defendant, and William
     SPENCER and Mary, his wife.

2 & 6 He having some discourse with defendant in the house
       of Robert TOWN in Addingham about a year ago concern-
       ing a bond for £100 or more entered into before that time
       by the complainants to the defendant, which the defendant
       said he had in his custody but confessed withal the money
       due thereupon to be paid by Thomas CURRER to him
       (defendant). He said nevertheless the defendant could
       make the complainant pay the money over again inasmuch
       as he had the bond in his hand uncancelled; and further
       he said that if Thomas CURRER would become bound with
       him, the defendant, to Abraham BOULTON of Ilkley for
       £23 (a debt he said he owed Abraham BOULTON) he would
       have given Thomas CURRER the said bond to be cancelled.
       Thomas CURRER refused to become bound with the defend-
       ant to Abraham BOULTON, whereupon he threatened to
       sue him, which he subsequently did.

Isaac LOFTHOUSE of Ilkley, carpenter, aged 47.

1.   He knew all the parties.

4 & 5 He was working for the defendant in Addingham, and the
       defendant, standing by him in his (defendant's) barn as
       he was at work there, Thomas CURRER came to them
       and demanded a bond, an acquittance or some sufficient
       discharge. Thomas CURRER said to the defendant, in
       LOFTHOUSE's hearing that he, Thomas, had paid the
       defendant and William SPENCER and Mary SPENCER
       £150 or more, viz; £50 to SPENCER and £100 to
       GREENE ... But Thomas CURRER denied and said
       he had over paid the defendant, and by his order the
       money due upon the bond, and would not become bound

as desired for him to Abraham BOULTON.   LOFTHOUSE
says that from this discourse, he truly believes that Thomas
CURRER does not owe anything on the bond, and that one
reason why the defendant would not deliver it over to be
cancelled was that if the children of Samuel GREENE
understood that the defendant had delivered the bond to
the complainants they would sue the defendant for their
portions entrusted in his hand for which the bond was
given to the defendant.

6.   He says he believes that the refusal of Thomas CURRER
to be bound to Abraham BOULTON with the defendant for
the money the defendant then owed to BOULTON was the
reason why the defendant put the bond in suite.

John VERLEY of Harden, Bingley, yeoman, aged 34.

1.   He knows all the parties except Samuel GREENE.

4.   Being a tenant to the defendant of a mill and lands in
Addingham at £44 per annum about four years ago he
lived in part of the defendant's house in Addingham.
Thomas CURRER came to the defendant's house and
paid the defendant some money, which to the best of
VARLEY's memory was about £15 or £16. On receipt
of this money, the defendant said to VARLEY and others
present, but who he cannot remember, that the money
he had just received was the last payment of £100 he
had received of Thomas CURRER upon bond for the use
of his cousins, the children of Samuel GREENE, his
uncle and for which he (defendant) said he was to give
an account. VARLEY also says he had seen Thomas
CURRER several times pay money to the defendant,
but how much he does not know, yet he believes from
what he has heard that Thomas CURRER does not owe
the defendant anything.

Henry WRIGHT Rector of Addingham.

4.   He says he has seen a bond entered into by the complainants of £200 to the defendant for the payment of £118 or
thereabouts for the use of Mary and Anne GREENE,
daughters of Samuel GREENE, but the date thereof he
does not remember. He remembers that there was endorsed on the back of the bond the receipt of £60, i.e.
£50 paid to William SPENCER, who married the said
Mary GREENE and £10 to the defendant, and he believes
that the endorsement was of the defendant's own hand.
He further says that the writing now showed to him
purporting to be a bond of £100 dated 27 June 1683
entered into by the complainants to William SPENCER
conditioned for payment of £50 at two times then following

269

viz; £30 on 29 September next ensuing and £20 on 24 December next ensuing, was sealed and delivered by Thomas CURRER to William SPENCER in his presence, and he subscribed his name to it as witness, which bond is since paid and cancelled.

Jane SMITH, wife of Joshua SMITH, of Addingham aged 29.

1. She knows or knew all the persons named except Samuel GREENE.

4. She being a servant to Thomas CURRER about five years ago by the space of one year and a half did several times for her then master pay the defendant several sums of money, but not being required, did not take notice what sums were paid, save only one time of her own mind and will she observed Thomas CURRER take out of the trunk about £10 and paid the same to the defendant in the then dwelling house of the complainant in Addingham.

Thomas WEST of Bolton Bridge, Innholder, aged 56.

1. He knows all the persons named.

5. About Christmas now two years past Thomas CURRER and the defendant were both at his house and had some discourse about a bond which the complainants had entered into unto the defendant, which Thomas CURRER then told the defendant he had really satisfied before that time, and demanded a release for the same. Thomas CURRER showed this release which was drawn by Mr. Richard SQUIRE, solicitor to the defendant, which release the defendant had in his hand and read and perused the same. The defendant then replied that he was then on his journey to Ripon and in haste and had not then time, but at his return he would seal and deliver the same unto Thomas CURRER at Addingham. He says Mr. Richard SQUIRE was present at the same time.

Martin METCALFE of Skipton, mercer, aged 50

4. He says he was in company with Thomas CURRER and defendant at Skipton on 8 September 1681 and saw Thomas CURRER and the defendant count a sum of money upon a table, and the defendant desired him to draw a bill of sale to Thomas CURRER for several goods of the defendant to the tune of £24 14s. 0d. which induces him to believe that Thomas CURRER did not then owe the defendant any money, for Thomas seemed unwilling to lay

down any money for the defendant, or to become bound with him to one John WALKER of Hungerhill unto whom the defendant was then endebted, and questioned how he should be reimbursed by the defendant, but with many speeches and promises the defendant prevailed with the complainant for security given to the said Mr. WALKER.

Edward BARROW of Skipton, Fellmonger, aged 50 and upwards.

6. About March 12 months ago he was in Addingham in company of the defendant and George BURNETT, then Chief Bailiff of the Wapentake of Skirack, who said he had a writ against Thomas CURRER at the suite of the defendant, and the defendant then desired him (Edward BARROW) to go to Thomas CURRER and to acquaint him that if he would according to his promise become bound with the defendant to Abraham BOULTON of Ilkley for the sum of £23 which he, the defendant, owed to Abraham BOULTON, he would deliver Thomas a bond of his he had. BARROW went to Thomas CURRER and told him what James GREEN desired, but he refused and said he would not be bound with him as desired.

William SPENSER of Addingham, yeoman, aged 34.

3 & 8 Four years ago he married Mary, one of the daughters of Samuel GREENE, deceased, and he received £60 in payment of a bond entered into by the complainants untl the defendant, that is to say £50 from the complainant, Thomas, and £10 from the defendant, which the defendant received from the complainant Thomas. The writing showed to him at the time of his examination purporting to be a release of all debts etc. from him to the complainants was signed by him according as the same is underwritten. A bond given to him by the complainant Thomas dated 27 June 1683 in £100 for payment of £50 was paid to him and another bond dated 3 December 1683 of £60 for payment of £30 was also paid accordingly by Thomas CURRER.

John CROSSLEY of Addingham, aged 25

1. He knows all the parties except Samuel GREENE.

4. About three years ago, being a servant to Thomas CURRER he saw him pay the defendant some money which seemed to be about four or five pounds.

*****

271

133.   SP 23/79
            Sworn before the Commissioners for Compounding
            21 Sept. 1651.

William CURRÈR of Stainton maketh oath that he was present when the
deed dated 20 Aug 1651 made between Richard SWINGLEHURST and
Ralph FABER of the one part and Hugh CURRER of the other part, was
sealed and delivered, and that the same was sealed and delivered upon
the day of the date thereof by the said Richard SWINGLEHURST and
Ralph FABER. He further saith that Hugh CURRER did authorise him to
take livery and seisin of the lands and premises mentioned in the deed,
and that accordingly on 20 Aug 1651 Thomas WALMESLEY departed and
FABER did give livery and seisin unto this deponent for the use of Hugh
CURRER according to the endorsement on the said deed.

                                                    Will. CURRER

                            *****

134.   Sworn before the Commissioners
            17 Sept. 1651.

Hugh CURRER of Bradford in the County of York, yeoman, maketh oath
that he did authorise and depute William CURRER of Stainton, yeoman,
his lawful attorney to take livery and seisin for this deponent's use of
the lands and premises mentioned in the indenture dated 20 Aug 1651
made between Richard SWINGLEHURST and Ralph FABER etc; and he
further saith that livery and seisin was taken accordingly by Wm. CURRER
and that he did agree with the same.

                                                    Hugh CURRER

                            *****

135.   29 Aug 1650.

            PETITION of Henry GOODGEON of Skipton and
            Anthony WALKER of Burnsall, gent.

The Sequestrators for the County of York have sequestred certain lands
and tenements (being all the lands and tenements of Henry CURRER, a
delinquent) lying in Skipton, and one tenement in Gargrave, belonging
to your petitioners, which they purchased from Henry CURRER after he
had compounded and paid one moiety of his fine and secured the other,
which latter moiety the said delinquent neglected to pay. They therefore
beseech your Honours to give them liberty to pay into the Treasury at
Goldsmiths Hall for proportion of the latter moiety of the said fine due

for the premises with interest; and to order that upon payment thereof the said sequestration may be discharged.

Henry GOODGEON
Ant. WALKER

*****

Henry CURRER of Skipton in the County of York, gent. His delinquency that he was in arms against the Parliament. He rendered in November 1645, his estate in fee per annum - £59 8s. 8d; for two years to come per annum - £9 10s. 0; for five years yet to come per annum - £7, after eight years per annum - £30 for which he was fined at a tenth £158 17s. 0d.

*****

29 Aug 1650

PETITION of Robert FERRAND of Harden Grange, Yorks., gent.

The sequestrators for the county of York have sequestred the moiety of Silsden and Kildwick Mill and one farm or tenement of Widow ATKINSON's and two farms in Farnhill and Horton belonging to the petitioner, he having purchased the same of Henry CURRER after he had compounded and paid one moiety of his fine and secured the other, which latter moiety he neglected to pay. He craves the liberty to pay into the Treasurey at Goldsmiths Hall the proportion of the latter moiety of the fine due for the premises with interest for the same, and to order that upon payment thereof the sequestration may be discharged.

Robert FERRAND

*****

29 Sept 1652

PETITION of Hugh CURRER

Your Honours on 6 November 1651, upon Mr. BRERETON's report, were pleased to allow of your petitioner's title to the Rectory of Chipping in the County of Lancaster sequestred for the delinquency of one HARRIS and ordered the Commissioners for the County to pay your petitioner the arrears of the profits of the said Rectory from 24 December 1649.

Notwithstanding your said Order the Commissioners refuse to pay the arrears pretending they have been paid to Ministers by order of the Committee for Plundered Ministers.

Your petitioner about 7 years since disbursed £140 as a purchase for the said premises but for the life of one Richard SWINGLEHURST, who is very aged and infirm, and hath been at about £100 charge in repairs of the house and barns and in the recovery thereof so that he like to be a great loser thereby.

He pleads that the said Commissioners be ordered to pay the arrears out of some other sequestration or take such other course for the petitioner's relief in the said premises as to your wisdom shall be thought most fit.

Hugh CURRER

*****

139.   By the Committee for Sequestrations
         29 Jan 1651/2

Whereas we have received an Order from the Committee for Compounding dated 6 November last (1651) made in the case of Mr. Hugh CURRER upon the report of Mr. BRERETON whereby the said Mr. CURRER's title to the glebe and tythes mentioned therein (excepting the tythes assigned by deed dated 15 May 17 Caroli to Christopher HARRIS for 21 years) is approved and allowed of, and that the said Mr. CURRER be permitted to have and enjoy the same freed and discharged from sequestration and that he have all arrears thereof which have incurred since 24 December 1649. In pursuance whereof it is ordered that the agent for Blackburn Hundred where the said tythes lie shall yield obedience to the said Order and shall observe the same in all things as thereby is required excepting payment of the said arrears; and that the tythes mentioned in the said deed of 15 May 17 Caroli growing upon the lands of these persons following viz; Robert PARKER, Henry CUTLER, Thomas PARKER, James ROGERSON, William WEANE, Robert HACKINGE, John WALTON, Mr. Richard SHERBURNE, William TRUNLEY, James WILKINSON, Christopher KENICN, William CUTLER, Robert ERRLIS, John DILWORTH, Thomas ERRLIS for Mr. RODES land, James RODES, Allan BATTELL, James DILWORTH, John WILKINSON, Thomas DILWORTH, Thomas ALSTON, William LANCASTER, Evan ERRLIS, Richard SIMPSON, John RODES of Priesthill, George ALSTON and Edward BRADLEY lying on the West side of Thornley, Wheatley and Studley within the parish of Chipping be continued under sequestration for the Popery and delinquency of Christopher HARRIS till further order. And as to payment of arrears due since 24 December 1649 as aforesaid, the same having been paid for the maintenance of Ministers according to orders from the Committee for Plundered Ministers, it is ordered that it be certified to the Committee for Compounding how the same have been disposed on and their further directions therein desired. And whereas there is a rent charge of £25 1s. 8d. due out of all the said tythes in Chipping Parish formerly due to the late Bishop of Chester and sequestred from him and now payable to the use of the State, it is ordered that the said Mr. CURRER shall pay his proportionable part of the said rent due to the State and the (? farmer) of the tythes aforesaid yet under sequestration to pay likewise the sum of £6 13s. 8d. being the proportionable part of the rent due for the tythes till further order. And the farmers of the housing and glebe lands mentioned in the said report are upon notice hereof to appear before us at our next sitting for Blackburn Hundred to shew cause why they have suffered the said housing to fall into decay and have not repaired the same according to the contract otherwise we shall certify their default to the Committee for Compounding to be further proceeded against as they shall see cause.

> Robt. CUNLIFFE
> G. PIGOT

*****

6 Nov. 1651

In the Case of Mr. Hugh CURRER; upon reading the report of Mr. BRERETON, Hugh CURRER therein desiring that the Rectory of Chipping, Lancs., sequestred for the delinquency of one HARRIS may be discharged from sequestration, and upon consideration had upon the matter, it is resolved and so ordered that title of the said Mr. Hugh CURRER to the glebe and tythes therein mentioned (except the tythes assigned by deed 15 May 17 Caroli to Christopher HARRIS for 21 years) be allowed of and that the said Mr. CURRER be permitted to have and enjoy the same freed from sequestration and that he have the arrears thereof which have incurred since 24 December 1649 whereof the Commissioners for Sequestrations in the County and all others whom it concerns are to take notice and see performed accordingly.

> Edward WINSLOW
> Jo. RUSSELL
> William MAKINS
> Ric. MOORE

I have taken notice of this Order
20 Jan 1651/2

Richard SHERWINGE. Auditor

*****

REPORT of Peter BRERETON

According to yours of 12 July 1650 upon the petition of Hugh CURRER desiring that the Rectory of Chipping in the County of Lancs. sequestred for the delinquency of one HARRIS may be discharged from sequestration, I have examined his case and find Hugh CURRER in 1646 petitioning the Committee of Lords and Commons; it was ordered that the Committee for the said County of Lancs. should examine and certify, which they did in May 1647. Afterwards the stating of the Case being referred by the Barons the same was reported by the now Recorder of London 27 October 1649; but the Barons concerning they had no power to determine titles and Hugh CURRER applying himself unto you copies of the said Examination of the Recorder's Report and all other proceedings attested by Mr. VAUGHAN and deposed by Hugh CURRER were transmitted hither upon perusal whereof and of other examinations taken since by me I find the Case to be this:-

275

Richard, Bishop of Chester, by Indenture dated 20 December 1598 demises the Rectory of Chipping, Lancs., with all glebelands the (? maines) of all tenements all tythes belonging to the said rectory unto Robert SWINGLE-HURST during the lives of the said Robert, Thomas SWINGLEHURST, Christopher and Richard SWINGLEHURST the younger, cousin to the said Robert, reserving rent with a clause of re-entry for non-payment a copy of which Indenture is deposed by John BLAGEBURNE. In February 1644 the said Robert SWINGLEHURST died leaving only a daughter married to Christopher HARRIS.

Richard THORNTON deposeth that Robert SWINGLEHURST 15 May 1641 did by Indenture demise some part of the tythes lying in Thorneley to Christopher HARRIS for 21 years after the expiration of the former grants of the said Robert and Richard SWINGLEHURST so long live.

And I find by the examination of Edward PARKER, a lawyer, that Robert SWINGLEHURST in his sickness delivered the lease of the rectory and gave (? orders) to the said Edward PARKER for drawing an assignment thereof to uses but died before the same was brought to him by the deponent, and further deposeth that he acquainted Robert SWINGLEHURST jr that Robert SWINGLEHURST by the said assignment had given him the said Richard £6 13s. 4d. per annum and some other things he shewed himself thankful and promised all things touching the said rectory to follow the directions of the said deponent who (? advised) him to keep possession in the Parsonage House to those uses the (? deceased) had declared unto the deponent and where expressed in the said assignment unto which the said Richard did assent. And Christopher FOULES and William TROUGHTON depose they heard the ... said intended assignment of Robert SWINGLEHURST read whereby he deposed of the said rectory to Christopher HARRIS and that Richard SWINGLEHURST said he would go and take possession for the said HARRIS; and Christopher FOULES further deposeth that the said Richard did take possession accordingly, but William TROUGHTON deposeth that Richard did not take possession, but did send unto his wife who took possession for the use of her husband. I find by a paper dated 12 February 1644/5 and deposed by John BOULTON and Henry WINDER two of the witnesses subscribed that Elizabeth, wife of the said Richard SWINGLEHURST, the said 12 February did enter into a close called Parsonage Heye, being part of the glebe, in the name of the ... Rectory claiming to hold the same unto her and her husband as occupant during all such estate as was in the said Robert SWINGLE-HURST and not by him assigned. And further deposeth that at the death of the said Robert SWINGLEHURST, Richard SWINGLEHURST lived in the Parsonage House and was in possession of the same and of the land.

I find further that Richard SWINGLEHURST by an Indenture dated 6 February 1645/6 reciting the original lease to Robert SWINGLEHURST that he died without assigning and that the said Richard SWINGLEHURST being the surviving life had entered in a Close called Parsonage Heye part of the glebe land in the names of all the glebelands, houses, tythes, etc. belonging unto the said rectory demised unto Robert SWINGLEHURST claiming the same as occupant unto him and his assigns during such estate as was in Robert SWINGLEHURST and not by him assigned, the said Richard SWINGLEHURST, for the consideration expressed in the said grant, and assigns the said rectory and premises unto Ralph FABER, his son-in-law, for ever to the use of the said Ralph FABER and his assigns for ever; the sealing and delivery of which Indenture is deposed by John (? SANDER) one of the witnesses and Ralph FABER by an Indenture dated 13 February 1645/5 reciting the said assignment in consideration of £140 granted and assigned the said lease and all his estate, right, title, claim and demand in and to the said rectory etc. unto your petitoner, Hugh CURRER, and his assigns for ever, the sealing and delivery whereof is deposed by Robert FABER one of the witnesses.

And Richard MARSDEN, John ROWCLIFFE and George MILES depose that at the time of the sequestration Richard SWINGLEHURST was in possession of the Parsonage House and glebelands and John ROWCLIFFE and Geo. MILES depose to the collecting of tythes for the said Richard SWINGLEHURST. In find by the examination of Richard MARSDEN and John HAWORTH that the rectory was sequestred for the delinquency of Christopher HARRIS and by the information upon the oath of Robert CUNFLIFFE, late one of the Committee, now one of the Commissioners for Sequestrations in Lancashire, that Richard SWINGLEHURST before the said Committee did make title and claim unto the rectory by virtue of an entry made by him, or in his name, into the same or some part thereof, which claim being not admitted as good by the Committee the said Richard desired to be farmer thereof, which would not be granted until he disclaimed all title and interest by his entry as (? first occupant) which he did in writing under his hand, and thereupon was admitted tenant for the year ensuing. He deposeth unto the time of the disclaimer, and John HAWORTH and Thomas WHALLEY depose fully to the disclaimer of Richard SWINGLEHURST and to his becoming farmer and John HAWORTH and Thomas WHALLEY depose it was in the year 1644 or thereabouts.

This I find to be the Petitioner's Case wherein you may please to consider whether the said rectory be conveyed by Robert SWINGLEHURST unto Christopher HARRIS the delinquent, or to any other in trust for him, whether the entry of Elizabeth SWINGLEHURST for herself, or her husband, into part of the glebelands in the name of the whole rectory and the subsequent agreement of her husband do vest all the rectory in him or her as occupant or occupants or only the glebeland. Admitting an (? occupancy) then whether the disclaimer have divested the frank tenement out of him, and if it have, in whom is the same vested. Admitting it have not, whether the glebeland by his assignment to Ralph FABER and by FABER's assignment to the petitioner do pass, ... appearing to have been made upon neither, and upon the whole, more it is submitted to judgement whether the sequestration ought to be discharged or not.

1 May 1651   Pet. BRERETON

*****

PETITION of Hugh CURRER of Bradford.

Robert SWINGLEHURST, gent., at the time of his death was seised of a freehold for the term of the natural joint and several lives of himself, Thomas SWINGLEHURST his brother, and of Richard SWINGLEHURST his cousin of and in the Rectory of Chipping in the County of Lancs. by virtue of a lease made to him by Richard, late Bishop of Chester, then imparsoned of the said rectory, and being of such estate seised thereof the said Robert SWINGLEHURST died without assigning thereof having only one daughter, who is heir of his lands immediately after his death, the said Richard SWINGLEHURST made an actual entry into the parsonage house and into part of the glebelands in the name of all the said rectory with the rights thereunto appertaining as first occupant, by force of which entry Richard SWINGLEHURST conceived and was informed by ... of sound judgement in the law that he was lawfully entitled to hold the same as first occupant during all the term of his life, for that the said estate being no inheritance cannot descend to the heir, and being freehold the executors cannot be capable of it wherefore for necessity of a tenant to the freehold the law hath vested the same in the said Richard SWINGLEHURST during the remainder of the lease. Now the said Richard SWINGLEHURST hath assigned the same for good consideration to Ralph FABER who married his daughter, and he to your petitioner for the sum of £140, who is now encumbered in enjoying the estate he so paid for by the Sequestrators of that County pretending the profits of the said lease ought to belong to the public by reason the daughter of the said Robert SWINGLEHURST is married to one HARRIS, a delinquent, and have ordered that the profits thereof be sequestred accordingly, although he was never invested therein, or ever had any possession thereof. Now for as much as your petitioner's case was formerly referred by the Barons of the Exchequer to Mr. Recorder STEELE to peruse and report, who accordingly prepared his said report, but before the same could be despatched and allowed of by the said Barons their power in such cases was dissolved. It is therefore humbly desired that Your Honours will be pleased to peruse the said report and to allow your petitioner's title and to discharge the sequestration of the premises, or else refer him to a trial at law, the sequestration notwithstanding.

Hugh CURRER

To the Commissioners for Sequestrations and Compounding.

*****

143.   The Case of Hugh CURRER wherein the opinion
         of Baron THORPE is desired by the Commissioners
         for Compounding.

Robert SWINGLEHURST lessee for his own life and the life of Richard SWINGLEHURST of the Rectory of Chipping in the County of Lancs. consisting of glebe and tythes, hath issue a daughter married to Christopher HARRIS, unto whom Robert assigned part of the tythes, and afterwards in 1644 directed an Assignment to be drawn of all the rectory to the use (among others) of Christopher HARRIS, and died before the said draft brought unto him; Richard SWINGLEHURST entered into part of the glebeland in name of the whole rectory not assigned, claiming the same as occupant, and received the profits of the glebe and collected the tythes, until the whole rectory was sequestred by the Committee of the said County for the delinquency of Christopher

HARRIS, who never had any possession of the glebelands, nor of any other part of the tythes, excepting the said portion assigned to him. Richard SWINGLEHURST disclaimed his title of occupancy before the said Committee and accepted of a lease for a year and afterwards assigned the estate which he had gained by occupancy in the said rectory unto FABER, who assigned unto Hugh CURRER in consideration of £140 really paid.

Querie 1st.   Whether the said Richard SWINGLEHURST by his entry and claim and his receiving the profits of the glebe, and collecting the tythes hath not gained an estate of franktenement as occupant.

Querie 2nd.   Whether Richard SWINGLEHURST hath gained an estate as occupant in the glebe alone, or in the tythes also.

Querie 3rd.   Whether the disclaimer of Richard SWINGLE-HURST have divested the franktenement out of him.

Baron THORPE's Reply
5 November 1651

In this case Robert SWINGLEHURST dying before he had made the assignment which he intended of the glebe and (? residew) of the tythes not assigned to HARRIS and Richard SWINGLEHURST entering upon the glebe, he thereby became an occupant both of the glebe and residew of the tythes not assigned. And so he gained an estate of freehold therein by the act and ... of Law in respect of his first entry. And therefore this was not liable to sequestration for the delinquency of HARRIS. Touching Richard SWINGLEHURST his disclaimer before the Committee of his title and occupancy and taking a lease for a year. It will not alter the law nor divest the freehold out of him. Howbeit he ...   ... to pay the rent agreed upon for that year.

F. THORPE

*****

Gentlemen,

In observance of your order of the twelfth of July last upon the petition of Hugh CURRER requiring us to certify the cause of the Sequestration of the Rectory of Chipping, and in whose possession the same was at the time of the Sequestration, we have proceeded to examine all such witnesses as were produced as well in behalf of the State as upon the part and behalf of the said Hugh CURRER (Copies whereof are herewith sent) referring the same to your further consideration we rest,

your humble servants,
Peter HOLT
Geo. PIGOT

Preston: 14 Sept 1650

To the Honble. Comm. for Compounding with Delinquents
at Westminster.   these present   For the Service of the State.

*****

146.   Rt. Honble.

In obedience to your Honours' order of 28 August last in the case of
Hugh CURRER concerning the Rectory of Chipping in this County of
Lancaster, we have examined witnesses on both sides on oath and have
herewith sent copies of the said examinations attested with the Clerkes
hand of this Committee, humbly referring the same to your Honours
consideration and rest,

Your Honours' humble servants,

J. BRADSHAWE
Peter EGERTON
H. FLEETWOOD

Preston: 20 May 1647

*****

147.   Preston at the Committee
           5 December 1646.

FABER in the presence of this Examination and others and that this
Examination endorsed his mark as witness to the same

Signed: John SOWER

Robert FABER of Kenringe in the County of York, gent., sworn and
examined saith that he was by and present when the assignment now
showed unto him and whereupon some of this Committee have endorsed
their names dated 13 January 21 Caroli R 1646 was sealed and delivered
by Ralph FABER named in the said assignment unto Hugh CURRER of
Halifax, gent. and that this examinant subscribed his name as a witness
to the same and that in consideration thereof the said Hugh CURRER paid
unto the said Ralph FABER the sum of one hundred and forty pounds at
the least to this examinant's best remembrance.

Robert FABER

*****

148.   Captain Richard MARSDEN examined upon oath saith that after the death
of Robert SWINGLEHURST of Farick House, gent., Mr. PARKER of
Brousholme told ... ... (incomplete)

*****

280

29 April 1651
William CURRER of the City of London,
Doctor of Physick.

His delinquency, that he hath adhered to the forces raised against the
Parliament in the late wars.   He petitioned here 25 April 1651 and
saith he was never yet sequestred. He compounds upon a particular
delivered in under his hand whereby he submits etc. and whereby it doth
appear that he is possessed of a personal estate consisting in books,
wearing apparel and other necessaries amounting to the sum of £10.

Jo. BRADINGE
13 May 1651

Fine at a 6th £1 13s. 4d.

*****

25 April 1651
PETITION.

He hath adhered to the forces raised against the Parliament in the late
wars for which his small estate is liable to sequestration, but not yet
sequestred.

He humbly prays to be admitted to compound for his said delinquency upon
his own discovery.

Wm. CURRER

*****

1 Sept 1646
Henry CURRER of Skipton in the County
of Yorks., gent.

His delinquency that he was in arms against the Parliament and came into
the Parliament long since, and took the National Covenant before Daniel
EVANS, Minister of St. Clement Danes, London, 25 November 1645, and
now again for more satisfaction before William BARTON, Minister of
John Zacharies 17 July 1646 and the Negative Oath here 23 July 1646. He
compounds upon a particular returned out of the country and upon another
delivered in under his hand by which he doth submit to such fine etc. and
by which it doth appear that he is seised in fee to him and his heirs in
possession of and in certain lands and tenements lying and being in Skipton
in the County of York, and of a farm in Horton and Farnhill in the said
county which by the Committee of York are returned to be worth together
before these troubles £58 8s. 8d.

That he is possessed of the remains of a term for two years to come of
other lands and tenements lying there, holden by demise from the Earl of
PEMBROKE, of the yearly value before these troubles £9 10s. 0d.

281

That he is possessed of the remains of a term for 5 years yet to come of and in other lands and tenements lying there holden of the Guardians of the School of Clitheroe under the yearly rent of £2 6s. 8d. and was yearly worth before these troubles over and above the rent reserved £7.

That there is to remain and come unto him and his heirs, after eight years expired the moiety of other lands and tenements lying in Silsden in Kildwick of the yearly value before these troubles £30.

That he is seised to him and heirs in possession of and in one other house situate in Gargrave in the said county of the yearly value before these troubles £1.

Personal estate he hath none.

D. WATKINS

Fine £158 17s. 0d.

*****

152.   25 November 1645

This is to certify that Henry CURRER of Skipton in the County of York, gent., did freely and fully take the National Covenant and subscribe the same upon 17 July 1646. The said Covenant being administered unto him according to order by me,

William BARTON,
Minister of John Zacharies,
London.

These are to certify to whom it may concern that Henry CURRER of Skipton in Craven in the County of York, gentleman, hath taken the solemn League and Covenant before me.

Daniel EVANS
Minister of St. Clement Danes,
London.

*****

153.   To the Rt. Hon. the Committee for Compositions for Delinquents' Estates sitting at Goldsmiths Hall

      The humble petition of Henry CURRER of Skipton in Craven in the County of York, gent., humbly showeth

That your petitioner's whole estate lies in and about Skipton which is yet kept by the King's party, where he with his wife and children have lived until 2 August last past, from whence at that time he came and hath left his whole estate to the mercy of the enemy, who threaten your petitioner's life ever since, yet your petitioner confessing his estate to be sequestrable for his offences below specified, humbly desires that this Hon.

Committee would be pleased to give him leave to give such satisfaction as your honours will think fit in this his distressed case.

Your petitioner has lived at his own house in Skipton since these unhappy troubles and took, though unwillingly, a commission for being a captain under the Earl of NEWCASTLE, but never raised any men, neither acted anything against the Parliament.

Henry CURRER

*****

A particular of the estate real and personal of Henry CURRER of Skipton in Craven in the County of York which he desires to compound 13 March 1646/7.

	£	s.	d.
He is seised of an estate in fee simple to him and his heirs of two tenements and pertaining lands in Skipton of the yearly value before these troublous times	22	-	-
He is also seised of a like estate of tenement and pertaining lands in Horton, Yorks., of the yearly value of	3	-	-
He is also seised of a like estate of one other tenement and lands in Farnhill, Yorks., of the yearly value of	3	-	-
He is also seised of a like estate of two closes of land lying in Collinghead worth per annum before troubles	1	10	-
Also of a tenement in Gargrave worth per annum		10	-
He is also seised of a like estate in reversion after the determination of a lease for 8 years and above yet to come of the moiety of the Mills of Kildwick and Silsden in the County of York worth per annum	20	-	-

As for his personal estate he hath none left to compound.

Henry CURRER

*****

PART V

CHANCERY CASES 1550-1650

BRIEF EXTRACTS

155   C.1./1223/17-20; Elizabeth GLANFYLDE v. Nicholas GARDNER;
Land in Drinkstone, late of John GLANFYLD, dec., father of
complainant; Suffolk.

156   C.1./1225/25; John GREY, clerk, v. Arthur RAY (?) & others;
Tithes of houses in St. John's in Watling Street; London.

157   C.1/1240/77-78; Marion KYRBYE & others v. Christopher
BOLTON; Lands in Friston, Buxlow, Knodishall, late of
John POLLYNG, whose heirs the female complainants are.
Pedigree given; Suffolk.

158   C.1/1240/67-68; John KYNG v. Robert WADE; Lands in
Brandeston; Suffolk.

159   C.1/1245/20-23; Ralph MARSHAM v. Margaret CHAPMAN; Lands
of William TOMPSON (clerk, dec.,) of Norwich; Norfolk.

160   C.1/1245/30-33; Robert MARTIN of Kersey, Clothier v. Simon
CLERKE & wife; Bond given on behalf of Alice before her marriage
for price of wheat, barley, and "Mystelen"; Suffolk.

161   C.1/1246/14-15; John, son & heir of John MARTEN v. William
LYNNE, husband of Alice, late wife of the said John the father;
Messuages & lands in Warmingford & Fordham, and Legacy;
Essex and Suffolk.

162   C.1/1248/53; Thomas MOUNTFORD of Little Massingham (Norfolk)
v. John CORNELL; Land in Radwinter; Essex.

163   C.1/1250/51; William NEYNES, husbandman, v. Robert WADE &
others; Lands in Woolpit, bought off Thom. HARRYES of Bury
St. Edmunds; Suffolk.

164   C.1/1252/39-40; Robert, nephew and heir of John PERHAM v.
William BISSHOPPE and Robert MARTEYN; Land in Burgh;
Suffolk.

165   C.1/1317/19; Lewis SERGEANT, fishmonger, v. John WILLOUGHBY,
Esq., of Denver, Norfolk, and Robert MARTEN, Constable of
Denver; Stray gelding laden with fish; Cambs, Norfolk. (Damaged).

166   C.1/1272/14-16; Nicholas THOMSON, guardian of the King's masons
of Calais, v. John DEBNEY of Colchester, Merchant; Loans (scheduled)
by Alice BAKER, since married to the complainant; Calais. Essex.

C.1/1280/19-21; John WEBBE of Lidget, Suffolk, executor of Rose RANDE of Sudbury, Suffolk, v. Thomas RANDE; Annuity charged on a messuage in Ashen, bequeathed to defendant by Richard RANDE, husband of Rose; Essex.

C.1/1281/1; Robert WADE of Debenham v. John, son and executor of John SPARROWE; Marriage settlement of Joan, late wife of complainant and sister of defendant, on consideration of which the former purchased lands in the Manor of Cosford; Suffolk.

C.1/1285/59; . . . of Co. Cambs, fisherman, v. John WILLOUGHBY, Esq., and Robert MARTEN, Constable of Denford (ie Denver?) (See C.1/1317/19); Arrest of complainants cart carrying fish to Ely; (Norfolk?). (Mutilated).

C.1/1286/14; Robert ANDREWES and Roger THOMSON of Carlton Colville, v. Henry WINDERICKE; Detention of bond for a debt to Thomas SMYTH partly paid in corn; Suffolk.

C.1/1288/2; Robert, son and heir of William BACON and of Margaret his wife a daughter and heir of Robert BROKE, v. George WADE of Ringstead, Suffolk; Detention of deeds relating to land in Woodton, Seething, Kirstead, Langham, Barrow and Mundham; Norfolk.

C.1/1291/30-31; Thomas BEAMOND of Norwich, Draper, v. Thomas HENDRY and Margaret his wife, executrix of William TOMPSON of Norwich, clerk; Part price of cloth, said by the defendants to have been plundered by the rebels at Norwich; No Norfolk.

C.1/1296/36-39; Thomas DERESLAY and Beatrice his wife v. John son and heir of Robert RAYE; Detention of deeds relating to a messuage and land in Denston, of the bequest of Henry SPALDINGE; Suffolk.

C.1/1300/3-4; Robert GARDENER v. Barbara, late the wife of Richard BALLES, and administrtrix of his goods; Refusal to rebuild a Manor or Messuage in Benacre, burnt down during the said Richard's tenancy; Suffolk.

C.1/1300/5-7; William GARDNER and Margaret his wife v. Nicholas LYNGWOOD; Dentention of deeds re. messuages and land in Badingham and Dennington, formerly of Robert BANHAM, great-grandfather of Margaret, and father in law of defendant; Suffolk.

C.1/1305/47-48; John, son and heir of John KYRBYE v. Thomas PARKER of Ashley, son and heir of Thomas YATYS, alias PARKER; Close of pasture in Cheveley; Cambridgeshire.

C.1/1305/16-18; Thomas KNEVETT and William SCRYMSHAWE v. William, Son of Nicholas RICHARDSON, dec., and Thomas RAYE; Messuages and land in Shelton and Laxton, parish of Howden; Yorkshire.

178   C.1/1309/35; Francis MICHELL, Yeoman of the Household, and
Jane his wife, late the wife of Christopher CARLETON of Theydon
Garnon, v. George TOMPSON and William COLTHURST, executors
of the said Christopher; Farm of Eppingbury, late of Christopher,
and guardianship of George and John, his sons; Essex. (Damaged).

179   C.1/1314/47; Robert ROBOTHAM and Grace his wife, v. Thomas
WYTTON of London, scrivener, John STEPHENS, and Armiger
WADE, gent; Debts due to Robert BULLE, former husband of
Grace; London. (Mutilated. D.VII.41).

180   C.1/1314/89-91; Robert ROTHERY and Thomas COOKE, servants of
Alice, late the wife of John TOMSON of Cheshunt, Herts, Yeoman,
v. George WRYGHT and John WHYTYNG, understeward of the
Manor of Waltham Holy Cross; Action of trespass re. land in said
Manor; Essex.

181   C.1/1318/53-55; John TOMPSON, Yeoman, and Margery his wife v.
Anthony SMYTHSON; Annuity charged on land in Walpole; Norfolk.

182   C.1/1318/56; James TOMSON v. William MANNE, husbandman;
Detention of deeds re. pasture in Murrow (in Wisbech); Cambs.

183   C.1/1320/1; Andrew WADE of Tower Hill, son of John WADE, dec.,
v. William ATKYNSON and his wife Ellen, late the wife of the said
John; Messuage and land in Little Cattal; Yorkshire.

184   C.1/1320/2-4; Lionel WADE of Brandeston v. John KYNGE; Land
in Cretingham, late held of the manor of Monewden by Thomas WADE,
dec., father of complainant; Suffolk.

185   C.1/1320/5-7; Lionel WADE v. Andrew REVETT of Brandeston,
surveyor of the manor of Monewden; Obtaining lease by false
statements; Suffolk.

186   C.1/1321/48-49; Robert WRIGHT of Debden, son and heir of John
WRYGHT and Alice his wife, v. John WYSEMAN esq.; Land held
of defendant at manor of Tendring; Essex.

187   C.1/1322/1-3; (Armiger) WADE, Esq., v. John, son and heir of
John WAGER; Messuage in Wragby, late of John WADE, dec.,
brother of complainant; Yorkshire.

188   C.1/1323/50-54; William WILSON and Othell (sic) his wife, formerly
Othell BOLTON, v. Margaret, late the wife of Thomas WOODHOUSE,
Esq; Bedding entrusted to said Thomas for said Othell, by Richard
ROBARDES, late parson of Kelsall; Suffolk.

189   C.1/1333/6-7; Edmund BARKER, yeoman, grandson and heir of
Edmund BARKER v. Robert GARDYNER and Thomasine his wife;
Detention of deeds relating to messuage and lands in Sibton; Suffolk.

190   C.1/1334/86; Henry BULLYVANT, John GARDENER and Agnes his
wife v. Robert HARRY; Messuages and lands in Frostenden sold to
the defendant by Robert his father, dec., also father of Agnes and
Margaret, wife of Henry; Suffolk.

C.1/1339/64-69; Philip CURSON and Bridget his wife v.
Elizabeth and Robert KARVYLE; Messuage and land in
Watlington late of Thomas KARVYLE of Rowton Holme,
gentleman, former husband of Bridget; Norfolk. (Mutilated.
D. XIV, 64).

C.1/1344/32-35; Thomas COLWELL of Hitchin v. John GARDYNER
and others; Messuages and lands in Saffron Walden (Walden Audley)
and Littlebury, late of John COLWELL, dec., brother of complainant; Essex.

C.1/1345/1; Robert DADE of Great Thornham in Suffolk, executor
of Robert WARREN of Sturton in Suffolk v. John SHELTON, Knight,
and others; Detention of deeds re. messuage and land in Shelton and
Fritton; Norfolk.

C.1/1353/7; Alexander GATE, parson, of Tolleshunt Knights
(Tolson Militis) v. Thomas BAKER; Lease of the parsonage made
to Jerome SONGER by Edward POPLEY, late parson, deprived
for marriage; Essex.

C.1/1354/58-63; John GOODLADE v. Nicholas RICHARDSON,
Edward KYRBY and John COPLEDIKE; House and land in the
manor of Ross-in-Holderness; Yorkshire.

C.1/1357/78; Robert HALL v. Henry THOMSON of Gargrave;
Money entrusted to the defendant; Yorkshire.

C.1/1362/35-38; Nicholas JAGGES v. Edward HALL, James
GARNETT and others of Newcastle-upon-Tyne, Archibald
THOMPSON and Leonard MERES; Bond delivered by John
HILL of Corpusty, complainants factor, since drowned, to
THOMPSON and MERES for goods bought of him by the other
defendants; Northumberland; Norfolk.

C.1/1367/25-30; Reynold, son and executor of Geoffrey LEE
v. Christopher and Ursula MOUNTFORDE and others; Farm in
Bishopburton and wardship of Geoffrey, brother of complainant;
(Yorkshire) - but could be Nottinghamshire: see C.1/1306/24.
(Mutilated).

C.1/1370/32-34; Richard MARTIN Esq., and others, feoffes to
uses, for themselves and all the inhabitants of Long Melford v.
Edward and Thomas ABBOT; White rents and woods of the manor
of Bower Hall in Pentlow, granted by John HILL of Melford, clothier,
for payment of the King's (tax) of Melford, or for alms when there
was no tax; Suffolk.

C.1/1375/48-51; Giles POOLEY, gentleman, and Alice his wife, v.
John PULHAM, yeoman; Meadow in Framlingham 'at Castell', late
of Giles TENDESLOWE, dec., father of Alice; Suffolk.

201   C.1/1381/32-33; Thomas, son and heir of Thomas SEXTEN, and Robert WALLSHE, his tenant, v. John WYSEMAN; Lands (described) in defendant's manor of Maplestead, forfeit-by the verdict of a jury not all of the homage; Essex.

202   C.1/1386/18; Richard THOMSON v. James ASLABY; Horse and gown late of James THOMSON, dec., father of complainant; (Yorkshire ?).

203   C.1/1386/19-22; The same v. Francis ASLABY, son and executor of James; Reviver of the preceeding.

204   C.1/1388/26; William THOMPSON of Ripon, miller, v. Richard SEYLL, clerk; Money promised in marriage with Jennet, sister of defendant; Yorkshire.

205   C.1/1391/9-10; William WALGRAVE v. Richard and Thomas GARDYNER and Robert SMYTH; Messuage and land in Brent Pelham; Essex.

206   C.1/1394/67-69; Eleanor WYSEMAN, guardian of Edmund, son and heir of John WYSEMAN v. Charles WYSEMAN; Composition concerning lands in Thornham Magna and Parva, Stoke (Ash) and Wetheringfelde (ie Wetheringsett?), late of Thomas WYSEMAN, dec., father of John and Charles; Suffolk.

207   C.1/1394/70; (The said?) John v. the said Charles; Lands in Thornham, Brockford (in Wetheringsett) and Stoke (Ash); Suffolk. (Mutilated).

208   C.1/1397/18; . . . of Hurstbourne, Esq., v. John KYRKBY, gentleman; Detention of deeds re. a farm called Payne's Hole; Hampshire.

209   C.1/1398/51; Francis ARMIGER v. John KYNGE; Detention of deeds re. lands in Stratford and Glemham of the grant of John, son of Thomas TRUSTON; Suffolk.

210   C.1/1398/66; Richard AWNGER of Chesterton, husbandman, v. Geoffrey SWAYNE, of the Middle Temple, student; Vexatious suits and contrivance of the complainants non-appearance; Cambridgeshire. London.

211   C.1/1399/61-63; John ATMER v. Roger WODEHOUSE, Knight, and John WALTER; Detention of a deed relating to turbary in Great Breccles, claimed by complainant, together with a fold course and common of pasture; Norfolk.

212   C.1/1406/42-44; Richard BENNYS of Harling, Norfolk, husbandman, grandson and heir of John BENNYS v. William, son and heir of William GARDENER; Detention of deeds re. land (described) in Dalinghoo; Suffolk.

213   C.1/1407/45-46; Robert, son and heir of Richard BLYANTE v. John POOLEY, Esq.,; Detention of deeds re. a messuage and lands (described) in Great Bricett and Ringshall. Suffolk.

C.1/1420/7-9; Giles CHARNDELER and Alice his wife v. Joan GARDENER; Messuages and land in Hartest, late of William FREEMAN, dec., grandfather of Alice; Suffolk.

C.1/1423/43-45; Richard RUSBURGH and Henry CLERKE, churchwardens of St. Dunstan's-in-the-West, and William PAYHEN and others, parishioners of same v. Richard LYSTE, vicar of same, and Peter NEWCE; Messuages and gardens in Shoe Lane, St. Brides, conveyed for the said church. (Defendants plead sale and purchase as chantry lands); London.

C.1/1426/3; Giles EDMUNDES and Alice his wife v. Joan GARDYNER; Messuage and land in Hartest, late of William FREEMAN, dec., grandfather of Alice; Suffolk. (faded) (See 1420/7-9).

C.1/1428/1-2; John FABYAN, citizen and draper of London, Jane his wife, and John GARDENER v. The Mayor and Alderman of London, and William PLEASANCE, yeoman, surviving executor of George PLEASANCE; Action on a bond given by Robert GARDENER, draper and citizen of London, whose executors are Jane, and John GARDENER, for a payment to Charles PLEASANCE, bestowed son of the said George; London.

C.1/1429/58-59; Roke GRENE, Esq., son and heir of Sir Edward GRENE, Knight, v. Margaret GRENE, late the wife of the said Sir Edward, and formerly of Robert, Lord CURZON; Actions for dower of the manors of Great and Little Sampford and Exning, barred by a grant of dower which is in the defendants hands; Essex; Suffolk.

C.1/1433/1-6; William, son and heir of John GARDENER v. William COLE and Richard GARDENER; Detention of deeds re. a tenement in Bramford; Suffolk.

C.1/1452/15-17; Robert, grandson and heir of Margaret, late the wife of John MARTEN v. Thomas HOLTON and Margery PECOKE, wife of the said John at the time of his death; Messuage and land in Kirton, late of John BRENDE, dec., father of the said Margaret; Suffolk.

C.1/1461/37-41; John POLEY, Esq., v. Elizabeth, executrix and late the wife of John HARRYE, Esq; Marriage settlement of the complainant's daughter with William son of the said John; Suffolk.

C.1/1464/31-33; Thomas ROCHESTER and John WALGRAVE, gentleman v. William CURSON and William ANDREWE, Esqs.,; Detention of deeds re. manor of Becke in Billingford, and messuages and lands in Billingford, Beelaugh, Foulsham, Wood Dalling, Wood Norton, Brisley, Bawdeswell, Hoo, Foxley, Worthing, Swanton, Over and Nether Guist, Sparham and elsewhere; Norfolk.

C.1/1466/56; Lionel ROULSTON of Pontefract v. Agnes, executrix and late the wife of John LAWE of Saxby; Barley which the said John had contracted to deliver; Yorkshire, Lincolnshire.

224 C.1/1467/1-3; John SECKFORD v. Anthony RUSSHE, Esq.,;
Lease of the manor of Mere Hall in P(layford), Bealings and
Rushmere, and of lands, sheepcourses and fisheries there and
in Bucklesham, Mantlesham and Newbourne; Suffolk. (Mutilated).

225 C.1/1475/25; Richard THOMSON, labourer, v. James ROBYNSON,
yeoman and Agnes his wife; Cottages in Nawton Dale and Beadlam
(Bodelam), late of William THOMSON, clerk, dec., brother of
complainant; ---.

226 C.1/1475/51; John THOMPSON of London, haberdasher, and
Elizabeth SUTTON, v. Richard ARGENTYNE, parson of Brantham
(Brame, otherwise Brentham) and George SUTTON, late parson;
Lease by said George of the parsonage of Brantham with the
chapel of Bergholt annexed; Suffolk.

227 C.1/1475/60-63; William TOTTENHAM, labourer, v. William,
son and heir of Hugh MARTEN; Tenements in Great Wenden, late
of Thomas SMYTH, dec., uncle of complainant; Essex.

228 C.1/1482/1-3; William WADE of Wilby v. Roger WADE; Legacy
of William WADE of Brundish, father of both parties, who died
seized of lands in Earl Soham; Suffolk.

229 C.1/1483/68-69; Francis WODEHOUSE, gentleman, v. John
ATTMER; Manor of Great Breckles and lands there and in Hockham,
(Heokkham), Shropham, Stow and Thompson, the deeds of which
were seized during Ket's rebellion; Norfolk.

230 C.1/1485/31-32; Thomas WILSON of London, brewer, v. Margaret,
late the wife of Giles KYRBY, and administratrix of his goods;
Money received by the said Giles as complainant's servant; London.
(Mutilated).

231 C.1/1486/70-72; Thomas WRAYE of Kensington, smith, v. Richard
AYRE of Shimfield, husbandman; Failure to deliver a ton of iron
promised in marriage with Alice FAWCE, servant of defendant;
Middlesex. Berkshire.

232 C.1/1488/40-41; . . . . . . v. Sir Roger WODEHOWSE and John
WALTER; Turbary and fisher in Breckles; (Norfolk). (Mutilated).

The following 4 cases are in a special section at the end of C.1.
in which dates are given where possible.

233 C.1/1505/57-60; Sir Anthony HEVENINGHAM, knight, and Mary
his wife, v. Dame Anne SHELTON; Legacy of John SHELTON
knight, dec., husband of defendant and father of Mary; Norfolk;
1547-53.

234 C.1/1514/27; William TOMPSON, baker, v. Mayor and Sherriffs
of London; Action of debt by John GRENE of Navestock Hall, yeoman,
and Ralph DYER, husbandman. Corpus cum causa; London. Essex;
Date: Reign of Henry VIII or later.

235   C.1/1522/2; Robert MARTEN v. Thomas HOLTON, Margaret PECOKE; Title deeds of land at Kirton; Suffolk; Philip and Mary. (ie 1554-58).

236   C.1/1522/46; William TOMSON and Agnes his wife v. William BALDWIN and Joan his wife; Bequest under will of Gilbert WACY; ---; Edward VI (ie 1547-53).

    Note: In the printed index the name ARMIGER has sometimes been emended by hand to AUNGER or ANGER, so references to these names have been included.

237   C.2.Eliz. A.4/59; Robert ARMIGER (AMIGER) (AUNGER) and Ann his wife, and Thomas GLOVER and Margaret his wife v. Erasmus NICHOLLS and Margery his wife; Messuages etc in Bramford, Burstall, Blakenham Magna and Blakenham Parva; Suffolk.

238   C.2.Eliz. A.8/52; Francis ARMIGER and Douglas his wife v. Roger GOADE, D.D., Provost of King's Coll. Cambridge, and Richard THORNEY; Copyholds of King's Coll. and it's manor, and lands in Barton conveyed to William ARMIGER, father of complainant; ?.

239   C.2.Eliz. B.14/33; Armiger BROWN v. Robert BARRETT and his wife Margaret, John BRAMES and his wife Rose, and Francis HABERD; Lands in Howlesley and Alderton, devised by the will of Robert ARMIGER, dec.,; ? Suffolk.

240   C.2.Eliz. F.5/9; Robert FORTHE, Esq., v. The Rt. Hon. the Earl of SURREY, William DIX and William CANTRELL, Esquires, and Robert ARMIGER, Gent; Right to a sheepwalk at Forthe's manor at Tangham; Suffolk.

241   C.2.Eliz. G.1/38; John GLOVER v. Geoffrey ARMIGER; Performance of agreement re. manor of Morehall, in Ashe; Suffolk.

242   C.2.Eliz. G.10/16; John GLOVER and son v. John BRAME and Rose his wife; Performance of agreement re. manor of Morehall, which the plaintiff and Jeffrey ARMIGER had agreed to purchase jointly; Suffolk. (see above).

243   C.2.Eliz. A.1/13 and A.6/43 concern Michael and Margaret AMIGER or AUNIGER and lands in Ely, Cambridgeshire.

244   C.2.Eliz. A.6/55; William AMIGER (AUGER ?) v. John LUCAS; Lands in Stratford, Suffolk; Suffolk.

245   C.2.Eliz. A.4/23; AUNGER v. PARRIS.

246   C.2.Eliz. B.11/53; Thomas BUTTS v. Humphrey BREWSTER, Arthur CHOWTE and William BATEMAN; Freehold and Copyhold lands in Wrentham, Suffolk; Suffolk.

247   C.2.Eliz. B.9/24; John BREWSTER alias ALBY v. Mary CROPLY, widow; Tenements and lands called Albys in the parish of Stoke-by-Clare; Suffolk.

248   C.2.Eliz. B.24/39; William BREWSTER v. Robert NORMAN, William NORBERY, Robert PORTLER; Messuage in Bridgegate Street, Lynn; Norfolk.

249   C.2.Eliz. B.31/1; William and Mary BREWSTER v. William and Francis HOBSON; Lands in Doncaster; Yorkshire.

250   C.2.Eliz. C.6/14; Arthur CLERKE v. Cicelye MARTYNE and Thomas CLEYBORNE; Manor of Hemingford Grey; Huntingdonshire.

251   C.2.Eliz. C.7/12; Arthur CLARKE v. Thomas CLEYBORNE &c; Lease of manor of Hemingford Grey; Huntingdonshire.

252   C.2.Eliz. C.14/57; William CURSON, on behalf of himself and his 3 daughters, v. Anthony STEPLEY, Esq., and Anne his wife; Lands, late of John STUBBE, Esq., dec., Ann's former husband, at Thelveton, Dickleborough, Shimpling, Frense and Stole, alias Osmonston; Norfolk.

253   C.2.Eliz. C.7/35; The printed index gives: G. COPLEY, Esq v. C. COPLEY, Esq., The complete index gives: COPLEY v. WRAY, &c; Manors and churches of Sprotborough and Plumtree; Yorkshire. (Pedigree stated).

254   C.2.Eliz. C.12/44; Arthur CLARKE v. Cecily MARTYN, widow; Manor of Hemingford Grey. (Only defendant's answer); Huntingdonshire.

255   C.2.Eliz. C.20/44; COLE v. A(U)NGER; Lands in Tendring, late of Thomas ANGAR; Essex.

256   C.2.Eliz. F.4/47; Alex. and Ann FOUNDE, and Thomas LEDGER v. Sir Nicholas BACON (The complete index gives the defendant as: MARTYN &c.); Privilege of searching for mines of metal or mineral, originally granted to W. HUMPHREY; Miner's Company.

257   C.2.Eliz. C.23/45; Sir Robert CAREY, Knight, v. John GARDENER and Agnes his wife, Martha CAREY, and Sir George CAREY; Messuage and lands connected with Collumbyne Hall in Stowmarket, alias Thorney Collumbers; Suffolk.

258   C.2.Eliz. C.12/56; Robert GARDENER and Christian his wife, and Richard MOORE and Agas his wife v. William GREENE, Elizabeth GREENE, and Thomas ALLIN; Capital messuage and small tenement in Dunwich, late of William BARRE, brother of Christian and Agas; Suffolk.

259   C.2.Eliz. G.8/45; Thomas GARDENER v. William BROWNYNGE, Thomas FURNESS and others; Manor and lands at Maldon, once of Henry BOURCHER, Earl of ESSEX, and late of Sir William PARRE, Knight, granted to Thomas GARDENER, father of the complainant, on Parre's being attainted of high treason; Essex.

C.2.Eliz. G.1/2; Thomas GARDINER v. William BROWNINGE;
Deeds re. lands called Downes and Pont Downes, but . . .;
. . . in what place does not appear.

C.2.Eliz. F.1/63; Elizabeth FOWLE and Edward FOWLE v.
William GARDINER, esq.,; Leasehold tenement of an inn, but
no place mentioned.

C.2.Eliz. G.14/23; Hugh GARDYNER v. Richard PHILLIFES;
Messuage and lands in Sutton, conveyed to the plaintiff by
Theophilus and Robert ADAMS; Yorkshire.

C.2.Eliz. G.13/14; John GARDYNER v. John TYRELL and
Haulnut HALES; Manor of Collumbyn Hall and lands in Stowmarket,
Newton and Gyppynge, some time the estate of John TYRRELL, dec.,
and by him mortgaged to Thomas STANBRIDGE; Suffolk.

C.2.Eliz. G.8/24; Raffe GARDYNER and Mawde his wife v.
Richard BURTON; Lands and cottage in Waltham, late the estate of
Thomas HOLBROOKE the testator, father of Mawde; Essex.

C.2.Eliz. F.6/30; John FROST v. Thomas GIBSON and Ann his
wife; Freehold and copyhold lands in Little Riburgh, let on lease
by Richard GOTTES to Richard GARDYNER; Norfolk.

C.2.Eliz. B.11/29; John BROWN, Esq., v. Thomas DOWNINGE
and Thomas his son; Lands, tenements and hereditaments in
Wrentham, purchased by the plaintiff of Robert GARDYNER; Suffolk.

C.2.Eliz. G.5/10; Christopher GARDENER v. Thomas GAUNTLETT,
(answer only).

C.2.Eliz. G.5/1; Robert GARDNER v. John STEPHENS and another.

C.2.Eliz. G.7/18; Christopher GARDINAR v. John DUNCOMBE and
another.

C.2.Eliz. G.12/47; John GARDINER v. Henry PALMER.

C.2.Eliz. G.3/57; Christopher and Thomas GARDINER v. John
PRESTON.

C.2.Eliz. G.7/8; Christopher GARDNER v. Thomas GAUNTLET.

C.2.Eliz. G.5/33; George GARDNER, D.D. and another v. Henry
RYSE.

C.2.Eliz. G.7/14; Mary GARDNER, widow, v. John REDSTON.

C.2.Eliz. G.3/35; William GARDNER v. Edward LYLE.

C.2.Eliz. G.3/30; Thomas GARDYNER v. John PARTRYCKE
and wife.

277   C.2.Eliz. G.9/2; Thomas GARDYNER v. John PATRICKE and wife.

278   C.2.Eliz. G.12/16; Thomas GARDYNER v. John CHAPMAN.

279   C.2.Eliz. G.15/27; Thomas GARDYNER v. Richard PEASE.

280   C.2.Eliz. D.10/7; Kenelm DIGBY, Esq., v. John JACKSON,
       Christopher KIRBYE, Richard STEVENSON and Robert TENANTE;
       A rent charge of 20 marks issuing out of the manor of Bedale, granted
       by King Henry VII in the 13th year of his reign to Everard DIGBY,
       Esq., and heirs male of his body, from whom the plaintiff deduces
       his pedigree; Yorkshire.

281   C.2.Eliz. B.16/6; Richard BROWNE v. Margery KIRBYE and
       John BROWNE; Messuage and land in Thaxted, descended to
       plaintiff as heir of W. BROWNE his grandfather; Essex.

282   C.2.Eliz. D.2/46; Simon DAVY v. John KIRKBY; Capital messuage
       and other houses and land in Howden, sold and conveyed by plaintiff
       to defendant; Yorkshire.

283   C.2.Eliz. C.24/4; Christopher CLAXTON v. John and Thomas
       WARTON; Messuages and land in Kirkbie-Thore, formerly the
       estate of William KYRKBIE, from whom plaintiff traces his
       pedigree; Westmoreland.

284   C.2.Eliz. F.4/37; Clement FINCHE and Grace his wife, daughter
       and heir of Thomas KENDALL, dec., v. the Wardens of the Company
       of Leathersellers, Rowland MARTIN, and others; The scite,
       circuit and precinct of the late priory of St. Helens, and the church,
       sometimes called the Nuns church, and the tenements thereto belonging,
       sold and conveyed by Sir Richard WILLIAMS, alias CROMWELL, kt,
       anno 35 of Henry VIII to said Thomas KENALL in fee; London.

285   C.2.Eliz. G.2/56; Thomas GRAYE and Johan his wife v. Thomas
       MARTYN; A garden and certain tenements near Bethlem, in the
       parish of St. Botolph, without Bishopsgate, demised by Thomas
       MARTIN to Bartholomew TALIAFERRO dec., former husband of
       Johan; London.

286   C.2.Eliz. H.2/38; George HOULTON v. John MARTYN and John
       WADE; Messuage and 18 acres of freehold and copyhold land in
       Little and Great Brissett, held by plaintiff and defendant WADE
       as tenants in common, and agreed to be sold for their mutual
       benefit; Suffolk.

287   C.2.Eliz. C.6/45; William COE, Peter WHITE, Nicholas MARTYN
       and John COE v. Robert WADE, Edward BULLOCKE and Robert
       WESTBROWNE; Manor of Netherhall in the parish of Gestingthorpe,
       which plaintiff W. COE stood bound to settle on his marriage with
       Elizabeth POLLEY, widow; Essex.

288   C.2.Eliz. G.4/5; William GARRARD v. Thomas MONFORD and
       William BATTELYE; Windmill in Yarmouth; Norfolk.

9   C.2.Eliz. B.14/25; The town of Bury St. Edmunds by 14 people
    (named) including Francis MOUNFORD v. Edward GOODING +
    5 others (named); The chantry of Kirketon, alias Shotley, with
    apputenances, lands and tenements called Hauslett, Stirpe, Houles,
    Crowes tenements and Cokes in Kirketon and Chelympton, alias
    Chelmson; a parcel of the possessions of the said chantry held by
    plaintiffs in the right of King Edward VI's Grammer School. Also
    capital messuage and garden in Shotley, late in the occupation of
    John DAVERS; Suffolk.

0   C.2.Eliz. A.1/53; George ADAME v. Samuel NEWCE; Lands
    etc belonging to the manor of Temple Roydon; Essex.

1   C.2.Eliz. C.15/15; Philip CONINGSBYE and Anne his wife, and
    Elizabeth POLLIE v. William BAKER; Manor of Somerton Hall,
    alias Somerton, late the estate of Francis POLLIE Esq., dec;
    Suffolk.

2   C.2.Eliz. G.5/41; Thomas GOOCHE the younger v. Thomas POOLEY,
    Esq., Theophilus ADAMS and others; Messuages, lands and tenements
    called Pakeman's and Giles in Hoo and East Derham, formerly the
    inheritance of the prior and convent, and afterwards of the Dean and
    Chapter of Norwich, and by the latter devised to the plaintiff's father;
    Norfolk.

3   C.2.Eliz. B.2/58; William BURROUGH, William ALLINGTON,
    William AVIS, Thomas BUNN and Simon RAY v. William and
    Thomas WORLICK; Lands etc in Wickhambrook, Stradshill and
    Denston, co. Suffolk, of which John WORLICK was seised, who
    by will dated 1558 devised them to his eldest son Charles; he
    also devised to his 3 other sons, Arthur, Thomas and William,
    rents issuing thereout etc; Suffolk.

4   C.2.Eliz. C.19/16; Thomas COLLE v. Alex RAYE and others;
    Lands in Walden, Wimbyshe and Radwinter, entailed by the will
    of John COLLE, plaintiff's grandfather; Essex.

5   C.2.Eliz. A.1/40; Pawle ALEXANDER v. Will DYER, elder and
    younger; Manor of St. Peter's, Ipswich, tenement etc called Brock,
    complainant's father seised of a moiety thereof, and Thomas SECK-
    FORD, one of the masters of requests, of the other; Suffolk.

6   C.2.Eliz. B.14/3; Harry BRANTHWAIT v. William GOLDSMITH;
    Messuage and lands in Fritton, Sir Ralph SHELTON, kt., being
    lord; Norfolk.

7   C.2.Eliz. A.6/25; John ALLEN v. Edward DOWNS and Elizabeth
    DOWNES, Elizabeth THOMPSON and Robert HARTLEY; Complainant
    seised of the manor of Erleham, Norfolk; Norfolk.

8   C.2.Eliz. F.9/53; Robert FORBYE v. John THOMPSON; House
    and ground in Southminster agreed to be let to plaintiff; Essex.

9   C.2.Eliz. B.13/2; Henry BARRETT and Joan his wife v. Robert
    THOMPSON and Margaret his wife; Lands in Wigenhall, Tylney
    and Islington; Norfolk.

300   C.2.Eliz. F.4/61; William FRESTON, Thomas THOMSON and Frances his wife v. Robert BURTON and William BURTON; Tenement in the lordship of Whitwood and Meare, sometime the estate of Robert BURTON, settled to divers uses; Yorkshire.

301   C.2.Eliz. F.9/34; Sir Charles FRAMLYNGHAM, kt., v. Nicholas GARNEYS Esq., Lionel WADE, George JAKYS and Merrible his wife; Lands lately held of Lawrence AWOOD, dec., of plaintiff's manor of Debenham Butley, late parcel of the possessions of the dissolved monastery of Butley; also land lately held by John WYETH, of plaintiff's manor of Crowes Hall in Debenham, and land lately held by --- WYETH, of plaintiff's manor of Abbotts Hall and Crowes Hall; Suffolk.

302   C.2.Eliz. D.1/31; Gabriel DENNE and Annes his wife, late the wife of Thomas DUDLEY v. Thomas WADE; Messuages, lands and a windmill in Walsoken, devised by Thomas DUDLEY to plaintiff to be sold for payment of his debts; Norfolk.

303   C.2.Eliz. B.31/30; John BOWTELL and Richard BOWTELL v. William CLARKE, alias WEBB and Francis CLARKE, alias WEBB; Messuage and land in Stoke-by-Clare; Suffolk.

304   C.2.Eliz. C.20/34; Thomas COLLE v. John COLLE and Jane WEBB; Land in the parish and fields of Walden, and in the parish and fields of Radwinter, devised by the will of John COLLE, plaintiff's grandfather; Essex.

305   C.2.Eliz. G.3/16; Reynold GLEYDELL and Elizabeth his wife v. Robert CHANDELOR, alias WEBB; Messuage and land in the parish of Wyckham, late the estate of Thomas CHANDELOR, alias WEBB, father of plaintiff Elizabeth, and formerly of Thomas CHANDELOR his grandfather; Suffolk.

306   C.2.Eliz. B.23/47; Pernell BOULTON, widow of Thomas BOULTON, dec., v. William BOULTON and William WEBB; The manor of Heywood Hall in Diss and Burston, Norfolk; Norfolk.

307   C.2.Eliz. C.2/1; William CLARKE v. Richard WEBBE, William COWELL and John WILLIAMS; Lease for divers belonging to the parsonage and rectory; Essex.

308   C.2.Eliz. B.3/47; Edmund BOKENHAM v. --- TASBOROUGH, gent, and others; Manors, lands &c. in Great Thorneham &c, co. Suffolk, of which Edmund WISEMAN was seised; Suffolk.

309   C.2.Eliz. F.10/34; Susan FEILDE, widow, as prchein amy to her son William FEILDE, v. Margaret WISEMAN, Thomas WISEMAN, and George THORNBACKE; Lands in West Mersey, mortgaged to William DARCYE, Esq; Essex.

310   C.2.Eliz. B.22/18; Edward, Earl of OXFORD, Lord Great Chamberlain, on the part of Henry BULLOCK, a minor, v. Richard WISEMAN; Lands etc in West Mersey, called Dawes, alias Bacons, holden of complainant the Earl of OXFORD, as of his manor of . . .by knight's service; ---. (Probably Essex. See F.10/34).

311   C.2.Eliz. B.12/48; Henry BAKER Esq., v. Ralph WYSEMAN,
      Esq., and Anne his wife; A farm called Owtings in the manor of
      Bures Gifford and Thundersley; defendant being lord of the said
      manor of Thundersley; Essex.

312   C.2.Eliz. A.8/15; Richard ALEXANDER v. Thomas WOODHOUSE;
      Messuage &c. in Eldersham, sold by Thomas WOODHOUSE to
      complainant; Norfolk.

313   C.2.Eliz. G.2/14; Thomas GRESHAM esq., v. Sir Henry
      WOODHOUSE, kt.,; Divers messuages and gardens in the parish
      of St. Giles-without-Cripplegate, and of St. Alphage-within-
      Cripplegate, in Milk St., the estate for life being in Dame Cicely,
      wife of the defendant, and the reversion in plaintiff; London.

314   C.2.Eliz. B.4/4; Edward BLENNERHASSETT v. Jermyne GOODWYNE
      and Sir Henry WOODHOUSE; Manor of Pawling &c, Norfolk, of which
      defendant Sir Henry was seised for years, who demised a messuage
      called Pawling Grange to the other defendant; Norfolk.

315   C.2.Eliz. B.17/26; Edward BLENNERHASSETT v. Sir Henry
      WOODHOUSE kt., Amphilis GRYME, widow, Thomas GRYME,
      George GRYME, John HOE and Elizabeth his wife; A barn called
      the Tythe Barn of Happesborough and the tithe corn of the said
      town and other towns adjoining, held by lease from the abbott
      and convent of the Blessed Mary of Wymondham. In answer said
      to be now the estate of the Bishop of Norwich, in right of his
      church; Norfolk.

316   C.2.Eliz. C.7/41; Sir Edward CLERE, kt., v. Sir Henry
      WOODHOUSE, kt; The manors of Happesborough and Wynterton,
      land in Ormsbie and Caster, messuage and lands and the advowson
      of the church of Winterton and the wreck of the sea in Winterton.
      Copyhold land held of the manor of West Somerton. The answer
      mentions the manor of Erles in Winterton, the advowson of the
      benefice of Winterton with the chapel of East Somerton, with a
      seigniory called Botolphe's in East Somerton, and lands in East
      Somerton; Norfolk.

317   C.2.Eliz. H.2/4; William HORNE v. Thomas MARTIN.

318   C.2.Eliz. F.8/24; John FRANKLINE v. Ambrose MARTINE.

319   C.2.Eliz. B.27/61; John BOLLE v. Henry MARTYN.

320   C.2.Eliz. B.29/31; Robert BROWNE v. Thomas MARTYN.

321   C.2.Eliz. B.27/51; William BUTTER v. William TOMSON.

322   C.2.Eliz. P.3/52; William PRYCE v. John TOPP and Christopher
      GARDENER; A freehold messuage called the Saracen's Head in
      the parish of Allhallows, Bread St., and a leasehold messuage called
      The Ram, in Watling St., in the said parish, belonging to defendant
      TOPP; London.

323 C.2.Eliz. H.24/12; Robert HEYWARD v. Martin HAYLOCK, Henry GARDENER, and Joan his wife; A tenement and lands in Wangford, late the estate of John HAYLOCKE, dec.,; Suffolk.

324 C.2.Eliz. R.8/57; John RAFFE v. William GARDENER; Lands in the towns and fields of Baddingham and Hokenhill, hamlet of Baddingham, purchased by plaintiff of defendant; Suffolk.

325 C.2.Eliz. P.11/6; John PETTIT v. George GARDINER, D.D., Dean of Norwich; Defendant, pretending himself to be parson of the parish church of Blofield, demised the said rectory or parsonage, and the tithes thereof, to the plaintiff; after which Edward PASTON Esq., being owner of the patronage of said church, presented another person, and plaintiff was deprived of his lease; Norfolk.

326 C.2.Eliz. R.11/55; Edmond RYVETT v. John GENT, John BRASYER, William POPE and William GARDINER; Divers lands in Bawdsby, holden of John, Lord DARCYE, as of his manor of Walton, by John GENT and Elizabeth his wife, and John BRASYER, being the estate of the said John GENT, who mortgaged same to plaintiff's father; Essex.

327 C.2.Eliz. H.8/9; Christopher HODSON v. John HOLFORD; The manor of Landbeach, called Brayes, and lands in Landbeach, held under leases from Richard KIRBYE and John MARTIN; Cambridgeshire.

328 C.2.Eliz. P.12/50; Robert PENNYNGTON v. Richard KYRBIE and James BOWLTON; Land in the parish of Henham, holden by plaintiff of Frances, Countess of SUSSEX, widow of Thomas, Earl of SUSSEX, as of her manor of Henham Parsonage, alias Henham Cannons; Essex.

329 C.2.Eliz. K.1/20; Thomas KYRBY and Matild his wife, Benedict FAVERALL and Eme his wife and Christian GEDHOE v. John TREWFOTE; A messuage and ground in the parish of St. Peter in the town and burgage of Dunwyche, late the estate of Thomas GEDHOE, dec., grandfather of plaintiffs Matild, Eme, and Christian; Suffolk.

330 C.2.Eliz. H.12/18; Ralph HEYES v. William ALLEN, Thomas ALLEN, Robert KYRBYE, and William WIGGINS; Tenement with shops in Tower St, St. Dunstan's-in-the-East, late of Agnes, wife of Thomas WHITBY, which plaintiff claims as cousin and next of heir of said Agnes; London.

331 C.2.Eliz. N.2/29; Richard NAYLER and Margery his wife, William PARFIELD, and Thomas DALLOOKE v. Thomas MARTEN, Michael MARTEN, Charles GOODMAN and Jane his wife, and Robert WARREN; Two messuages in Walden, sometime inheritance of William GASELEY, former husband of Margery, and by him alleged to have been conveyed to trustees to divers uses; Essex.

332 C.2.Eliz. M.14/53; Roger MARTEN of Melford, Suffolk v. William SHETTLE; Certain land, meadow, pasture and wood. Place name effaced; Suffolk.

333   C.2.Eliz. H.9/9; George HAGARTH v. John HOWE, Ewin MARTIN
       and William FLEETWOOD; Two tenements on the south side of
       Knight Rider St. in the parish of St. Benet, nigh Paul's wharf, held
       under a lease from the Dean and Chapter of St. Paul's; London.

334   C.2.Eliz. M.10/46; Roger MARTIN v. William WIGAROUS,
       William SWEETING and others; Three messuages and lands in
       Halsted and Castle Hedingham, late the estate of William MARTIN,
       dec., which plaintiff claims as his cousin and heir; Essex.

335   C.2.Eliz. K.5/62; John KINGE, clerk, B.D., parson of St.
       Andrew's, Holborn, and Thomas MARTIN, executor of Mabel
       RICARDS, executrix of William RICARDS v. John DEAN and
       others; Respects debt due from William PAGE, dec., to said
       William RICARDS; ---. (Presumably London).

336   C.2.Eliz. M.13/34; Henry MARTON v. Mathewe ALDERSON;
       Manor of Tabsley or Tobsley Hall, divers lands and tenements in
       Marton, late the estate of Christopher MARTON, dec., plaintiff's
       father; Yorkshire.

337   C.2.Eliz. M.11/56; Henry MARTYN v. Edward WORLEY, Edward
       GLEMHAM and Thomas POWLE; A fraudulent insurance imposed on
       plaintiff by defendants as stated in bill; ---.

338   C.2.Eliz. P.3/42; John PARKER v. Sir Richard MARTYN, kt.,
       Richard MARTYN his son, and Anthony MARLOWE; A messuage
       and certain shops in Cheapside and Bread St., holden by lease from
       the Goldsmith's company; London.

339   C.2.Eliz. M.10/20; John MOUNTFORD v. Robert WRIGHT and
       Richard BARNARD; The manor of Deans in Debden, purchased by
       Philip MOUNTFORD, plaintiff's father, and defendant WRIGHT
       jointly, of Christopher ALLEYN; Essex.

340   C.2.Eliz. P.8/56; Roger POPELEY v. Giles ESTCOURT, Esq.,
       George SNELGAR, Francis VAUGHAN, Edmond MATHEWE, John
       GRAFTON and Roger TANNER; Tenements in parish of St. Michael
       Bassishaw, late the estate of Johan POPELEY, dec., plaintiff's
       mother, who demised the same to plaintiff for a term of years, and
       afterwards conveyed the inheritance to his use; London.

341   C.2.Eliz. P.12/24; Alvary COPLEY and Edmund SHILLETO v.
       John ROBYNSON, Ralph AYRIE and Thomas COOKE; Certain
       tenements in Pomfrett (Pontefract), and lands in the fields of
       Ferrybridge and Pomfret, holden under a lease granted by Elizabeth
       TYAS, widow; Yorkshire.

342   C.2.Eliz. R.1/8; Raynold RAYE and Anne his wife v. Thomas
       STODDERD; Tenement which defendant claims as his inheritance,
       but in what place or county is not mentioned. (Answer only).

343   C.2.Eliz. R.4/3; As for R.1/8, above; Re. land claimed by plaintiff
       under a devise by the will of John STODDARD, brother of defendant.

344   C.2.Eliz. R.10/12; Thomas RAYE v. William ADAMS; Tenement
and land in Walden, agreed by defendant to be purchased of plaintiff,
being parcel of the manor of Mitchells in Walden Parva; Essex.

345   C.2.Eliz. R.12/12; Silvester ROULSTON v. Thomas BULLOCKE;
Bonds entered into by plaintiff re. the office of bailiwick or collector-
ship of the Queen's manor of Bawtry, parcel of the possessions of
the late Duke of CLARENCE, attainted, within . . .; Yorkshire.

346   C.2.Eliz. H.24/9; Seckford HEMSBY v. Henry SECKFORD esq.,;
Re. a legacy bequeathed by the will of Humphrey SECKFORD, who
purchased certain lands, but where is effaced.

347   C.2.Eliz. L.3/52; William LUSKYN, clerk, and Johan his wife, v.
Henry WYNDHAM Esq.,; Lands held in the manor of Overhall and
Netherhall in Dedham, late the estate of William LITTLEBURY,
alleged by defendant to have escheated to Thomas SECKFORD, Esq.,
dec., late lord of said manor; Essex.

348   C.2.Eliz. L.7/40; Robert LAUNDE, alias PALLANT, John LAUNDE,
alias PALLANT, and John TYRRELL, Esq. v. Elizabeth SHELTON,
widow, and Thomas, Lord HOWARD; The manor of Shelton, and the
park called Shelton Park, and the lands thereto belonging in the
towns, fields and parishes of Shelton, Hardwycke, Morningthorpe,
Stratton St. Michael, Hempnalls, Alboroughe, Pulham Market and
Pulham St. Mary which, having been conveyed by Thomas SHELTON
Esq., dec., to defendant Lord HOWARD, to secure a debt due to
him, had been demised by both of them to Robert LAUNDE, alias
PALLANT; Norfolk.

349   C.2.Eliz. L.1/37; Edward LENG (this bill filed 1638) v. Thomas
GELL, Stephen THOMPSON, and Anne his wife; A messuage
and lands in Eskrigg, demised by the Lord KNEVETT to Dame
Elizabeth his wife, and plaintiff's father; Yorkshire.

350   C.2.Eliz. R.2/10; James ROBINSON v. Edward PYPE, Thomas
ORAMS and Mary his wife; Capital messuage and divers tenements
in the parish of St. Gregory in Norwich, late the estate of Martha
THOMPSON, widow; Norfolk.

351   C.2.Eliz. M.2/20; William MALLETT and Elizabeth his wife v.
John HANSON; Messuage and land in Cley St. Peters (in the answer
called Cokley Cley), late the estate of John WADE; Norfolk.

352   C.2.Eliz. H.12/13; Nicholas HANSON v. Samuel WADE; A moiety
of lands and tenements in the township and parish of Hothersfield,
alias Huddersfield, holden by Robert WADE, dec., of W. RAMESDON
Esq., farmer to the Queen of her manor of Hothersfield, which
premises the said Robert demised to plaintiff for 1000 years, and
afterwards by his will devised to plaintiff the inheritance; Yorkshire.

353   C.2.Eliz. M.12/38; Thomas MYLDMAY Esq., and others v.
William BROWNE, Dorothy his wife, and Robert WADE; Certain
lands and tenements called Tomlyn's Wicke and Tawney's Wicke,
in the county of Essex, (but in what part therof does not appear)
late the estate of John BROOKE of Much Badow in the said county;
Essex.

C.2.Eliz. O.2/28; William OSBORNE v. Thomas WADE and
John CLIFTON; Certain houses and lands in Wittelingham, the
inheritance of plaintiff, and by him demised to Richard CUBIT;
Norfolk.

C.2.Eliz.N.3/48; Raffe NORTH v. Edward WEBBE; Assignment
of lands in parish of Althorne, held for a term of years by
defendant, and assigned by him to plaintiff for payment of his debts;
Essex.

C.2.Eliz. P.4/60; John PRATT for himself and his brothers and
sisters v. Abel CLARKE and Edward WEBBE; The estate of
John PRATT the father, who was possessed of a lease for years
of the manor of Althorne, and divers lands in the parish of Althorne,
granted to him by Edward HARRESSE; Essex.

C.2.Eliz. P.5/38; William PAYNE v. John JOHNSON, Robert
WEBB, Edmund LEVEROOK; The manor of Wridlynton, alias
Worlington Tyndalls, demised to plaintiff by Henry PAYNE, the
owner of the fee, situate in Worlington, Frickenham, or Kelham;
Suffolk.

C.2.Eliz.R.3/21; Hugh RAYLAND v. Robert WEBBE and George
MAULE; A legacy given to plaintiff by the will of Thomas MOYS,
charged on his lands and mansion house in St. Osyth, near
Colchester; Essex.

C.2.Eliz. K.1/52; Jeffrey KNAPWOOD of Badwell Ash, Suffolk,
v. Sir John CARELL, kt., and W. WEBBE, gent; A farm and
lands in Suffolk, late the estate of the defendant CARELL, who
demised same to plaintiff, and since of defendant WEBBE; Suffolk.

C.2.Eliz. P.6/58; William PARTRIDGE and Bridget his wife v.
Margaret WISEMAN, widow; Messuage and land in West Mersey,
late the estate of Thomas DARCYE, dec., father of Bridget, who
by his will devised the same to his wife Margaret upon divers trusts;
Essex.

C.2.Eliz. M.2/9; Thomas MAWDISLEY v. Amiston WRAY and
Jennett CLERKE; Messuage and land in township of Long Preston-
in-Craven, granted by the Queen's letters patent to John EAMERTON
and others, for a term of years, and by them assigned to plaintiff;
Yorkshire.

C.2.Eliz. O.3/45; Thomas OSBORNE v. John ANDREWES,
Christopher GASCOYNE, John WORMLEY and Henry BUTTER;
Freehold lands in Barnham, and copyholds there holden of Thomas
CROFTS Esq., as of his manor of Baggotss, by Agnes the wife
of Robert BARRYTT, alias BURRARD, and which plaintiff purchased
of the devisees of the said Agnes; Suffolk.

C.2.Eliz. I.4/41; Nicholas JUDD v. Thomas BREWSTER and
William REYNOLDS; The manor of Catch Vaches in Old Buckenham,
held under a demise from Hugh WILKINSON, gent., owner of the
inheritance; Norfolk.

364   C.2.Eliz. M.7/38; Margaret MILLER v. Dorothy CLAIBORNE.

365   C.2.Eliz. R.4/19; Thomas ROBINSON v. John CURSON.

366   C.2.Eliz. M.11/59; George MIDDLEMORE v. Gilbert GARDENER.

367   C.2.Eliz. H.8/32; John HAMBYE v. Thomas GARDENER Esq.,
       and wife.

368   C.2.Eliz. L.8/16; Thomas LANCASTER v. Thomas GARDINER
       and wife.

369   C.2.Eliz. M.11/68; Robert MURGATRODE v. John GARDYNER.

370   C.2.Eliz. K.1/29; Adrian KIRBYE v. Thomas DEANE and others.

371   C.2.Eliz. K.1/49; Robert KIRKBYE v. --- ---.

372   C.2.Eliz. K.1/25; Walter KYRBYE, clerk, v. Henry DONNYNGE.

373   C.2.Eliz. M.6/58; George MARTEN v. Thomas COVELL.

374   C.2.Eliz.M.1/24; John MARTEN v. Thomas BOSTON and another.

375   C.2.Eliz. M.1/46; Richard MARTEN v. Thomas THOMASYN and
       others.

376   C.2.Eliz. M.10/12; Richard MARTEN v. John JAMES.

377   C.2.Eliz. M.10/63; Robert MARTEN and wife v. James HOBSON and
       others.

378   C.2.Eliz. K.2/53; Richard KELING v. Thomas and W. MARTEN.

379   C.2.Eliz. R.11/17; Thomas ROBYNS, alias JOHNS v. William
       MARTEN.

380   C.2.Eliz. N.4/18; Robert NEWTON v. Anthony MARTIN.

381   C.2.Eliz. H.9/3; John HOWYTT v. William MARTYN and others.

382   C.2.Eliz. H.14/1 and H.9/9; George HOGARTH (HAGARTH) v.
       John HOWE, Ewin MARTIN, William FLETWOOD and others.

383   C.2.Eliz. M.8/11; Alexander MASON v. John MARTIN and others.

384   C.2.Eliz. P.16/27; Francis PENDRETH v. Sir Richard MARTIN and
       Sir George GIFFORD, Kt.

385   C.2.Eliz. M.14/33; George MARTYN v. Roger SAMUEL.

386   C.2.Eliz. M.14/46; Christopher MARTYN v. Nicholas DYER.

387   C.2.Eliz. M.14/17; Elizabeth MARTYN, widow, v. Sir Alexander
       COLEPEPER and others.

C.2.Eliz. M.7/55; George MARTYNE v. Sir Richard MARTYN, kt.

C.2.Eliz. M.10/1; Henry MARTYN v. Sylvester WILLIAMS.

C.2.Eliz. M.11/56; John MARTYN v. Ralph BRESSIE and another.

C.2.Eliz. M.13/15; John MARTYN v. John WEAVER.

C.2.Eliz. M.9/54; Thomas MARTYN, jun., v. Henry MUNDAY
and another.

C.2.Eliz. M.7/35; Thomas MARTYN v. James HAMPTON and another.

C.2.Eliz. M.14/11; Richard MARTYN v. Robert MARTYN and others.

C.2.Eliz. R.2/16; William READE Esq., administrator of Dame
Anne GRESHAM, widow, v. Sir Richard MARTYN, kt.

C.2.Eliz. R.9/57; Dame Anne GRESHAM, widow of Sir Thomas
GRESHAM, v. Sir Richard MARTYN, kt.

C.2.Eliz. H.19/1; William HORNE and others v. Thomas MARTYN.
(answer only).

C.2.Eliz. R.3/24; Robert RADFORD v. Thomas MARTYN.

C.2.Eliz. M.4/3; Thomas MONFORD v. Robert SCARTHE.

C.2.Eliz. M.11/36; Francis MOUNFORD esq., v. Raffe SHELDON
esq.

C.2.Eliz. M.3/60; Clement NUCE v. Richard FISH and another.

C.2.Eliz. P.4/5; John POLLYE v. Robert REEDE.

C.2.Eliz. P.10/50; Sir William POOLEY, kt., v. William BEECHER.

C.2.Eliz. M.3/35; Rowland MYNORS v. William POOLEY.

C.2.Eliz. P.7/53; William POOLEY v. Rowland MYNORS.

C.2.Eliz. I.3/69; Robert JERRARD v. Roger POPLEY and another.

C.2.Eliz. P.1/59 and P.7/56; Roger POPLEY v. John WARMAN
and others.

C.2.Eliz. P.6/22; Roger POPLEY v. Robert JERRARD.

C.2.Eliz. R.9/35; Thomas RAYE and another v. Edmond COOKE.

C.2.Eliz. L.5/22; Richard LARDYE v. Thomas THOMPSON and
others.

C.2.Eliz. P.12/14; Agnes PAGE and John ARSCOTT her son v.
Mathew THOMSYN and others.

303

412 C.2.Eliz. M.14/30; John MOODYE v. Anthony WEBB.

413 C.2.Eliz. L.9/34; John LEY v. John WEBBE.

414 C.2.Eliz. H.21/6; Robert HAWKINS v. Richard WEBB and another.

415 C.2.Eliz. P.6/59; Nicholas PILL v. Robert WYSEMAN.

416 C.2.Eliz. M.11/15; Edward MARSON v. Michael WOODHOUSE and another.

417 C.2.Eliz. W.25/49; John WICKS and William CURZON, Thomas COLLEY, William HOOPER, Richard SPARKES and John BALDEWYN v. Richard ARCHDALE, Henry and William KEBLE, Robert LAPWORTH, Adam TURNER and Agnes TURNER, widow; Personal matters; 1574.

418 C.2.Eliz. W.18/13; Owen WILLIAMS v. John GARDENER; Personal matters; 34 Eliz. (ie 17th Nov. 1591 - 16th Nov. 1592).

419 C.2.Eliz. T.7/27; John THOMPSON and another v. William GARDINER; Personal matter. Relief against action at law.

420 C.2.Eliz. S.6/60; Samuel SHETTERDEN and Jacob LAWE v. Thomas NEWCOMAN and John GARDNER; For relief against a fraudulent lease re. 60 acres of ground at West Walton, pretended to be proper and fit for the growth of Wood; Norfolk.

421 C.2.Eliz. T.5/3; Henry TRAPP v. John GARDYNER and William TWIST; Object of this bill not discoverable, being much decayed, but it seems to respect a lease made by the plaintiff to Peter, Thomas and Edward DAVIES of a messuage called Frampton's Place, with land belonging.

422 C.2.Eliz. W.14/8; John WHARFE v. Philip GARDYNER; Personal matters; 1595.

423 C.2.Eliz. T.8/37; John TAILER and another v. George MARTIN; Personal matters. Praying a writ of certiorari to remove a cause by scire facias.

424 C.2.Eliz. S.26/21; Thomas SUTTON v. Sir Richard MARTIN, kt; Personal matters. Relief against an action upon a bond.

425 C.2.Eliz. S.24/35; George SIDNAM v. Robert BATT and Thomas MARTIN; Personal matters. Relief against a bond.

426 C.2.Eliz. S.19/48; Thomas and John SOMASTER v. William MARTIN; Personal matters. Relief against a bond.

427 C.2.Eliz. W.6/15; John WALTER v. William MARTIN, Alice JENETT, and Elizabeth JENETT; Land called Mole Croft (but where situated is not mentioned in this answer) demised by Sir Edward RODNEY to Thomas WALTER and the plaintiff, and William WALTER the plaintiff's brother, for their lives. (Answer only).

428   C.2.Eliz. Y.1/5; Thomas YOUNGE, clerk, v. Robert POWLTER, ~~William SILKE, Jerome RABYE,~~ Samuel WISEMAN, John RIGGES, John LURST, Hugh MARTYN and Humfrey RAWLEY; Personal matters.

429   C.2.Eliz. T.1/3; Paul TRIGGE v. John MARTYN; Personal matters; Discovery as to money lent by plaintiff.

430   C.2.Eliz. Y.1/24; Jane YETSWEIRT, widow, v. Sir Richard MARTYN kt; Personal matters; 1596.

431   C.2.Eliz. S.5/12; Richard SAVERYE v. Thomas MARTYN and others; Personal matters.

432   C.2.Eliz. S.22/32; Joane SMYTH v. Edward MARTYN; Lands called Grenestreet Park in East Ham; Essex.

433   C.2.Eliz. S.6/8; Thomas SARES and Katherine his wife v. William PENYNGTON; Bill of Revivor - claim by descent. One messuage, with the appurtenances, in parish of St. Mary-at-Hill. Reviver in consequence of marriage; London.

434   C.2.Eliz. S.10/36; Gilbert SMITH v. William POLLYE and John MILLER; Personal matters. Relief against a bond.

435   C.2.Eliz. S.13/48; William SMITH and Thomas WORTHAM v. Christopher POOLEY; Rectory and parsonage of Great Massingham; Norfolk; Temp.Car.I* (* This footnote seems odd since this volume concerns Elizabeth's reign; however - Charles I, 27th March, 1625-1649.).

436   C.2.Eliz. W.4/17; Thomas WENTWORTH esq., and Grace his wife, v. Suzan ALLEN, widow of Thomas ALLEN, dec; To recover rent in arrear. Sir Arthur INGRAM, kt., being seised in fee of a farm called Gibson Farm in Cleaveland, in a town called Swainby in the county of York, demised the same to Francis POPELEY, dec., late father of the plaintiff Grace, who shortly after made a lease thereof to the said Thomas ALLEN; the said Francis POPELEY was also possessed of two leases for years from the Lord BRUCE, one of them a farm called Brackenhill in the lordship of Walton, Yorkshire, and the other of certain closes called Little Shewghes (but where situated is not mentioned), but also let the same on lease to the said Thomas ALLEN, from whose widow plaintiffs now claim arrears of rent; Yorkshire.

437   C.2.Eliz. W.23/16; John WEBBE v. Thomas ROLSTON and Thomas KESTELL; Personal matters; 16 Eliz. (ie 17th November 1573 - 16th November 1574.).

438   C.2.Eliz. S.16/41; Thomas STAINER and wife v. Humphrey SECKFORD and William SMYTH, George GOODWYN, and Robert MYLES; Messuages and lands in the parishes of Bradfield, Melton, Woodbridge, and Hasketon Bowlye; Suffolk; 1588.

439   C.2.Eliz. S.25/1; Randell SMYTH v. William SCLATER; The
       third part of a piece of ground lying between the Satterbald and
       the Rowney, and the third part of the herbage of a wood called
       Knowle, and another wood called Rowney.

440   C.2.Eliz. S.12/27; Robert SKYNNER and wife v. Henry SECKFORD
       Robert SMITH, and Nicholas WOODFEN and wife; Personal matters.
       Claim under nuncupative will.

441   C.2.Eliz. S.13/22; Mary SECKFORD v. Richard FYSHER; Manors
       of Great Bealings, alias Seckford and Bough; Suffolk.

442   C.2.Eliz. Y.1/45; Robert YORKE (addressed to Sir Thomas
       BROMLEY) v. Thomas WRIGHT; To set aside an award of
       arbitrators re. dispute between defendant and plaintiff respecting
       certain freehold lands in the manors of Burghe and Hasketon, of
       which manors Sir Robert WINGFEILD, kt., and --- SEKEFORD
       esq., are lords; Suffolk. (see S.16/41, above).

443   C.2.Eliz. T.4/45; Robert TOWER v. Richard SMITH and Richard
       HARDINGE; Sir J. SHELTON, kt., being seised in fee of the
       manor of Shelton, granted an annuity of £10, charged thereon, to
       Ralph SHELTON his brother, and his wife Amy. Plaintiff, and
       defendant SMITH afterwards purchased jointly certain parcels of
       land holden of the said manor; and on making partition plaintiff
       gave to defendant SMITH a bond to indemnify him against the said
       annuity, and which bond had been put in suit by reason of a distress
       being made for the annuity upon the lands occupied by SMITH;
       Norfolk.

444   C.2.Eliz. S.21/44; John, Wynyfrede, and Ann SHELTON v.
       Bartholomew KYGHTELEY and Robert THOMPSON; Messuages
       and lands, parcel of the abbey of Creake; Norfolk.

445   C.2.Eliz. S.26/41; Elizabeth SHELTON, widow, v. John GUYBON
       and Robert PALLANT alias LANE; Rent of the scite of the manor
       of Eaton, demised to plaintiff's late husband by defendant GUYBON;
       Norwich.

446   C.2.Eliz. S.21/5; Elyanor STURGES v. Raffe SHELTON;
       Personal matters. Relief against a bond.

447   C.2.Eliz. S.22/5; John STANNOWE v. Thomas SHELTON, James
       HARTSTONG, Thomas KERSYE, John BRANTINGHAM and William
       ROGERS; (Bill half lost through decay) It seems plaintiff had become
       security for the late Sir Ralph SHELTON for payment of his debts,
       and that Sir Ralph intended to secure plaintiff by assigning over
       to him the manor of Amrynghall, but died before he could carry same
       into effect. Defendant SHELTON, as heir to his father, refused to
       pay his debts or cooperate with plaintiff. The other defendants are
       creditors of Sir Ralph; Norfolk.

448   C.2.Eliz. S.14/39; Thomas SHEREWOOD v. Thomas MAKYN,
       Richard SANDERS, John CLERK, Richard SHEREWOOD, Thomas
       SLATER and Richard JACKSON; Messuages and lands, holden of
       the manors of Walkington, and freehold land in Walkington; Yorkshire;
       1594.

C.2.Eliz. S.2/33; Dorothy SLATER v. Richard BUNTING; Personal matters. For Performance of contract.

C.2.Eliz. S.4/31; Geoffrey SLATER v. Richard and Dorothy SLATER; Messuage or tenement in parish of North Wooton; Norfolk.

C.2.Eliz. S.5/19; Henry SLATER v. John CALLIARD and wife, Richard HUDSON, Thomas GESSOPP and another; Personal matters.

C.2.Eliz. S.5/11; Nicholas SLATER v. John SONTE; Personal matters.

C.2.Eliz. T.5/29; Alice THOMPSON v. Simon HORSPOOLE and Thomas HORNE; Messuage in Gracechurch Street; London.

C.2.Eliz. T.5/37; Peter THOMPSON and Frances his wife v. George and Marmaduke CONYSTON; Lands and tenements in Hornsey in Holderness, devised by William CONYSTON to defendants, upon condition they should pay to plaintiff Frances (testator's daughter, and sister to defendants) £10, upon her attaining the age of 21 years; Yorkshire.

C.2.Eliz. T.10/18; John TURNER v. John DIXON; Messuage and land in Bowes, demised to plaintiff for a term of years, by John THOMPSON; Yorkshire.

C.2.Eliz. U.1/14; James VENABLES v. Joseph and Roger THOMPSON; Personal matters. Relief against a bond.

C.2.Eliz. T.10/58; Robert THOMPSON v. Francis REYNOLDS; Personal matters. Relief against a bond.

C.2.Eliz. T.11/47; Robert THOMPSON and others v. Thomas DUTTON; Personal matters. Relief against a bond.

C.2.Eliz. T.6/18; Nicholas THOMPSON v. William WALPOLE; Personal matters. Performance of an award.

C.2.Eliz. S.1/25; Peter SAVAGE v. Samuel THOMPSON; Messuage in the parish of St. John ZACHARY, underlet to plaintiff by defendant, who holds under the dean and chapter of St. Pauls; London.

C.2.Eliz. T.11/43; Samuel THOMPSON v. Robert COOKE, alias CLARENCIEUX, and Edmond KNIGHT, alias Chester, Executors; Claim under the will of Robert GREENWOOD. A messuage in Fenchurch Street, London ; London.

C.2.Eliz. S.17/18; William STRUDWICKE, an infant, by William GORYNGE and John ASTREATE his guardians v. Henry STRUDWICKE and Thomas THOMPSON; Personal matters. To compell defendants (overseers under the will of the plaintiff's father) to account for assets received and to perform trusts under the same.

463   C.2.Eliz. T.1/58; Thomas THOMPSON v. William HUNTLEY and wife; Personal matters. Discovery as to a contract and bargain made by defendants.

464   C.2.Eliz. T.5/4; Thomas THOMPSON v. Thomas PASTOWE; A messuage, with the appurtenances, in Cawthorne, formerly belonging to the dissolved chauntry of St. Ann in Budsworth; Yorkshire.

465   C.2.Eliz. T.7/24; Thomas THOMPSON v. Thomas CHAUNTRY and others; Personal matters. For relief against a discharged bond.

466   C.2.Eliz. T.2/20; William THOMPSON v. Hugh COUNSEL; Personal matters. Relief against a bond.

467   C.2.Eliz. T.1/15; George THOMSON v. Robert WOOD and Robert SPARKE; Messuage and land at Millgate in Aylsham and Sextens field, formerly in possession of Gregory HOUSEGOE, and part of which land was taken in exchange by the said GREGORY, with Sir Robert WOOD, then lord of the manor; Norfolk.

468   C.2.Eliz. T.1/2; Henry THOMSON v. John GRAY; Certain deeds re. lands of Mrs. Mary HOLCROFT, but . . .; . . .where situated is not expressed.

469   C.2.Eliz. T.5/24; John TCMPSON v. George ROBARTS; Messuage and shop in the parish of Christ Church, London, holden of defendant; London.

470   C.2.Eliz. T.10/9; William and Catherine TOMPSON v. William RANDOLL; Answer, replication and rejoinder only; bill apparently filed to redeem a mortgage and recover possession of a house in Grub Street, Cripplegate, demised to John THOMPSON by the chamberlain of . . . ; . . . the city of London.

471   C.2.Eliz. Y.1/34; Henry YAXLEY exq., v. Robert HARTLEY, John HARTLEY and John LATHE; Claim as heir in tail. The manor of Spilmans, sometime the estate of Myles SPILMAN, LL.D., who granted a lease thereof to Elizabeth TOMPSON, and afterward conveyed the reversion to the plaintiff's father, W. YAXLEY esq., in tail; Norfolk; 1598.

472   C.2.Eliz. T.4/32; George TOMPSON . . . (other details as for 467).

473   C.2.Eliz. T.11/51; George TOMPSON v. Robert WOOD and John BROWNE; To compel the defendants, who are lord and steward of the manor, to admit the plaintiff, and for relief against excessive suit and service. 11 acres of customary land, parcel of the manor of Aylesham Sexteyns, sold to plaintiff by Richard BREVYTER, which manor was late parcel of the possessions of the dissolved monastery of Bury St. Edmunds; the custom of the manor, with regard to suits and services, is fully set forth in the bill; Norfolk.

C.2.Eliz. S.18/40; Robert SMITH v. William GARDINER, Nicholas SMITH, Thomas NEWMAN and John TOMPSON; Messuages in Bermondsey; Surrey; 1599.

C.2.Eliz. Y.1/28; Edward YARE v. John TOMPSON; Personal matters; 1601.

C.2.Eliz. T.2/1; Margaret TOMPSON v. Anne ANDERSON; Personal matters. Claim under a will.

C.2.Eliz. T.7/7; Richard TOMSON v. --- HOCLEY and others; Personal matters. Discovery as to bonds and other writings in the hands of the defendant.

C.2.Eliz. T.10/11; William TOMSON v. Henry BETTS and William RANDOLL; (same objects and premises as 470).

C.2.Eliz. W.23/42; Anthony WADE v. Stephen HILL, Leonard BESSON, Thomas CLARKE, John CLARKE, Gerrard LOWTHER, Henry PULLEN, and Reynold FURLEY; Claim by purchase. Two messuages and divers large parcels of land in Ledstone, and the tithes of corn and hay of the premises, purchased by plaintiff of defendants HILL and BESSON; Yorkshire; 1599.

C.2.Eliz. W.25/23; Edward WEBB v. Bartholomew WADE; To redeem a messuage and ground in Hitchin, late of Richard WEBB, dec., who mortgaged to defendant; Hertfordshire.

C.2.Eliz. S.19/53; Inglebright SMYTH and wife, Thomas FRAMSON and Robert SALTER v. John WADE; To recover possession of messuage and land in Finbarrow, obtained by defendant under breach of trust; Suffolk.

C.2.Eliz. W.21/23; Lionel WADE v. John WENDEN; Claim under a deed of gift and to set aside a lease. - A tenement in Brandeston, late the estate of Lionell, plaintiff's father, who conveyed it to him in fee; Suffolk; 1594.

C.2.Eliz. W.14/34; Ralph WADE v. William TURNER and Thomas COLE; Claim under a will. - A farmhold called Bovelles in Maylond, held by Robert WADE, plaintiff's brother, for a term of years, and bequeathed by him to defendant TURNER, in trust for the plaintiff during his minority; Essex; 1571.

C.2.Eliz. W.22/26; Richard WADE v. Thomas BARKER; For protection against an alleged forfeiture. - A messuage and land in Wimbish, which plaintiff rented of defendant; Essex; 1591.

C.2.Eliz. W.1/42; Tobias WADE v. Edmund THWAYTES, Nicholas FOSTER, and Henry BEARTE; Re. a purchase made by plaintiff from Thomas COLVILE, of a quantity of timber and firewood growing on the lands of the said COLVILE, in North Glemham, in the occupation of the defendant THWAYTES; Suffolk; A° 37 Eliz. (ie 17th November 1594 - 16th November 1595).

486   C.2.Eliz. S.15/17; Bernard SALTER v. William WADE; Claim by descent as son and heir. Messuage and land in Billeston, parcel of the manor of Billeston; Suffolk.

487   C.2.Eliz. W.1/14; Benedict and William WEBB v. Jasper WOOD-ROFFE and another; Personal matters.

488   C.2.Eliz. W.4/61; Edward WEBB v. Raphe NORTHEY; Re. plaintiff's having pledged with defendant a lease of the manor of Stokes, which said plaintiff then held as an indemnity to said defendant against sundry obligations he had entered into on plaintiff's account; Essex; 41 Eliz. (ie 17th November 1598 - 16th November 1599).

489   C.2.Eliz. S.16/5; Thomas SHORTE v. John BARTHOLOMEW and John WEBB; Personal matters. Relief against a bond.

490   C.2.Eliz. W.3/6; John WEBB v. Thomas GOODALE; Demurrer only. Re. a close of pasture called Grove Close, which was to be conveyed to defendant, but . . .; . . . it's situation does not appear; Temp.Car.I. (see note to 435).

491   C.2.Eliz. W.3/42; John WEBB v. John GILLY, the elder, and John GILLY, jun.,; The reversion of certain freehold lands and tenements in Risby, which plaintiff had conveyed to defendant GILLY sen., as indemnity; Suffolk; 1600.

492   C.2.Eliz. W.16/33; Mary WEBB, widow, v. John HIPSLEY and Dorothy his wife, and John WEBB; Personal matters; 1600.

493   C.2.Eliz. W.18/14; John WEBB (addressed to Sir Thomas BROMLEY) v. Thomas CURE and others, wardens of the sadlers company; Claim by descent. - A messuage called The White Horse, in the parish of St. Catherine Creechurch, and a house and garden in the parish of St. Botolph without Aldergate, late of John WEBB, dec., plaintiff's grandfather; London.

494   C.2.Eliz. W.20/60; John WEBB, an infant, son and heir of Robert WEBB, v. Thomas SPINKE senior, Thomas SPINKE jun., and Richard and George BAKER; To redeem - Freehold land in Shelland, and copyhold land holden of the manor of Fenhall in Buxhall, mortgaged by Robert WEBB to Thomas SPINKE jun; Suffolk; 1602.

495   C.2.Eliz. S.17/27; Robert SUCKERMAN v. Andrew FORSTER and William WEBB; Personal matters. Relief against a bond.

496   C.2.Eliz. W.22/16; Edward WEBBE v. Katharine NORTH, widow; Personal matters.

497   C.2.Eliz. W.9/38; George and Thomas WEBBE v. William WEBBE; Personal Matters; 1595.

498   C.2.Eliz. W.6/19; John WEBBE v. John WENTWORTH and Mark MOTT; A tenement and land in Bocking, the inheritance of plaintiff, and by him mortgaged in fee to defendant; Essex; 1577.

C.2.Eliz. W.6/58; John WEBBE v. William HOLLAS and another; Personal matters; Filed during the usurpation (? of Lady Jane GREY July 1553).

C.2.Eliz. W.16/2; John WEBBE v. Ralph WISE and another; Personal matters. Demurrer only.

C.2.Eliz. W.9/40; Katharine WEBBE, widow, administratrix of Thomas WEBBE v. Jane CONINGESBY, widow; Personal matters; 32 Eliz (ie 17th November 1589 - 16th November 1590).

C.2.Eliz. W.2/10; Nicholas and William WEBBE v. Richard WYE; Personal matters.

C.2.Eliz. S.11/52; James STEWARD, an infant, by William TYFFIN his guardian, Peter WYTHAM, and Agnes his wife v. Thomas BENDISHE, Robert WEBBE, and John PARKER; Claim under will, and to compel defendants, as executors, to account for rents, issues and profits &c. - Moiety or half deale of Dangewell Hall, and house and land called Parkers, a meadow called Queen's meadow lying in Okeley, and copyhold houses and lands called Brownings, Soninies, Dobles, Plomers, Pypers and Goddardes, and a customary tenement and land in Walton; Essex.

C.2.Eliz. W.16/45; Robert WEBBE v. Robert GAGES and Henry GAGES; To complete a purchase. - Lands in Shelland, and an outhouse holden by Robert GAGES of James RYVETT esq., as of his manor of Fenhall in Buxhall, and of the manor of Shellands, agreed to be sold to plaintiff; Suffolk; 1857. (probably a misprint for 1587).

C.2.Eliz. W.14/58; Thomas WEBBE v. John ELKINGTON and another; Personal matters; 1595.

C.2.Eliz. W.19/57; Dorothy WISEMAN, widow, v. John WELBECKE; Touching the personal estate of Thomas WISEMAN, dec., plaintiff's late husband, who died seised of divers lands and tenements in the . . .; . . . county of Essex; 1585.

C.2.Eliz. T.7/31; Nicholas THURGOOD and Johan his wife, Thomas RAMESEY and Juliana his wife, and William JOHNSON, an infant, v. Robert NEWMAN, William JUDD, and Leonard MUNCKE; Claim by descent. Houses, lands, tenements and hereditaments, free and customary, in Much Canville, holden of John WISEMAN esq., as of his manor of Canville Hall, and also customary lands &c. in Little Eiston, holden of the same manor, and lands &c in Much, or Great Eiston, and holden of Richard WARREN esq., as of the same manor, descended to plaintiffs in right of their wives as grandchildren of Henry DOVE, and to plaintiff JOHNSON as Great-grand-child; Essex.

C.2.Eliz. W.3/8; John WISEMAN v. Richard SHUTE; Personal matters; 1594.

509 C.2.Eliz. W.10/52; Rauf WISEMAN esq., v. William ATKINSON;
To protect title by purchase. A messuage called the Helmet, or Helme,
in Fornhill, sold by Robert TRAPPES esq., to William ATKINSON
and Ralph FLEETE, alias ATKINSON, and by them sold and conveyed
to plaintiff; London; 1598.

510 C.2.Eliz. W.24/33; Reynold WYLIE v. William WISEMAN and Ralph
WYLIE; Claim as heir in tail. A messuage and land in Debden, holden
of defendant WISEMAN's manor of Weldebernes by Robert WYLIE,
plaintiff's grandfather, and by him surrendered to divers uses;
Essex; 1570.

511 C.2.Eliz. S.20/52; Rychard STUBBS v. Myles HUBBARD and
wife, and Thomas WOODHOUSE; Personal matters. Bill filed by
plaintiff as executor for discovery as to assets of testator in
defendant's hands.

512 C.2.Eliz. W.8/42; Henry WOODHOUSE v. Sir William HEYDON kt.,;
Personal matters., being the office of vice-admiralship within the county
of Norfolk, of which plaintiff was possessed, and conveyed the same
of defendant (who married his sister) upon certain conditions; ---
(Presumably Norfolk.); 1596.

513 C.2.Eliz. W.12/42; Sir Henry WOODHOUSE, kt., v. Ann GOSLING,
widow, administratrix of John GOSLING; Principally re. payment
of money due to plaintiff from said GOSLING, who in his lifetime was
possessed of two leases of the parsonage of Great Yarmouth; Norfolk.

514 C.2.Eliz. W.1/61; William WILSON, in his own right, and as
executor of William WILSON his father, v. William HAMEND, John
DURREL, Thomas THORPE, and Margaret HORTON; To carry
into execution a special agreement. Ralph HALL and Thomas HALL,
or one of them, being seised in fee of 320 acres of land in Leverton,
did in Michaelmas term 38 Henry VIII by deed and fine convey the same
to William WILSON, plaintiff's father, and John WOODHOUSE, for
the term of 60 years, with remainder to the aforesaid Ralph HALL in
fee, and said John WOODHOUSE being dead, the term of 60 years
survived to the said William WILSON, plaintiff's father; and William
HAMOND, father of defendant HAMOND, having purchased to reversion
in fee, sundry particulars were agreed upon between him and plaintiff
re. their interest in the premises, which it is the object of the bill to
carry into execution; Yorkshire; A.40.Eliz. (ie 17th November 1597-
16th November 1598.).

515 C.2.Eliz. W.5/18; John WOODHOUSE and Margery his wife v. Jeane
HASWELL, widow, William HOOD her son, and Thomas FOOTE,
clerk; Answer only. A copyhold tenement, holden by John HASWELL,
dec., the late husband of defendant Jeane, but the name of the manor
is effaced from the record.

516 C.2.Eliz. W.15/61; Ralph WALLER esq., v. Francis SPILMAN,
Henry SPILMAN, Erasmus SPILMAN, Frances SAUNDERS, Robert
HILL, Thomas WHITE, and William SWANSON; To protect title by
purchase against encroachment. The manors of Ryden and Congham,
in Ryden and Congham, late the estate of Sir Thomas WOODHOUSE

kt., and purchased by plaintiff of Roger WOODHOUSE his son; and defendants having set up a title to a tenement or manor called Rustins, parcel of the said manors, they claim a right of foldcourse for 360 sheep in the demesne lands of the plaintiff; Norfolk; 38 Eliz. (ie. 17th November 1595 - 16th November 1596).

C.2.Eliz. W.21/40; Roger WOODHOUSE esq., (addressed to Sir N. BACON) v. James ALTHAM, William and Richard BENSON, and Nicholas MYNNE esq; For relief against a recognizance given as surety for and with the defendant MYNNE to warrant the title of the rectory or parsonage of Wesenham, which said defendant MYNNE sold and conveyed to defendant ALTHAM; Norfolk.

C.2.Eliz. W.21/26; Sir Roger WOODHOUSE kt. v. Edward CLERE and Mathew GREY; Personal matters; 1581.

C.2.Eliz. W.19/41; Nicholas WYNTER v. John CLIPPESBY esq; To recover rent. The Bishop of Norwich, who was seised in fee of the manor of Thyrne, granted a lease thereof to Sir Thomas WOODHOUSE kt., which is now vested in the plaintiff, of whom defendant holds lands, parcel of the said manor, by the rent of fourscore mynes of wheat, every myne containing 3 bushels; Norfolk; 1578.

C.2.Eliz. W.14/15; Thomas WRAY v. Margaret WORMELEY, widow; Re. a settlement agreed to be made on the marriage of plaintiff's father with Margaret REYNEY, widow, by money to be laid out in lands.

C.2.Eliz. W.13/18; Reignold WARY and Anne his wife, daughter of Thomas STODDARD, dec., v. Thomas STODDARD, Susan his wife, and John SALTMARSH; Claim under a will and an award. Thomas STODDARD and Johan his wife, both dec., being seised in fee of certain messuages and land in the parish of Barking, in right of said Johan, settled a part thereof on plaintiff Anne, which settlement was afterwards confirmed by an award, but defendant STODDARD, heir at law, opposes same; Essex; 1590.

C.2.Eliz. W.18/40; Sir Christopher WRAY kt., Lord Chief Justice of England; Sir Walter MILDMAY kt., Chancellor of the Exchequer; Sir Gilbert GERRARD kt., Master of the Rolls; Sir John PETER kt., Sir Thomas MILDMAY kt., Thomas WROTH and Edward ANLABYE esqs., v. James CLAPOLE, John JOISE and Richard EWING; To recover deeds &c. The manor of Molton, and divers lands in Molton, of which the plaintiffs were seised in fee, as trustees for performance of the will of Thomas, late EARL OF SUSSEX; Lincolnshire; 1587.

C.2.Eliz. W.8/5; Plaintiffs as for 522 (addressed to Sir Christopher HATTON) v. Sir John HIGHAM kt; For an account and payment of monies received for the dec., Thomas, EARL OF SUSSEX had appointed defendant to be high steward of his courts, of his manors in Suffolk, Norfolk, Essex and Lincoln, and he had received divers sums of money, and particularly from falls and sales of woods within the said Earl's manors of Moulton, Lincolnshire, for which the bill prays an account; Lincolnshire.

524   C.2.Jas I B.17/36; Bury St. Edmund's School v. Matthew CRACH-
WOOD (alias CRACHROOD), Brian SMITH, John REVELL, William
BAXTER, Ambrose BREWSTER, Margaret BARRETT, Margaret
EVERARD, Thomas WALE and Edward and John FRENCHE; Land
belonging to the manor of Coddingham Hall, leased by the former
governors of the school to John SMITH. (The bill contains a history
of the foundation of the grammar school by Edward VI); Suffolk;
(Cases B.19/48 and B.41/63 also deal with this subject, though
the defendants for those are, respectively, CRACHROODE and
WALE. -G.W.).

525   C.2.Jas I A.9/10; Samuel ARGALL, governor of Virginia, v. Lady
Cicely DE LA WARE and Edward BREWSTER; Goods belonging to
the late Lord DE LA WARE.

526   C.2.Jas I C.15/56; Francis CATTON v. Richard BREWSTER;
Meadow in Havering-at-Bower in Hornchurch; Essex.

527   C.2.Jas I B.28/46; Thomas BREWSTER and others, (inhabitants
of Old Buckenham) v. Sir Philip KNYVETT, lord of the manor, Sir
Francis RAVELL, and William BIDWELL; Right of common in Old
Buckenham, on land called the Lowes, or Netherdownes, near to
Wilby Warren, which defendant KNYVETT ploughed up as belonging
to his manor of Buckenham Castle or Buckenham Lathes; Norfolk.

528   C.2.Jas I H.28/47; William HARRYSON v. Edward COLISTON;
Lands in Sutton, in the isle of Ely; Cambridgeshire.

529   C.2.Jas I D.4/39; John DAUNTESEY v. William SHERSTON and
George COLSTON; Messuage and lands in West Yeaton, late of
William and Peter SHERSTON; Wiltshire.

530   C.2.Jas I C.19/1; John COLSTON, married to defendant's daughter,
v. Andrew ABINGTON and Margaret his wife; Manor and Demesnes
of Battleborough; Somerset.

531   C.2.JAs I G.12/21; Henry GODDARD v. Henry CURSON, John
SCOTT, Mary and Grissell MAXTER; Manors of Marches in
Stanhow, alias Calthorpes in Stanhow and Docking; Norfolk.

532   C.2.Jas I E.1/1; George ELVY (uncle and next friend to Francis
ELVY, an infant) v. Maud ELVY, widow, Andrew LYGHTWYN and
Katherine his wife, Matthew CURSON and Anne his wife, John
READE, Thomas POYNTER and Robert MURTON; Land held of
manor of East Dereham by Maud ELVY, widow, late mother of
plaintiff Francis; Norfolk.

533   C.2.Jas I C.18/50; Robert CURSON and Mary his wife v. Roger
WIGGOTT; Lands in Geiswicke, Thorninge, and Woodawlinge, late
of Symon THOMPSON, clerk; Norfolk.

534   C.2.Jas I B.25/14; Jeremy BLOFIELD v. Thomas WILSON, elder and
younger; Annuity on Hastings in Byntrey, formerly of Thomas CURSON;
Norfolk.

C.2.Jas I F.8/51; Robert FRANCKE v. William MOORE (heir of
George HOLTBY), Peter HOPPERTON, and Elizabeth KIRBY;
Lands and tenements late of John KIRBY; Yorkshire.

C.2.Jas I K.4/2; Matthew KIRBY v. Fridiswith KIRBY, widow;
Moiety of messuage and land in Watlington, late of John MANNING;
Norfolk.

C.2.Jas I A.7/13; John ALMON v. John KIRBY(E); Claim under
will of Richard KIRBYE.

C.2.Jas I F.10/12; Cuthbert FENWICKE v. Anthony COCKSON,
Ambrose APPLEBIE, and John KIRKBIE; Tenements and lands
called Colpighill in Lanchester, part of possessions of Robert
TEMPEST, attainted of High Treason; Durham.

C.2.Jas I G.17/2; Edward GALLAND v. William KIRKBY and
Elizabeth his wife; Messuage called the 'Bull' in High street,
Winchester; Southampton.

C.2.Jas I & J.1/64; Robert JACKSON v. William KIRKEBY; Messuage
in Scarborough; Yorkshire.

C.2.Jas I K.4/56; William KIRBIE and Elizabeth his wife, v.
Ellice HEWES, vicar of Sparshott; Tithes in Sparshott, held
by W. BURTON, late husband of plaintiff Elizabeth; Southampton.

C.2.Jas I K.8/8; William KIRKBY and Elizabeth his wife (executrix
of William BURTON) v. Peter BLAKE; 2 tenements in Winchester;
Southampton.

C.2.Jas I A.5/35; Thomas ANDREWES v. Walter PRICKETT alias
PRICHARD, and Francis MARTIN, churchwardens; Messuage in
St. Clement's Lane, demised by one WILKINSON to Jeffery LODGE,
who left two children, of whom defendants are guardians; London.

C.2.Jas I H.6/52; Robert HODGESON v. William and Ann DIXON
and Henry MARTIN; Land in Cawood, late of John LAW, and by
him surrendered to use of plaintiff for a term of years; Yorkshire.

C.2.Jas I A.7/8; Michael AUSTIN and Lucy his wife v. John
MARTYN and Alice his wife and others; Estate of Walter
CHYNOCKE, father to plaintiff Lucy;

C.2.Jas I D.11/1; Humphrey DRYWOOD v. John MARTIN; Messuages
and lands in Rayleigh; Essex.

C.2.Jas I H.5/49; John HUDSON and Margaret his wife v. John
MARTIN and John STEWARD; Inn in St. Clement's lane, in the
parish of St. Edmund-the-King; London.

C.2.Jas I A.3/7; Richard ARDLEY v. Robert MARTYNS and Mary
his wife; Messuage &c. in Romford, devised to plaintiff under will
of his uncle Thomas ARDLEY; Essex.

549　C.2.Jas I C.4/24; Thomas COOKE and Philippa his wife (late wife of Stephen MARTIN) v. Felix CHAMBERS and Amy his wife; Lands and tenements in Clavering and Langley; Essex.

550　C.2.Jas I F.7/9; John FETTWELL v. Robert BARKER and Thomas MARTYN; Manor of Westbury (locality not specified.) (Rejoinder only).

551　C.2.Jas I H:29/65; Sampford HEPES, clerk v. Edmund MUNDEFORD; Manor of Nonnes and lands in Gayton Lyziate, late of Jeffery MIGHT; Norfolk.

552　C.2.Jas I C.2/10; Meryell CLERE, late wife of Sir Henry CLERE, v. Sir Edward CLERE, Anthony HOBART, and John ATHOWE; Marriage settlement re. messuage and lands in Thelvetham and Mundford, the estate of plaintiff before her marriage by gift from Sir Edmond MOUNDEFORD her father, and the manors of Ormesby, Pedhams, Castons, Burghe (alias Burroughe Vaux), Stalham Hall, Scrotbye, Winterton, Buckenham Ferry, and Hassingham alias Haslingham, lands in Ormesby, Burghe, Scrotby, Winterton, Buckenham, Hassingham, Burlingham and Scrumshawe, and advowsons of Burghe, Buckenham Ferry, and Hassingham, which Sir Edward CLERE covenanted to settle upon said Sir Henry CLERE and his heirs; Norfolk.

553　C.2.Jas I B.2/62; Pawle BOWCHER and John SEX (alias SACKS) v. Ann PENNINGTON, late wife of William PENNINGTON; Discovery of assets.

554　C.2.Jas I C.6/6; Richard COOKE and Margaret his wife v. Thomas and Richard PENNINGTON; Lands in London and Tottenham High Cross, late of Thomas PENNINGTON, former husband of plaintiff Margaret; London. Middlesex.

555　C.2.Jas I & J.1/34; Robert JOHNSON v. Ralph FOX and W. PENINGTON; Messuage of St. Andrew, Holborn, late of Richard WIGGINGTON; Middlesex.

556　C.2.Jas I H.9/50; Elizabeth HOWE and John HOWE her son v. Sir John POLEY, John HOWE and John KEBLE; Annuity from tenements and lands in Stowmarket; Suffolk.

557　C.2.Jas I B.38/47; William BEECHER v. Sir William POOLEY; Debt due from the late Sir John POOLEY.

558　C.2.Jas I & J.2/22; Francis JACOB v. Edmund POOLEY; Messuage and land in Combs; Suffolk.

559　C.2.Jas I G.12/63; William, second son of William GERY (late of Rushmeade, Co. Bedford) v. Dr. Thomas POOLEY; Lands and tenements (not specified); (? Bedford.).

560　C.2.Jas I A.1/49; William ALDBURGH v. John POPELEY and Jane his wife; Messuage at Mexburgh; Yorkshire.

C.2.Jas I B.11/57; William BATE v. Francis POPLEY and
Leonard SIVETON; Meadow within the manor of Wherleton
demised to Thomas BATE, first by the Duchess of LENNOYES
(LENNOX), after that by Queen Elizabeth, and next by Edward,
Lord BRUCE, Master of the Rolls; Yorkshire.

C.2.Jas I G.14/17; John GARLAND v. William RAY, William RICHE
and Robin FENNE; Messuages and lands in Hickling, Ludham and
Winterton; Norfolk.

C.2.Jas I B.19/65*; Ralph BOSVILE v. Lyonell ROWLSTON and
Dorothy his wife, and Christopher COPLEY; Lordship of Cunthwayte
in Pennystone, and of lands and tenements in Kexforth, alias
Keresforth Hill, Barnsley, Denby, Over Denby and Nether Denby;
Yorkshire. (*Footnote: The index refers also to cases B.7/70 and
B.13/25, but no relevant names appear in them).

C.2.Jas I B.31/58; Walter BUTLER and John SLATER v. Michael
KIRK, Margaret his wife, Francis THACKERAY and Gilbert
CAWDREY; Messuage and land in Cookeridge; Yorkshire.

C.2.Jas I G.1/21; George and Thomas GRIME v. Sir Edward
BOTELER, John TANFIELD, Robert BACON, Thomas OXBOROUGH,
and Richard SLATER; Manors, lands and tenements late of George
GRIME of Fulsham; (Norfolk).

C.2.Jas I C.5/37; Sir Charles CORNEWALLIS v. Henry SECKFORD;
Annuity for Mary CAVENDISH, widow. Secured on manor of Trymley
and other lands; Suffolk.

C.2.Jas I B.35/39; Sir Robert BROOKE, John SOUTHCOTE, Francis
PLOWDEN, Thomas STICHE, and Ann COPLEY, widow, v. Robert
NAPPER, Daniel SHELTON, Richard HEMINGE, --- WAVERINGE,
and Mary OLDHAM; Manor of Battels and Ongar Park, sometime of
William SHELTON, who settled the same on the marriage of William
COPLEY the younger with Ann DENTON, niece of said SHELTON;
Essex.

C.2.Jas I C.27/85; William COPLEY (married to Ann DENTON) v.
Robert NAPPER and Daniel SHELTON; Manor of Battelles and
Onger Park, late of William SHELTON; Essex.

C.2.Jas I C.28/29; Christopher CALTHORPE, Maud his wife, Edward
HANCHETT, Elizabeth his wife and John CROFTER v. William
COOKE, and Mary his wife; Manor of Broome and patronage of the
church of Broome, fulling mill in Ditchingham and lands and tenements
in Broome, Ditchingham, Ellingham, Thwayte and Haddescoe, late of
Ralph SHELTON; Norfolk.

C.2.Jas I H.22/25; Elizabeth HANCOCKE and George THOMPSON
and Susan his wife, her daughter v. William WALKER; Messuage
in St. Ellens, . . . ; . . .York.

C.2.Jas I C.12/68; Nicholas COOKE, executor of Joseph THOMPSON,
v. Maryan TALBOT, John KING, Benjamin ROBLETT, and John
TALBOT; Lands and tenements in Farnham, Benhall, Blaxall, Sweff-
ling, and Iken, late of Joseph THOMPSON; Suffolk.

572   C.2.Jas I B.13/20; Richard BILBROUGHE v. Richard THOMPSON,
Thomas WETHERELL, George APPLEYARD and John KNAPTON;
•Messuage and lands in Wetherby, held under lease from Queen
Elizabeth, and formerly belonging to the hospital of St. John of
Jerusalem; Yorkshire.

573   C.2.Jas I D.9/40; Robert DOBSON (heir and administrator of
Robert GIBSON his uncle) v. Sir John BOUCHER, George ELLIS,
Michael ASKWITH, William LAMPLEY, William JOHNSON and
Richard THOMPSON; Messuages and lands in Newton-upon-Ouse,
and mill and pasturage in Grymston; Yorkshire.

574   C.2.Jas I F.2/8 (also F.10/75); John FEILD v. Richard THOMPSON,
George APPLEYARD, Thomas WETHERALL and John KNAPTON;
Messuage and land in Wetherby in Spofforth, held under a crown lease;
Yorkshire.

575   C.2.Jas I D.2/46; James and John DAGGER v. Samuel THOMPSON;
Tenement, being one of several in St. John Zacharies, held under
lease from the Dean and Chapter of St. Paul's; London.

576   C.2.Jas I B.7/48; Henry BREWER v. Alice TOMPSON; Messuages
in Gracechurch St. in Allhallows-in-the-Elms, Lombard St.,; London.

577   C.2.Jas I F.4/29; Amy FULLER, widow, v. John STRICKLAND;
Messuages and land (not specified), late of John TOMPSON, of
Ingatestone, plaintiff's grandfather; (? Essex).

578   C.2.Jas I D.2/5; William DOWGILL v. William STEVENSON,
Robert GODFREY and Anne his wife; Pannell Banks in Pannell,
late of Richard WADE; Yorkshire.

579   C.2.Jas I B.19/47; Sir Francis BACON, Attorney General, v.
Thomas WADE and Richard WRIGHT; Lease of customs upon
tabacco. (Answers only).

580   C.2.Jas I D.12/46; Henry DADE and Elizabeth his wife (executrix
of Thomas SHAWE, her former husband) v. Thomas WADE and
Thomas JENNER; Messuage and land in Reydon, late of Jonas
COOKE; Norfolk.

581   C.2.Jas I B.8/24; John BURTON, Sara BRUN (late wife and
administratrix of Thomas BRAMLYE), Edward WISEMAN and
William KELLET, Sir William CRAVEN, William GARRAWAYE,
and Thomas COLDWELL v. Sir William ROMNEY, Edward QUARLES,
Thomas CLARKE, Master and Wardens of the Haberdashers Company,
Martha SMITH, and Thomas ALLEN; Messuages in Bartholomew
behind the Royal Exchange; London.

582   C.2.Jas I C.16/26; Sir Robert CROSSE v. Edward DANIELL,
John BURDER, John WISEMAN and William BOYTON; House in
St. Mary-le-Strand; Middlesex.

C.2.Jas I B.34/22; Edmund BOKENHAM and Barbara his wife
(sister and co-heir of Mary WISEMAN) v. Ursula and Frances
HONYNGE; Meadows in Eye, formerly of Sir John WISEMAN, and
from him descended to plaintiff in right of his wife Barbara; Suffolk.

C.2.Jas I E.3/81; John ELDRED v. George CAMPE, John SHEPARD,
John DOVER , Stephen WISEMAN, Richard RIDNALL, Brice BROWNING,
William BROOKE, Robert COBBE and John TOVELL; Manor of
Mendlesham, purchased of Sir Philip KNYVETT; Suffolk.

C.2.Jas I B.34/19; John BROCKETT v. Robert, Lord RICH,
Richard YOUNG and Ann his wife, Ellen SANFORD and Robert
WISEMAN; Manor of Waltons Hall, alias Wardens Hall, alias
Willingale Doe, Willingale Spain and Shellowbowells, formerly
of Richard SANFORD, by him sold to William WISEMAN, and
by said WISEMAN to Thomas FITCH; Essex.

C.2. Jas I F.2/22; Elizabeth FITCH, widow, v. Sir Thomas
WYSEMAN and Thomas FITCH; Farm and premises called
Crasenheade. (Replication only).

C.2.Jas I B.15/66; Paul BAYNING v. Philip COLLYNS; Pretended
lease of Smalland Hall, alias Mershes, in Hatfield and Wyckham,
purchased by plaintiff from Sir William WYSEMAN; Essex.

C.2.Jas I B.36/36; John BAKER v. William WISEMAN, Sir William
SMITH, John CLERK, Simon SPATCHURST and Henry GOWERS;
Manors of Brockells, Broadoaks, Yardley Hall, Weild, and Tendring,
purchased by plaintiff from John WISEMAN; Essex.

C.2.Jas I D.1/45; Sir Robert DOLMAN v. Sir William WISEMAN,
Sir John MORGAN, Sir Edward CULPEPER and Michael WENTWORTH;
Rent charge of 60l. payable out of the manor of Great Wenden, alias
Wenden; Essex.

C.2.Jas I D.7/67; Arthur DENHAM, clerk, William CRUMPE,
Benjamin HULKE, Thomas MUNDY and Henry BAFFORD v.
William WISEMAN and Edward BAYLEY; Donation for establishment
of a charity school made by the will of one PUCKLE of lands held
of the Bishop of London's manor of Layndon. (Replication and rejoinder
only); (Essex).

C.2.Jas I C.10/2; Sir Charles CORNEWALLYS and Dorothy his wife
(late the wife of John JEGON, late Bishop of NORWICH) v. Sir Henry
WOODHOUSE and --- JOHNSON; Rent of manors of Gelham Hall,
Duling Cross, Blackburgh, Grancoats and Wrongay (Wormegay) and
lands in Fowlsham; Norfolk.

C.2.Jas I C.19/32; Thomas CREAKE v. William CREAKE, Henry
WOODHOUSE and Roger HARRIES; Messuage on Ludgate Hill
near the 'Bell Savage', late of Dr. Thomas CREAKE; London.

C.2.Jas I F.10/76; Robert FLYNT v. John WOODHOUSE; Manor
of Little Ellingham and messuages and lands in Hadleigh; Norfolk,
Suffolk.

319

594   C.2.Jas I C.19/39; John CUDDEN and Mary his wife, William
       SPARROWE and Amye his wife, and John GRAYE and Katherine
       his wife (daughter of William PIGEON) v. Sir Edward BLENERHASSET,
       John BLENERHASSET and Robert DEBNEY; Messuage and lands in
       Pockthorpe and lease of the manor of Pockthorpe granted by the
       dean and chapter of Norwich to Sir Thomas and Henry WOODHOUSE;
       Norfolk.

595   C.2.Jas I D.6/80; Sir William DE GREY, Sir Henry BEDINGFEILD,
       Sir Francis LOVELL and William PASTON v. Sir Thomas WALSING-
       HAM, Sir Thomas WOODHOUSE and Sir John SHERLEIGH; Manors
       and lands of Hingham, Hockering, Harling, and Brettenham; Norfolk.

596   C.2.Jas I F.3/84; William FAGG v. Sir William WRAY; House
       and lands in manor of Barden; Yorkshire.

597   C.2.Jas I A.3/9; Edmond ARMINGER v. Richard DAWTREY; Bonds.

598   C.2.Jas I A.13/20; Edmond ARMINGER v. Richard DAWTREY;
       Injunction.

599   C.2.Jas I B.24/63; Blaze BREWSTER v. Jane SMYTH, widow;
       Agreement.

600   C.2.Jas I C.12/43; Sir Henry CARYE (administrator of Sir Thomas
       COMPTON) v. John BREWSTER; Payment on account.

601   C.2.Jas I C.30/39; Sir Henry CARY v. John BREWSTER; Fragment
       of answer only.

602   C.2.Jas I B.36/20; Richard BREWSTER v. William STONYNGE;
       Answer only.

603   C.2.Jas I C.22/17; Thomas CLEBORNE v. Marmaduke FRANCKE;
       Stay of legal proceedings.

604   C.2.JasI C.9/62; Edward COLSTON v. John LANGHAM; Sale of
       goods.

605   C.2.Jas I C.13/13; Edward COLSTON v. Bishop of LINCOLN;
       Bond on administration.

606   C.2.Jas I C.16/52; George and William COLSTON v. Jerom
       RAWSTORN and Thomas RYCE.

607   C.2Jas I C.23/67; George COLSTON v. Alice ROBERTS, widow;
       Trade accounts.

608   C.2.Jas I A.3/76; Andrew ABINGTON v. John COLS(T)ON; Relief
       against suit.

609   C.2.Jas I & J.5/19; Edward ILLS v. John COLSTON; Suretyship.

610   C.2.Jas I K.4/21; George KNIGHT (?) v. Richard and Thomas
       COLSTON; Payment of marriage portion.

C.2.Jas I E.3/65; William ELSDON alias ELSON v. Humphrey CURSON; Ship accounts.

C.2.Jas I C.18/82; Sir John CURSON v. John SOUTHCOTT and Nicholas RUGGELEY; Suretyship.

C.2.Jas I H.8/11; Sir John HARPER v. George CURZON; Marriage agreement.

C.2.Jas I B.2/66; John BROWNE v. William KIRKBY and wife; Injunction.

C.2.Jas I H.4/4; Peter HALL v. Thomas KIRKBY; Replication only.

C.2.Jas I K.4/59; Richard KIRBY v. Margaret MASON, widow; Trust money.

C.2.Jas I K.7/29; William and Richard KIRBY v. John ROBINSON and John TURNING; Bond.

C.2.Jas I K.7/38; Margaret, late wife and executrix of John KERSE, v. Alexander MARTIN; Bond.

C.2.Jas I C.25/45; William CROWE v. Francis and Edward MARTIN; Suretyship.

C.2.Jas I B.31/65; Sir Edward BARKHAM v. Francis MARTYN; Answer only.

C.2.Jas I C.19/28; Ferdinando CALFIELD v. Henry MARTIN and Alexander CALFIELD; Share of deceased's estate.

C.2.Jas I A.6/20; John ALLEN v. John MARTYN; Bond.

C.2.Jas I B.2/70; Nicholas BREWSE v. John MARTYN and wife; Bond.

C.2.Jas I B.4/35; John NARGRAVE v. John MARTINE; Performance of trust.

C.2.Jas I B.13/65; Huntington BEAUMONT v. John MARTIN (administrator of Sir Philip STRELLY); Relief against action at law.

C.2.Jas I B.25/13; Richard BREMELCOMBE v. John MARTYN; Answer only.

C.2.Jas I H.26/47; Robert HEYSED v. Thomas CHAPPELL and John MARTYN; Bond.

C.2.Jas I D.2/52; John DEELEY v. Ralph MARTYNE; Payment of money.

C.2.Jas I B.13/1; Richard BREERTON v. Sir Foulke GREVILL and Robert MARTIN; Replication only.

630   C.2.Jas I G.1/16; William GANDER v. Robert MARTIN and John ROBINSON; Deceased's effects.

631   C.2.Jas I H.19/11; Anthony HONEY v. Sibell MARTEN; Payment of money.

632   C.2.Jas I B.29/46; John BUCKNER v. William MARTIN; Debts.

633   C.2.Jas I C.4/44; Richard COLLYN v. William MARTIN; Bond.

634   C.2.Jas I H.4/53; William HAVERCROFT v. William MARTIN; Purchase of barley.

635   C.2.Jas I D.1/34; Andrew DAILL v. Thomas PENNINGTON; Trade accounts.

636   C.2.Jas I G.8/44; Thomas GRAYE v. Josiah PENNINGTON; Estate of Richard BRACKENBURY.

637   C.2.Jas I C.21/44; Anthony CRESWELL and Francis MOORE (executors of John MOORE) v. Humphrey ROLSTON; Deceased's effects.

638   C.2.Jas I D.9/20; Dame Oliffe DINELEY v. Jennet SLATER, widow; Answer only.

639   C.2.Jas I D.11/21; William DEANE v. Jennet SLATER, widow; Accounts.

640   C.2.Jas I & J.10/25; Lord Bishop of the Isles of Scotland v. Allan THOMPSON; Bail.

641   C.2.Jas I & J.5/14; Richard JOHNSON v. Christopher THOMSON and Elizabeth his wife ; Claim under will.

642   C.2.Jas I D.2/72; Richard DRAPER v. Francis MARSHE and Edmund TOMPSON; Trade accounts.

643   C.2.Jas I K.3/27; Henry KEYNE and Alice his wife v. Jane THOMPSON, widow; Marriage portion.

644   C.2.Jas I D.12/3; John DUFFEILD v. Nicholas THOMPSON and wife; Bond.

645   C.2.Jas I A.7/11; Thomas ALDRIDGE v. Peter THOMPSON; Bond.

646   C.2.Jas I H.36/49; John HARDINGE v. Robert TOMPSON and Nicholas FEILDER; Answer only.

647   C.2.Jas I B.13/31; John BANE v. Robert TOMPSON; Performance of marriage contracts.

648   C.2.Jas I C.2/67; William CRIPS v. Robert TOMPSON; Household goods.

C.2.Jas I G.17/85; Richard GRAVENOR v. Thomas TOMSON; General replication only.

C.2.Jas I E.1/21; William ELLENOTT v. William TOMPSON; Answer only.

C.2.Jas I E.1/39; William ELINOTT v. Henry BRANCH and William TOMPSON; Trade matters.

C.2.Jas I & J.6/33; William ILSLEY and W. BLANCHERD v. William TOMPSON; Bond.

C.2.Jas I C.17/33a; THOMPSON v. WANNERTON; Trade matters.

C.2.Jas I G.3/34; Sir Edward GRYFFYN v. Robert WADE; Suretysip.

C.2.Jas I G.3/40; Sir Edward GRYFFIN v. Robert WADE; Bonds

C.2.Jas I H.1/17; Christopher HORNER v. William WADE; Replication only

C.2.Jas I A.4/1; William ALEXANDER v. Sir Richard WYSEMAN; Performance of contract.

C.2.Jas I C.13/59; Sir Robert GARDINER and John WEBB v. John COCK and Edmund SARJANT; Right of common in manor of Cony Weston, alias Cunston; Suffolk.

C.2.Jas I P.15/55; Ambrose PALMER v. Thomas ARMYGER; Site of messuage of Canewden Hall; (Essex) (Answer only).

C.2.Jas I R.15/61; Margery, late wife of Edmund RUSHE, v. Robert RUSHE, John LANE, (LAME?) and Robert BREWSTER; Messuage and land held of the Manor of Lopham; Norfolk.

C.2.Jas I L.8/24; Humphrey LEE v. Andrew CHARLTON, Elizabeth BEVAN, Andrew and William KYRBIE and --- CHARLTON; Inclosure of wastes in manors of Rodon and Upton; Salop.

C.2.Jas I L.12/5; John LOTT v. John KERBY, the elder and younger, and Adam KERBY; Annuity out of lands in Alkham; Kent.

C.2.Jas I L.16/63; Aslack LANY v. William HOLLY; Manor of Bardolfe in Great Ringstead and land in Holme-by-the-sea; Norfolk.

C.2.Jas I P.8/28; Sir William POPE and Ann his wife (late wife of Henry, Lord WENTWORTH) v. John LANY and Edmund BREWSTER; Manors of Stebenheath (alias Stepney) and Hackney; Middlesex.

C.2.Jas I M.3/67; John MARTEN v. Stephen PATRICK; Messuage and land held of the manor of Shrimpling; Suffolk.

666   C.2.Jas I M.16/61; John MARTEN v. Agnes SEABROOKE, Robert MARTIN and John BYATT; Messuage and land in Thaxted held of the manor of Thaxted; Essex.

667   C.2.Jas I M.1/62; George MARTIN and Ralph CLARKE v. Susanne and Elizabeth MARTIN; Tenements near Bowling Alley in Westminster; Middlesex.

668   C.2.Jas I M.8/30; John and Moses MARTIN v. George BUTLER; Messuage, tenements and land in Bradfield, held of the manors of Wixehall, alias Wixe Abbey, and Wixe Parkhall; Essex.

669   C.2.Jas I M.17/47; Edward, son of Robert MIGHELL and Joan his wife (daughter of Edward GODDING) v. Robert MIGHELL, Anthony COLLETT, George WINNISSE and Richard MARTIN: Messuages, tenements and lands in Ipswich and Westerfeild; Suffolk.

670   C.2.Jas I M.22/43; Robert and Edward MIGHELL v. Richard MARTIN; Messuages and lands in Westerfield and Tuddenham; Suffolk.

671   C.2.Jas I M.2/26; William MARTIN v. John BENNETT, Elizabeth KNIGHT and William PINCH; Messuage called Scroope Place in the parish of St. Andrew, Holborn; London.

672   C.2.Jas I M.19/61; Thomas MARTINS v. John DIGBY and Robert WOOLSEY; Tenements and lands in Edgefield; Norfolk.

673   C.2.Jas I M.5/53; Thomas MUNN v. John FOWKE, Ralph YARDLEY, Robert BRANCHWORTH, Robert BOWYER, John CORDELL, Robert COXE, Francis DORRINGTON, Arthur SHEERES, Thomas HYCKES, Morris ABBOT, Thomas NORDEN, Francis BARNHAM, Thomas IVATT and Giles MARTYN; Houses in Mark Lane; London.

674   C.2.Jas I M.20/2; John MARTYN v. Michael GISBYE and Ellis ELIOTT; Lease of a Brick field in Stepney; Middlesex.

675   C.2.Jas I M.19/6; John MOUNDFORD v. Edmund FRAMINGHAM; Land in Wighton; Norfolk.

676   C.2.Jas I M.21/31; Edmund MOUNDFORD and Elizabeth his wife, and Robert HILL and Ann his wife, v. Richard BOND; Messuages and lands in Wyveton, Blakeney, Langham, Merston and Bayfield; Norfolk.

677   C.2.Jas I L.11/3; John LASSELL v. Martin MUNFORD; Houses and lands in Stoke; Norfolk.

678   C.2.Jas I M.15/56; Edmund MAUNSELL v. Robert PENNINGTON and Joan his wife; Annuity issuing out of messuages and lands in Tottenham; Middlesex.

679   C.2.Jas I L.10/25; Edward LOCKINGTON v. Beatrice DUGGETT, widow, John EGMERE, alias POLLY, Mary his wife, and William WOOLWARD; Messuage in Beccles; Suffolk.

C.2.Jas I P.18/16; Edmond POOLEY v. Thomas and William
LOCKWOOD and Robert DENNY; Tenement and land in Combs;
Suffolk.

C.2.Jas I P.27/13; William POOLEY v. Sir Edward BOTELER;
Messuage and land called Boxted Hall in Boxted; Suffolk.

C.2.Jas I P.8/1; Christopher POPELEY v. Richard RAYNER;
Lands in Gomersall and Popeley; Yorks.

C.2.Jas I P.8/69; Henry POPELEY and Cicely his wife (daughter
of William HARRIS) v. Sir William, Sir Francis, and Sir Thomas
HARRIS, James BRETT, Thomas BYAT, Henry PYE, William
WAKES, John SAFEFILD and Richard FULLER; Messuages of
Eastwick and Westwick, in the parish of Barnham, Leigh Heath,
Triggs, Shopland Hall, Gristead Hall, Beckney, Stocks and
Tutherness in Althorne, Reculver and Rattyborough and lands in
South Fanbridge, Purleigh, Canewden, Munden, Shopland,
Prittlewell, Rochford and Tellingham; Essex.

C.2.Jas I P.9/47; Henry POPELEY and Cicely his wife (daughter
of William HARRIS) v. Sir Thomas HARRIS, Ralph HUTTON, John
NASHE and John EVE; Tenements and lands in Tillingham, held of
the manor of Reculver; Essex.

C.2.Jas I L.7/29; John Lloyd v. Roger POPLEY; Messuages in
Westminster; Middlesex. also L.7/53: John LOYD v. Roger
POPLEY; Bond.

C.2.Jas I P.2/7; Charles PARMAN v. John DUFFRING, Edmond
PAYNE, Henry SKEGG, Edward MILLICENT, William BUNYARD,
John RAYE and John ROSSE; Farm and land in Winston; Suffolk.

C.2.Jas I R.1/20; Richard ROSSE, alias WROSSE, and Elizabeth
his wife v. Silvester ROLSTON, John NUTTALL, Bartholomew
WHITEACRES and William HARRYSON; Messuage and land in Newhey
in the parish of Drax; Yorks

C.2.Jas I R.11/54; Lionel ROWLSTON v. Ann HAMMERTON and
Thomas THOMPSON; Messuage in Wathe (Waith) held according to
the custom of the Soke of Grantham; Lincoln.

C.2.Jas I P.22/39; William PEMBERTON, clerk, v. William SHELTON;
Tithes of High Ongar; Essex.

C.2.Jas I P.15/7; Thomas PROCTOR v. John TENNANT, William
WALLOCK, Simon WILKINSON, Henry and Edward THOMPSON
and Thomas RYDDE; Common land of the manor of Bordley; Yorks.

C.2.Jas I P.12/10 and P.7/41; (In latter, defendants called PURS-
GLOVE and THORNETT); William PEPPER v. Robert PURSLEY,
Edward THORNELL, Thomas SCARTH and John THOMPSON;
Messuages in Ellerby and Hinderwell; Yorks.

692   C.2.Jas I M.7/38; John MUGGERIDGE v. Matthew SWIBNER, Richard BURTON and John THOMSON; Inn called The Bush in Staines, and the office of postmaster; Middlesex.

693   C.2.Jas I O.2/16; Samuel OAKLEY v. Robert THOMSON, George KILLINGBECK, George NETTLETON, John COOPER, John BATT, Seth SKELTON and William SMITH; Lands (Not specified); Yorks.

694   C.2.Jas I M.14/1; Thomas MAWE, Robert MATHER, Jonas JAMES, John ENGLISH, clerk, John GOODING, John BARRETT, John HERRING, John KEMP, John TOMPSON, Edward FOSDICK, Thomas HALL, Henry JOLLY, John DICKENSON, Elizabeth MEADOW and Thomas TAYLER v. William and Rebecca GODBOLD, Peter COOKE, Henry GARDNER, and William and Henry MANNING; Tenements and lands in Little Bealings; Suffolk.

695   C.2.Jas I P.15/56; Ann, Mary, and Prisca PLOMBE v. Nicholas TOMPSON and John WILKINSON; Tenement in Newgate Street, St. Stephens, Norwich; Norfolk.

696   C.2.Jas I P.5/9; John and Lawrence PAYCOCK v. Richard and Robert WISEMAN; Stay of legal proceedings respecting tenements in the manors of Grinton, Harkerside and Whiteside; Yorks.

697   C.2.Jas I N.2/30; William NICHOLSON v. Ellen HOWETT, William WISEMAN and William ANSELL; Lands in Walsoken, and messuages in Peterborough; Norfolk and Northampton.

698   C.2.Jas I N.7/49; Robert NATSON, Thomas WOODHOUSE and others v. Adam SCAMBLER; Manor of Neateshead; Norfolk

699   C.2.Jas I R.10/73; Henry CAREY, Viscount ROCHFORD, Sir Thomas WOODHOUSE and Blanch his wife v. Sir Philip WOOD-HOWSE and John LOVETT; Messuage and advowson of Litcham and manors of Carleton and Gelhams, Thuxton, Yaxham, Deepham and Hackford, East Lexham, Ranhall Popes and Waterhouse; Norfolk.

700   C.2.Jas I L.13/64; Rice LLOYD, Katherine his wife (late wife of Thomas BREWSTER) and Edward BREWSTER, infant, v. Edward DORSETT and Magdalene his wife; Deceased's effects.

701   C.2.Jas I Q.1/1; Henry QUINTYNE and Alice his wife v. Ann COLSTON; Deceased's effects.

702   C.2.Jas I P.5/56; William PITT v. George COLSTON; Bond.

703   C.2.Jas I R.7/67; Humphrey RASTELL v. William COLSTON and Thomas and Daniel ADAMS; Answers only.

704   C.2.Jas I P.22/34; John and Joan PARRIS v. Humphrey CURSON; Bond.

705   C.2.Jas I P.18/66; Edward POLE, Gracian TAYLOR, Thomas HIBBERT and John AUNTILL v. John CURSON; Bond.

5   C.2.Jas I L.16/5; William LEE v. Henry KIRKBY and Helen his wife; Debt.

7   C.2.Jas I L.5/48; John LANY v. Robert and William CATFORDE; bonds.

8   C.2.Jas I N.5/33; Lettice, late wife of Denis NEVELL, v. Christopher MARTEN; Deceased's effects.

9   C.2.Jas I M.22/31; John MARTEN v. John CULPEPPER; Debt.

0   C.2.Jas I M.17/24; Peter MARTEN v. Ralph TURNEY; Bond.

1   C.2.Jas I M.22/32; Stephen MARTEN v. John PARKER; Breach of Agreement.

2   C.2.Jas I M.21/18; Thomas MARTEN v. William and John BLIGHE and George GREYNVILE; Bonds.

3   C.2.Jas I M.13/12; William MARTEN v. John KNIGHT; Debts.

4   C.2.Jas I M.18/57; William MARTEN v. John WEBSTER and William CHAMBERS; Debt. (Very imperfect).

5   C.2.Jas I L.1/7; Edward LUCAS v. Elizabeth MARTIN, widow, Thomas SCARGEN, Joseph KETTLE, John JERMYN and Richard AUGER (ANGER ?); Alleged misuse of goods.

6   C.2.Jas I M.6/53; Francis MARTIN v. Anthony and Daniel MORGAN and John, Elizabeth, Ann, Francis and Mary WARREN; Bond.

7   C.2.Jas I M.3/48; Henry MARTIN v. Maximilian BUCKE, Nicholas POLHILL and Chris BROUGH; Injunction.

8   C.2.Jas I M.12/75; John MARTIN v. Elizabeth THREELE; Debt.

9   C.2.Jas I R.11/37; John ROSE v. Humphrey STOCKS, George COLUMBELL, Edward ASHTON, Thomas WALKER, John MARTIN, Robert GREAVES and William ALLEN; Debt.

0   C.2.Jas I M.3/4; Peter MARTIN v. Thomas HALL, George THORPE, Arnold and Edward OLDESWORTH, Thomas HILL and Thomas BEAND; Bond.

1   C.2.Jas I R.12/62; Sir William RUMNEY v. Sir Richard MARTIN; Debt.

2   C.2.Jas I M.4/33; Richard MARTIN and Robert HOWE v. Ann ALLOTT; Bonds.

3   C.2.Jas I M.14/49; Robert MARTIN v. Michael MARTIN; Ship accounts.

4   C.2.Jas I M.2/14; Thomas MARTIN v. William GILLING, George DENNY and Edmund FERRIS; Injunction.

725   C.2.Jas I M.9/55; Sir William MARTIN v. Sir Robert LEE; Non performance of marriage settlement.

726   C.2.Jas I M.12/40; Lewes MARTINE v. Thomas DREW, Dorothy his wife, and Simon WOLCOTT; Bond.

727   C.2.Jas I M.13/56; Nicholas MARTON v. Thomas BROWNE; Bond.

728   C.2.Jas I M.12/20; Bartholomew MARTYN v. Thomas BROOKE; Bonds.

729   C.2.Jas I M.21/53; Edith MARTYN v. Philip NICHOLLS; Money Payment.

730   C.2.Jas I M.9/16; Sir Henry MARTYN v. Thomas LEAKE; Replication only.

731   C.2.Jas I M.11/23; Henry MARTYN v. William and Rowland WILMOTT; Debts.

732   C.2.Jas I M.16/32; Hugh MARTYN v. John and William WYKE; Replication only.

733   C.2.Jas I P.22/3; Sir George PECKHAM v. John MARTYN; Replication only.

734   C.2.Jas I M.19/3; Lewis MARTYN v. Valentine TEDBERRY and Winifred his wife; Bond.

735   C.2.Jas I M.20/9; Lewis MARTYN v. Christopher ADAMS and Joan his wife; Bonds.

736   C.2.Jas I M.13/50; Margaret MARTYN, widow, v. Thomas JESSOP; Replication only.

737   C.2.Jas I P.16/69; Amy PYNCOMBE v. Nicholas and John MARTYN; Sale of cloth.

738   C.2.Jas I M.13/28; Nicholas MARTYN and Susan his wife (daughter of John SHEER) v. George SHEER, Roger MALLOCK, Nicholas BOLT, Joseph TROBRIDGE, John WEST, and Nicholas BAKER; Legacy.

739   C.2.Jas I M.18/10   Nicholas MARTYN and Ann his wife (daughter of Sarah HARRIS) v. George Langrack; Legacy.

740   C.2.Jas I M.15/10; Edmund MANSELL v. Edward SHERWOOD, Richard MARTYN, and Eleanor his wife; Deceased's effects.

741   C.2.Jas I M.20/7; Robert MARTYN v. John REEDE, Thomasin his wife, and Ann CLOTWORTHY; Debt.

742   C.2.Jas I L.8/27; Thomas LONGE and Robert MARTYN v. Arthur ANVYLE, alias WOLGAR; Bond.

3 C.2.Jas I R.11/24; Nicholas, executor of William RYLAND, v.
   ~~Robert MARTYN~~, Thomas RAWLYNS and Nicholas RYLAND; Bond.

4 C.2.Jas I L.7/1; Rebecca LONGE (late wife and executor of Henry
   LONGE), Henry his son and heir, John MAY, William ALLEN,
   Thomas CHAFYN, Thomas LOVYBAND and Roger MARTYN v.
   Sir Francis POPHAM, Sir John and Jeremy HORTON, John
   SACHFEILD and Robert CHAMBERS; Deceased's estate.

5 C.2.Jas I M.7/14; Thomas MARTYN v. William GAME; Bonds.

6 C.2.Jas I M.7/30; William MARTYN, Isabel his wife, (daughter
   of Richard BURNOPPE) v. Eleanor HUTTON, Ralph WILKINSON,
   Robert ELINOR (?) and Isabel his wife; Legacies.

7 C.2.Jas I M.11/74; MOUNDEFORD v. DREWRY. (This case was
   not listed in the modern (handwritten) index, but appears in the
   manuscript index list).

8 C.2.Jas I M.11/6; John MOUNTFORD and John SPELLER v. Moses
   WALL and John BURLE; Replication only.

9 C.2.Jas I M.4/50; Cicely, late wife of Thomas MUNFORD, v. Nicholas
   and Thomas LOCKINGTON, William STEDMAN and Richard WAKEFIELD;
   Bond.

50 C.2.Jas I R.11/17; Nicholas RINGOULDE v. John YATES and John
   MUNFORDE; Debt.

51 C.2.Jas I P.27/30; John PENNINGTON v. John DALE, Elizabeth
   his wife, and John BELLYE; Marriage settlement.

52 C.2.Jas I P.25/44; Richard PENNINGTON v. Edward CASON and
   William HUTTON; Debt.

53 C.2.Jas I P.11/45; Robert PENNINGTON v. Sir Francis FANE;
   Bond.

54 C.2.Jas I O.3/22; William OGLESTHORPE v. Stephen PENNINGTON;
   Debt.

55 C.2.Jas I P.9/34; Thomas PENNINGTON v. Thomas HOLMES; Debt.

56 C.2.Jas I R.12/20; Mary RYVES, widow, v. Chris SMYTHE,
   Robert PENNYNGTON and Elizabeth and Abdias DURDANTE;
   Deceased's effects.

57 C.2.Jas I P.11/52; Philip POLIE (executor of Thomas GALE) v.
   Nicholas BICKFORD and Nicholl his wife; Debt.

58 C.2.Jas I P.3/34; Francis POPLEY v. John Warman, Thomas
   POPLE and John HAGGARDE and Barbara his wife; Deceased's
   effects.

759   C.2.Jas I R.1/24; Charles RAY and Ann his wife v. Richard CRANE; Answer only.

760   C.2.Jas I R.11/25; Ralph PARYS v. Gilbert ROLLESTON and Jane his wife; Debt.

761   C.2.Jas I R.7/18; John ROLSTON v. Richard RECKLES; Bond.

762   C.2.Jas I R.14/33; John ROLSTON and Elizabeth his wife (daughter of John CHAMBERS) v. Humphrey SNOWDEN and Katherine his wife; Deceased's effects.

763   C.2.Jas I P.25/54; Simon PATTERICK (Administrator of Sir Ambrose WILLOUGHBY) v. Robert SLATER; Deceased's effects.

764   C.2.Jas I M.22/41; Freeholders of the towns of Marston and Pebworth (Rebworth?) v. John SLATER; Common of Pasture.

765   C.2.Jas I R.1/28; Thomas RUGGE v. Edward and Bertram THOMPSON; Debt.

766   C.2.Jas I M.16/53; Richard, Samuel and Edmund MERRYWEATHER v. William TAYLOR, John TURNER, William BATSON, Thomas COSSUM, Robert HUDSON, John PREDDYE, Richard TOMPSON, James BRUCE, Thomas WRIGHT, Samuel MONCK and Thomas RICHARDS; Debts.

767   C.2.Jas I M.9/44; Mary MORGAN v. Thomas THOMPSON and Peirse WILLIAMS; Bond.

768   C.2.Jas I L.5/54; Samuel LISTER and John WHITLEY (executors of Robert HEMINGWAY) v. Francis WADE; Loan.

769   C.2.Jas I L.9/69; William LANGDON v. William WADE and Mensbe his wife, Roger WADE, William PIPER, John WADE and Frances his wife; Bonds.

770   C.2.Jas I N.2/76; William NEGUSSE v. Thomas NEGUSSE and Gilbert WISEMAN; Stay of legal proceedings.

771   C.2.Jas I N.2/73; James NUTTALL and Jane his wife (administratrix of Martha WISEMAN) v. William and Humphrey WISEMAN; Deceased's effects.

772   C.2.Jas I R.6/61; Francis READE v. Simon WISEMAN, Richard BURNBY, Thomas CARTER, William BURMAM, Henry MYLNER, Richard BALL, Giles SYMPSON, Robert FEAKE, Robert WOOD-CROFTE, Richard GRYSMEND, Richard BUCKLEY, Thomas DENT, Francis ALLEN, William HAYES, Edward CARTWRIGHT, Ralph WOODCOCK, and Cuthbert HASELWOOD; Bonds.

773   C.2.Jas I P.11/7; Richard PAGE v. Sir Thomas WOODHOUSE and Edward YELVERTON; Bond.

774   C.2.Jas I P.5/59; John PYE v. Edward WREY; Bond.

PART VI

EXTRACTS FROM THE NOTARIAL RECORDS
OF ROTTERDAM: 1644-1669

Not. A. Rotterdam, No. 436. Notary: B. BAZIUS

p. 143 29 June 1644

Jean de LANGE, merchant of Amsterdam, associate in the voyage, certifies at the request of Hendrick BROOCQ re Master Francis HURDIDGE
that the latter, coming from Virginia, refused to sail into the Goereesche
Gat and had sailed to the Downs in England.

p. 159 16 Aug 1644

Isaacq LAURENS, aged 28, certifies on behalf of Mr. Jan GLOVER, that
he has been with him in Hellvoetslius to discharge there from the vessel
under the command of Master Francois HURDIDGE, a parcel of tobacco
from Virginia. He certifies that GLOVER has met the farmer of the im-
post (tax official) and has agreed to pay 7 guilders per cask six weeks
after unloading. An agreement to be made where casks are found to be
damaged. Confirmed by Master Reijnier LEENDERTS, aged 25.

p. 162 29 Aug 1644

Hendrick BROOKE, English merchant, at present resident in this city,
authorises Joh. GLOVER to deal with his business, and to receive from
the hands of Francis HURDIDGE 748 casks of tobacco, which BROOKE
has loaded on board the vessel in Virginia to bring them to this country
to the Goereesche Gat. 506 casks are for his own use or for that of his
uncle, Laurens GRIJN, the balance for others unnamed. It would appear
that there are difficulties with the master, because it is twice mentioned
that the master should have enforced a bill of lading.

p. 164 29 Aug 1644

A difference having arisen between Frans HAMER, tax official, and Mr.
Jan GLOVER concerning the tax on 841 casks of tobacco, arbitrators
have been appointed, viz: Franchois VERBOOM and Dirck van der
WOLFF.

p. 165 12 Sept 1644

The parties appeared before the arbitrators and it was agreed that Jan
GLOVER should pay 1,000 guilders to HAMER on that day, and that he
would give orders for the payment of 3,000 guilders, payable by Daniel
PINTO at Amsterdam, three days after sight of his order. The remaining
amount to be remitted to the arbitrators by GLOVER on the following
Monday, failing which he may pay a fine of 100 guilders.

p. 166 19 Sept 1644

Jan GLOVER owes a total of 5,200 guilders, which is paid by him and for
which Frans HAMER gives him a receipt.

p. 187 12 Oct 1644

IOU of Henry BROOKE, English merchant of this city, for 10,057 guilders, 10 pence which he has borrowed from Mr. Jan GLOVER. To be repaid 50% within three months and the balance within nine months.

780   p. 188 12 Oct 1644

Jan GLOVER promises Hendrick BROKE to give a good account for the 90 casks of tobacco he holds for him.

781   Not. A. Rotterdam, No. 332. Notary: A. van der GRAEFF

        p. 730 24 Oct 1644

IOU of John GLOVER who owes Willem VIRULY, broker, and Jan Jacobs van der HOUVEN 10,000 guilders for money borrowed this day. To be repaid in 6 weeks, or at most three months from today's date with interest at 8% p.a. Security: 250 casks of Virginia tobacco.

782   Not A. Rotterdam, No. 436. Notary: B. BAZIUS

        p. 197 4 Nov 1644

Hendrick BROOKE jr English merchant, now of this city, certifies that Mr. Jan GLOVER having underwritten £138 for him, which Jan ANSWOORT being proxy for Robert LOUW, of London, claims against him, engages as an assurance of this security one-twelfth part of the vessel "De Spiegel" Master, Havick COOK, in which Hendrick BROOKE jr intends to sail to the West Indies or Virginia. If GLOVER is ordered to pay the debt, this share of the vessel may be sold to, and received by Deputy Wessel van der HEUL, or anyone appointed by the sheriffs of this city.

783   p. 227 11 Nov 1644

Have KOCX, master of the ship "De Spiegel", about 100 tons, and Hendrick BROOCKE, assisted by Jan GLOVER, of this city, have made the following contract of freight:- The master shall provide the vessel with 8 guns and another 4 guns to be paid for by BROOKE, and shall prepare the ship with sufficient ammunition and victuals to sail with the first good wind from the Maas to Virginia or thereabouts, and to another locality if they be not allowed to land in Virginia. The master will stay there three and a half months and will use his boat's crew to load 300-400 casks. During loading the expenses of the crew's victuals will be paid for by the freighters, and if the ship stays longer than three and a half months then the freighters will be obliged to pay for this. After returning to Rotterdam an amount of 35 caroli guilders will be paid per cask. In case 300-400 casks are not loaded, every cask will cost 70 guilders, 10 pence. All cost and charges for damage at sea to be paid by the freighters.

784   p. 229 27 Sept 1644

Willem HENDRICKS, aged 33, and Reinier LEENDERTS, aged 26, both masters of this city, certify that at the request of Jan GLOVER, when at Hellevoetsluis at the beginning of August last to unload tobacco, which had arrived from Virginia in the ship "Mary", master Francis HURD-IDGE, they saw that the crew had to pump continuously. They had then said that they thought the vessel must be an old one because it was so leaky, but were told that it was not so old, but that it had not been cleaned in 2 or 3 years, nor had it been caulked. On the voyage over it was hard to make it manoevre one way or another on account of its being so dirty.

At the request of Jan GLOVER, Notary B. BAZIUS has proceeded against
Hendrick BROOKE and presented him with the following Bill of Exchange:-

> 15 March 1643. I pray pay this my first bill of exchange, my
> second and third being under paid within forty days after sight
> thereof to Mr. William PRYOR or his assigns the full sum of
> £82 13s. 10d. lawful English money for so much received of
> him. Pray make him good payment and put it to account as per
> advice. Your loving friend Arg: YARDLEY. To his loving
> friend Henry BROOKE, jr, merchant in London.

Asked whether he wanted to pay BROOKE replied that he had no shares to
that effect in hand from the drawer and could not honour the bill, after
which the bill was protested.

p. 231   25 Aug 1644

At the request of Jan GLOVER, Notary B. BAZIUS has proceeded against
Hendrick BROOKE and presented him with the following Bill of Exchange:-

> Virginia, 19 March, 1643. Thirty days after sight of this my
> first bill of exchange, my second and third being not paid, I
> pray pay to Capt. Peter ANDREWES, or his assigns, the just
> sum of £11 sterling, it being for so much received here, pray
> make good payment and put it to account as per advice. Your
> friend and brother Arg: YARDLEY. To my loving friend Mr.
> Henry BROOKE jr and my loving brother Capt. Francis
> YARDLEY in London.

Asked whether BROOKE wanted to honour the bill of exchange, he replied
that it was also addressed to the brother of the drawer, and he had only
to be put on it in case this brother were not present here. The notary
then went to Capt. Francis YARDLEY, and when presenting the document
received the following reply: "No. Let Mr. BROOKE accept it and pay
it." After which the bill was protested against both persons.

Not. A. Rotterdam No. 480 Notary: Joannes van WEEL.

p. 105   20 Apl 1644

William BARKER, English broker, aged 36, and Humphrey HODGES,
English merchant, aged 26, issue a statement on behalf of John GLOVER
and Richard MAYHEVE (MAYHEW), as follows:- GLOVER arrived at
the house of Isaacq LAURENSSEN, who lives on the Nieuwe Haven on
13 April last. A certain Joris HARWOOD, an English merchant, also
arrived there. After some discussion during which HARWOOD called
GLOVER and MAYHEW liars there was a quarrel.

Not. A. Rotterdam. No. 444. Notary: B. BAZIUS

p 217 8 Aug 1646

Michiel COLEPRIJS, apprentice, at present of this city, now being ill,
appeared before the notary and stated that his former testamony before
Notary Gerrit COREN at Amsterdam must be annulled. He stated that he
made it on 25 Oct 1644. He now wishes to appoint the children of John
GLOVER, his brother-in-law, and Anna COLEPRIJS, his half-sister, as
his heirs for the sum of 3,300 caroli guilders which were given to him by

his late father for his mother's legacy. John GLOVER and his wife to have
the use thereof during their lives, with remainder to their children. The
poor of the Reformed Church to have 100 guilders and the orphans 50 guilders, payable with interest. The rest of his goods he leaves to his half-
sisters Sara and Janneken COLEPRIJS.

789   Not. A. Rotterdam. No. 438. Notary: B. BAZIUS

        p. 185 6 Nov 1643

Johan GLOVER appeared for Richard GLOVER, his brother, and admitted
receiving from Cornelius CONING, a member of the Town Council, the
sum of 2,000 caroli guilders which he is keeping on bottomry on the vessels
and merchandise mentioned below, as long as these vessels sail to Virginia
and back again to this city. GLOVER to make monthly payments for interest at 3% from 18 September until such time as the vessels have returned
here from Virginia and the full capital sum and interest has been paid. If,
however, the vessel "Hope", Master Jop AERTS, which sailed to Virginia
on 18 September, should be lost, Jan GLOVER shall claim 1,000 guilders
on it, raised on bottomry, but CONING shall receive this sum from Adriaan
VROESEN and Cornelius de GRAEFF, who have both insured it for 1,200
guilders. If the ship "De Valck" (Falcon), Master Reijer HARMANS, on
which the remaining 1,000 guilders have been raised on bottomry should be
lost, then CONING may not claim from GLOVER, but he will have to obtain
it from Willem de CRIJER, Adriaan VROESEN and Cornelius de GRAEFF,
who have togehter insured this ship for 1,600 guilders.

790   p. 187 8 Nov 1643

A supplement to the above respecting the premium and in case the vessels
should be captured by the English. GLOVER would then have to pay 1,000
guilders himself.

791   Not. A. Rotterdam. No. 475. Notary: Johan van WEEL

        p. 182 26 Feb 1647

Johan GLOVER, resident in this city, sells to Jean HABEN (?) a certain
ship called "De Liefde", 125 lasts, length across stern 101½ feet, width
24¾ feet, mounted with 8 iron castings, 4 stone pieces and all accessories,
which he bought in Amsterdam on 18 January last, and now berthed in this
city. Also ¼ part in the ship "Hope" about 50 lasts, being now in Virginia,
Master Jop AERTSEN, together with one quarter of her cargo, and also
one quarter share of the vessel "Sanct Peter", Master Ocker DIRKSZ,
about 130 lasts, now berthed in this city, together with ⅛ part of all that
belongs to the vessel, as it has recently come from sea, and also all the
rights, actions and claims of certain insurance policies dated 22 October,
1646, for the sum of 1,000 guilders on Jop AERTSEN's vessel. Also the
right of insurance for the sum of 2,000 guilders on Reijer HARMAN's
ship, "De Valck", dated 28 January 1647. He certifies receipt of settlement and payment with which he is, according to a certain account of the
above-named HABEN, in arrear and endebted.

792   Not. A. Rotterdam. No. 335. Notary: A. van der GRAEFF

        p. 95 2 May 1647

John GLOVER states that Cornelis van SLINGERLANT has bound himself as security on 6 December, 1646, for 2,000 guilders and interest thereof, on behalf of Madam Agata WELHOUX, widow of Cornelius HARTOCHSVELT. SLINGERLANT's security is all the casks of leaf-tobacco recently arrived in good condition in the ship "De Valck", Master Reijer HARMANS, now lying in the warehouse of Willem OCKERS in De Boompjes in this city, as due to him for his part in the cargo.

Not. A. Rotterdam. No. 499. Notary: V. MUSTELIUS

p. 728 9 May, 1647

John GLOVER sells to Gillis JORISSEN, balance maker, of this city, two yards with two small houses situated thereon in the Manor of Blommersdijk.

Not. A. Rotterdam, No. 439. Notary: B. BAZIUS

p. 57 16 May 1647

IOU of John GLOVER, who owes Isbrant van HOUTEN, Sheriff of Schieland, and company 5,000 caroli guilders for the purchase of tobacco satisfactorily received. To be paid within two months exactly. Security: the house at Nieuwe Haven North side, in which GLOVER presently lives. Witness: Michiel COLEPRIJS.

Not. A. Rotterdam. No. 445. Notary: B. BAZIUS.

p. 50 6 Feb 1648

John SHEPHERD and John GLOVER witness the marriage contract of John WIMIS, sexton of the English Church and Helena HAUWES.

Not. A. Rotterdam. No. 582 Notary: Willem SONNEVELT

p. 3 27 Feb 1649

Robert CUSTER, English skipper, and John PENDIER, also an English skipper, living in England, who have a difference of opinion appoint as arbitrators Mr. Robert ETON and Mr. John GLOVER, both of this city.

Not. A. Rotterdam. No. 441 Notary: B. BAZIUS

p. 73 24 Sept 1649

Seth VERBRUGGE, owner of the ship "Prinsesse Royale", Master Jan Jansz VISSCHER, with co-owners on the one side and Jan GLOVER on the other side agree that GLOVER shall appoint three persons to take charge of and bring over the said vessel, which is ready to sail to Virginia. Eight days after the ship's arrival in Virginia Richard LEE will pay 500 pounds of tobacco in cask. GLOVER holds himself responsible for damage.

Not. A. Rotterdam. No. 502 Notary: V. MUSTELIUS

p. 398 5 Nov 1650

Johan GLOVER appeared as the freighter on behalf of Francis MANSELL and Company, merchants of Chichester, England versus Willem WILLEMSZOON of Rotterdam, Master of the ship "Het Valckenhoff", about 30 lasts. They state they have agreed about the chartering terms; the master to have the vessel ready in good condition within four or five working days, and to have it loaded with merchandise to sail with the first good wind and weather, and convoy to Chichester to be unloaded there. The ship shall there be loaded again within the next ten or eleven days by Francis MANCELL or his partners, after which it shall return to Rotterdam at the first opportunity, where unloading shall take place within the next five or six working days. The amount to be paid for the freight shall be 500 caroli guilders, one half at Chichester and the other half on the return to Rotterdam. Damage and pilotage shall be settled according to the custom at sea.

799   p. 458 7 Jan 1651

John GLOVER acknowledges a debt to Richard GLOVER, of Amsterdam, of 2,000 guilders, which he borrowed from him. To be repaid in instalments of 400 guilders every three months at 5%.

800   p. 456 7 Jan 1651

IOU of John GLOVER in favour of Dirck LAECKENS, spice merchant, of this city, in the sum of 2,000 guilders, for the sale of merchandise, to be paid at the rate of 400 guilders every three months with interest at 5%. First payment to be made on 7 Apl 1651.

801   p. 457 7 Jan 1651

IOU in favour of Leendert de JONGH, spice merchant, by John GLOVER, also a merchant in spices, for 1,000 guilders. To be repaid at the rate of 200 guilders every three months.

802   Not. A. Rotterdam. No 493 Notary: Johan van WEEL

        p. 18 19 Jan 1651

John GLOVER leases premises at the Nieuwe Haven on the southern side of the Houttuin known by the name of "De Gulde Arke", for the following 15 months from 1 Feb 1651, for 330 guilders.

803   Not. A. Rotterdam. No. 666. Notary: Pieter de PAUS.

        p. 676 25 Jan 1651 (In English in the original)

Charter ... of freight made between Mr. John GLOVER of Rotterdam on behalf of Francis MANCELL of Chichester and Company on the one part, and William GAYE of Middelburg in Zeeland, Master of the Hoeker ship "St. George" of 26 tons or thereabouts and now for the present here at Rotterdam on the other part, witnesseth that the said William GAYE, with the aforesaid hoeker ship fully laden is to sail to the Isle of Wight and from thence to Chichester, and there being unladen to go from thence to the Isle of Wight, and there to take in his full lading according to order and to return to Rotterdam, on condition to have £35 sterling for his freights thereof.

804   Not. A. Rotterdam, No. 502. Notary: V. MUSTELIUS

        p. 477 27 Jan 1651

Francis MANCELL, of Chichester, for himself and Symon KELBEY, Edward HABSON and Francis HABSON, his partners, authorise John GLOVER to act in their name in all rights, actions and claims which they have at charge of Captain Jan GRIFFITH, being the sum of 2,086 guilders according to invoice, to wit, a parcel of groceries having been shipped for their account on board the ship ... (illegible), Master Willem Bastiaansz de MAN of Schiedam, on or about 20 Dec 1650, on which the party concerned has prosecuted an action before the Court of this city. GLOVER is ordered to arrange the matter.

Not. A. Rotterdam. No. 493. Notary: Johan van WEEL.

p. 30   2 Apl 1651

Certain bonds are offered by Michael DUNCUMBE, dwelling at the Hague, on behalf of his son-in-law Johan GRIFFITH, for a sum of 4,500 guilders, to those mentioned in the instrument of 15 Apl below, for which GRIFFITH was sentenced in an action prosecuted before the Admiralty of this city.

p. 30   15 Apl 1651

Samuel van der LANEN, Willem THEUNEMANS, Hendrick WEBSTER, Richard FORD, Willem EMPEREUR, and Jacob GISEN appeared on behalf and with the instructions of John GLOVER, all of this city and all merchants. They have obtained the ownership of a bond from Michael DUNCOMBE in the Hague on behalf of Michael EDWARDS for 1,500 Flemish pounds and now transfer it to Johan Reijersz van BEAUMONT, of this city.

Not. A. Rotterdam. No. 502. Notary: V. MUSTELIUS

p. 594   29 Apl 1651

Francis MANCELL, as drawer of the following bills of exchange, with Johan GLOVER having endorsed them authorises the notary to proceed with two witnesses to Jan ROGELDAN, and Englishman now living in this city, to ask the latter to return the bills of exchange of the 6th of this present month of April, at the hand of the above-names MANCELL ... at the charge of Jan WHITE, merchant of London, containing the sum of £200 against the rate of exchange of the draft on London. In default whereof all damage due to the lower rate of the bills of exchange and all other costs of delay on the part of Master William GAY, in whose ship the goods are loaded, will be charged to him.

Not. A. Rotterdam. No. 683. Notary: B. ROOSE.

p. 70   18 Mar 1655

Willem CORNELIS, skipper of the ship "De Twee Gebroeders" appeared at the request of Francois HUYS, broker of this city, and certified it to be true that he has loaded in London 70 barrels of figs, 20 baskets of raisins, 40 barrels of tobacco and 3 barrels of sugar, all consigned to the requisitioner, and certified not to belong to John GLOVER, but to certain merchants in London. Francois HUYS acts as broker to John GLOVER. This declaration is confirmed by Henrick HANT, merchant of Amsterdam.

Not. A. Rotterdam. No. 487. Notary: Johan van WEEL.

p. 1.   17 Sept 1655

Henrick TOUWER, wine merchant, of this city authorizes M. van AERSEM merchant of London to claim in his name from Johan GLOVER, English

merchant, formerly dwelling in Rotterdam, but now at London, or in the
event of his death, from his heirs, 142 guilders, 16 pence, for the purchase and supply of wines to which amount the said GLOVER is sentenced
by the sheriffs of this city.

810   Not. A. Rotterdam. No. 656 Notary: Pieter de PAUS

        p. 952 3 Feb 1659/60 (English style)

Derick LAKENS of Rotterdam has constituted William DRABE, gentleman,
to recover of John GLOVER, of London, merchant, the sum of 2,000 guilders according to his bond dated 7 Jan 1651.

811   Not. A. Rotterdam. No. 636 Notary: A. van ALLXER

        p. 27 8 Dec 1665

Anna COLEPRIJS, widow of Johan GLOVER, aged 44 and Anna GLOVER,
aged 17 issue a statement at the request of Jacomijntgen JANSDR.

812   Not. A. Rotterdam. No. 733 Notary: Dirck BLOCK.

Anna GLOVER, widow of Johannes GLOVER, of this city appeared and
certified that she owed Gideon DUYTS, dwelling at Amsterdam, 300
caroli guilders, received from him today and due for repayment in a year's
time. Receipt signed by Gideon DEUTZ 26 June, 1668.

813   p. 315 26 June 1668

Anna GLOVER again borrowed from Gideon DUYTS the sum of 1,500
guilders.

814   Not. A. Rotterdam. No. 935 Notary: Philip BASTEEIS

        p. 1 2 Jan 1669

Lease contract. The family KOOL leases a house belonging to them situated at the end of the Hoofstraat, in the neighbourhood of the Roode
Brugge, then occupied by the lessee, to Anna COLEPRIJS for one year
from 1 May, 1669, for the sum of 400 caroli guilders. Anna is the widow
of Johannes GLOVER, formerly an English merchant of this city.

815   p. 921 24 Dec 1669

Catharina COCK, widow of Meester Ulrick van ZOELEN, leases to Anna
COLEPRIJS, widow of Johan GLOVER, a house called "Den Witten
Eenhoorn" with the stores situated behind it, at present being leased by
Lowijs ELSEVIER, located at Noordzijde Nieuwe Haven for 456 caroli
guilders from 1 May 1670. Gideon DEUTZ, now dwelling in this city,
appeared as surety for the said Anna COLEPRIJS.

816   Not A. Rotterdam. No. 595. Notary: ....

        p. 345 - Mar 1670 (?71)

Anna GLOVER, widow of John GLOVER of London, and mother of Benjamin
GLOVER, late of Boston in New England, appeared and stated that to her
great grief she has been informed that her son Benjamin has unfortunately
by accident been drowned at sea and has left behind some goods and estate,
which by right of law become hers. She authorises Ezichiel SWISELETON
and Humphrey DAVICE to act on her behalf.

PART VII

EXTRACTS FROM THE NOTARIAL RECORDS
OF AMSTERDAM: 1644-1653

Not. A. Amsterdam, No. 848 Notary: Joseph STEIJNS

p. 56 19 Mar 1644

Johannes GLOVER, merchant of Rotterdam, aged about 28, appeared and
certified at the request of Sr. Gillis SUMPTER, merchant of Rotterdam,
that he, at the command of the producer, who lived with him at Rotterdam,
about the beginning of January this year, has had loaded in the ship
" 't Groenevelt", Master Thomas TAYLOR, 31 pieces of linen, of which
30 pieces are in three cases and one piece loose. He intends to ship them
to Topsham in England. Certified that he has also at the command of the
producer, ordered at Amsterdam to have the goods insured for 2,000
guilders.

Not. A. Amsterdam, No. 848 Notary: Joseph STEIJNS

p. 85 19 Apl 1644

Richard GLOVER, merchant, and Maria BROECK, his wife, now dwelling
at the Prinsengracht, the wife being sick in bed, appeared to make their
will and testament. The longest living heir to pay to the parents of the
deceased that which lawfully is due to them. The child of the testatrix
(she being great with child) is made heir, with exclusion of the Orphan's
Court. Guardians: Hendrick WEBSTER, merchant of Rotterdam and
Pieter JANSE, tobacco merchant, of this city. Acknowledged at the house
of Richard GLOVER. Signed: Richard GLOVER Mary BROOK.

p. -- 1 Nov 1644

Richard GLOVER, merchant of this city, who, although sick but of sound
mind, appeared and certified to approve the will of 19 April 1644, appointing as guardians instead of the persons mentioned in the will, his
brother, Jan GLOVER, merchant of Rotterdam and Hendrick WHITAKER,
merchant of this city, to have the guardianship of his daughter, Anna
GLOVER, and of the child, or children, he might still leave behind.
This guardianship to be executed by the above-named gentlemen and his
wife, Mary BROECK.

p. -- 10 Nov 1644

Hendrick BROECK, English merchant, now dwelling at Rotterdam,
appeared and promised to supply Richard GLOVER, English merchant,
with 20 hogsheads of leaf-tobacco within eight days, as received by him
from Virginia by the ship "Maria St Jan", and now lying the the warehouse
of Sr. Jan GLOVER at Rotterdam. Richard GLOVER has already paid
about 500 guilders for freight and expenses on this shipment, and
Henderick BROECK promises that a normal settlement will be made in
case of any difference of opinion. This is agreed to by Edward BOECKER
brother-in-law to Richard GLOVER, who was present. Given at
Amsterdam in the presence of Michiel COLEPRIJS and Joris Stevens
BOUGEON. Signed by Henry BROOKE, jr, Edward BOOKER, Michael

COLEPRIJS, Joris Stevenson BOUGEON and the Notary.

821   Not. A. Amsterdam, No. 2434. Notary: Johan CROSSE

        p. -- 24 June 1653

Janetje POTTS, widow of Edward KERBY, late wine merchant, appeared and authorized Johannes FOULAER, of this city, to claim and cash all her debts within the city of Leiden. Signed Janneken KIJRKBY.

822   p. -- 15 Nov 1653

Sr. Arthur KERKBY, wine merchant of this city, appeared and authorized Dirck VOGEISANG to receive from the heirs of Claes DOMMERS, late innkeeper at Franeker in Vriesland, the sum of 55 caroli guilders for one hogshead of French wine, received on the 12 July this year, with expenses incurred.

Extracts from the Register of Banns
of Marriage for the City of Amsterdam

823   No. 436. p. 171 8 Oct 1630

Dirck DIRCKSEN of Deventer, tailor, living in the Jonkerstr, aged 26 and Trijntie BAERENTS van EEMDEN, widow of Jan IJDES, living in Leliegracht. She declares she has been a widow for one year. Signed: Derck DERCKSEN.

Children baptized at the Reformed Church, Amsterdam.

      10 Aug 1631   Grietje DERCKSEN
      18 Dec 1633   Henrick DERCKSEN
       2 May 1638   Dirck DIRCKSEN
      23 Sept 1640   Aeltje DIRCKSEN

824   No. 451. p. 6 21 Apl 1639

Eduwaert KERCKBIJ (Edward KIRBY) of Ritsmond (?Richmond), French brandy distiller, now dwelling in the Binnenaemster, aged 24, and Janettje POTTS, aged 22, of Vlissingen, appeared with Sara POTTS, her mother. Signed: Edward KIRKBIJ Janneken POTTS

Children baptized in the English Church at Amsterdam.

       1 Jul 1640   Sarah KERBY
     29 Dec 1641   Thomas KERBY
      2 Nov 1643   Mary KERBY
     21 May 1645   Edward KERBY
     23 Dec 1646   Joseph KERBY
     31 Oct 1649   Jasper KERBY

825   No. 455. p. 36. 15 Feb 1641

Johannes GLOVER, of Hilledny, aged 25, parents still living, now dwelling at Rotterdam and Anna COLEPRIJS of Amsterdam, aged 19, appeared with her father, Michiel COLEPRIJS, now dwelling on the Noordzijde Voor- burgwall. Signed: Jo. GLOVER Anna COLEPRIJS
Banns approved at Rotterdam, 7 Mar 1641. Signed Segnerus BERCKEL,
                               Minister

Children baptized at the Reformed Church, Rotterdam.

| 11 June 1643 | Anna GLOVER | Witnesses: | Richard GLOVER |
| | | | Maria ADRIAANS |

20 Sept 1644 Caterina GLOVER No witnesses

3 Mar 1647 Johannes GLOVER Witnesses: Philippus de RET
                                         Thomas DOSTELWIT
                                         (POSTLETHWAITE)

26 Nov 1648 Anna GLOVER   Witnesses: Thomas POSTLETH-
                                         WAITE,
                                         Brigit CLAVER
                                         Michiel COLEPRIJS

10 Nov 1650 Caterina GLOVER Witnesses: Nyclaes HARRIS
                                         Maria de GRAVEN

11 Aug 1652 Peroni Bennet
              GLOVER   No witnesses

Buried at Rotterdam

26 May 1647 A child of Johan GLOVER, of Nieuwe Haven
16 June 1677 A child of Jan GLOVER

No. 456. p. 20. 1 June 1641

Eduart BOUCKER (Edward BOOKER) of London, now dwelling in Nieuweleliestraat, aged 28, (mother living in England) showed a certificate from Johannes HEYDANUS, Minister at Rotterdam, and Elizabeth GLOVER, of Rotterdam. Signed: Edward BOCKER

(Elizabeth, daughter of Robert GLOVER, was baptized at the English Church in Amsterdam on 30 Oct 1619)

Child baptized at the English Church, Amsterdam

16 Mar 1642 Richard BOOKER

No. 467. p. 531. 1 Apl, 1650

Thomas KERKBIJ (Thomas KIRBY) of Ritsmond (?)Richmond), distiller, aged 25, now dwelling at the Goutseveer, was present with Eduwart KERKBIJ (both parents living in England) and Naeltje van HOECK of Amsterdam, dwelling in the Elanstraat (no parents living), aged 25, appeared with Lijsbeth van HOECK, her sister. Banns passed in the English Church. Signed: Thomas KIRKBY Naeltje van HOECK

Child baptized in the English Church, Amsterdam.

28 May 1651 Thomas KERKBY

No. 471. p. 65. 22 Mar 1653

Thomas KERKBIJ, widower of Naeltje van HOECK, living on the Prinsengracht and Jannetje JASPERS, widow of Johannes KLERCK, now dwelling on the Elantsgracht.

The marriage of Richard GLOVER did not take place at either Amsterdam or Rotterdam. His wife's name was Mary BROOK. Children baptized at Amsterdam:-

```
English Church      8 May 1644  Anna GLOVER
Reformed Church    7 Jan 1646  Richard GLOVER    Witnesses: Richard
                                                  GLOVER sr
                                                  Maria GLOVER
Reformed Church 16 May 1647  Bennet GLOVER       Witness: Aeltje
                                                  GARLICKS
English Church    23 May 1649  Edward GLOVER
English Church    16 Apl 1651  Richard GLOVER
```

830   Child baptized at the Reformed Church, Rotterdam

                26 Dec 1650   Thomas, son of Thomas GLOVER
                               and Lijsbeth GLOVER

831   No. 487 p. 507. 13 Nov 1665

Thomas KIRKBY of Amsterdam, merchant, aged 24, appeared with his
mother,, Jannetje POTTS, living at the Goudseveer, and Maria PECOCKX
of Amsterdam, aged 19, appeared with her father William PECOCKX,
living on the Heregracht. Signed: Thomas KIRKBY Maria PEACOCK.

(Mary, daughter of William PEACOCK, Deacon, was baptized in the
English Church, 28 Jan 1646)

Child baptized in the English Church at Amsterdam

                12 May 1669   John KERBY

832   No. 497. p. 240. 13 Nov 1671

William GLOVER of Utrecht, wine merchant, aged 25, appeared with his
mother, Anna MOISER, living on the Cingel, and Catrine LAMS of
Amsterdam, aged 26, appeared with her mother, Josijntje DIRCKS,
living in the Halsteeg. Signed: Willem GLOVER Katrijna LAMS

Children baptized at the Reformed Church at Amsterdam

                30 June 1673   Anna GLOVER
                14 Oct 1674   Anna GLOVER
                12 Sept 1679   Josina GLOVER

833   No. 507. p. 397. 17 Aug 1680

Jan SCHRENDER of Hamburg, widower of Anna BARENTS, living on the
Norddijk, and Catharina LAMS of Amsterdam, widow of Willem GLOVER,
living on the Nordzijde Voorburgwall. Married: 31 Aug 1680.

APPENDIX 1

Numerical List of CHADWELL (males) 1528-1710

	Name	Abode	Born	Marr.	Alive	Died	Father's Name	
101	William	Rissington				1529	William	101
202	Richard	Rissington		1543		1567	"	"
203	John	Broadwell				1577	"	"
204	Robert	Shipton					"	?
205	William	Rissington			1543		"	?
306	William	Broadwell	1554			1551/2	?	203
307	Richard	Burford	1544	1578		1613	John	202
308	Michael	Chip. Norton				1591	Richard	"
409	Simon	Rissington	c.1566	1588	1624	1609	"	307
410	John		1570		1624		Richard	"
411	Henry		after 1578	1st 1617 2nd 1619	1650		"	"
412	Richard	Broadwell	1578			1634	"	306
413	William	Woodstock	1579	1606	after 1649		William	"
414	John	Donnington	1580			1636	"	"
415	Thomas	Donnington	c.1588			1637	"	413
516	William	Broadwell	1613			1660	William	
517	John	Donnington	1623		1672		"	308
518	Edmond		1630				"	"
419	Michael	Chip. Norton	before 1572	1st ? 2nd 1612		before 1609	Michael	
420	Edward		c.1572			1631	"	
521	Thomas	Chip. Norton	1600			1656	John	410
522	Michael	Donnington	1613	?		1614	Edward	420
523	Thomas	Lt. Barrington	1610			1684	Thomas	415
224	Thomas	Lt. Barrington			1554		? John of Burford	189
325	Richard					1601	Thomas	224
426	John	Stroud	c.1565				Richard	325
427	Simon		c.1568		1608		"	"
428	Moses	Lt. Barrington	?1570		1605		"	"
529	Thomas	Lt. Barrington	1595			1668	John	425

No.	Name	Abode	Born	Marr.	Alive	Died	Father's Name	No.
530	Thomas	Kempley	1631	1554	1571	1695	Thomas	529
531	John	Blackbourton	c.1640			1577	"	"
532	Samuel		c.1642				"	"
633	William	Broadwell	c.1645		1695		William	516
634	William		c.1635		1571		Simon	427
535	John	Stroud	c.1590		1674	1674	John	535
636	John	Stroud	c.1639		1674		"	"
637	Thomas	Stroud	c.1640		1674		"	"
638	Benjamin	Stroud	1642	1570				
639	Richard	Stroud	1647	1578			Thomas	637
740	Thomas		after 1650		1674		"	"
741	Nathaniel		"		1674			
742	John		"		1674			
343	John	Burford	1521		1543	1617	Robert	204
444	Richard	Upton (? 412)	c.1530		1630	1684	Richard	444 or 412
545	David	Upton	1650		1571		Lawrence	" 546
546	Lawrence		1653				"	"
547	Robert		1659				"	"
648	Lawrence				1684			
649	John	Burbage			1584			
150	William				1575	1617	William	150
251	Edmund	Ebbesborne	1595			1617	Edmund	251
352	Edmund	Ebbesborne	1622	c.1621		1682	Edmund	352
453	Edmund	Wroughton			1682			
454	Francis			1658				
455	Oliver					1670		
456	William			1667		1682		
457	John	Mappowder	c.1530		1682	1672		
458	Nicholas				1682			
459	Joseph		c.1534					
460	Thomas		after 1542	? 1696		1679		
561	Robert		"		1682		Edmund	453
552	William		"		1682		"	"
553	Thomas				1682		"	"

344

No.	Name	Abode	Born	Marr.	Alive	Died	Father's Name	No.
564	John		1634	1687		1724	Francis	454
565	Edmund		1635				"	"
566	Samuel		1655				"	"
557	Edmund		1688	1680		1595	Oliver	455
668	Thomas		1688			1703	John	564
669	Francis		1693			? 1705		
370	Henry		1539		1551		William	205
371	Ambrose		1594					
573	Simon		1589		1627		Simon	409
572	Edmund		1598				"	"
575	Michael		1597				"	"
574	John		1611				"	"
576	Thomas	Salem, Mass.		1. 1649 / 2. 1651 / 3. 1656		1683	? Moses	428
577	Richard	Saugus, Mass.	1637				Moses	428
678	Moses	Salem, Mass.				1651	Thomas	537
679	Benjamin	Salem, Mass.					Moses	378
780	Thomas		1652				Moses	378
781	Moses		1673			1676	"	"
782	Benjamin		1669				Benjamin	679
783	Joseph		1671				"	"
784	Jeremiah		1673				"	"
785	Samuel		1676				"	"
186	Thomas	Greenwich	1602	1632	? 1655	1534	Thomas	186
287	William		1534				John	412
588	Edmund		1599					
189	John	Burford			1501		Richard	196
290	Henry	Stanton Harcourt			1635		? Samuel	403 or 408
591	Samuel				1650		? John	631 or 636
694	John	Southwark	1640	1603				
196	Richard	Stanton Harcourt	1608		1588			
699	John	Camberwell	c.1640			1641	? John	574
601	Thomas						Thomas	576

	Name	Abode	Born	Marr.	Alive	Died	Father's Name	
403	Samuel		c.1657	c.1700		1676	Francis	454
504	Edward		1700			1710	Edward	504
305	William							
408	Samuel	Everleigh				1629		
211	William	Gt. Bedwyn			1611		? William	150 or son of 150 ?

Miscellaneous

Name	Abode	Marr.	Alive	Died
Anthony	Glympton			
Stephen	Cassington	1606	1641	
Robert	Whitechapel			1555
Oliver	Hackney			1562
John	Gt. Bedwyn	1599	1576	
Thomas	Gt. Bedwyn	1598	1576	
Edward			1576	
Thomas	Burbage			1557
Walter	Mere		1675	
Matthew	Mere		1670	

Gloucestershire 1671

Barrington
John CHADWELL	4 Hearths	(probably 631)
Mr. CHADWELL	3 "	" 632 or 633)

Donnington
Mr. CHADWELL	8 "	" 517

Broadwell
William CHADWELL Esq.	9 "	634

Stroud Town and Upper Lippyatt
Thomas CHADWELL	2 "	637
John CHADWELL	6 "	(probably 535)

Lechlade
David CHADWELL	2 "	545

Bibury
Widow CHADWELL	3 "	(unknown)

Kempley
Thomas CHADWELL	1 "	630

Oxfordshire 1665

Stanton Harcourt
Henry CHADWELL	1 "	290

Burford Upton and Signett
Lawrence CHADWELL	1 "	546

Wilts and Dorset 1662-4

Handley
Mr. CHADWELL and Richard SAUNDERS	8 "	(probably 457)

Mappowder
Mr. John CHADWELL	5 "	457

APPENDIX II

Numerical list of CURRER (males and females) 1503-1836

	Name	Abode	Born	Marr.	Husband or wife's name	Died	Father's Name
Generation I							
101	Thomas	Rotherham				1503	
Generation II							
201	Thomas	Skybeden	alive		Elizabeth	1551/2	
202	Hewe	Dacrebanks	"		Ellen	1571/2	
203	Peter	? Pateley Bridge		1572			
204	William	"		"			
205	Peter	Giggleswick	alive	1550			
206	Henry	"				1550	
207	Hugh	Hamsthwaite	alive				
208	Hugh	Kildwick	alive	1515-40	?	1573	
Generation III							
301	William	Marley	c.1535	c.1555	Isabel Maude	1604	Hugh 208
302	Henry	Kildwick		c.1550	Anne Wade	1566	" "
303	Thomas	Langbar		c.1550	Lucy ...	?1596	" "
304	Peter	Cowling		c.1550	Thomasine ...	?1598/9	Thomas 201
305	William	Skybeden			Agnes ...		" "
306	Christopher	"					
307	William ?	Dacrebanks					Hewe 202
308	Christopher	"					" "
309	Peter	"	c.1547	c.1567	Dorothy Jaike	1577/8	" "

	Name	Abode	Born	Marr.	Husband or wife's name	Died	Father's name	
310	Francis	? Collingham	c.1540		? John Gill or Hill or Wm. Coulthwaite	1608	Hewe	202
351	Isabel						"	"
352	Anne						"	"
353	Grace						"	"
311	Peter	Clint			Elizabeth	1590	Hugh	207
312	Thomas	B. Hamsthwaite					"	"
313	Francis	"					"	"
314	Matthew	"					"	"
315	Henry	"					"	"
316	Jerome	"					"	"
354	Elizabeth	"					"	"
355	Joane	"					"	"
356	Margaret	"					"	"
317	Peter	York				1603	"	"

Generation IV

	Name	Abode	Born	Marr.	Husband or wife's name	Died	Father's name	
401	William	Staintoncotes	1549 or 50	c.1586	Ellen Halstead	1624	Henry	302
402	Hugh	Kildwick	c.1560			1617	"	"
403	Christopher	"		died young without issue			"	"
453	Agnes	"	c.1555	1576	William Bawdwen		"	"
457	Margaret	"		1576	Hugh Bawdwen		"	"
458	Anne			1582	Alex Horrocks		"	"
459	Jane			1583	Steven Dixon		"	"
460	Isabella			1592	Edmund Hird		"	"
461	Lucy			1585	Miles Gill		"	"
462	Mary			1593	Edmund Bawdwen		"	"
463	Agnetta			1580	Rowland Watson		"	"
404	Henry	Middleton	1571	c.1600	Alice	1633	William	301
405	Henry	Hollinhall	c.1555	c.1591	Dorothy Maude	1598	"	"
406	William	Marley	c.1555		Isabel Parker	1643	"	"

	Name	Abode	Born	Marr.	Husband or wife's name	Died	Father's name
407	Walter	Linton/Craven	?1560		unmarried ?	1602	William 301
408	Arthur	Morton	c.1570	(1591 (1612 (1619	Edith Ryley Alice Oldfield Susan Lupton	1623	" "
451	Isabel	Marley		1593	Christopher Hodgeson		" "
452	Jane	"		1604	Andrew Skatchand		" "
453	Mary	Langbar	before 1586		... Barlett		Thomas 303
454	Margaret	"	between 1586 & 1599		... Cogill		" "
409	William	"	c.1565	c.1595-97		1635	" "
455	Isabel	Cowling		1583	John Emmott		Peter 304
410	William	Skybeden	before 1560		Alice	1625	William 305
411	Gregory	Embsay	before 1595		Janet	1612	
412	Edward	Skipwith		1583			
413	Christopher	Dacrebanks	c.1568			1628	Christopher 308
414	John	York/London	1580	(1605 1614	Eliza Williams Ruth Rousse		Peter 317
415	Edward	B. York		1607	Susan Harvey	1598	" "
416	Christopher	Leeds					"
464	Katherine	Clint					Peter 317

Generation V

	Name	Abode	Born	Marr.	Husband or wife's name	Died	Father's name
501	Henry	Kildwick	1587	c.1607	Ann Harrison	1652/3	Hugh 402
502	Hugh	Steeton	1588	1618	Mary Bawdwen	1637	" "
503	Christopher	Kildwick	1590		unmarried	1611	" "
504	William	Kildwick Grange	1592	1612	Grace Whaler	1637	" "
505	Samuel	Kildwick	1592		unmarried	1593	" "
506	William	Middleton	1603	1635	Dorothy Jackson	1654	Henry 404
507	Hugh	b. "	c.1606				" "
551	Anne	"	1601	(1631 (?	Israel Dodsworth Henry Penrose		" "

No.	Name	Abode	Born	Marr.	Husband or wife's name	Died	Father's name	
552	Jane	Middleton	1602	1630	John Topham	1611	Henry	404
553	Mary	"	1609		George Oldfield	1645	"	"
554	Isabel		1611	unmarried			"	"
555	Alice	York	1612				"	"
556	Elizabeth	b. Middleton	c.1616				"	"
557	Margaret	York	1618	unmarried		1644	"	"
558	Agnes	b. Middleton	1617	1638	Matthew Lee		"	405
508	William	Skipton	1592	1617	Ellen Parker	1643	Henry	"
509	Walter	b. Skipton	c.1595				"	"
559	Isabel	"	c.1597		? Nicholas Walker		"	"
560	Elizabeth ?	"	? 1598		?	? posth	"	"
561	Agnes	b. Morton	1591		Christopher Standeven		Arthur	408
562	Jane	"	1593	1612	Samuel Waddington		"	"
510	William of	" Angram	1595 ? 9				"	"
563	Isabel	"	1600	? 1624	? Alexander Squre	1602	"	"
511	Walter	"	1601	unmarried			"	"
504	Anne	"	1604			1614	"	"
512	Arthur	"	1614	unmarried			"	"
505	Susan	"	1620	1637	William Wigglesworth		"	"
506	Ellen	"	1621	unmarried		1624	"	"
507	Martha	"	1623			1623	"	"
508	Mary	"	1598	{ 1618 / 1639	Thomas Currer (513) / John Walker		"	"
513	Thomas	Ilkley	c.1597	1618	Mary Currer (508)	1629	William	409
514	William	?	1597 alive 1629				"	"
515	Hugh	Langbar	c.1600			1659	"	"
516	Peter	Langbar	c.1595	{ 1615 / 1635	Alice ...., Elizabeth Banister	1657	William	401
517	Henry	Staintoncoates	c.1595		Isabel Staw		"	
518	Hugh	Bradford	1595-1605	unmarried ?		1666		
519	William	Marley ?	1607			? 1612	William	406
520	Thomas	Skybeden	c.1592	1613	Agnes Ingmyre	1651	William	410
569	Margaret	"	1597				"	"

No.	Name	Abode	Born	Marr.	Husband or wife's name	Died	Father's name
521	William	Skybeden	1605	unmarried		drowned 1630	William 410
570	Ann	? Embsay	1597				Gregory 411
522	Gregory	"	1599				"
523	John	London		alive 1528			John 414
571	Frances	"		"			"
572	Jennett	Leeds	1585				Christopher 416
524	Richard	Leeds	1587	1613	Margaret Pickard		"
525	John	"	1588	unmarried		1588	"
526	John	"	1588			1590	"
527	William	"	1590	1633 "	Elizabeth Smithson	1635 ?	"

Generation VI

No.	Name	Abode	Born	Marr.	Husband or wife's name	Died	Father's name
501	Henry	Skipton	1621	c.1642	Catherine Loraine	1659	William 508
651	Anne	b. "	1622			1623	"
652	Mary	"	1622	1635	Henry Goodgion	1671	"
653	Ellen	"	1623				"
554	Dorothy	Wighill	1623	unmarried		1619	"
602	William	Ilkley	1629	c.1650		1589	Thomas 513
655	Isabel	Stead	1618	unmarried		1681	"
503	William	? Ilkley	1620	c.1645	Jane Garforth	1632	"
504	Henry	b. Ilkley	1623	unmarried		1627	"
656	Jane	"	1622	"			"
657	Lucy	"	1625				"
658	Isabel	"	1628				"
659	Jane	Langbar	1632	1652	Michael Dunwell		Peter 516
560	Anne	"	c.1635	c.1655	Anthony Taylor	1655	"
505	William	"	1641	1638	Alice		"
661	Dorothy		1645	1667	Henry Currer (510)		"
606	Thomas	Addingham			Anne Raikes		"

No.	Name	Abode	Born	Marr.	Husband or wife's name	Died	Father's name	
607	Hugh	Kildwick	1608	(c.1549	Blanche Ferrand	1590	Henry	501
				(	Anne Haworth	1685		
				(1687	Jennet Watkinson			
659	Helen	b. Kildwick	1610		Roger Whalley		" "	" "
608	Henry	London	1614	? 1635	Anne Watkinson	1553	" "	" "
					or Anne Millington			
609	John	Bradley	c.1615	c.1650	Mary	1586	" "	" "
670	Mary	b. Kildwick	1618		Thomas Hammond		" "	" "
671	Anne	"	1620		William Watson		" "	" "
633	William	"	1623	unmarried		1624	" "	" "
672	Sara	"	1621	"		1623	" "	" "
673	Susan	"	1621	"		1623	" "	" "
674	Martha	"	1625					
675	Alice	Middleton	1635		Edmund Bawdwen		William	506
676	Jane		1638					
677	Mary	Ilkley	1639	1659	Richard Whitehead	1691	" "	" "
610	Henry	Middleton	1642	1668	Dorothy Currer (561)	1644	" "	" "
611	William	b. Middleton	1643	unmarried			" "	" "
678	Anne	"	1645				" "	" "
612	William	Bradford	1617	Probably unmarried		1667	Henry	517
613	Hugh	Staintoncotes	1618			1675	" "	" "
614	Henry	b.	1619	Probably unmarried		c.1660	" "	" "
615	John	"	1623	unmarried		1623	" "	" "
616	John	Staintoncotes	1637			1674	" "	" "
617	Thomas	b. Staintoncotes	1639				" "	" "
652	Mary		1648	unmarried		1662	" "	" "
663	Elizabeth	"	1649				" "	" "
664	Anne	"	c.1656		Nicholas Stowe		" "	" "
618	Christopher	b. Bradford	c.1645	1669			Hugh	518
619	William	"					" "	" "
620	John	Gawthrop Hall	1621	? 1645		1672	" "	" "
621	Henry							

No.	Name	Abode	Born	Marr.	Husband or wife's name	Died	Father's name	
622	Hugh	Steeton	1622	(1642 (1656	Elizabeth Hargreaves Mary....	1670	Hugh	502
623	William	London	1624	1658	Ann Farrington		"	"
665	Helen	b. Steeton		unmarried		1628	"	"
624	Henry	" "	1621				"	"
666	Anne	" "	1629				"	"
625	Hugh	Kildwick	1612	unmarried		1613	William	504
626	Henry	" "	1614	1635	? Ann Watkinson (see 308)	167. ?	"	"
627	Hugh	Dedford	1616	164. ?		167. ?	"	"
628	William	London	1618	Probably unmarried		1668	"	"
629	Samuel	Kildwick Grange	1620	unmarried		1623	"	"
667	Anne	b. "	1620				"	"
630	Samuel	Cottingham	1622	c.1642	Dorothy Creyke	1650	"	"
631	Christopher	Kildwick	1624	unmarried		1635	"	"
668	Helena	b. Kildwick	1626	unmarried		1626	"	"
632	John	London	1627	155. ?	Eliz. Chillingworth	1670	"	"
634	William	Skybeden	1613			1675	Thomas	520
635	Francis	b. Skybeden				1657	"	"
679	Anne	" "	1616				"	"
635	Thomas	" "	1618				"	"
680	Ellen	" "	1620	1659	John Becroft		"	"
637	Edward	Skybeden	1627	1657	Abigail Goodgeon	1678	"	"
638	Richard	Eastby	1629			1685	"	"

Generation VII

No.	Name	Abode	Born	Marr.	Husband or wife's name	Died	Father's name	
777	Grace	b. Skipton	1643	unmarried		1650	Henry	601
701	William	" "	1648	1681	Alice Jackman	1691	"	"
778	Mary	b. " "	1653	unmarried		1666	"	"
779	Catherine	b. Wighill		1682	Robert Goodgeon jr		William	602
780	Mary	" "					"	"

No.	Name	Abode	Born	Marr.	Husband or wife's name	Died	Father's name	Ref.
781	Mary	b. Ilkley	1647	1670	Peter Langthorne		William	603
702	William	Ilkley	c.1649	1683	Ann Banks		"	"
782	Dorothy	b. Ilkley	1650	? unmarried		? 1551	"	"
703	William	Bolton Abbey		c.1694		? 1720	William	605
783	Alice	b. Langbar	1668	unmarried			Thomas	505
704	Peter	Langbar	1675			1577	"	"
784	Anne	b. Langbar	1678				"	"
705	Henry	Kildwick	before 1649	unmarried		before 1649	Hugh	607
751	Anne	b. Kildwick	1650	(1670) (1685)	William Busfield / Robert Ferrand		"	"
706	Henry	Grays Inn	1651	(1683) after (1697)	Margaret Fothergill / Mary Watson	1724	"	"
752	Eleanor	b. Kildwick	1652	1685	Richard Entwhistle		"	"
753	Grace	"	1653	1682	William Raines		"	"
754	Mary	"	1654	1577	Robert Pickering		"	"
755	Elizabeth	"	1656	1675	Ellis Meredith		"	"
757	Dorothy	b. Ilkley	1673	1697	Nathaniel Wright		Henry	610
758	Mary	"	1673	1693	Richard Cook		"	"
707	William	" Middleton	1670			1733	"	"
708	Henry	Nappa	1665			1692	John	616
709	William	"	1669			1695	"	"
759	Elizabeth	"	1650				Henry	621
728	Henry	b. Draughton	1647				"	"
760	Eleanor		1648	unmarried		1650	"	"
761	Catherine	? London	1650	unmarried		1658	"	"
762	Mary	Steeton	1651				"	"
710	Hugh	Steeton	1643	1670	Ann Watson	1693	Hugh	622
711	William	? London	1644				"	"
763	Anne	b. Steeton	1651	unmarried		1652	"	"
712	John		1646				"	"
713	Henry		1647				"	"
714	Christopher	Morton	1652	1674	Jane Turner		"	"
764	Mary	b. Steeton	1653		.... Winstanley		"	"

Name	Abode	Born	Marr.	Husband or wife's name	Died	Father's name
765 Ellen	b. Steeton	c.1653	1677	Jonathan Rawson		Hugh 622
766 Margaret	"	1658				" "
767 Anne	"	1660				" "
768 Elizabeth	"	1663				" "
715 Thomas	b. Keighley	1664	1691	Sarah Ferrand		Henry 626
769 Mary	b. Kildwick Grange	1635		unmarried	1636	" "
770 Anne	"	1637		unmarried	1645	" "
716 William	b.	1639			1690	" "
771 Grace	b.	1642				" "
717 Henry	b.	?1640				" "
772 Mary	b.	1648	1670	John Colbeck		" "
773 Elizabeth	b.					" "
718 John	London	1549	1670	Susan Elton		Hugh 627
719 Henry	? Heptonstall	1644				" "
720 William	b. Cottingham	c.1643				Samuel 630
721 John	"	c.1644			? before 1673	John 632
722 William	" Islington					" "
723 Nicholas	Westminster	1665	(1715	Priscilla Osborn		" "
774 Elizabeth	London					
775 Diana	"					
776 Katherine						
724 Christopher	Bradley ?	1657			1707	John 609
725 Henry	Bradley ?	1662			1664	" "
756 Anne	Bradley ?	1650				" "
726 Hugh	Bradley	1658	c.1684	Ann	1729	" "
785 Mary	b. Skybeden	1660		unmarried	1677	Edward 637
727 Thomas	Skybeden	1662		unmarried	1660	" "
786 Ann	b. Skybeden	1665				" "
787 Margaret	"	1668	1693	Robert Hardacre		" "
788 Isabel	"	1670		unmarried	1687	" "
789 Elizabeth	"	1675		unmarried	1676	" "
790 Frances	"					" "

Generation VIII

No.	Name	Abode	Born	Marr.	Husband or wife's name	Died	Father's name	
801	Hugh	Kildwick	1684	unmarried		1684	Henry	706
802	Hugh	"	1689	unmarried		1690	"	"
851	Anne	b. Kildwick	1686	1707	Benjamin Ferrand	1727	"	"
852	Dorothy	"	1687	1705	Richard Richardson	1763	"	"
803	Haworth	Kildwick	1691	1722	Sarah Harvey	1744	"	"
853	Margaret	b. Kildwick	1692	unmarried		1767	"	"
854	Elizabeth	Kildwick	169. ?	unmarried		1704	"	"
855	Mary		1694	unmarried		1694	"	"
856	Henrietta Maria	York	1695	unmarried		1771	"	"
804	Henry	Middleton	1696	unmarried		1706	William	707
866	Mary	b. Middleton	1699	unmarried		1712	"	"
805	William	"	1706	unmarried		1709	"	"
806	Henry	Skipton	1683	(1703 (1715	Mary Pollard Jane Banks	1750	William	701
807	William	b. Skipton	1688	unmarried		1690	"	"
874	Catherine	Skipton	1682		.... Crook		"	"
875	Martha		168.		.... Constantine		"	"
808	William	b. Ilkley	1685				William	702
809	Henry	Bolton Abbey	1695	unmarried		1695	William	703
810	Peter	"	1697	1733	Susan Birtwhistle	? 1751	"	"
811	William	"	?				"	"
812	John	"	1708				"	"
813	Henry	Bradley	1685				Hugh	726
858	Mary	b. Bradley	1687				"	"
859	Martha	"	1689				"	"
860	Ann	"	1692				"	"
861	Elizabeth	Bradley	1693	unmarried		1694	"	"
862	Ellen	"	1695	unmarried		1729	"	"
863	Margaret	"	1698				"	"
814	John	"	1700				"	"
864	Grace		1702	unmarried		1705	"	"

	Name	Abode	Born	Marr.	Husband or wife's name	Died	Father's name
865	Sarah	Bradley	1704	unmarried			Hugh 726
815	Hugh	Upper Bradley	1707	1727	Sarah Sturke	1723	Hugh 710
816	Hugh	Steeton	1673	c.1705	Bridget	1738	" "
817	William	b. Steeton	1675	unmarried		1676	" "
818	Henry	" Steeton	1677	unmarried		1684	" "
867	Elizabeth	Steeton	1680	unmarried		1692	" "
868	Ann		1682	? 1704	? Thomas Barcroft		" "
869	Mary	"	1684	1707	William Lupton		" "
819	Henry	Stonegap/Glusburn	1686	1711	Isabel Hartley		" "
820	William	Steeton	1688			? 1718	" "
870	Martha	"	1690				" "
871	Elizabeth	"	1692	unmarried			Christopher 714
872	Grace	Morton	1677	1699	Bernard Hartley	1692	" "
821	John	"	1680				" "
873	Mary	"	1684				" "

Generation IX

	Name	Abode	Born	Marr.	Husband or wife's name	Died	Father's name
901	Henry	Kildwick	1728	1756	Mary Ferrand	1756	Haworth 803
951	Sarah	Kildwick	1729	unmarried		1759	" "
902	William	Clapham	1716	1745	Anne Stokoe	1803	Henry 806
962	Ann	b. Skipton	1710		{ .... Rushforth		" "
963	Katherine	Skipton	1713	1738	{ .... John Maude	1807	" "
964	Jane	b. Skipton	1718	unmarried		1803	" "
965	Alice	" "	1721	unmarried		1784	" "
955	Mary	" "	1723	1753	Abraham Chamberlain	1811	" "
967	Sarah	" "	1726	unmarried		1728	" "
903	Henry	" "	1727	unmarried		1799	" "
968	Margaret	" "	1730	1754	William Moorhouse		" "
904	William	b. Steeton	1705			? 1748	Hugh 816

No.	Name	Abode	Born	Marr.	Husband or wife's name	Died	Father's name	
958	Isabel	b. Steeton	1710	1745	Wray Atkinson		Hugh	815
959	Anne	"	1708				"	"
960	Sarah	b. Glusburn	1711			? 1748	Henry	819
906	William	"	1713				"	"
961	Anne	" Glusburn	1715				"	"
907	Hugh	b. Glusburn	1718				"	"
952	Grace	b. Bradley	1732	unmarried		1732	Hugh	815
953	Anne	"	1733		Thomas Gill		"	"
908	Henry	" Bradley	1735			1756	"	"
909	George	"				1763	"	"
910	John	"	1727	unmarried		1737	"	"
954	Sarah	b. Bradley	1737				"	"
955	Mary	"	1740	unmarried		1741	"	"
956	Martha	"	1744	unmarried		1744	"	"
957	Agnes	"	1749				"	"
911	William	" Addingham	1737				Peter	810

Generation X

No.	Name	Abode	Born	Marr.	Husband or wife's name	Died	Father's name	
1001	William	Luddenden	1749	(1777 (1795	Elizabeth Swire Fanny Mellin	1807	William	902
1002	Henry			unmarried			"	"
1003	Henry			unmarried			"	"
1051	Jennet	Halifax	1747		Roger Swire	1789	"	"
1052	Elizabeth			unmarried			"	"
1053	Elizabeth			unmarried			"	"
1054	Ellen		1766		Thomas Langton	1846	"	"
1055	Alice	Canada	1769	unmarried		1846	"	"
1056	Anne		1763	1791	Rawdon Briggs	1802	"	"

Generation XI

	Name	Abode	Born	Marr.	Husband or wife's name	Died	Father's name
1101	Henry	Luddenden	1784	unmarried		1817	William 1001
1151	Alice		1780	unmarried		1791	"
1152	Jennet		1782	unmarried		1814	"
1153	Elizabeth		1795	unmarried		1836	"
1102	William	Jamaica	1789		Sarah	1834	"
1103	Edward	St. Vincents	1796	unmarried			"
1154	Frances		1800	1834	Thomas Margerison		"
1155	Ann	b. Luddenden					"

360

References are to item numbers, <u>not</u> to pages.

Austin, Elizabeth 70; Joan 57; Lucy 545; Michael 545
Avis, William 293
Awnger, Richard 210
Awood, Lawrence 301
Aylworth, Anne 103; Bray 103; Edward 103,104; Thomas 103
Ayre, Richard 231
Ayrie, Ralph 341

Bacon, Sir Francis 579; Margaret 171; Sir Nicholas 256; Robert 171,565; William 171
Badger, Henry 57
Baerents Van Eemden, Trijntie 823
Bafford, Henry 590
Bayley (Bailye, Bayly), Edward 590; Robert 128; Thomas 63
Bainbrigg, Peter 92
Baker, Alice 166; Capt. --- 102; George 494; Henry 311; John 57,588; Nicholas 738; Richard 494; Thomas 194; Walter 69; William 291
Baldocke, John 77
Baldwin (Baldewyn), Joan 236; John 417; William 236
Ball, Richard 772
Balldryke, Richard 29
Balles, Barbara 174; Richard 174
Bamford, Elizabeth 46
Bane, John 647
Barnham, Robert 175
Banister, John 128; Sir Robert 128; William 103,104
Barebone, Thomas 67
Barents, Anna 833
Bargrave, John 624
Barker, Edmund 189; Thomas 484; William 787
Barkesdale, Simon 57
Barkham, Sir Edward 620
Barnam, Francis 673
Barnard, John 113; Martha 27; Richard 339; Robert 64
Barners, Robert 95; William 95
Barnes, Robert 59
Barnesdale, Nicholas 57
Barre, Agas 258; Christian 258 William 258
Barrett (Barrytt), Agnes 362; Henry 299; Joan 299; John 694; Margaret 239,524; Robert 239,362

Barrow, Edward 132
Barry, John 46
Barrytt, alias Burrard
Bartholomew, John 489
Barton, William 12,151,152
Bass, George 60
Basteels, Philip, Notary 814, 815
Bate, Thomas 561; William 561
Bateman, William 246
Baterbie, William 75
Bates, --- 57
Batherne, Margaret 12; Roger 11
Batson, William 110,111,119 766
Batt, John 693; Robert 425
Battell, Allan 139
Battelye, William 188
Baugh, Rowland 95
Bawdwen, William 127
Baxter, Francis 93; Grissell 531; John 129; Mary 531; William 524
Bayning, Paul 587
Bazius, B --- notary 775-780, 782-786,788-790,794,795,797
Beale, Jeffery 13; Robert 57
Beand, Thomas 720
Bearte, Henry 485
Beaufew (Beaufoy), Henry 114, 115,119
Beaumond (Beaumont), Christopher 49; Huntington 625; Johan Reijersz Van 806; Sir Richard 124; Thomas 172; Robert 115
Bedford, Robert 55
Bedingfield, Sir Henry 595
Beecher, William 403,557
Belcher, William 109
Bell, Henry 80; Robert 41,92; Thomas 80; William 80
Bellye, John 751
Belson, Augustine 116
Belwood, William 88
Beminster, Richard 57
Bendish (Bendishe), Edmund 30; Thomas 503
Bennet (Bennett), John 115,116, 671; Peter 5,6,7; Symon 47
Bennys, John 212; Richard 212
Benson, Richard 517; William 517
Berckel, Rev. Segnerus 825
Bernard alias Crispe, William 63
Berners, see Barners
Berrisse (Ber(r)isse), Edmund 108; Thomas 107,108

Besson, Leonard 479
Best, Edward 71
Betts, Henry 478
Bevan, Elizabeth 661
Beynham, William 69
Bickford, Nicholas 757; Nicholl
    757
Bidwell, William 527
Bigmore, Allen 42; Margaret
    42; Thomasine 42
Bilbroughe, Richard 572
Billingsley, John 46
Bingham, John 4
Birch, Francis 12
Bird, --- 103
Birkett, Stephen 89
Bishopp (Bisshoppe), Robert
    12; William 164
Blackall, Richard 25
Blageborne, John 141
Blake, Peter 53, 542
Blanchard, W --- 652
Blenkinsop, Thomas 89
Blennerhassett, Edward 314,
    315; Sir Edward 594;
    John 594
Blighe, John 712; William 712
Block, Dirck, notary 812,813
Blofeld, Jerome 534
Blore, Christopher 110
Blount, Thomas 47
Blower, Francis 22
Blyante, Richard 213;
    Robert 213
Boake, Elizabeth 85; Thomas
    85
Bohun, Michael 26
Bokenham, Barbara 583;
    Edmund 308,583
Bolle, John 319
Bolt, Nicholas 738
Bolton, Christopher 157;
    Othell 188
Bonaby, Thomas 55
Bond, Richard 676
Boecker (Booker), Edward 820,
    826; Richard 826
Boothbie, William 75
Boston, Thomas 374
Bosville, Ralph 563
Boteler, Sir Edward 565,681
Boucher (Bowcher) Sir John
    573; Pawle 553
Bourgeon, Joris Stevenson 820
Boulton (Bowlton), Abraham
    132; James 328; John 141;
    Pernell 306; Thomas 306;
    William 306

Bourchier, Henry, Earl of
    Essex 259
Bowle, Thomas 116
Bowtell, John 303; Richard 303
Bowyer, Robert 673
Boyden, Alice 32; John 32;
    Seakin 32
Boyton, William 582
Brabant, Anne 40; Susan 40
Brackenbury, Richard 636
Bradford, Charles 129; John
    129
Bradinge, John 149
Bradley, Edward 139
Bradshaw (Bradshawe), J 146;
    John 34
Brakyn, Richard 29
Brames, John 239,242; Rose
    239,242
Bramlye, Thomas 581
Branchworth, Robert 673
Brancome, Robert 116
Brangwin, Castle 15; Francis 15
Branthwait, Harry 296
Brantingham John 447
Brasyer, John 326
Bray, Elizabeth 105
Breerton, Richard 629
Bremelcombe, Richard 626
Brende, John 220; Margaret 220
Brent, Sir Nathaniel 1
Brereton, Peter 138,139,140,141
Bressie, Ralph 390
Brett, James 682; Samuel 117
Brevyter, Richard 473
Brewer, Henry 576; John 10
Brewis, Valentine 68
Brewse, Nicholas 623
Brewster (Bruster), Ambrose 524;
    Blaze 599; Edmond 664; Edward
    525,700; Humphrey 246; John
    600,601; Katherine 700; Mary
    249; Richard 526,602; Robert
    102,660; Thomas 363, 527,700;
    William 248,249; alias Alby,
    John 247
Bridgeman, Robert 115,116
Briggs, Sybil 32
Brigstock, Ellen 60
Bringley, see Brymley
Bringley, Elizabeth 38
Britton, Baron 39; Martha 39
Brockett, John 585; William 92
Brodway, --- 57
Broke, Robert 171
Broker, William 70
Bromley, Sir Thomas 442, 493
Bromwell, Robert 92

Bronden, Ingram 129
Brooke (Broeck), Elizabeth
  72; Henry (Broocq Hendrick)
  775,777,779,780,782,783,785,
  786,820; John 353; Mary 818
  819,829; Richard 69,72; Sir
  Robert 567; Thomas 69,728;
  William 584
Broom, Robert 3,5,6,7
Brough, Christopher 717
Browne (Brown), Armiger 239;
  Dorothy353; Henry 57; John
  92,114,266,281,473,614;
  Katherine 92; Richard 281;
  Robert 320; Thomas 727;
  W. 281; William 75, 353
Browning, Brice 584; William
  259,260
Bruce, Edward, Lord 561;
  James 766
Brun, Sara 581
Bryan, William 21,22; John 52
Brymley, Jane 35,36,38; Job
  (or Brimlye, John) 35,36,38
Bucke, Maximilian 717
Buckley, Richard 772
Burckner, John 632
Bulle (Bull), Charles 132;
  Grace 179; Robert 179
Bullocke (Bullock), Edward 287;
  Henry 310; Thomas 345;
  Toby 11
Bullyvant, Henry 190; Margaret
  190
Bunn, Thomas 293
Bunting, Richard 449
Bunyard, William 686
Burder, Henry 34; John 582
Burle, John 748
Burnham, William 772
Burnby, Richard 772
Burnett, George 132
Burnoppe, Isabel 746; Richard
  746
Burrough, William 293
Burton, Elizabeth 53,541,542;
  John 581; Richard 51,264,692;
  Robert 300; William 51,53,300,
  541,542
Butler, George 668; John 11;
  Mrs. --- 57; Walter 564
Butter, Henry 362; William 321
Butts, Thomas 246
Buxston, Rowland 75
Byatt, John 666; Thomas 683
Bynns (Binns) Abraham 123,130;
  John 124

Bywater, Ann 33,34; Thomas 34

Calfield, Alexander 621;
  Ferdinando 621
Calliard, John 451
Calthorpe, Christopher 569;
  Maud 569
Campe, George 584
Cantrell, William 240
Carell, Sir John 359
Carey (Cary, Carye), Alice 70;
  Christopher 70; Sir George
  257; Henry 699; Sir Henry
  600,601; Martha 257; Sir
  Robert 257
Carleton, Christopher 178;
  George 178; Jane 178;
  John 178
Carpenter, Robert 13; William
  17
Carrick, Jane 106; Richard 106
Carter, Edmund 9; Ellen 40;
  Francis 130; Joan 16; Richard
  16; Thomas 772
Cartwright, Edward 772; John
  115
Case, Richard 34
Cason, Edward 752
Catforde, Robert 707; William 707
Catton, Francis 526
Cave, John 60; Philip 115,116;
  Thomas 126
Cavendish, Mary 566
Cawdrey, Gilbert 564
Chadwell, Anne 102,108,109,111;
  Deborah 117; Edmund 117;
  Edward 102,103,106,109,110,
  111,114,115,116,121; Eliza-
  beth 103,105; John 103,107,
  108; Joyce 102,109,111;
  Katherine 102; Michael 102,
  106,114,115,116,119,120,
  121; Richard 107,108; Simon
  103,104,105,107,108; Thomas
  112,114,116,122; William 112,
  113,118
Chafyn, Thomas 744
Chamberlaine, --- 47
Chambers, Amy 549; Elizabeth
  762; Felix 549; Henry 115;
  John 762; Robert 744; William
  714
Chandelor, Elizabeth 305;
  (alias Webb) Robert 305;
  (alias Webb) Thomas 305
Chandon, Adam 4; Elizabeth 4

367

Evans, Daniel 151,152
Eve, John 684
Everard, Margaret 524
Ewint, Richard 522
Eyre, Robert 75
Eyrman alias Fronman Francis
116

Faber, Ralph 133,134,141,142,
143,147; Robert 141,147
Fabyan, Jane 217; John 217
Fagg, William 596
Fairfax, Sir Thomas 118
Fane, Sir Francis 753
Fanner, Katherine 130;
Robert 130
Farmer, Samuel 115,116
Farrow, William 90
Faverall, Benedict 329; Eme
329
Fawce, Alice 231
Feake, Robert 772
Feilde, Susan 309; William 309
Fell, Agnes 59; Isabel 90;
Oliver 59; Richard 90
Fenne, Robin 562
Fenwicke, Cuthbert 538
Fermor, Sir John 59
Ferrand, Robert 137
Ferris, Edmund 724
Fetherstonhalgh, John 92;
Ralph 92; Thomas 92
Fettwell, John 550
Field, Elizabeth 12; John 574
Filkins, Isabel 59; John 59
Finche, Clement 284; Grace
284
Fish, Richard 401
Fisher (Fysher), --- 57;
Hugh 115,116; Richard 441
Fitch, Elizabeth 586; Thomas
585,586
Flaxman, Robert 45
Fleete, alias Atkinson, Ralph
509
Fleetwood, H 146; William 333,
382
Flower, Elinor 94; George 94;
William 94
Flynt, Robert 593
Foot, Rev. Thomas 515
Forbye, Robert 298
Ford, James 28; John 28,94;
Richard 806
Forder, James 57
Forestone, Robert 129
Forster, Andrew 495
Forth, Robert 240
Fosdick, Edward 694

Foster, Joan 102; Nicholas 485
Foulaer, Johannes 821
Foules, Christopher 141
Founde, Alexander 256; Ann
256
Fowke, John 673
Fowle, Edward 261; Elizabeth
261
Fox, Ralph 555
Foxall, Ambrose 67
Framingham (Framlyngham),
Edmund 675; Sir Charles
301
Framson, Thomas 481
Francke (Frank), Elizabeth 132;
Marmaduke 602; Robert 535
Franklin (Frankline), Anthony
22; John 318
Freeman, --- 57; Alice 74;
Anthony 112; Edward 113;
Michael 112; Thomas 74;
William 112,214,216
Freer, John Frederick 66,67;
Sarah 66,67
Frenche, Edward 524; John 524
Freston, William 300
Frost, John 265
Fuller, Amy 577; Edward 35,36;
John 28; Richard 683;
Furley, Reynold 479
Furness, Thomas 259
Furser (or Fusser) Mary 8
Fyncher, Richard 14n

Gabites, Thomas 129
Gage, Edward 116
Gages, Henry 504; Robert 504
Gale, Thomas 757
Galland, Edward 539
Gamble, Henry 124; William 124
Game, William 745
Gamlin, Frances 57; John 57
Gander, William 630
Gandy, William 45
Gardener (Gardner, Gardiner,
Gardyner), Agnes 190,257;
Christian 258; Christopher
267,269,271,272,322;
George 93, 273; Dr. George
D.D. 325; Gilbert 366;
Henry 323,694; Hugh 262;
Joan 214,216,323; John 190,
192,216,219,257,263,270,
369,418,420,421; Margaret
175; Mary 274; Maud 264;
Nicholas 155; Philip 422;
Raffe (Ralph) 264; Richard
219,265; Robert 174,189,
217,258,266,268; Sir Robert

315,565; Thomas 315,565
Grymshagh, Roger 130
Grysmend, Richard 772
Guybon, John 445
Gwilliam, John 11,12

Haben(?), Jean 791
Haberd, Francis 239
Habson, Edward 804; Francis
  804
Hackinge, Robert 139
Hadducke, Thomas 28
Hagarth (Hogarth), George
  333,382
Haggard, Barbara 758;
  John 758
Hales, Haulnut 263
Hall, Edward 197; Peter 81,
  615; Ralph 514; Randall
  29; Robert 196; Thomas
  514,694,720; William 64
Halsteed, John 33,34
Hambrook, Richard 9
Hambye, John 367
Hamer, Frans 778
Hammerton (Hamerton), Ann
  688; Nicholas 75
Hammon (Hamon), Adam 7;
  Elizabeth 7; John 55;
  William 514
Hampton, James 393
Hancocke (Hancock), Eliza-
  beth 570; William 57
Hanchett, Edward 569;
  Elizabeth 569
Handon, Christian 7
Hands, Henry 115
Hanson, John 351; Nicholas
  352
Hant, Henricj 808
Hanwell, --- 114
Harber, --- 7
Harding (Hardinge, Hardinte),
  Gyles 74; Joan 74; John
  646; Joseph 12; Richard
  443
Hare, Edward 67
Hagest, Margaret 13
Hargreaves, Mary 130
Harmans, Reijer 789,791,
  792
Harper, Sir John 613;
  Thomas 62
Harris (Harresse, Harries),
  Ann 739; Christopher 138,
  139,140,141,142,143,144;
  Cicely 683,684; Edward
  356; Elizabeth 141,143; Sir
  Francis 683; Nyclaes
  (Nicholas) 825; Richard 13;

Roger 592; Sarah 739;
  Sir Thomas 683,684;
  William 683,684; Sir
  William 683
Harryson, William 528,687
Harry (Harrye), Agnes 190;
  Elizabeth 221; Margaret
  190; John 221; Robert
  190; William 221
Harryes, Thomas 163
Hartley, Isabel 130; John
  130,471; Robert 297,471
Hartochsvelt, Cornelius 792
Hartstong, James 447
Harwood, Joris (?) 787
Hasell (or Hasyll), George
  29,30
Haselwood, Cuthbert 772
Hastings, Dorothy 76; William
  116
Haswell, Joan 515; John 515
Hatton ---, Scrivener 41;
  Christopher 47; Sir
  Christopher 523; Lord 47
Hauwes, Helena 795
Havercroft, William 634
Hawkesworth, Peter 57
Hawkings, Robert 414
Hawlett, Francis 4,7
Haworth, John 141
Hayes, John 27; Ralph 330;
  William 772
Haylock, John 323; Martin 323
Hayter, --- 57; Richard 27
Hayward, Ann 13; John 13;
  Richard 13
Heaman, Richard 57
Heath, Thomas 71
Heber, Thomas 129 130
Heblethwaite, Robert 129
Heminge, Richard 567
Hemingway, Robert 768
Hemsby, Sackford (?Seckford)
  346
Hendricks, Willem 784
Hendry, Margaret 172; Thomas
  172
Henry VI, King 61; VII, King
  61; VIII, King 61,106
Herring, John 694
Heul, Wessel Van Der 782
Heveningham, Sir Anthony
  233; Lady Mary 233
Heydanus, Johannes 826
Heydon, Sir William 512
Heynes, Enoch 73; Margaret
  73; Robert 73; William 73
Heysed, Robert 627
Heyward, Robert 323
Hibbert, Thomas 705

Hickman, Andrew 55
Hide, Roger 55
Higgison, William 67
Higham, Sir John 523
Hill, Ann 676; John 197,199;
    Robert 516,676; Stephen
    479; Thomas 720
Hilliard, George 70
Hilton, George 89; James 89;
    John 89; Nicholas 89;
    Robert 89; Thomas 89
Hipsley, Dorothy 492; John
    492
Hobart, Anthony 552
Hobday, Stephen 4
Hobson, Francis 249; James
    377; William 249
Hocley, --- 477
Hodges, Anthony 112;
    Humphrey 787
Hodgesson (Hodgeson), John
    70; Robert 544
Hodshon, John 91
Hodson, Christopher 30,327
Hoe, Elizabeth 315; John 315
Hoeck, Lijsbeth Van 827;
    Naeltje Van 827,828
Holbrooke, Maud 264; Thomas
    264
Holcroft, Mary 468
Holford, Henry 13; John 30,
    327; Thomas 115,116,120
Hollas, William 499
Holly, William 663
Holmes, Thomas 755
Holt, --- 117
Holtby, George 535
Holton, Thomas 220,235
Honey, Anthony 631
Honynge, Frances 583;
    Ursula 583
Hood, William 515
Hooke, Christopher 67
Hooper, William 417
Hopkins, William 22
Hopperton, Peter 535
Horne, John 23,24; Mary 23,
    24; Peter 129; Thomas 453;
    William 317,397
Horner, Christopher 656
Horrell, William 57
Horspoole, Simon 453
Horton, Jeremy 744; Sir John
    744; Margaret 514
Hough, John 64
Houghton, Thomas 50
Houlton, George 286

Housegoe, Gregory 467
Houten, Isbrant Van 794
Houven, Jan Jacobs Van
    Der 781
Howard, Thomas Lord 348
Howe (How), Elizabeth 556;
    Jane 38; John 333,382,
    556; Robert 722
Howes, Daniel 35,36; Jane
    35,36
Howett (Howytt), Ellen 697;
    John 381
Howlett, Nicholas 77
Howson, Thomas 130
Hubbard, Myles 511
Hudson, John 547; Margaret
    547; Richard 451; Robert
    766
Huffam, Mercy 1; Susan 1
Huffgate, Michael 2
Huggins, Thomas 115,116
Hughes, Ellis 51,541; Henry
    38
Hulke, Benjamin 590
Humphrey, W. 256
Hungerford, Edward 98
Hunt, Elizabeth 67; John 13;
    Richard 75; William 67
Huntley, William 463
Hurdidge, Francis 775,776,
    777,784
Hutchinson, Christopher 91;
    Thomas 81
Hutton, Eleanor 746; John
    30; Ralph 684; William 752
Huys, Francois 808
Hyckes, Thomas 673
Hyett, Thomas 12
Hynde, Francis 29

Ijdes, Jan 823
Iliffe, William 66,67
Ills, Edward 609
Ilsley, William 652
Ilston, --- 61; Richard 62
Ingram, Sir Arthur 436;
    Thomas 22; William 22
Ireland, Elizabeth 34; Henry
    34
The Isles of Scotland, Bishop
    of 640
Ivatt, Thomas 673
Ives, Elizabeth 49; Richard 49

Jackman, John 130; Thomas 129
Jackson, Henry 92; John 34,92,
    280; Richard 448; Robert 540;

371

Pinto, Daniel 778
Piper, William 769
Piston, --- 53
Pitt, Sir James 40; William 702
Pleasance, Charles 217; George 217; William 217
Plombe, Ann 695; Mary 695; Prisca 695
Plowden, Francis 567
Pole, Edward 705
Poley (Polie, Pollie, Polley, Polly - see also Egmere -, Pollye), Elizabeth 287,291; Francis 291; John 221,402; Sir John 556; Philip 757; William 434;
Polhill, Nicholas 717
Pollarde, William 4
Pollyng, John 157
Pooley, Alice 200; Christopher 435; Edmund 558,680; Giles 200; John 213; Sir John 557; Thomas 292; Dr Thomas 559; William 404,405,681; Sir William 403,557
Pope, Lady Ann 664; Dudley 37; Mary 37; William 326; Sir William 664
Popeley, Christopher 682; Cicely 683,684; Francis 97,436; Grace 436; Henry 683,684; Johan(Jane) 340, 560; John 97, 560; Martha 97; Robert 97; Roger 340
Popham, Sir Francis 744
Pople, Thomas 758
Popley, Bridget 95; Edward 98,194; Derrick 94,98,99; Francis 95,96,561,758; Mary 98,99; Roger 95,406, 407,408,685
Porter, Brian 109; William 75,93
Portler, Robert 248
Postlethwaite, Thomas 825
Potter, Francis 67
Potts, Jannetje 821,824,831; Sara 824
Powell (Powle), Cadwallader 34; Thomas 337
Powlter, Robert 428
Poynter, Thomas 532
Pratt, John 356
Preddye, John 766
Preston, John 271
Price (Pryce), James 26; William 322

Prickett, Alan 89; William 120; alias Prichard, Walter 543
Priddie, John 74; Mary 74
Prince, Philip 87
Prior (Pryor), Efram 57; William 785
Proctor, Thomas 690
Prowd (Prude, or Prowde), William 4,5,7
Pulham, John 200
Pullen, Henry 479
Purdy, --- 57
Pursley, alias Pursglove, Robert 691
Pusey, Richard 28
Pyarde, Peter 4
Pye, Henry 683; John 774
Pyncombe, Amy 737
Pype, Edward 350

Quarles, Edward 581
Quintyne, Alice 701; Henry 701

Rabye, Jerome 428
Rackham, Henry 4
Radburne, Mark 115,116
Radford, Robert 398
Raffe, John 324
Ramesdon (Ramsden), W. 352; William 124
Ramesey, Juliana 507; Thomas 507
Rande (Rand), John 60; Richard 167; Rose 167; Thomas 167
Randall (Randoll), Margaret 57; William 470,478
Rastell, Humphrey 703
Ratcliffe, Agnes 74; Hugh 74; Thomas 74
Ravell, Sir Francis 527
Rawche, Francis 9
Rawley, Humfrey 428
Rawlyns, Thomas 743
Rawson, John 124
Rawstorn, Jerome 606
Raye (Ray, see also Wraye), Alexander 294; Anne 342, 759; Arthur 156; Charles 759; John 173,686; Raynold 342; Robert 173; Simon 293; Thomas 177,344,409; William 562
Raymont, Richard 34; Robert 34
Rayner, Richard 682
Raynolds, --- 95

Saverye, Richard 431
Saville, Robert 130
Sayer, Jonathan 28; Joseph 24
Scambler, Adam 698
Scargen, Thomas 715
Scarlet, Matthew 75
Scarthe (Scarth), Robert 399; Thomas 691
Scattergood, Roger 47
Schrender, Jan 833
Sclater, William 439
Scott, John 531; William 44
Scrymshawe, William 177
Seabrooke, Agnes 666
Seale, --- 103
Seckford (Sackford), --- 442; Henry 346,440,566; Humphrey 346,438; John 224; Mary 441; Thomas 295,347
Sergeant, Lewis 165
Sex, alias Sacks, John 553
Sexten, Thomas 201
Seyll, Jennet 204; Richard 204
Sharp, Mark 42; Thomasine 42
Shawe, Elizabeth 580; Thomas 580
Shayle, John 12
Shayler, John 112
Sheer, George 738; John 738; Susan 738
Sheeres, Arthur 673
Sheldon, Raffe 400
Shelleto, Edmund 341
Shelley, Sir John 116,119
Shelton, Amy 443; Ann 444; Dame Anne 233; Daniel 567,568; Elizabeth 348, 445; Sir J 443; John 193, 444; Sir John 233; Mary 233; Ralph 443,446,569; Sir Ralph 296,447; Thomas 348,447; William 567,568, 689; Winifrede 444
Shepheard, John 115,116,584, 795
Sherborne, Richard 139
Sherewood, Richard 448; Thomas 448
Sherleigh (Sherley), Sir John 595; Robert 116
Sherston, Peter 529; William 529
Sherwinge, Richard 140
Sherwood, Alice 19; Edward 740; Ralph 19

Shetterden, Samuel 420
Shettle, William 332
Shippobottom, Robert 82
Shorte, Thomas 489
Shotblocke, Christopher 91 Elizabeth 91
Shute, Richard 508; Robert 30; Themasyn 30
Shutt, John 131
Sidnam, George 425
Silke, William 428
Simmons, Bartholemew 45 Richard 7
Simpson, Giles 772:Richard 139
Sims, William 57
Siveton, Leonard 561
Skegg, Henry 686
Skelton, Seth 693
Skynner, Robert 440
Skinner, William 119
Slaney, Moreton 67
Slater, Dorothy 449.450; Geoffrey 450; Henry 451; Jennet 638.639 John 564; Nicholas 452; Richard 450.565; Robert 763; Thomas 448
Slatter, John 764
Slaughter, William 103
Slingerlant, Cornelis Van 792
Smallwood, William 85
Smith, Brian 524; Christopher 756; Gilbert 434; Inglebright 481; James 57; Jane 132.599; Joane 432; John 87.115.116.524; Joshua 132; Martha 581; Nicholas 474; Randell 439; Richard 57.443; Robert 205. 440.474; Thomas 16.75.170.227; William 435.438.693; Sir William 588.
Smithson, --- 129; Anthony 181.
Snat, --- 57
Snelgar, George 340
Snowden, Humphrey 762; Katherine 762
Somaster, John 426; Thomas 426
Songer, Jerome 194
Sonnevelt, Willem 796
Sonte, John 452
Southcote, John 567.612
Southend, John 17
Southropp, Robert 102
Sower, John 147
Spaine, William 55
Spaldinge, Henry 173
Sparepoynt, Michael 7
Spark, Robert 467; Richard 417
Sparrowe, Amye 594; Joan 168; John 168: William 39.594
Spatchurst, Simon 588

Speller, John 748
Spencer, Mary 132; Robert 57; William 57.132
Spicer, Christopher 6; William 71
Spier, Elizabeth 16
Spilman, Erasmus 516; Francis 516; Henry 516; Miles 471
Spinke, Thomas 494
Spottell, --- 103
Sprigge, Richard 65; Thomas 65
Squire, Richard 132
Stainer, Thomas 438
Stampe, Thomas 115
Stanbridge, Thomas 263
Stancombe, George 1
Stanhope, Sir Edward 111.114
Stanly, John 4.7.
Stannowe, John 447
Stedman, William 749
Steele, Mr Recorder 142
Steijns, Joseph, Notary 817.818
Stephens, John 179; John 286; Oliver 107.108
Stephenson, --- 117
Stepley, Anne 252; Anthony 252
Stevenson, Richard 280: William 578
Steward (Styward) Edward 29.30; James 503; John 547
Stiche, Thomas 567
Stocks, Humphrey 719
Stockwood, Dunstan 43; Ellen 43
Stoddard, Anne 521; Johan 521; John 343; Susan 521; Thomas 342.521
Stone, Thomas 109
Stonynge, William 602
Stratford, Thomas 57
Strelly, Sir Philip 625
Stretton, Priscilla 40; William 40
Strey, Dorothy 77; Nicholas 77
Strickland, John 577
Strudwicke, Henry 462; William 462
Stubbe, Anne 252; John 252
Stubbs, Richard 511
Sturges, Eleanor 446
Suckerman, Robert 495
Summers, Thomas 4
Sumpter, Gillis 817
Sunderland, Richard 124
Surrey, Earl of 240
Sussex, Frances, Countess of 328; Thomas, Earl of 328.522.523
Sutton, --- 130; Elizabeth 48.49. 226; George 49.226; Thomas 424; William 48.49
Swanson, William 516

Swayne, Geoffrey 210
Sweeting, William 334
Swibner, Matthew 692
Swinglehurst, Elizabeth 141.143; Christopher 141; Richard 133. 134.138.141.142.143.144; Robert 141.142.143.144.148; Thomas 141.142
Swiselton, Ezichiel 816

Tailboys, Richard 95
Tailer, John 423; Nicholas 57
Talbot, John 571; Maryan 571
Tallentine, Richard 59
Tanfield, John 565
Tanner, Roger 340
Tatham, Roland 129
Tawyer, --- 34
Taylor, John 13: Gracian 705; Ralph 92; Robert 13; Thomas 694.817: William 766
Tedberry, Valentine 734: Winifred 734
Tempest, John 92; Robert 538
Temple, Thomas 102
Tendeslow, Alice 200: John 200
Tendringe, John 41
Tennant, Elizabeth 130: Isabel 130: James 130: John 130.690: Richard 130
Tenante, Robert 280
Thackeray, Francis 564
Thackham, Francis 14; Margaret 14
Thatcher, John 116
Theaker, Edward 127; Diana Posthuma 127; John 127; William 127
Theunemans, Willem 806
Thomas, Daniel 28; Peter 421; William 115.116.119.120
Thompson, --- 653
Tomson, Agnes 236
Thompson, Alice 166.180.453.576; Allan 640; Anne 349: Archibald 197; Bertram 765; Catherine 470: Christopher 641; Edmund 642: Edward 690.765: Elizabeth 297.471. 641; Frances 300. 454; George 178. 467.472.273.570; Henry 196.468. 690: James 182.202; John 180.181. 226.298.419.455.469.470.474.475. 577.691.692.694; Joseph 456.571; Margaret 299.476; Margery 181; Martha 350; Nicholas 166.459.644. 695; Peter 454.645; Richard 202. 203.225.477.572.573.574.766: Robert 92.299.444.457.458.646. 647.648.693; Roger 170.456; Samuel 460.461.575: Stephen 349; Susan 570; Symon 533 ;

INDEX OF PLACES

References are to item numbers, <u>not</u> pages

SHIPS

393